The Economics of Recreation, Leisure and Tourism

The Economics of Recreation, Leisure and Tourism

FOURTH EDITION

John Tribe

Routledge
Taylor & Francis Group

LONDON AND NEW YORK

First published by Butterworth-Heinemann

This edition published 2012 by Routledge
2 Park Square, Milton Park, Abingdon, Oxon OX14 4RN
711 Third Avenue, New York, NY, 10017, USA

Routledge is an imprint of the Taylor & Francis Group, an informa business

British Library Cataloguing-in-Publication Data
A catalogue record for this book is available from the British Library

Library of Congress Cataloging-in-Publication Data
A catalog record for this book is available from the Library of Congress

ISBN 978-0-08-089050-0

Typeset by MPS Limited, a Macmillan Company, Chennai, India
www.macmillansolutions.com

Printed and bound in India by Replika Press Pvt. Ltd.

Contents

Contents

Preface to the fourth edition

Recreation, leisure and tourism continue to provide a fascinating field of study for economists. The first edition of this book was written just after a period of intense recession in the UK economy. The second edition was prepared during a period of growth in the economies of the UK, the USA and Europe. But elsewhere, the economies of Japan – the second largest in the world – Brazil, Russia, and what were once referred to as the Asian tiger economies had suffered decline. The third edition was written in a period where the economic significance of China had continued to grow whilst the rest of the world economy showed a mixture of growth and economic stagnation. Additionally, tourism suffered a severe shock in the wake of 9/11 and the war in Iraq. This new fourth edition is particularly overshadowed by the (near) global recession and its effects on recreation, leisure and tourism. It is, of course, impossible to predict the economic conditions that will prevail in the year when, or the region where, this book will be read. But it is important to understand what has happened over the course of economic business cycles to prepare for what may happen in the future.

The changes in fortunes of various economies are mapped out through the updated statistics which are a central feature of this fourth edition. The effects of these changes on the leisure sector are also evident in these statistics and more so in the many new and updated exhibits that illustrate the text. In some cases, original exhibits have been retained and updated so as to provide the reader with contrasting evidence and a sense of the dynamics of the economy. In terms of geographical coverage, this book attempts to use examples from around the world to illustrate its points.

The aim of this book remains that of offering those involved in the business of recreation, leisure and tourism an understanding of the practicalities of economics. To support this aim, real-world examples continue to be emphasized in this book rather than economic theory for theory's sake. Thus, in contrast to general economics introductory texts, the marginal productivity theory of labour is excluded, but pricing of externalities is included on the grounds that the latter is more useful to students of leisure and tourism than the former.

The key themes of the book focus on a series of questions:

- How is the provision of leisure and tourism determined?
- Could it be provided in a different way?
- How are organizations affected by the competitive and macroeconomic environments?
- What are the economic impacts of leisure and tourism?
- What are the environmental impacts of leisure and tourism?

- How can economics be used to manage leisure and tourism?
- How has economics failed recreation, leisure and tourism?

The other key features of this book are:

- Visual mapping of the content of each chapter.
- Liberal use of press cuttings to illustrate points.
- Chapter objectives.
- Learning outcomes.
- Key points summarized.
- Data response questions.
- Short answer questions.
- Integrated case studies.
- Useful websites.

The fourth edition also includes illustrations in each chapter, multiple choice questions at the end of each chapter and a set of PowerPoint slides available on the companion website.

It is hoped that this book will create a lasting interest in the economics of recreation, leisure and tourism and generate a spirit of critical enquiry into leisure and tourism issues affecting consumers, producers and hosts.

John Tribe, 2011

Introduction

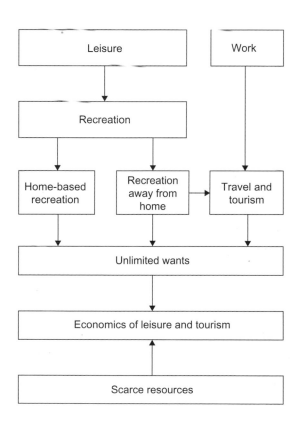

Objectives and learning outcomes

- Are the recreation, leisure and tourism industries more important to national economies than banks?
- Why do these industries provide so many new jobs?
- What is the globalization of recreation and leisure?
- Are recreation, leisure and tourism shares good investments?
- Is air travel sustainable?
- Why do we spend more days at work than at play?
- Economics is a social science but is it human?

This book will help you investigate these issues. The objectives of this chapter are to define and integrate the areas of study of this book.

First the scope of recreation, leisure and tourism will be discussed, and second the scope and techniques of economics will be outlined. The final part of the chapter explains how the study area of recreation, leisure and tourism can be analysed using economic techniques.

By studying this chapter students will be able to:

- understand the scope of recreation, leisure and tourism and their interrelationship;
- explain the basic economic concerns of scarcity, choice and opportunity costs;
- outline the allocation of resources in different economic systems;
- explain the methodology of economics;
- understand the use of models in economics;
- understand the use of economics to analyse issues in recreation, leisure and tourism;
- access sources of information.

DEFINITION AND SCOPE OF RECREATION, LEISURE AND TOURISM

Like all definitions, those pertaining to recreation, leisure and tourism encounter some problems. For example, a common element in many definitions of leisure is that of free time. Thus working, sleeping and household chores are excluded. However, should we then include people who are sick or recovering from illness? Similarly, recreation is commonly applied to the pursuits that people undertake in their leisure time. But what about things people do to support their employment in their spare time? For example, is a computer programmer's use of computers in non-working time a leisure activity? Similar questions arise in defining tourism. The common element in definitions of tourism is that of 'temporary visiting'. Questions of scope immediately arise. Are people who are engaged in study overseas tourists? Are people travelling on business tourists? Aware of the problems involved, some working definitions of travel and tourism are now attempted.

WORKING DEFINITIONS

- Leisure: *Discretionary time* is the time remaining after working, commuting, sleeping and doing necessary household and personal chores which can be used in a chosen way.
- Recreation: *Pursuits undertaken in leisure time*. Recreational pursuits include home-based activities such as reading and watching television, and those outside the home including sports, theatre, cinema and tourism.
- Tourism: *Visiting for at least one night for leisure and holiday, business and professional or other tourism purposes*. Visiting means a temporary movement to destinations outside the normal home and workplace.
- Recreation, leisure and tourism sector organizations: *Organizations producing goods and services for use in leisure time*, organizations seeking to influence the use of leisure time and organizations supplying recreation, leisure and tourism organizations. Many organizations produce goods and services for recreational and non-recreational use, for example, computer manufacturers. Figure 1.1 shows the relationship between recreation, and tourism and the constituent parts are discussed later.

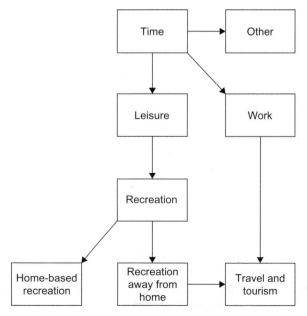

Figure 1.1 Leisure and tourism.

Home-based recreation

This includes:

- listening to music
- watching television and videos
- listening to the radio
- reading
- do it yourself (DIY)
- gardening
- playing games
- exercise
- hobbies
- leisure use of computers.

Recreation away from home

This includes:

- sports participation
- watching entertainment
- hobbies
- visiting attractions
- eating and drinking
- betting and gaming.

Travel and tourism

This includes:

- travelling to destination
- accommodation at destination
- recreation at destination.

DEFINITION, SCOPE AND METHODOLOGY OF ECONOMICS

The nature of economics

Resources and wants

Economics arises from a basic imbalance that is evident throughout the world. On the one side, there are resources which can be used to make goods and services. These are classified by economists into land (raw materials), labour and capital (machines). Additionally, we sometimes include the entrepreneur (the person that brings factors of production together) as a resource. On the other side, we have people's wants. The worldwide economic fact of life is that people's wants appear unlimited and exceed the resources available to satisfy these wants. This is true not just for people with low incomes, but for people with high incomes too. Clearly, the basic needs of rich people are generally satisfied in terms of food, clothing and shelter, but it is evident that their material wants in terms of cars, property, holidays and recreation are rarely fully satisfied.

Scarcity and choice

The existence of limited resources and unlimited wants gives rise to the basic economic problem of scarcity. The existence of scarcity means that choices have to be made about resource use and allocation. Economics is concerned with the choice questions that arise from scarcity:

- What to produce?
- How to produce it?
- To whom will goods and services be allocated?

Opportunity cost

Since resources can be used in different ways to make different goods and services, and since they are limited in relation to wants, the concept of opportunity cost arises. This can be viewed at different levels.

At the individual level, consumers have limited income. So if they spend their income on a mountain bike, they can consider what else they could have bought with the money, such as an air ticket. Individuals also have limited time. If an individual decides to work extra overtime, leisure time must be given up.

At a local or national government level the same types of choices can be analysed. Local councils have limited budgets. If they decide to build a leisure centre, then that money could have been used to provide more home help to the elderly. Even if they raised local taxes to build the new leisure centre, there would be an opportunity cost since the taxpayers would have to give up something in order to pay the extra taxes. Similar examples exist at a national government level. For example, subsidizing the arts means that there is less money available for student grants.

Opportunity cost is defined as the alternatives or other opportunities that have to be foregone to achieve a particular thing. Figure 1.2 illustrates this concept by use of a production possibility frontier (PPF). It is assumed first that the economy only produces two types of goods (leisure goods and other goods) and second that it uses all its resources fully.

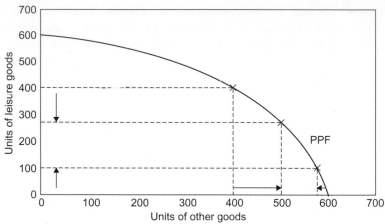

Figure 1.2 Opportunity cost and the PPF.

Curve PPF plots all the possible combinations of leisure goods and other goods that can be produced in this economy. It is drawn concave to the origin (bowed outwards) since, as more and more resources are concentrated on the production of one commodity, the resources available become less suitable for producing that commodity.

Curve PPF shows that if all resources were geared towards the production of leisure goods, 600 units could be produced with no production of other goods. At the other extreme, 600 units of other goods could be produced with no units of leisure goods. The PPF describes the opportunity cost of increasing production of either of these goods. For example, increasing production of leisure goods from 0 to 100 can only be done by diverting resources from the production of other goods, and production of these falls from 600 to 580 units. Thus, the opportunity cost at this point of 100 units of leisure goods is the 20 units of other goods that must be foregone. Similarly, if all resources are being used to produce a combination of 400 units of leisure goods and 400 units of other goods, the opportunity cost of producing an extra 100 units of other goods would be 100 units of leisure goods.

Allocative mechanisms

The existence of scarcity of resources and unlimited wants means that any economy must have a system for determining what, how and for whom goods are produced. The main systems for achieving this are:

- free market economies
- centrally planned economies
- mixed economies.

Figure 1.3 The price mechanism in action.

Free market economies work by allowing private ownership of firms. The owners of such firms produce goods and services by purchasing resources. The motive for production is profit and thus firms will tend to produce those goods and services which are in demand. Figure 1.3 shows the market mechanism in action and how resources are allocated away from the production of compact disc (CD) players in favour of MP3 players in response to changes in demand.

Centrally planned economies do not allow the private ownership of firms which instead are state owned. Production decisions are taken by state planning committees and resources are mobilized accordingly. Consumers generally have some choice of what to buy but only from the range determined by state planners.

Mixed economies incorporate elements from each system. Private ownership of firms tends to predominate, but production and consumption of goods and services may be influenced by public ownership of some enterprises and by the use of taxes and government spending.

The allocative mechanism has important implications for leisure and tourism. The collapse of communism in the eastern bloc meant that many economies are now in transition from centrally planned to market systems. Tourism facilities, such as hotels and restaurants, in these countries are having to revolutionize their organizational culture and become more customer oriented. The economies of Cuba and China are still nominally centrally planned, but free enterprise is continuing to flourish in China, and a visit to the Great Wall is greeted by privately owned souvenir shops jostling for custom. Plate 1 shows a McDonald's outlet in Beijing and the expansion of MacDonald's into communist countries illustrates the gradual softening of communist ideology. In 1988, McDonald's opened its first restaurant in a communist country, in Belgrade, Yugoslavia (now Serbia). In 1990, the first Soviet McDonald's opened in Moscow and was for a time the largest McDonald's in the world. In the same year the first McDonald's opened in mainland China, in the city and Special Economic Zone of Shenzhen, Guangdong province. However,

Plate 1 The McDonald's Golden Arches in Beijing, China.

Exhibit 1.1 demonstrates that despite the rapid growth of private enterprise in China there still remain some challenges and bottlenecks caused by state involvement and these are illustrated here in the area of Sport.

In the UK, the 'Thatcher Revolution', which involved 'rolling back the frontiers of the state', represented a key shift in the political economy away from state participation in the economy towards a greater role for private enterprise. This had an important impact on recreation, leisure and tourism production. It involved privatization of British Airways (BA) and the British Airports Authority (BAA), and also limited the spending powers of local government, thus reducing public provision in arts and leisure. Exhibit 1.2 discusses the spread of privatization in the airline industry and some of the consequences of this for consumer satisfaction.

The debate surrounding the mix of private versus public provision tends to centre on several key issues. Advocates of the free market argue that the system allows maximum consumer choice or sovereignty. They point to the efficiency of the system as firms compete to cut costs and improve products, the fact that the system does not need wastefully to employ officials to plan and monitor production, and lower taxes under free market systems. Their evidence is the one-way flow of human traffic observed across the Florida Straits from Cuba and past the former Iron Curtain from Eastern Europe in search of the free market.

Critics of the free market argue that choice is an illusion. Thus, although by day the shops in major shopping districts in London, New York and Paris are full of every conceivable product, by night their doorways are full of homeless people. What this illustrates is

Exhibit 1.1 The business of sport in China

The 2008 Beijing Olympics proved that China had the capability to host world-class sporting events and to produce world-beating athletes. The Games boasted dazzling opening and closing ceremonies, they were held in state-of-the-art venues and China won 51 gold medals.

In the light of this a report from the Economist Intelligence Unit asked questions about the nature of China's sports business and in particular how it compares with the cash rich sporting leagues in Western markets. The report focussed on three sports: basketball, football and golf.

The press release following the publication of the report noted the following headline features:

1. Despite the fact that China has liberalized and globalized many of its industries, sport has remained largely sheltered from commercialization.
2. Since Beijing was awarded the right to host the Olympic Games in 2008, more private money has flowed into the industry and the beginning of a market for sponsorship has developed.
3. Almost all of China's top athletes are products of the state system.
4. Commercialization is developing and for example in basketball several teams in the Chinese Basketball Association (CBA) league are now privately owned.
5. More Chinese athletes are leaving their sport associations to become independent agents where they are able to choose their own coaches and keep more of their winnings.
6. Major equipment suppliers including China's Li Ning and the international brands of Nike and Adidas are trying to enter the market by investing money in training programmes for young and developing sportspersons.
7. China has not yet created the kind of virtuous circle found in more developed markets. This occurs where popular events expand the fan and participant base. This in turn attracts sponsors and creates more demand for merchandise and more events.
8. Sport marketing is undeveloped with few of the sport federations in China focussing on issues like branding and marketing.
9. Consumers do not show the obsession with teams or individual players that are evident in the Western with no mass markets for club clothing or equipment featuring with team logos.
10. Broadcasting presents a financial constraint. The state-owned broadcaster CCTV-5 dominates the national television market and pays less for the rights to broadcast domestic sporting events than broadcasters in other countries who face strong competition with each other. The result is less money for sport and sport development.
11. Foreign games and leagues often outshine local ones especially in football where England's Premier League still dominates interest in the game.

All of these points demonstrate the complexity of business in China and that whilst the private sector continues to expand at a great pace, the state still plays a significant role in key parts of the economy and society. In this instance, state control of the media and its influence in training athletes has important repercussions for the development of the industry.

Sources: 'The big league? The business of sport in China' A report by the Economist Intelligence Unit http://graphics.eiu.com/upload/eiu_missionhills_sport_MH_main_Sept30 .pdf; Economist Intelligence Unit Press Release http://www.eiuresources.com/mediadir/ default.asp?PR=2009100501

Exhibit 1.2 Influence of the state-owned airlines on passenger satisfaction

López-Bonilla and López-Bonilla (2008) note that in the last three decades there have been major changes in the ownership of the airline industry. They note that a large number of state-owned airlines have been privatized and that the main motivations for privatization have included increased efficiency, improved service quality and reduction in state subsidies. The authors define a pure public sector airline as one where a state or states own 95 per cent or more of the airline. A mixed ownership airline is defined as one where the private sector controls voting stock of between 6 and 98 per cent and an airline is private where the private sector controls at least 99 per cent of the voting stock. The authors offer the following examples of these modes of ownership in 2005:

Public:
- Egypt Air, Egypt
- Olympic Airways, Greece
- Royal Air Maroc, Morocco
- Tap Portugal, Portugal.

Mixed:
- Alitalia, Italy
- SAS, Scandinavia
- Thai Airways, Thailand.

Private:
- American Airlines, USA
- British Airways, UK
- Lufthansa, Germany
- Varig, Brazil.

Their article investigates whether state-owned airlines exhibit poorer service levels than privately owned airlines. It examined such things as check-in, information service, courtesy, seat space, comfort, food service, in-flight entertainment services, delays, overbooking, positive word-of-mouth communication and overall satisfaction. The results show that state-owned airlines offer lower satisfaction levels than private airlines and mixed ownership carriers.

Source: López-Bonilla, J.M., López-Bonilla, L.M., 2008. Influence of the state-owned airlines on passenger satisfaction. J. Air Transp. Manage. 14 (3), 143–145.

that only those with purchasing power can exercise choice and purchasing power is unequally distributed in free market economies. Additionally, public provision is able to provide services which may be socially desirable but not profitable.

Macroeconomics and microeconomics

Economics is often subdivided into the separate areas of microeconomics and macroeconomics. Microeconomics studies individual consumer and household behaviour as well as the behaviour of firms. It analyses how these interact in particular markets to produce an equilibrium price and quantity sold. Thus, microeconomics investigates topics such as the price of air travel, the output of running shoes and the choice between leisure and work.

Macroeconomics looks at the economy as a whole. The national economy is composed of all the individual market activities added together. Thus, macroeconomics analyses aggregates such as national product and inflation and studies economic cycles of booms and recessions.

Marginal analysis

The concept of 'the margin' is central to much economic analysis. Consumer, producer and social welfare theories are based on the idea that an equilibrium position can be achieved, which represents the best possible solution. This position can theoretically be found by comparing the marginal benefit (MB) of doing something with the marginal cost (MC). For example, MC to a firm is the cost of producing one extra unit. MB is the revenue gained from selling one extra unit. Clearly, a firm can increase its profit by producing more if MB > MC. It should not expand such that MC > MB, and thus profits are maximized, and the firm is in equilibrium, because it cannot better its position, where MC = MB.

The methodology of economics

Economics is a social science. As such it draws some of its methodology or way of working from other sciences such as physics or chemistry but also has important differences. Social science can be broken down into its components of 'science' and 'social'.

The 'science' of social science

The science part of economics reflects the fact that it is a discipline that attempts to develop a body of principles. Economics attempts to construct theories about and explain the behaviour of households and firms in the economy. It therefore shares some common methods with other sciences.

The first of these is the need to distinguish between positive and normative statements. Positive statements are those which can be tested by an appeal to the facts. They are statements of what is or what will be. 'Swimming cuts cholesterol' is a positive statement. It can be tested, and accepted or refuted. Normative statements are those which are statements of opinion and therefore cannot be tested by an appeal to the facts. 'There should be a swimming pool in every town' is a normative statement.

Second, economics uses positive scientific method. This method acts as a filter which determines which theories become part of

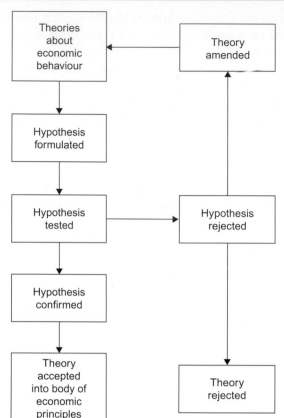

Figure 1.4 Scientific testing of theories.

the established body of principles of economics, which should be rejected and whether existing theories should maintain their place. Figure 1.4 illustrates the scientific testing of theories.

New and existing theories are subject to testing against empirical evidence and are accepted, rejected, amended or superseded according to the results of testing. Thus, the body of economic principles is, like that of other sciences, organic in the sense that knowledge is always being extended and some theories are shown to be no longer valid.

The organic and provisional nature of scientific understanding can be illustrated by considering the shape of the earth. Hundreds of years ago, people were in agreement that the earth was flat. This theory was confirmed by scholars who reasoned that if it was not flat people would fall off it. It was further reasoned that the stars were attached to a canopy above the earth and this fitted observations nicely. This then was the accepted set of principles until the theory no longer tested true. It was developments in geometry and astronomy that first led to serious questioning of the accepted principles of a flat earth and circumnavigation of the earth endorsed such findings. Modern space programmes continue to confirm our current belief in a round earth by providing supporting photographic evidence.

Academic journals in economics, leisure and tourism provide the arena for testing old and new hypotheses in this field.

The 'social' of social science

The difference between social sciences such as economics, sociology and psychology and natural sciences such as physics and chemistry is that the former study people rather than inanimate objects. This means first that their investigative methods are often different. It is difficult to perform laboratory experiments in economics and often data must be collected from historical records or from surveys. Second, it means that economic 'laws' are different from physics laws. If interest rates increase it can be predicted that the demand for credit will fall but we cannot predict that this will be true for every individual. This is called a statistical hypothesis. The law of gravity, on the other hand, applies universally. This is called a deterministic hypothesis.

Economic models

Economic models are built to describe relationships between economic variables and predict the effects of changing these variables. They can be compared to models used elsewhere. For example, civil engineers build models of bridges and subject them to stress in a wind tunnel. The purpose of the model is to predict what will happen in the real world, and in the case of a bridge ensure that the design is safe in extreme conditions.

Models are generally simplified abstractions of the real world. They have two key components. First, assumptions are made which build the foundations for the model. For example, the model of firms' behaviour under perfect competition assumes that firms maximize profits, that there are many buyers and sellers and that the products bought and sold are identical. Second, implications or outcomes are predicted by the working of the model. For example, theory predicts that firms operating under conditions of perfect competition will not be able to earn abnormally high profits in the long run. The predictions of competition theory can be tested empirically, or in other words by making observations. So for example as air travel operates in an ever-more competitive environment with the development of low-cost carriers, economic theory would predict that profits in the industry will fall.

The term *ceteris paribus* is often used in economic analysis, meaning all other things remaining unchanged. This is important because in the real world several factors often occur at the same time, some exaggerating a particular effect and some countering it. So for example it can be said that for most goods an increase in price will lead to a fall in demand *ceteris paribus*. Thus, a rise in cinema ticket prices should cause a fall in demand. Clearly, if other things are allowed to change this might not happen. For example, if incomes rose significantly this might more than offset the increase in price and we might observe demand for cinema tickets rising whilst prices rise.

THE ECONOMICS OF RECREATION, LEISURE AND TOURISM

To recap, economic questions in general as well as those specific to recreation, leisure and tourism result from scarcity. Scarcity arises from the imbalance between the resources available to make goods and services and people's demand for those goods and services. Economics is a social science which studies how limited resources are used to try to satisfy unlimited wants. Economic theories and models are constructed to describe the relationship between economic variables (e.g. the level of income and the demand for fitness club membership) and to make predictions. Economics is generally divided into microeconomics focussing on individuals, firms and markets and macroeconomics, focussing on the whole economy generally at the national level. There is also a growing movement concerned with environmental economics.

At the microeconomic level, in market economies, it is consumer preferences expressed through patterns of demand that largely determine which recreation, leisure and tourism goods and services will be supplied. On the demand side rising incomes have stimulated strong growth in this sector. On the supply side technological advances have led to the introduction of new leisure products (e.g. digital cameras and MP3 players) and the reduction in prices of many existing ones (e.g. televisions and stereos). Changing patterns of demand and supply create relative shortages, gluts and price changes in different recreation, leisure and tourism markets. These signals are picked up by profit-seeking producers who adjust production and economizing consumers who adjust purchases accordingly until there is an equilibrium reached in each market at a price where demand equals supply. This is the 'invisible hand' of the market which was first explained by the early economist Adam Smith. It demonstrates in general how leisure resources are allocated amongst competing uses and specifically how, for example, digital downloads over the Internet have replaced CDs and music stores. It also demonstrates why in a sports stadium a cleaner might earn US$5 per hour (high supply and limited demand) whereas a top international sportsperson can earn US$1000 per hour (limited supply and high demand).

Most economies incorporate a degree of government intervention and so recreation, leisure and tourism production and consumption is not left totally to market forces. For example, some leisure pursuits (e.g. the consumption of recreational drugs) are banned and not available through regular markets. Similarly, some leisure pursuits (e.g. gambling and smoking) are discouraged by governments through taxation. Other leisure pursuits (e.g. opera, arts and children's playgrounds) are deemed to be beneficial to society at large. These so-called merit goods are therefore encouraged by governments and offered at reduced prices or at no charge through government subsidy. In some instances (e.g. television stations, parks and swimming pools) leisure services are not provided by private firms (the private sector) but rather by state or local government (the public sector). However, over the last 20 years there has been a move towards privatization of public sector organizations – most notably airlines in the leisure sector. Privatization and deregulation of markets are both designed to promote competition which in turn encourages cost cutting, low prices and product innovation. Similarly, governments intervene in markets for the purposes of consumer protection which includes actions to prevent the formation of monopolies that may be against the public interest. The airline industry is a good example here. Airlines often wish to merge with other airlines to become more efficient. But if an airline becomes too big and competition becomes weak then consumers face ticket price hikes. So most countries set levels of maximum ownership by any single airline and do not allow mergers that would breach such a limit.

As well as making choices in the market between different leisure goods and services and other goods and services, individuals are also faced with the choice of allocating time between work and leisure. An interesting economic question is the way in which individuals react to an increase in wages. On the one hand, an increase in wages stimulates our desire for leisure time because we have more income to enjoy it. On the other hand, as earnings per hour increase workers are faced with a notional increase in the cost of not working (i.e. the opportunity cost of leisure increases). Hence, rational individuals may be tempted to reallocate time towards paid work or at least increase the intensity of their leisure consumption. Empirical evidence points to a modest reduction in time devoted to work and research in the UK suggests that in the second half of the twentieth century British people had decreased their working hours by 2 hours 40 minutes per week. The labour market is also subject to government intervention and in the European Union (EU), for example, the European Work Directive has capped the working week at 35 hours for most employees.

At the macroeconomic level, recreation and tourism are major contributors to national income and prosperity. Their main economic impacts include expenditure, incomes, employment and foreign currency earnings but is difficult to determine the exact contribution of recreation and tourism to the macroeconomy because the boundaries between leisure and other activities can be blurred. For example, motoring can include business and leisure uses as can computing and Internet use. Because of this Tourism Satellite Accounts (TSA) have been developed to try to more accurately measure the contribution of this sector to national economies. In some countries economic impacts are particularly strong and tourism for example represents approximately almost 80 per cent of the economic activity of the Caribbean islands of Antigua and Barbuda (http://www.wttc.org/bin/pdf/original_pdf_file/top_10_tables_summary.pdf). Different aspects of the leisure industry are of importance in different countries. For example, the film industry is particularly significant in the USA, the music industry in the UK and the tourism industry in Spain.

The economic importance of recreation and tourism also depends on the stage of a county's economic development. As countries become richer, leisure assumes an increased economic importance. In low-income economies, resources are typically used mainly to satisfy basic demands of food, clothing and shelter with little available for leisure. In high-income economies, resources and incomes are more plentiful and the production and consumption of leisure goods and services become significant economic activities. This is reflected in economic data so that for low-income countries the primary sector of the economy (agriculture, mining and so on) accounts for the majority of economic activity, whereas for developed economies it is the manufacturing and the services sector. However, in mature developed countries deindustrialization is a common phenomenon where traditional manufacturing industries decline and the services sector (especially financial services, leisure and information technology) has become the major source of economic growth.

The leisure industry is increasingly seen as an appropriate vehicle to aid economic growth. For developing countries, tourism especially can be an important part of an economic development strategy although resources need to be found for investment in infrastructure. Leisure projects are also important for developed countries. So for example there is always a lot of competition between countries to host the Olympic Games. Such projects bring income and employment both in the construction and running phases and can have significant multiplier effects on the local and national economy. Because of this governments may favour leisure developments as part of a regeneration strategy for regions which have been affected by a decline in traditional industries. In situations such as these where wider benefits beyond immediate profitability are important, governments may use cost–benefit analysis to determine whether a scheme should go ahead.

The growth of multinational corporations through integration, franchising and international tourism has led to an increasing globalization of leisure. In economic terms, this means that production and marketing of leisure goods and services are increasingly unconstrained by national boundaries. Examples of global brands in leisure include Nike, Manchester United Football Club and Carnival Cruises in tourism. Multinationals such as Nike are able to locate production where labour and other costs are lowest whilst marketing products to high-income consumers. Additionally, production for global markets enables multinationals to benefit from economies of scale. These factors can bring benefits to shareholders in higher profits and consumers in lower prices. However, some multinationals have been criticized for exploitation of labour in developing countries. Similarly, whilst multinationals can provide investment for tourism development, they may result in lower-multiplier benefits since they tend to import more and repatriate profits to their corporate headquarters.

The production and consumption of leisure goods and services also gives rise to a series of externalities. For example, on the positive side, increased use of fitness facilities results in lower use of public health provision; on the negative side, increased air travel causes environmental impacts of air and noise pollution and CO_2 emissions. Environmental economics seeks to extend conventional economic analysis to include consideration of environmental externalities, the use of renewable and non-renewable resources, and the carrying capacity of the environment. Taking the example of air travel, environmental economists would advocate the following. First, airlines should pay for the pollution they cause (e.g. they should finance double-glazing for those directly affected by aircraft noise). Second, airlines should monitor and control their effects on resources such as the ozone layer. Third, since the atmosphere has a limited carrying capacity for absorbing pollution before global warming occurs, airline contribution to this should be monitored and controlled. Environmental taxes are advocated so that polluting firms pay the full costs of any negative environmental impacts and non-government organizations (NGOs) such as Tourism Concern, World Wide Fund for Nature (WWF) and Greenpeace lobby governments to provide better environmental protection.

Finally, the limitations of economics in analysing the leisure world should be noted. Economics tends to concentrate on how markets work and how to increase economic efficiency and economic growth. It often incorporates somewhat unrealistic assumptions to enable modelling to take place. The market is in fact just one possible mechanism that decides which leisure goods and services will be produced and who will enjoy them. It lacks a human dimension, for that human dimension (which includes the dimensions of caring, or emotion, or hope, or justice, or empathy, or love) is specifically barred from the subject by its positivist rules. It does not raise or answer questions about what leisure goods and services should be produced or who should enjoy them or indeed about what kind of a leisure society would be desirable. Such questions are generally tackled under ethics and philosophy and neatly sidestepped by mainstream economists. Indeed, those with access to recreation leisure and tourism represent a minority of the world's population many of whom are still struggling to meet the more basic needs of food, shelter and clothing.

REVIEW OF KEY TERMS

- Leisure: discretionary time.
- Recreation: pursuits undertaken in leisure time.
- Tourism: visiting for at least one night for leisure and holiday, business and professional or other tourism purposes.
- Economic problem: scarcity and choice.
- Leisure and tourism sector organizations: organizations producing goods and services for use in leisure time, and organizations seeking to influence the use of leisure time.
- Opportunity cost: the alternatives or other opportunities that have to be foregone to achieve a particular thing.
- Free market economy: resources allocated through price system.
- Centrally planned economy: resources allocated by planning officials.
- Mixed economy: resources allocated through free market and planning authorities.
- Microeconomics: study of household and firm's behaviour.
- Macroeconomics: study of whole economy.
- Marginal analysis: study of effects of one extra unit.
- Positive statement: based on fact.
- Normative statement: based on opinion.
- *Ceteris paribus*: other things remaining unchanged.

 Data Questions

Task 1.1 **The uses and misuses of economics**

Economics is a discipline which can help to understand leisure and tourism and provides tools to help decision-making. But it is only one of a number of ways of looking at leisure and tourism. For example, the disciplines of sociology, psychology, anthropology and philosophy each investigate different aspects of leisure and tourism and use different methods and theories in their investigations. So philosophy may look at meaning (what is the concept of leisure?), aesthetics studies beauty and form (is a football stadium attractively designed?) and ethics is concerned with justice and rightness (are violent video games good or bad?). Focussing on video games can help to see how different disciplines tackle different issues. Psychology might investigate human motivation

Table 1.1 Differences between disciplinary and functional approaches to leisure and tourism

	Disciplinary	Functional
Knowledge	Knowing that	Knowing how
Site of knowledge creation	Universities	Industry
Interest	Is it true?	Does it work?
Emphasis	Theory	Practice

for playing video games. Economics may forecast the demand for them. Sociology can help to understand the effects of video games on society.

A complex field of study such as leisure and tourism often requires a multidisciplinary approach. That is we may seek understanding not just from one discipline but from a number of disciplines. In addition, there are approaches which are interdisciplinary. Here, a new set of methods, theories and language emerge from those working collaboratively across disciplines. Environmentalism, which uses economics, sociology, biology, physics and chemistry, is an example of an interdisciplinary approach.

Then there are functional approaches to leisure and tourism. These have a more distant relationship to disciplines and their specific focus is on management. Examples here include accounting, law, marketing and human resource management. Whilst disciplines are nurtured in universities and concentrate on the development of theories, functional approaches are developed in the practising field. The main differences between disciplinary knowledge and functional knowledge are summarized in Table 1.1. The importance of this discussion is that we live in a society of specialists with a highly developed division of labour. It is easy for people to become highly knowledgeable in one area while being ignorant of other significant aspects of a situation. It is therefore important to understand the limits of any single approach and the fact that most leisure and tourism issues are multifaceted. It is always worth asking what kind of a question is being investigated (is it an economic, philosophical, psychological question, or one of law or marketing or a multidisciplinary issue?). Of course, the wider the approach, the more difficult decision-making can become.

Recap Questions

1 What contribution can economics make to environmentalism?
2 What kinds of questions are each of the following?
   (a) The level of a minimum wage for the hotel industry.
   (b) Whether violent video games should be banned.
   (c) The effects of a rise in interest rates.
   (d) Maximizing profits from the sales of video games.
   (e) Imposing a tax on aviation fuel.
   (f) Ending tax-free sales at airports.
   (g) The location of the next Olympic Games.
3 Is there a correct answer to any of these questions?
4 Frame two leisure and tourism questions which are exclusively economic.

Task 1.2 **Active outdoor recreation and its contribution to the US economy**

A report by the Outdoor Industry Foundation found that three out of every four Americans participate in active outdoor recreation each year making this industry contribute $730 billion to the US economy. In addition to this the industry generates 6,435,270 jobs and $87,867 million in federal and state taxes. The report notes that the Active Outdoor Recreation Economy is a big business, it being equal to or bigger than other major economic sectors in the USA such as telecommunications, hospitals and motion pictures and videos.

The outdoor recreation sector covers the following activities:

- *Bicycling*: paved-road bicycling; off-road bicycling.
- *Camping*: RV camping at a campsite, tent camping at a campsite, rustic lodging.
- *Fishing*: recreational fly, recreational non-fly.
- *Hunting*: shotgun, rifle, bow.
- *Paddling*: kayaking, rafting, canoeing.
- *Snow sports*: downhill skiing – including telemark, snowboarding, cross-country skiing, snowshoeing.
- *Trail*: trail running on an unpaved trail, day hiking on an unpaved trail, backpacking, rock climbing.
- Wildlife viewing, bird watching, other wildlife watching.

The report divides expenditure into trip expenditure and expenditure on materials. Trip expenditure includes food and drink, transportation, entertainment and activities, lodging and souvenirs and gifts, amounts to retail sales of $243 billion. Expenditure on supply of materials includes apparel, footwear, equipment, accessories and services, accounts for retail sales of $46 billion. However, the report also identifies a ripple effect (called by economists 'the multiplier effect') which raises the total economic worth of retail sales to $622 billion and that of supply of materials to $108 billion. The report explains that the components of the ripple effect are:

- The direct effect consisting of the initial purchase made by the consumer.
- The indirect effect where sales create economic linkages in the industries that provide supplies and supporting activities.
- The induced effect where wages and salaries paid to those working in the direct and indirect effect industries circulate through the economy.

The report includes several case studies including the opening of a bike shop in the struggling town of Fruita, CO, USA. The shop 'Over the Edge Sports' was one of the few businesses in the town centre where businesses had been closing. Its success encouraged the community to build mountain bike trails and organize an annual Fruita Fat Tire Festival. Fruita has since earned a reputation as a world-class mountain biking destination that creates $1.5 million a year of spending in the local economy. The town's sales tax revenues increased by 51 per cent over 5 years, including an 80 per cent increase in sales tax revenues from restaurants.

Finally, the report emphasizes how active outdoor recreation improves the physical health of the nation. It notes that over 30 per cent of adult Americans are obese and that participation in outdoor recreation is a way to make Americans fitter and leaner so reducing medical costs and increasing their sense of well-being.

The Outdoor Industry Foundation is a non-profit organization dedicated to encouraging participation in active outdoor recreation and healthier lifestyles.

Source: Adapted from the Outdoor Industry Foundation Report
http://www.outdoorindustry.org/images/researchfiles/RecEconomypublic.pdf?26

Recap Questions

1 (a) Referring back to Task 1.1 is the knowledge produced in this report disciplinary or functional knowledge?

   (b) Why might some observers challenge the findings of this report?

2 What factors of production are used by the Active Outdoor Recreation Industry?

3 Explain the 'ripple effect' using the example of 'Over the Edge Sports' in Fruita, CO, USA.

4 How significant is the outdoor recreation sector in the country in which you are studying? How does it compare in importance to other major industries?

5 The report emphasizes the positive impacts of outdoor recreation in terms of health benefits – are there any negative impacts? Is it possible to quantify these broader impacts?

Task 1.3 Consultancy report: The economic impact of the london 2012 olympics

In his report on the economic impact of the Olympics Adam Blake notes that hosting the Olympics has brought mixed rewards in the past. Data cited for previous Olympics includes:

- **Los Angeles 1984**: The economic impact of the games on Southern California was estimated to be US$2.3 billion with 73,375 jobs supported.
- **Seoul 1988**: An economic impact of some $1.6 billion with an increase in employment of 336,000 jobs.
- **Barcelona 1992**: A direct economic impact of $30 million with 296,640 new jobs created.
- **Atlanta 1996**: The economic impact of the Olympics on Georgia was estimated to be $5.1 billion and with an additional 77,026 jobs generated.
- **Sydney 2000**: One key study estimated that the economic impact of the Games on Australia was estimated to be $4.5 billion with employment gains of 98,700 jobs.
- **Athens 2004**: A study showed the economic impact of the Games to be US$15.9 million with an employment impact of 445,000 jobs, respectively.

Blake continues his analysis by outlining the stages that must be undertaken in order to conduct an economic impact assessment (EIA) of the Olympics. First, it is necessary to calculate spending, by organizations such as the organizing committee as well as by individuals. Next, this expenditure must be aggregated and third, a model must be constructed and applied to the data to calculate how this spending translates into

Task 1.3 **continued**

income and employment. The two main techniques are input–output (I–O) analysis and computable general equilibrium (CGE) modelling.

He also notes the different time scales in which impacts occur. These are first the pre-Games impacts

- the construction phase
- other pre-Games costs
- visitor impacts in the run-up to the Games.

Next the during-Games impacts include:

- revenues from staging the Games
- during-Games visitor impacts
- costs of staging the Games.

Finally post-Games impacts include:

- legacy visitor impacts
- legacy infrastructural impacts.

The main conclusions drawn from Blake's analysis of the London Olympics are:

> the London 2012 Olympics would have an overall positive effect on the UK and London economies, with an increase in GDP over the 2005–2016 period of £1,936 million and an additional 8,164 full-time equivalent jobs created for the UK. The impacts are concentrated in 2012 (£1,067 million GDP and 3,261 FTE jobs) and in the post-Games period 2013–2016 (£622 million GDP and 1,948 additional FTE jobs).

Source: Adapted from The Economic Impact of the London 2012 Olympics by Adam Blake
http://www.nottingham.ac.uk/ttri/discussion/2005_5.pdf.

Recap Questions

1 How can projects such as hosting the Olympic Games help in regeneration? What examples are there of this?
2 What negative economic impacts might there be from the hosting of the Olympic Games?
3 What is the opportunity cost of hosting of the Olympic Games?
4 Which industries are most likely to benefit from hosting the Olympic Games?
5 Distinguish between micro- and macroeconomic impacts of hosting the Olympic Games.
6 What are the major non-economic impacts of hosting the Olympic Games and are they quantifiable?

MULTIPLE CHOICE

1 Which of the following is not considered a resource?
   (a) Demand.
   (b) Land.

(c) Labour.

(d) Capital.

2 *Ceteris paribus* means:

(a) Everything changes in the long run.

(b) All other things remain unchanged.

(c) Equal wages.

(d) Inflation is rising.

3 What does the term macroeconomic mean?

(a) An embedded programme in economics.

(b) The absence of scarcity.

(c) To do with the whole economy.

(d) The economy is growing.

4 Opportunity cost measures:

(a) An alternative that has to be given up in order to produce something

(b) Average cost (AC) plus MC.

(c) AC divided by MC.

(d) Environmental cost.

5 Which of the following is a positive statement?

(a) The minimum wage should be increased.

(b) Pigs can fly.

(c) The price of bacon is too high.

(d) Unemployment should be reduced.

REVIEW QUESTIONS

1 What is the opportunity cost of watching television?

2 Explain in terms of marginal analysis at what point you will turn off the television.

3 Formulate a hypothesis that links the level of unemployment to the demand for video rentals. How would you test this hypothesis and what problems might you encounter?

4 Explain how the market mechanism responds to a change in consumer tastes or demand using an example from the leisure or tourism sector.

5 Distinguish between the kinds of problems which physics, biology, psychology and economics might address in the area of sports. What similarities and differences in investigative methods are there between these disciplines?

6 'Economics is a social science but is it human?' Discuss this question with reference to recreation or leisure or tourism.

Websites of interest

Institute of Leisure and Amenity Management: www.ilam.co.uk

World Tourism Organization: www.world-tourism.org

World Travel and Tourism Council: www.wttc.org

Learning help in economics and business studies: www.bized.ac.uk

The ALTIS guide to Internet resources in hospitality, leisure, sport and tourism: www.altis.ac.uk

The London Olympics Website: www.london2012.com

PART 1

Organizations and Markets

CHAPTER **2**

Recreation, leisure and tourism organizations

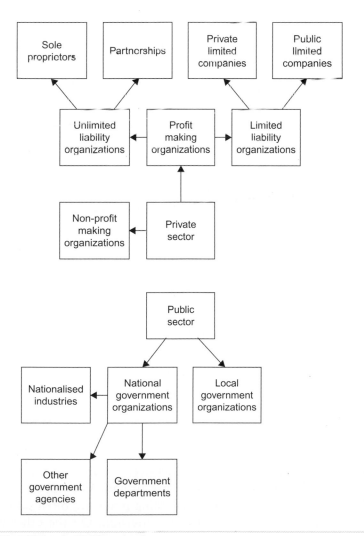

Objectives and learning outcomes

In order to analyse and understand the behaviour of organizations in the recreation, leisure and tourism sector, we need to be able to clarify their aims and objectives. An important initial question is whether the organization is in the private sector or government-run. For most private-sector organizations such as The Walt Disney Corporation, profits are the main objective. On the other hand, Tourism Concern is a not-for-profit organization and exists to encourage ethical and sustainable tourism. Organizations run by government were traditionally set up to provide services such as parks, museums and swimming pools that were desirable but not commercially profitable. But attitudes to the extent of government provision and use of subsidies vary across countries according to which party holds political power.

By studying this chapter students should be able to:

- distinguish between private- and public-sector organizations;
- understand the differences in finance, control, structure and objectives of organizations;
- understand ways in which capital can be raised;
- analyse movements in share prices;
- analyse the effects of different organizational structures on organizational behaviour.

PUBLIC-SECTOR ORGANIZATIONS

Public-sector organizations are those owned by the government. This can be national government or local government.

Local government organizations

Leisure and tourism provision in the local government sector may include:

- leisure centres and swimming pools
- libraries
- arts centres
- parks and recreation facilities
- tourism support services.

It should be noted that sometimes services are free, sometimes they are subsidized and sometimes they are provided at full commercial rates. For example, charges for swimming pools are often subsidized but sometimes cover the full cost of provision. On the other hand, facilities such as parks, libraries and children's playgrounds are generally provided without charge.

Sources of finance

The finance of these organizations comes from:

- charges for services where applicable
- central government grants
- grants from other sources (e.g. lotteries)
- local government taxation
- local government borrowing.

Ownership and control

In essence, local government organizations are owned by the local population. Policy decisions or decisions of strategic management are taken on their behalf by the local council. Each local government area elects councillors or members to represent them. The political party which holds the majority of seats on the council will generally be able to dictate policy and such policy will be determined through a series of committees such as:

- libraries and arts
- recreation and leisure
- planning and resources.

The planning and resources committee is a particularly powerful one as it determines the medium- to long-term strategy of the council and thus provides the financial framework within which the other committees must operate. The day-to-day or operational management of local government-run services depends on the nature of the service being provided. Council employees are responsible for overall management and services which are spread out across a local government area, such as parks, will be run from the council offices. Larger services such as leisure centres will have their own management which in turn will be responsible to a service director at the council offices.

Aims and missions

The aims of local government and its organizations are largely determined by the political party or coalition of parties who hold the majority. This often means that leisure provision, for example, will vary between neighbouring local authorities which have different political parties in power. Administrations to the right of the political spectrum favour lower local taxes and market-driven provision. Those to the left favour public provision financed out of tax revenues and offered free or at subsidized prices. To determine the differing aims of political parties we need to consult their manifestos as well as review their actual provision. However, political parties do not operate in a vacuum. They will be influenced by:

- pressure groups
- trade unions
- local press
- national government.

Edgecombe (2003) examined a major dilemma facing local government leisure facility managers in Australia – that of providing recreation services, whilst at the same time minimizing financial deficits and avoiding significant negative impacts on private enterprises providing similar services.

National government organizations

National government-owned organizations can be further subdivided into public corporations, government departments and other government agencies.

Public corporations are sometimes known as nationalized or state-run industries. They generally supply goods or services to the public. Examples of these include:

- the British Broadcasting Corporation (UK)
- Societe National des Chemins de Fer (SNCF; National Rail Network, France)
- Air India (Exhibit 2.1).

But the extent of nationalization of recreation, leisure and tourism industries depends on the politics of individual countries. So in the USA, most television stations and airlines are in the private sector, and in the UK, railways are run by private-sector organizations.

Government departments perform an executive role on behalf of governments in implementing policy. There are a number of government departments which impinge on the recreation leisure and tourism sector of the economy. Examples include:

- *The Department of Culture, Media and Sport (DCMS) (UK)*: This department has the responsibility for tourism, arts and libraries, sport and broadcasting.
- *The Department of the Interior (USA)*: This department protects America's natural resources and heritage, honours US cultures and tribal communities, and supplies the energy to power its future. Its responsibilities include overseeing the National Parks Service.
- *The Department of Resources, Energy and Tourism (Australia)*: This department provides advice and policy support to the Australian government regarding Australia's resources, energy

Exhibit 2.1 Nationalization of Air India

Air India, originally known as Tata Airlines, started life with two planes, one palm-thatched shed, one full-time pilot, one part-time engineer and two apprentice-mechanics. In its first full year of operations (1933), it flew 160,000 miles, carrying155 passengers and 10.71 tonnes of mail. Tata Airlines was converted into a public company and renamed Air India in August 1946.

However, by the early 1950s the financial condition of airlines operating in India had deteriorated so that the government made the decision to nationalize the air transport industry. On 1 August 1953, Indian Airlines was formed with the merger of eight domestic airlines to operate domestic services and Air India International was established to operate the overseas services.

Source: Author, adapted for Air India Corporate Information (www.airindia.com).

and tourism sectors. It also develops and delivers policies to increase Australia's international competitiveness, consistent with the principles of environmental responsibility and sustainable development.

Other government agencies tend to work at a smaller level than government departments and provide more specific services. Examples include:

- Tourism Australia
- Visit Britain.

Aims and missions

The aims of nationalized industries vary from country to country. In some cases, public corporations aim for public service provision without the limitations imposed by the profit motive and are able to provide services that are loss making. In these instances, the rigours of efficiency and private-sector management styles may not be apparent. In other parts of the world (notably in the UK and in the USA) public corporations have been subjected to efficiency targets, performance indicators and target rates of return on investment, all of which have made them more closely mimic private-sector organizations. Nationalized industry's aims are generally contained within their charters or constitutions.

The aim of government departments is to carry out the policy of the government of the day and includes planning, monitoring and reviewing of provision and legislation. Exhibit 2.2 illustrates the aims of the Government Department of Resources, Energy and Tourism in Australia. This department covers the three areas of energy, resources and tourism. From the exhibit it can be seen that this department, as with other similar departments worldwide, is to provide both policy advice and implement programme-delivery services. Sometimes

Exhibit 2.2 Australian Government Department of Resources, Energy and Tourism

This department covers the following areas:

- Resources
- Energy
- Tourism.

Statement of Purpose

We enhance Australia's economic prosperity by improving productivity, competitiveness, security and sustainability of the resources, energy and tourism sectors through the provision of high-quality policy advice and programme-delivery services for the Australian government.

Our Valued Behaviours

Minister: We are responsive to our Minister in delivering apolitical, honest and frank policy advice and in implementing the government's policies and programmes.

Stakeholders: We focus on achieving constructive and collaborative relationships with our stakeholders including portfolio agency partners and other government departments, underpinned by genuine consultation, feedback and robust service delivery.

Policy: We provide high-quality evidence-based advice, through informed judgement and prudent risk management.

People: We encourage a positive workplace and display high levels of personal leadership and integrity. We are results focussed and continuously strive to learn and innovate.

Strategy

Resources: The Australian government is committed to creating a policy framework to expand Australia's resource base, increase the international competitiveness of our resources sector and improve the regulatory regime, consistent with the principles of environmental responsibility and sustainable development.

Energy: The Australian government is committed to the provision of adequate, reliable and affordable energy to meet future energy consumption needs and to underpin strong economic growth, consistent with the principles of environmental responsibility and sustainable development.

Tourism: The Australian government is committed to maximizing tourism's net economic contribution to the Australian economy and to fostering an industry that promotes the principles of environmental responsibility and sustainable development.

Source: Adapted from the Department of Resources, Energy and Tourism Corporate Plan 2009–2013 http://www.ret.gov.au/Department/Documents/2009-13_RETCorporatePlan.pdf

leisure, tourism and recreation fall under the same government department, but sometimes as in this case they are separated. The aims of other government agencies are specific to each organization and are generally targeted to a quite narrow field.

Sources of finance

National government organizations in the public sector are financed in the main from:

- taxes
- trading income.

The dependence on tax funding can mean that public-sector organizations are very sensitive to the changing priorities of the government of the day. Equally if the state of the economy as a whole is unhealthy, spending cuts will generally be imposed through the public sector.

Ownership and control

National government organizations are owned by the government on behalf of the population at large. However, each type of organization is controlled in a different way.

- Nationalized industries are typically given some autonomy and generally have a legal identity separate from the government. At the point of nationalization a law is passed outlining the aims, organization and control mechanism for each industry.
  A typical structure is one where a board of directors is established responsible for the day-to-day running of the industry. The chair of the board and its other members are appointed by an appropriate government minister and strategic decisions will be taken by the minister in consultation with the government.
- Government departments are headed by a minister and staffed by government employees. Their actions are directly accountable through a minister to the national assembly such as parliament. The offices of government departments are generally located close to the national assembly. The degree of political control exerted over government departments is thus more direct than for nationalized industries.

PRIVATE-SECTOR ORGANIZATIONS

Private-sector organizations are those which are non-government-owned. They can be further subdivided into profit-making organizations and non-profit-making organizations.

Profit-making organizations

Profit-making private-sector organizations consist of those with unlimited liability, those with limited liability and companies which are quoted on the stock exchange.

Unlimited liability

Unlimited liability means that the owners of such companies face no limit to their contribution should the organization become indebted. Most of their personal assets can be used to settle debts should the business cease trading. This includes not only the value of anything saleable from the business, but also housing, cars, furniture and stereos. Because of the discipline that unlimited liability brings, there are often very few formalities required to start trading as this form of business. Sole proprietorships and partnerships are examples of this type of business organization and advantages include:

- independence
- motivation
- personal supervision
- flexibility.

Equally there are some disadvantages which include:

- unlimited liability
- long hours of work
- lack of capital for expansion
- difficulties in case of illness.

Limited liability

In contrast, the formation of a limited liability company enables its owners to create a separate legal identity and this enables them to limit their exposure and liability in the case of company failure. Incorporation confers separate legal identity on the company. This may be contrasted with the position of unlimited liability organizations where the owners and the organization are legally the same. Limited liability places a limit to the contribution by an investor in an organization to the amount of capital that has been contributed. Should one of these organizations cease trading with debts, an investor may well lose the original investment, but liability would cease there and personal assets would not be at risk.

The benefits of the limited liability company mean that they are bound by closer rules and regulations than are unlimited liability organizations. Typically such companies need to provide details of:

- the name and address of the company
- details of the directors
- the objectives of the company
- details of share capital issued
- details of the internal affairs of the company including procedures for annual general meetings
- audited accounts.

Limited liability companies are further subdivided into private companies and public companies. It is the latter's shares which are freely tradable on the stock exchange. There are benefits and drawbacks of moving from a private limited company to a public limited company. Ability to raise more capital is a key advantage of becoming a public limited company as the stock exchange provides access to thousands of potential investors. On the other hand, there are considerable extra costs associated with flotation. These include the costs of bringing a company to the market as well as the costs of reporting and more burdensome governance requirements. Also there is a constant need to perform and produce high profits in the short term as a public limited company, and the risk of loss of control. The free access to share ownership and lack of control on transfer of shares mean that it is more difficult to retain control of public than private limited companies as groups of shareholders can build up controlling interests. Exhibit 2.3 provides an illustration of a company flotation in the travel industry. Amadeus, a leading travel IT company, was refloated on the Madrid Stock Exchange in 2010 meaning its shares were made available to the public and that the owners of the company were able to raise a large amount of capital.

Exhibit 2.3 Amadeus flotation

Amadeus, the Spanish travel reservations firm, has achieved a position as a leading transaction processor for the global travel and tourism industry. It provides transaction processing to both travel providers (including airlines, hotels, railways, cruise lines, ferries, car rental companies and tour operators) and travel agencies. Amadeus' distribution and IT systems cover itinerary planning, fare-searching, reservations, ticketing, airlines schedule and inventory control, passenger check-in and departure control. It earned €2.46 billion in revenues in 2009.

The company which was originally listed on the Madrid Stock Exchange was delisted in 2006 when BC Partners and Cinven bought their stake from airlines Air France, Lufthansa and Iberia for €4.4 billion. This effectively meant that the company was taken into the ownership format of a private limited company. However, Amadeus returned to the Spanish Stock Exchange in 2010 to become one of Europe's largest flotations in that year. According to the prospectus lodged with stock market regulator Comisión Nacional del Mercado de Valores (CNMV), Amadeus offered 98.9 million shares in a primary offering and 36.9 million existing shares to institutional investors. This share offer represented about 25 per cent of the firm. The price range expected for the listing was estimated at between €9.2 and €12.2 per share. In the event it raised over €1.3 billion in the listing which meant it had a market capitalization of around. €4.9 billion. On the day of the flotation the share price rose by 7.36 per cent by midday to reach a figure of €11.81.

Source: Press Cuttings.

Examples of companies that are quoted on the stock markets include:

- Royal Caribbean (USA)
- Carnival (USA)
- MGM Resorts (USA)
- Avis Budget Group (USA)
- Qantas (Australia) (see Exhibit 2.4)
- Living and Leisure Australia Group (Australia)
- Innovo Leisure Recreation Holdings Limited (Hong Kong)
- British Airways (UK)
- EasyJet (UK).

Exhibit 2.4 examines the case of the Qantas group – the major national and international airline operating in Australia. As the exhibit explains Qantas was formerly a nationalized industry run by

Exhibit 2.4 Qantas

Qantas is Australia's largest domestic and international airline. It employs around 35,000 staff and serves 173 destinations in 42 countries (including those covered by its codeshare partners) in Australia, Asia and the Pacific, the Americas, Europe and Africa.

The Qantas Group's main brands are:

- Qantas
- Jetstar
- QantasLink
- Jetstar Asia
- Jetstar Pacific.

The Qantas Group's long-term vision is to operate the world's best premium airline, Qantas, and the world's best low-fares carrier, Jetstar.

Qantas is a public limited company listed on the Australian Stock Exchange. However, Qantas was at one stage a nationalized industry owned by the Australian government. But in the 1990s, the government moved to privatize the airline. A public share offer was launched on 22 June 1995. The privatization was completed and Qantas shares listed on the Australian Stock Exchange on 31 July 1995 with a float price of AUS$1.90.

Since then key variations in its share price have included:

- 1995 AUS$1.90
- 1999 AUS$4.50
- 2001 AUS$2.60
- 2007 AUS$6.00.

and in 2008 the share price of Qantas fell below its flotation price to a level of AUS$1.40.

Source: Adapted from Qantas Fact File http://www.qantas.com.au/infodetail/about/ FactFiles.pdf

the Australian government and this was the case for many airlines. Government ownership meant that the airline was funded mainly from taxes. Some governments still maintain ownership of national airlines since it is believed that they play a strategic role in the economy. Additionally, airlines need to make very large capital purchases and these can be difficult to finance in the private sector. However, nationalization often means that competition and enterprise are stifled resulting in a poorer service for air travellers. Also as air travel is still something of a luxury it is argued that the state should not subsidize this sector out of taxes. Finally, state-run industries can be run on bureaucratic lines meaning that they are inefficient and inflexible.

Sources of finance

Sources of finance available to sole proprietors and partnerships are limited to:

- capital contributed by the owners
- ploughed-back profits
- bank loans.

Since these sources generally are only available to supply limited funds, this is a key reason why small firms remain small. On the other hand limited liability, incorporated firms are able to raise capital through the additional routes of:

- shares (equity)
- debentures.

A share, or equity or stock (USA), represents a small portion of ownership of a company that is sold. The company issues shares certificates in return for capital. The price of shares goes up and down according to relative demand and supply in the market place – in this case a stock exchange. Shares can be seen from the perspective of a shareholder and of a company. From the company's point of view, share capital is generally of low risk since if the company does not make any profits then no dividends are paid. So unlike with bank loans a company is not saddled with the need to make payments if it is going through an unprofitable period. Shareholders are attracted to shares by the prospect of dividend payments (related to the level of company profits) as well as growth in the capital value of shares. Of course, there is some risk as there is no guarantee of dividend payments and the value of shares can go down as well as up, indeed the value of shares in failing companies will often become worthless.

Debentures can be seen as a form of loan as they carry a fixed rate of interest. Thus to the company they pose a problem when profits are low because they still have to pay out the fixed interest, but their

Table 2.1	Financing Eurotunnel
1986	Concession to build the channel Tunnel awarded to Eurotunnel £46 million seed corn equity raised £206 million share placing with institutions
1987	£5 billion loan facility agreed with 200 syndicate bank 770 million equity funding from public offer in the UK and France
1990	£1.8 billion additional debt from syndicate £300 million loan from European investment bank £650 million rights issue
1994	£700 million raised from banks £850 million rights issue, priced at 26 per cent discount and entirely underwritten.

Source: Adapted from Press Cuttings.

fixed interest rate is attractive when profits are high as the company will retain more of its profits. Debenture holders get a guaranteed rate of return and are paid before shareholders so they are generally less risky than shares. On the other hand, there is no opportunity to benefit from higher dividends when a company is growing and making good profits.

Table 2.1 illustrates many of the aspects of financing mentioned earlier through the case of Eurotunnel. Eurotunnel is the name given to the rail tunnel that was built between England and France in the 1990s. Of course, a massive amount of capital was required to finance this project. Several points emerge from Table 2.1 which illustrates the financing of Eurotunnel. First, Eurotunnel's capital represents a mixture of loans from banks which carry interest payments until they are repaid, and share issues which will not pay dividends until profits are earned. If profits from the tunnel are insufficient to repay loans and interest, the company may be forced into liquidation by the banks. The assets of the company would then be sold to repay the banks. Under this scenario, shareholders would get nothing. This is because shareholders are assigned a lower priority than loan providers. However, because their liability is limited, neither would they stand to lose any personal assets, just the value of their shares. Under a more optimistic, high-profit scenario, payments to the banks are limited to previously negotiated rates, leaving substantial profits to be distributed in the form of high dividends to shareholders. Second, three different forms of share issue are illustrated by this case:

- A *placing* in 1986: This is where Eurotunnel's shares were placed directly with institutions such as pension funds and insurance companies. This represents a direct negotiation between the merchant bank selling the shares and the target groups they wish to sell to.

- An *offer for sale* in 1987: This is where shares are advertised and offered to the public. This is a more open and competitive market, but there is a risk that not all the offer will be taken up or that the price offered will be lower than anticipated.
- A *rights issue* in 1990 and 1994: This is where existing shareholders are able to buy new shares at a discount. Their *right* to buy new shares is related to the size of their existing shareholding.

Finally, the *underwriting* of share issues means that insurance has been taken out against the eventuality of shares remaining unsold. Should this be the case the *underwriting* firm would purchase the unsold shares at a pre-agreed price.

Share prices and the stock market

Shares which are sold on the stock market are second-hand shares and thus their purchase does not provide new capital to companies. Prices of shares are determined by supply and demand. The stock market approximates to a perfect market (see Chapter 3) and thus prices are constantly changing to bring supply and demand into equilibrium. The demand for and the supply of shares depend upon the following:

- *Price of shares.*
- *Expectations of future price changes*: This can be very important when the market suffers a long period of price falls (bear market) or a period of sustained price rises (bull market).
- *Present and future profitability of the firm*: This increases the prospect of higher dividends.
- *Price of other assets:* The price of gold and property prices can influence the attractiveness of holding shares.
- *Interest rates*: A rise in interest rates can cause a fall in demand for shares by making savings more attractive.
- *Government policy.*
- *Tax considerations.*

Exhibit 2.4 illustrates the changing fortunes of the shares in the airline Qantas. It shows how share prices can go up and down. In particular, it shows how global economic events can affect share prices. The worldwide economic recession that was evident in 2008 saw the price of Qantas shares fall from a high of AUS$6.00 the previous year to a price of AUS$1.40. This also represented a fall in value of more than 20 per cent as compared with even the flotation price 13 years earlier in 1995. It also demonstrates the potential benefits and risks of holding shares. Anyone investing AUS$1000 in Qantas in 1995 would have been able to purchase 526 shares. If they had sold those shares in 2007 they would have earned AUS$3156 – a profit of

AUS$2156. However, if they had sold the shares in 2008 they would have earned only AUS$736 representing a loss of AUS$244.

Aims, missions, ownership and control

The main aim for organizations in the private sector is generally to maximize profits. For example, Exhibit 2.5 illustrates the objectives of 'The Walt Disney Company' where it can be seen that maximizing long-term shareholder value is a prime concern. The private sector consists of both small- and medium-sized enterprises (SMEs) and large corporations. These have previously been classified as sole proprietors and partnerships and limited liability corporations. Understanding small-business organizations is straightforward. The owner is the manager and this can act as a strong incentive to maximize profits. However, it may also mean that profit maximization is subject to personal considerations such as environmental concerns or hours worked. Indeed, the term 'Lifestyle Entrepreneur' has been used to describe small-business owners who construct a business around a hobby that enables them to earn an income whilst pursuing their interest.

For corporations, size of operations and number of shareholders make the picture more complex. Companies are run along standard lines: the managing director is responsible for directing managers in the day-to-day running of the organization. The board of directors is responsible for determining company policy and for reporting annually to the shareholders. This can lead to a division between ownership (shareholders) and control (managers) and a potential conflict of interests. Shareholders generally wish to see their dividends and capital gains, and thus company profits, maximized. Managers will generally have this as an important objective since they are ultimately answerable to shareholders. However, they may seek other

Exhibit 2.5 The Walt Disney Company's objectives

The Walt Disney Company, together with its subsidiaries and affiliates, is a leading diversified international family entertainment and media enterprise with four business segments:

1. media networks
2. parks and resorts
3. studio entertainment and
4. consumer products.

The Walt Disney Company's objectives is to be one of the world's leading producers and providers of entertainment and information, using its portfolio of brands to differentiate its content, services and consumer products. The company's primary financial goals are to maximize earnings and cash flow, and to allocate capital toward growth initiatives that will drive long-term shareholder value.

Sources: http://corporate.disney.go.com/investors/index.html

objectives – in particular, maximizing personal benefit – which may include kudos from concluding deals, good pension prospects and a variety of perks such as foreign travel, well-appointed offices and high-specification company cars.

NON-PROFIT MAKING ORGANIZATIONS

Non-profit organizations in the private sector vary considerably in size and in purpose. They span national organizations with large turnovers, smaller special interest groups, professional associations and local clubs and societies, and include:

- *The National Trust (UK)*: This is a charity trust and independent from the government. It derives its funds from membership subscriptions, legacies and gifts, and trading income from entrance fees, shops and restaurants. It is governed by an act of parliament – the National Trust Act 1907. Its main aim is to safeguard places of historic interest and natural beauty.
- *The New York Road Runners/NYC Marathon (USA)*: This non-profit organization is dedicated to promoting the sport of running for health, recreation and competition. It organizes over 75 races each year.
- *Surf Life Saving Australia (SLSA)*: This is Australia's major water safety and rescue authority and one of the largest volunteer organizations in the world. Their mission is 'to provide a safe beach and aquatic environment throughout Australia'. SLSA provides lifesaving patrol services on most of Australia's populated beaches in the swimming season.
- *Indigenous Tourism Rights International (USA)*: This is an indigenous peoples' organization collaborating with indigenous communities and networks to protect their territories, rights and cultures. Their mission is to exchange experiences in order to understand, challenge and take control of the ways in which tourism affects our lives.
- *Tourism Concern (UK)*: The vision of Tourism Concern is 'A world free from exploitation in which all parties involved in tourism benefit equally and in which relationships between industry, tourists and host communities are based on trust and respect'. Tourism Concern's mission is to ensure that tourism always benefits local people. Tourism Concern works with communities in destination countries to reduce social and environmental problems connected to tourism and with the outgoing tourism industry in the UK to find ways of improving tourism so that local benefits are increased.

The aims and missions of voluntary groups are generally not profit driven. They include protection of special interests, promotion

Plate 2 Non-profit-making organization: The Orphan Elephant Project, Nairobi, Kenya
Source: The author.

of ideas and ideals, regulation of sports and the provision of goods and services which are not catered for by the free market. Andersson and Getz (2009) offered a helpful examination of the differences between private, public and not-for-profit concepts with using festivals as their context. Plate 2 shows tourists (including the author on the right of the photo) at the David Sheldrick Wildlife Trusts' Orphans' Project in Nairobi, Kenya. This is a charity organization which depends entirely on donations. It has the specific aim of rehabilitating orphaned elephants.

REVIEW OF KEY TERMS

- Public sector: government owned.
- Private sector: non-government-owned.
- Council member: elected councillor.
- Council officer: paid official.
- Private limited company: company with restrictions governing transfer of shares.
- Public limited company: company whose shares are freely transferable and quoted on stock market.
- Public corporation: public-sector commercial-style organization.
- Nationalized industry: industry owned and run by government.
- Dividend: the distribution of profits to shareholders.

- Limited liability: liability limited to amount of investment.
- Flotation: floating a private limited company on the stock market, thus becoming a public limited company.

Data Questions

Task 2.1 **Mission types**

- The National Trust of Australia (New South Wales, NSW) is a community-based charity organization. It relies almost entirely on donations, fundraising, partnerships and its bushland management services to fund its work. Other support comes from its 26,000 members and a 2000 strong team of volunteers throughout NSW.

The Trust's vision is 'to be trusted as a leading independent guardian of Australia's built, cultural and natural heritage, and defender of our sense of place and belonging in a changing world'. Its mission is to:

- 'advocate for the conservations of [the] built, cultural and natural heritage by engaging with the community and government
- conserve and protect [the] built, cultural and natural heritage by example, advice and support
- educate and engage the community by telling...stories in ways that awaken a sense of place and belonging'.

Source: http://www.nationaltrust.com.au/about/default.asp

- The Hong Kong Tourism Board (HKTB) is a government-sponsored body whose prime responsibilities are to market and promote Hong Kong as a destination worldwide and to take initiatives to enhance the experiences of its visitors once they have arrived. It also makes recommendations to the Hong Kong Special Administrative Region (SAR) Government and other relevant bodies on the range and quality of visitor facilities.

The HKTB's mission is to maximize the social and economic contribution that tourism makes to the community of Hong Kong, and to consolidate Hong Kong's position as a unique, world-class and most desired destination.

The six objectives of the HKTB, as defined under the HKTB Ordinance 2001, are:

- to endeavour to increase the contribution of tourism to Hong Kong;
- to promote Hong Kong globally as a leading international city in Asia and a world-class tourist destination;
- to promote the improvement of facilities for visitors;
- to support the government in promoting to the community the importance of tourism;
- to support, as appropriate, the activities of persons providing services for visitors to Hong Kong; and
- to make recommendations to and advise the chief executive (of the Hong Kong SAR) in relation to any measures which may be taken to further any of the foregoing matters.

Source: http://www.discoverhongkong.com/eng/about-hktb/about-us.html

Task 2.1 continued

- The BAA owns London Heathrow and other major U.K. airports. In 2006, BAA was bought by a consortium led by Ferrovial, the Spanish construction company. Ferrovial is one of the world's leading infrastructure companies, with 104,000 employees and operations in 43 countries in a range of sectors including construction, airport, toll road, and car park management and maintenance, and municipal services.

  BAA's objectives are to be:
  - a responsible custodian and developer of public assets
  - a good employer
  - a co-operative partner with government
  - an equitable partner to airlines
  - a good neighbour in the communities where our airports are located
  - an excellent business.

Source: www.baa.com

Recap Questions

1 Identify the different aspects of the mission agenda that are evident for each of the above organizations using Figure 2.1, and discuss these differences.
2 Which aspects of the mission agenda are most likely to be found for
   (a) A private sector corporation
   (b) A not-for-profit organization
   (c) A local government organization.
3 Why is it important for economists to identify organizational type if they are to understand the pricing policy of recreation, leisure and tourism organizations?

↓ Mission Agenda Example →	NTA	HKTB	BAA
Maximizing profits			
Corporate success			
Customer satisfaction			
Employee welfare			
Environmental sensitivity			
Product safety			
Employment policy			
Community activity			
Ethical considerations			
Benefits to society			
Political considerations			

Figure 2.1 What is in a mission?

Task 2.2 **Virgin**

London 1970s

Richard Branson started his business career at school with a student magazine at the age of 17. In 1970, he founded Virgin as a mail order record retailer, and shortly afterwards he opened a record shop in Oxford Street, London.

London 1980s

This was the beginning of the Virgin empire which demonstrated its maturity when Branson floated the company on the London Stock Exchange. However, in his autobiography, 'Losing My Virginity', Branson explains why he changed his mind about the benefits of being a public company so that the company's management executed a management buyout to take Virgin private again. He particularly pointed to the 'onerous obligations' which included the duty of appointing and working with outside directors. He also felt that he had lost the ability to make quick decisions: 'Our business was not one that could be boxed into a rigid timetable of meetings. We had to make decisions quickly, off-the-cuff: if we had to wait 4 weeks for the next board meeting before authorizing Simon to sign UB40, then we would probably lose them altogether'.

Branson found the British tradition of paying a large dividend difficult to fit with his business philosophy which was to reinvest profits to increase the company's value and stated that the one year when Virgin was quoted on the stock exchange was the company's least creative year because the executives were taken away from management and strategy by the need to explain their business to fund managers and financial advisers.

Sydney 2003

Virgin launched its low-cost carrier Virgin Blue in Australia in 2001. From that year to the end of March 2003 the airline had made a pre-tax profit of AUS$158 million on revenues of AUS$924 million and it is expected to report profits of about AUS$150 million for 2003–2004.

Its owner Richard Branson has announced plans to float the company on the stock market by Christmas 2003. Virgin Blue was originally expected to come to the market in summer 2003 but a listing was postponed because of the adverse effects on the aviation sector from the impact of the severe acute respiratory syndrome (SARS) outbreak and the war in Iraq.

The float valued the group at around AUS$2 billion (£832 million). The airline raised about AUS$400 million from the flotation on the Australian Stock Exchange. One of the principal reasons for the strategy is to give the company enough cash to expand internationally without having to obtain the money from existing shareholders. The airline wanted to use the cash raised to help fund its plans to launch a low-cost airline in the USA and Virgin Blue was also planning new routes to New Zealand, Papua New Guinea and the Polynesian islands. The group was also looking at speeding up the expansion of its Virgin Mobile operations in the USA.

Commenting on the float, Grant Williams of brokerage firm Reynolds & Co said, 'There seems to be a strong interest in Virgin Blue's float but this is not a lot of money and there won't be much around for the retail market'.

Task 2.2 continued

A Virgin spokesman said the money from Virgin Blue could be used to increase the Virgin group's 'war chest'. Plans for a low-cost carrier in the USA are described as 'quite advanced'.

California 2007

Launched in August 2007 with initial funding of $128 million, Virgin America is one of the best funded start-up airlines in history according to the *Wall Street Journal*. Virgin America positioned itself as a new, California-based airline. Its competitive edge is honed around a package that includes brand new planes, attractive fares, service excellence, in-flight Internet, mood-lit cabins, leather seats and on-demand menus.

Global position 2011

The Virgin Group has grown to become a leading global company operating in businesses in sectors ranging from mobile telephony to transportation, travel, financial services, media, music and fitness. It has created more than 300 branded companies worldwide, employing approximately 50,000 people, in 30 countries. Global branded revenues in 2009 exceeded £11.5 billion (approximately US$18 billion). Its portfolio includes:

- Virgin Atlantic Airways
- Virgin Active U.K.
- Virgin Active Portugal
- Virgin Holidays
- Virgin Galactic
- Virgin Trains
- Virgin Gaming
- Virgin Blue.

Recap Questions

1 What is meant by floating a company?
2 How does a flotation raise money for a company? Where does the money come from?
3 What does Grant Williams mean when he says 'there would not be much around for the retail market'?
4 What are the advantages and disadvantages of floating a company?
5 Why do you think Virgin has been such a successful company?
6 How do you think Richard Branson funded and managed his first venture as a mail order record retailer?

Task 2.3 Journal article: Ateljevic, I., Doorne, S., 2000. 'Staying within the fence': lifestyle entrepreneurship in tourism. *Journal of Sustainable Tourism* 8 (5), 378–392.

In their seminal article on Lifestyle Entrepreneurs, Ateljevic and Doorne noted that lifestyle and non-economic motives can be important stimuli for tourism entrepreneurship and represent a significant part of the small-business sector. The main hallmark of Lifestyle Entrepreneurs is a valuing of quality of life over profit. Because Lifestyle Entrepreneurs have found it difficult to find this combination in traditional business they find that the solution is to set up their own business. This desire for quality of life merged with running a business means that Lifestyle Enterprises can allow for flexible hours, or a favoured location, or the specializing is certain products or services (often developing out of a passionate interest or hobby) or a particular stance with regard to ethical practices. Examples of such businesses include small accommodation providers, yoga retreats, specialized restaurants and organizers of leisure pursuits.

Ateljevic and Doorne noted that the long-term survival of Lifestyle Entrepreneurs in tourism has been cited as a possible constraint on regional economic development. Their research is based on a cohort of Lifestyle Entrepreneurs in the New Zealand tourism sector. They focus on the values that motivate Lifestyle Entrepreneurs finding that typically the conscious rejection of economic and business growth opportunities is an expression of a specific, personal sociopolitical ideology. The authors found that this rejection of profit as an over-riding motive does not necessarily result in financial difficulties or a stagnation in the development of the business. Rather new opportunities are created to engage with niche consumers who portray common values. Their research also concluded that Lifestyle Entrepreneurs can be associated with the creation of innovative services and products and that this business format can make an important contribution to sustainability, the developing of a sense of place and community and be a point of stimulation for regional development.

Source: Adapted from http://www.informaworld.com/smpp/content~db=all~content=a908038878

Recap Questions

1 What particular issues of expansion and growth are pertinent to Lifestyle Enterprises?
2 How do aims, mission, ownership and control differ between Lifestyle Enterprises and profit-maximizing businesses?
3 What factors are likely to influence the business decisions of Lifestyle Entrepreneurs?
4 Why would Lifestyle Entrepreneurs be unlikely to float their business on the stock exchange?
5 Locate, read and critique this article.

MULTIPLE CHOICE

1 Which of the following is most likely to contribute to a fall in the share price of Qantas Airways?
   (a) A fall in interest rates.
   (b) A rise in profits.
   (c) A bear market.
   (d) None of the above.

2 Unlimited liability means:
   (a) A firm can be sued for damages.
   (b) A firm's owner is liable for all of its debts.

(c) A firm has been incorporated.

(d) A firm may be sued for libel.

3 Tourism Concern is:

(a) A non-profit-making organization.

(b) A local government organization.

(c) A nationalized industry.

(d) Quoted on the stock exchange.

4 Which of the following is a valid reason for holding shares:

(a) A chance to benefit from a company's profit.

(b) Guaranteed to get your investment back.

(c) The avoidance of risk.

(d) Guaranteed minimum dividends.

5 Which of the following statements is not true?

(a) Public-sector organizations are government owned.

(b) Debentures are less risky than shares.

(c) Shareholders are not liable for more than their initial investment.

(d) Nationalized industries always seek to maximize profits.

REVIEW QUESTIONS

1 Distinguish between the public sector, public limited companies and nationalized industries, giving examples of each in the recreation, leisure and tourism sector.

2 What is the major benefit of incorporation?

3 Who determines strategic policy for:

(a) Local government organizations?

(b) Public limited companies?

(c) Nationalized industries?

4 What are the benefits and drawbacks for a company thinking of floating on the stock exchange?

5 Identify four quoted corporations in the leisure and tourism sector.

(a) Research and record movements in their share prices over the past 24 months.

(b) Suggest reasons for the movements in these share prices.

Websites of interest

Air India: www.airindia.com

BAA: (British Airports Authority): www.baa.com

British Airways: www.ba.com

British Tourist Authority: www.visitbritain.com

Department for Culture, Media and Sport: www.culture.gov.uk

Department of Resources, Energy and Tourism: www.ret.gov.au

Department of the Interior (USA): www.doi.gov

Hong Kong Tourism Board: www.discoverhongkong.com

Indigenous Tourism Rights International: www.tourismrights.org

Qantas Airways: www.qantas.com.au

SNCF: www.sncf.com

Surf Life Saving Australia: www.slsa.asn.au

The British Broadcasting Corporation: www.bbc.co.uk

The National Trust: www.nationaltrust.org/

Tourism Australia: www.tourism.australia.com

Tourism Concern: www.tourismconcern.org.uk

Virgin Group: www.virgin.com

Walt Disney Company: www.corporate.disney.go.com

The market for recreation, leisure and tourism products

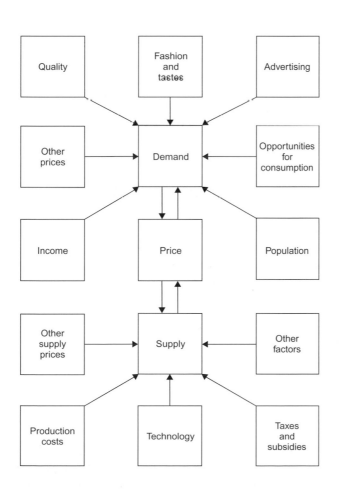

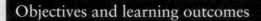

Objectives and learning outcomes

Prices in a market economy are constantly on the move. For example, the price of package holidays has fallen considerably in real terms over the last decade, whilst the price of foreign currency changes many times in a single day. Price has a key function in the market economy. On the one hand, it signals changes in demand patterns to producers, stimulating production of those products with increasing demand and depressing production of those products where demand is falling. At the same time, price provides an incentive for producers to economize on their inputs. This chapter will investigate how price is formed in the market. It will investigate the factors which determine the demand for and the supply of a good or service and see how the forces of demand and supply interact to determine price.

By studying this chapter students will be able to:

* identify a market and define the attributes of a perfect market;
* analyse the factors that affect the demand for a good or service;
* analyse the factors that affect the supply of a good or service;
* understand the concept of equilibrium price;
* analyse the factors that cause changes in equilibrium price;
* relate price theory to real-world examples.

DEFINITIONS AND ASSUMPTIONS

Effective demand

Effective demand is more than just the wanting of something, but it is defined as 'demand backed by cash'.

Ceteris paribus

Ceteris paribus means 'all other things remaining unchanged'. In the real world, there are a number of factors which affect the price of a good or service. These are constantly changing and in some instances they work in opposite directions. This makes it very difficult to study cause and effect. Economists use the term *ceteris paribus* to clarify thinking. For example, it might be said that a fall in the price of a commodity will cause a rise in demand, *ceteris paribus*. If this caveat were not stated then we might find that, despite the fact that the price of a commodity had fallen, we might observe a fall in demand, because some other factor might be changing at the same time, for example a significant rise in income tax.

Perfect market assumption

A market is a place where buyers and sellers come into contact with one another. In the model of price determination discussed in this chapter, we make a simplifying assumption that we are operating in a perfect market.

The characteristics of a perfect market include:

- many buyers and sellers;
- perfect knowledge of prices throughout the market;
- rational consumers and producers basing decisions on prices;
- no government intervention (e.g. price control).

The stock exchange is an example of a perfect market – equilibrium price is constantly changing to reflect changes in demand and supply. There is some evidence to suggest that the Internet is leading to markets becoming less imperfect as consumers are able to get more information about prices and products, and source their purchases from a wider range of suppliers.

THE DEMAND FOR RECREATION, LEISURE AND TOURISM PRODUCTS

Demand and own price

Generally, as the price of a good or a service increases, the demand for it falls, *ceteris paribus*, as illustrated in Table 3.1. This gives rise to the demand curve shown in Figure 3.1.

The demand curve slopes downwards to the right and plots the relationship between a change in price and demand. The reason for this is that as prices rise consumers tend to economize on items and replace them with other ones if possible. Notice that as price changes we move along the demand curve to determine the effect on demand so that in Figure 3.1 as price rises from $100 to $120, demand falls from 4400 to 4000 units a day.

The main exceptions to this are twofold. Some goods and services are bought because their high price lends exclusivity to them and thus they become more sought after at higher prices. A good example of this is the new generation of so called seven-star hotels such as the Burj Al Arab in Dubai. Also, if consumers expect prices to rise in

Table 3.1 The demand for four-star hotel rooms							
Price (US$)	220	200	180	160	140	120	100
Demand (per day)	2000	2400	2800	3200	3600	4000	4400

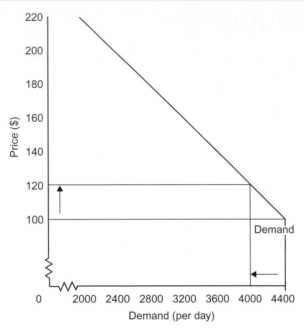

Figure 3.1 The demand curve for four-star hotel rooms.

the future, they might buy goods even though their prices are rising. However, this is difficult to do with services.

Demand and other factors

The following factors also affect the demand for a good or service:

- disposable income
- price of other goods
- comparative quality/value added
- fashion and tastes
- advertising
- opportunities for consumption
- population
- other factors.

Since the demand curve describes the relationship between demand and price, these other factors will affect the position of the demand curve and changes in these factors will cause the demand curve to shift its position to the left or the right.

Disposable income

Disposable income is defined as income less direct taxes but including government subsidies. The effect of a change in disposable income on the demand for a good or service depends on the type of

Exhibit 3.1 From exotic vacations to modest 'staycations'

In Victorian England, the place to be for the British monied, leisured classes was a British seaside resort. Queen Victoria herself had a residence at Osborne House near Cowes on the Isle of Wight and the Victorian boom brought railways, piers, promenades and seafront hotels to resorts such as Brighton, Ventnor and Eastbourne. Today, piers have collapsed, accommodation has shrunk and many resorts are in decline. The long-term trend since the 1970s is that holidays taken abroad by UK residents have increased and the number spent in the UK has shown a steep decline. Increased incomes made Spain the major destination for UK holidaymakers in the 1980s and 1990s, but as incomes continued to rise Spanish resorts themselves are in danger of becoming inferior substitutes for more exotic, distant destinations. However, the 2007–2009 recession witnessed a notable reversal in these trends. Lower incomes meant that 'staycations', where holidays are taken in the home country, have become more popular. Data from the UK Office of National Statistics showed a 15 per cent fall in British foreign holidays, the biggest decline since records began. Foreign destinations affected include Mexico, down 41 per cent; New Zealand, down 30 per cent; Spain, down 19 per cent and France, down 10 per cent.

Source: The author.

good under consideration. First, for normal or superior goods, as disposable income rises, so does demand. This applies to most hotels, holidays abroad and membership of leisure clubs. However, some goods or services are bought as cheap substitutes for other ones. These are defined as inferior goods and examples might include cheap hotel rooms, bed and breakfast accommodation, domestic holidays, cheap-range music systems or trainers without a leading brand name. As income rises, the demand for these goods and services declines as people start to demand the normal goods that they can now afford. Exhibit 3.1 shows that many UK seaside resorts can be classified as an 'inferior' destinations in economic terms. Despite the rise of the recession-induced 'staycation', they are likely to suffer continued decline as people's long-term standard of living continues to increase.

An income consumption curve shows the relationship between changes in income and changes in the demand for goods and services and Figure 3.2 shows the different income consumption curves for superior and inferior goods. As income rises from A to B, the demand for superior goods rises from C to E, whilst the demand for inferior goods falls from C to D.

Price of other goods

Changes in the prices of other goods will also affect the demand for the good or service in question. In the case of goods or services

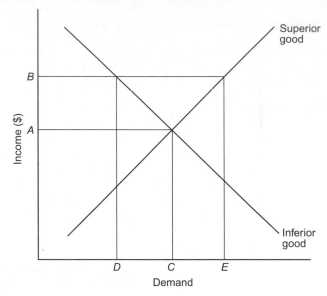

Figure 3.2 Income consumption curves for superior and inferior goods.

which are substitutes, a rise in the price of one good will lead to a rise in the demand for the other. In the skiing market, for example, Verbier in Switzerland, Ellmau in Austria and Courchevel in France are to some extent substitutes for each other and changes in relative prices will cause demand patterns to change. The same is true for air travel where there are often many competing airlines offering substitutes on major routes.

Some goods and services are complements or in joint demand. In other words, they tend to be demanded in pairs or sets. In this case, an increase in the price of one good will lead to a fall in the demand for the other. So in Exhibit 3.2 the demand for ski holidays in Bansko, Bulgaria may well be lifted by the relative cheapness of those items that are in joint demand with a ski holiday – drinks and meals since Bulgaria turns out to be a relatively cheap destination for these items. Other examples of joint demand include holidays in the USA and Dollars or holiday destinations and transport costs.

Joint demand in the tourism sector also encompasses other factors. Important amongst these are the weather and significant cultural events. Exhibit 3.3 reports on the influence of the weather (seasonality) and cultural events on tourism demand in Galicia, Spain.

Comparative quality/value added

Consumers do not just consider price when comparing goods and services – they also compare quality. Improvements in the quality

Exhibit 3.2 Skiing: unpacking the price

The demand for skiing at different resorts is affected by a range of price factors. The price of accommodation in the resort (own price) will be a key factor. But other prices will also affect demand. Demand will be sensitive to substitute prices which includes prices in other resorts and prices of other alternative activities (e.g. diving holidays). Demand will also be affected by the price of other essential parts of a ski package (complementary goods and services). Lift pass prices, equipment hire and tuition are key factors here. So are subsistence costs of food and drink in the resort. The table shows some of these for ski resorts in Europe by way of the Resort Price Index (RPI) which was prepared by the website *Where to Ski and Snowboard*. Here, prices of the following items were compared across resorts:

- cheap eats (pasta/pizza)
- proper meals, eg plat du jour
- coke
- beer
- wine
- cappuccino/hot chocolate/glühwein.

The resulting index included the following:

Country	Resort	RPI
Bulgaria	Bansko	40
USA	Breckenridge	70
Italy	Bormio	75
Austria	Ellmau	80
Italy	Livigno	80
Switzerland	Grindelwald	90
Switzerland	Wengen	90
France	Les Menuires	100
Switzerland	Davos	110
Austria	Zürs	115
France	Courchevel	145

Source: Adapted from Where to Ski and Snowboard http://www.wheretoskiandsnowboard. com/features/cutting-costs-resort-price-index/

of a good or service can be important factors in increasing demand, and Exhibit 3.4 describes how airlines have been rated by passengers over a number of key quality issues. Faced with similar prices for competing air services customers will generally choose airlines with superior service quality. This is an important consideration for airlines' strategies for increasing market share.

Exhibit 3.3 Tourism in Galicia: domestic and foreign demand

In a paper published in the journal *Tourism Economics* Teresa Garín-Muñoz analyses the main determinants of the demand for tourism in the region of Galicia, Spain. Galicia is located in the north-west of Spain and shares its southern border with Portugal. The author notes the increasing importance of tourism for the region so that by 2004 it accounted for around 11.6 per cent of GDP, 13.3 per cent of total employment and contributed 14.7 per cent to the total taxes revenues.

The article investigates factors which affect domestic and foreign demand for tourism to Galicia. But it also notes the importance of religious events and the weather. The religious calendar is seen to impact on the demand for tourism and the author notes:

> Each year, many thousands of people from all over the world are drawn to Galicia to make the ancient pilgrimage to Compostela. The flow is especially high during the Holy Years of Santiago, which occur when the 25 July, the celebration of the martyrdom of St James, falls on a Sunday. These historical assets make Galicia a potentially important religious and cultural tourism destination. (p. 755)

In terms of seasonality Garín-Muñoz notes that:

> The monthly distribution of tourism … shows that most tourism arrives in Galicia during the summer. In fact, more than half of the overnight stays take place during the summer months and August is the month with the greatest volume of tourism. (p. 760)

Source: Adapted from Garín-Muñoz, T., 2009. Tourism in Galicia: domestic and foreign demand. Tourism Economics 15 (4), 753–769.

Exhibit 3.4 Asiana Airlines win the title Airline of the Year 2010 at the World Airline Awards

Asiana Airlines was named the winner of the Airline of the Year Award at the 2010 World Airline Awards that took place in Hamburg, Germany. The awards were attended by over 40 airlines from around the world. The awards are based on reviews from airline customers and over 17 million air travellers representing over 100 different nationalities took part in the survey.

The survey included over 200 airlines, from largest international airlines to domestic carriers and measures over 38 items of airline product and service standards. These rate the customer experience both at airports and at inflight and include:

- check-in
- boarding
- seat comfort
- cabin cleanliness
- food
- beverages
- inflight entertainment
- staff service.

The award was received by Mr Young-Doo Yoon, Asiana Airlines' President and CEO who stated:

> Asiana has been committed to realise our company vision to achieve 'Customer Satisfaction' by providing the best in terms of safety and service since its establishment in 1988. Asiana will continue to provide the world's best quality and differentiated service to our customers … [and] will use this opportunity as further motivation to never cease in its continual improvement and development efforts while devoting ourselves to always go beyond satisfying each and every valuable customer.

Mr Edward Plaisted, Chairman of Skytrax who organized the wards said:

> …the real strength that was shining through for Asiana Airlines is their front-line staff. Across both the ground services environment at their home base at Incheon International Airport, and the exceptionally high quality and consistent cabin staff service, Asiana Airlines is setting a new world order when looking at the best airlines across the globe. They have been close to the top positions in previous year awards, and I am delighted to now see Asiana Airlines taking the highest accolade in being named Airline of the Year for 2010.

The runners up for Airline of the Year were:

#2 Asiana Airlines

#3 Singapore Airlines

#4 Qatar Airways

#5 Cathay Pacific Airways

#6 Air New Zealand.

Source: Adapted from www.worldairlineawards.com/Awards 2010/Airline2010.htm

Fashion and tastes

Fashion and tastes affect demand for leisure goods and services as in other areas. For example, the demand for tennis facilities and accessories rises sharply during tennis tournaments such as Wimbledon. Similarly, World Cup rugby and football events have a big impact on sales of sports clothing and merchandise as do the successes of teams in national leagues. Holiday destinations move in and out of fashion. Tourism to Israel is frequently affected by adverse publicity related to the Israel–Palestine conflict. Mexico has joined Columbia as a destination which is perceived as dangerous because of the drugs trade. Exhibit 3.5 shows how the fortunes of destinations can quickly change with Goa suddenly losing its status as a heaven of peace and tranquility after highly publicized bomb attacks and murders.

Advertising

The aim of most advertising is to increase the demand for goods and services. The exception to this is advertising that is designed to inhibit the demand for some goods and services. For example, many governments fund advertising campaigns to inhibit the demand for cigarettes and drugs. Plate 3 reproduces two graphic labels used

Exhibit 3.5 Goa's tourism woes

Goa in India has enjoyed a long period of growth in tourism fueled partly by its natural beauty, climate, value for money and reputation as a safe, secure and peaceful destination. Between September and December 2007, 82,515 foreign visitors arrived in Goa by chartered and scheduled flights. But by 2008, the number had dropped to 71,918 in the corresponding period. This represents a 13 per cent drop.

Much of Goa's tourism suffered because of the global economic recession in the same period. But tour operators have reported that other incidents have added to Goa's difficulties with tourists cancelling their travel plans. These include events such as the explosions in Madgaon that left two dead. Even more adverse publicity was generated by the death of British teenager Scarlett Keeling, aged 15, who was found raped and murdered on Anjuna Beach in February 2008. Adding further to the problems the Israeli government issued a travel advisory that suggests its citizens to keep away from Goa.

Source: Adapted from Mid Day www.mid-day.com/news

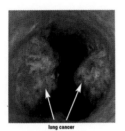

WARNING

CIGARETTES CAUSE LUNG CANCER

85% of lung cancers are caused by smoking. 80% of lung cancer victims die within 3 years.

Health Canada

WARNING

TOBACCO USE CAN MAKE YOU IMPOTENT

Cigarettes may cause sexual impotence due to decreased blood flow to the penis. This can prevent you from having an erection.

Health Canada

Plate 3 Health Canada anti-smoking campaign. *Source: Reproduced by kind permission of Health Canada.*

in cigarette packaging to dissuade people from smoking by Health Canada. In one case shocking pictures of lung cancer growths are used, in the other a direct link to sexual performance is made.

Opportunities for consumption

Unlike many sectors of the economy, many leisure and tourism pursuits require time to participate in them. Thus, the amount of leisure time available will be an important enabling factor in demand. The two main components here are the average working week and the amount of paid holidays. Table 3.2 illustrates time use in the USA. This shows that women still do the majority of the household chores, spending 2.24 hours a day on average on housework compared with 1.33 hours spent by men. Women also spent more time (almost double) than men on childcare and other household caring activities. However, men worked on average for nearly 1.5 hours a day more than women (4.26 hours a day for men compared with 2.85 hours for women). The average amount of time devoted to leisure

Table 3.2 Time (average hours per day) spent on primary activities by sex 2009

	Total	Men	Women
Personal care, including sleeping	9.45	9.25	9.63
Eating and drinking	1.22	1.26	1.19
Household activities	1.80	1.33	2.24
Housework	0.60	0.26	0.92
Purchasing goods and services	0.76	0.64	0.88
Caring for and helping household members	0.54	0.37	0.70
Caring for and helping non-household members	0.21	0.19	0.22
Working and work-related activities	3.53	4.26	2.85
Educational activities	0.46	0.43	0.50
Organizational, civic and religious activities	0.34	0.32	0.36
Leisure and sports	5.25	5.59	4.93
Telephone calls, mail and e-mail	0.20	0.14	0.25
Other activities	0.24	0.23	0.26

Source: Adapted from US Bureau of Labour Statistics http://www.bls.gov/news.release/atus.t01.htm

and sports activities is 5.25 hours, with men having 5.59 hours of leisure and sports in comparison to 4.93 hours for women. Aguiar and Hurst (2007) in an article titled 'Measuring trends in leisure: the allocation of time over five decades' use 50 years of time use surveys to analyse trends in the allocation of time within the USA. They find that leisure for men increased by about 6–9 hours per week (caused mainly by a decline in work hours) and for women by roughly 4–8 hours per week (caused mainly by a decline in homework hours). They also show a growing inequality in leisure that reflects the growing inequality of wages and expenditures in the country.

Population

Population trends are an important factor in the demand for recreation, leisure and tourism. Demand will be influenced by the size of population as well as the composition of the population in terms of age, sex and geographical distribution; for example, the leisure requirements of a country are likely to change considerably as the average age of the population increases. Football pitches may need to give way to golf courses. The location of leisure facilities similarly needs to be tailored to the migration trends of the population. Tourism marketing also needs to be informed by relevant population data. The dramatic growth in extended winter sun breaks in Europe reflects the demands of an ageing population. Table 3.3 shows

Table 3.3 Selected world population data

Demographic variable	Australia	USA	China	India	Spain
Population mid-2009	21,852,000	306,805,000	1,331,398,000	1,171,029,000	46,916,000
Birth rate (annual number of births per 1000 total population)	14	14	12	23	11
Death rate (annual number of deaths per 1000 total population)	7	8	7	7	8
Rate of natural increase (birth rate minus death rate, expressed as a %)	0.7	0.6	0.5	1.6	0.3
Population change 2009–2050 (projected %)	55	43	8	49	− 7
Population 2025 (projected)	26,917,000	357,452,000	1,476,000,000	1,444,450,000	46,164,000
Population 2050 (projected)	33,959,000	439,010,000	1,437,000,000	1,747,969,000	43,861,000
Population under age 15 (%)	19	20	19	32	14
Population over age 65 (%)	13	13	8	5	17
Life expectancy (years)	81	78	73	64	81

Source: Adapted from Population Reference Bureau website www.prb.org

different population trends from around the world. The population of India is set to increase by around 50 per cent between 2009 and 2050 and this growth in the population will mean the average age of the population remains low. In contrast, the population of Spain is forecast to decline in total size by 7 per cent between 2009 and 2050. This is because of a low birth rate and therefore the average age of the Spanish population is likely to increase. Notice a strong contrast in the age distribution of the populations of Spain and India. Table 3.3 shows that 14 per cent of the population in Spain is under 15 years, whereas in India 32 per cent of the population is under 15 years. Similarly, 17 per cent of the population of Spain is over 65 years but only 5 per cent of the population of India is over 65 years. Life expectancy to a large extent mirrors the stage of economic development and stands at 81 years in Australia but only 64 years in India.

Grant (2002) outlines the demand for active leisure in the Australian seniors market and concludes that those in the leisure industry need to understand not only the changing demographics but also the special demand characteristics of this group. Glover and Prideaux (2009) note that population ageing is a critical element of demographic change and a key driver for future consumer demand. Because of the size of the baby boomer generation, they argue that population ageing is likely to have a significant effect on the future choice of tourism activities and destinations. As the baby boomer generation retires, their demand patterns and preferences will change and strongly influence the future structure of tourism product development. The authors point to the possible emergence of a product gap, if these changing patterns of demand are ignored. On the same theme the future of leisure services for the elderly in Canada is explored in the light of ageing of the baby-boom generation by Johnson (2003). Schroder and Widmann (2007) note that destinations – which consciously cater to the senior segment, i.e. spas and health-oriented locations – will be able to profit from demographic change.

Other factors

Terrorism has had a significant impact particularly on some types of tourism in recent years. For example, Tate (2002) examines the impact of the 11 September 2001 events on the world tourism and travel industry and reviews some of the recovery strategies adopted by the industry. These are lower prices, shorter duration of visits, changes in booking habits, changes in motivation for travel and new approaches to product and service promotion. One commentator suggested the following impacts of 11 September 2001 on the tourism industry: a growing demand for security; a shift in focus towards tourism in domestic markets (i.e. less foreign travel); for foreign travel, an increasing tendency to travel to relatively close and familiar destinations (i.e. those in the same geographic region); greater importance being placed on visiting friends and relatives as a reason for travelling; a growth in the number of short trips and city breaks (although not to large city destinations); a decreasing interest in adventure tourism and a growing interest in travel that emphasizes experiencing local cultures or proximity to nature. Araña and Leon (2008) note that terrorism and threats to national security have impacts on tourism demand and their research focusses on the short-run impacts of the September 11 attacks in New York on tourist preferences for competing destinations in the Mediterranean and the Canary Islands. Their findings show that the attacks caused a shock to tourists' utility and a change in the image profile of destinations. However, it was found that whilst some destinations experienced a strongly negative impact on their image and attractiveness, others were upgraded as a consequence of terror events.

THE SUPPLY OF RECREATION, LEISURE AND TOURISM PRODUCTS

Supply and own price

Generally as the price of a good or a service increases, the supply of it rises, *ceteris paribus*. This gives rise to the supply curve which

Table 3.4 The supply of four-star hotel rooms							
Price ($)	220	200	180	160	140	120	100
Supply (per day)	4400	4000	3600	3200	2800	2400	2000

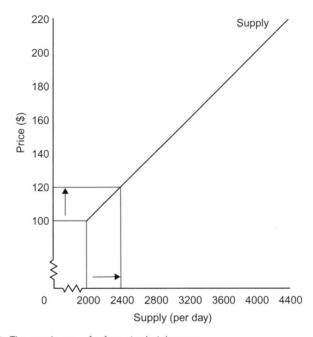

Figure 3.3 The supply curve for four-star hotel rooms.

is illustrated in Table 3.4 and Figure 3.3. The supply curve slopes upwards to the right and plots the relationship between a change in price and supply. The reason for this is that, as prices rise, the profit motive stimulates existing producers to increase supply and induces new suppliers to enter the market. Notice that as price changes, we move along the supply curve to determine the effect on supply so that in Figure 3.3, as the price of four-star hotel rooms rises from $100 to $120, supply rises from 2000 units a week to 2400 units a day.

Supply and other factors

The following factors also affect the supply of a good or service:

- prices of other goods supplied
- changes in production costs
- technical improvements
- taxes and subsidies
- other factors (e.g. industrial relations).

Exhibit 3.6 Carry on cruising

The Cruise Lines International Association (CLIA) is the world's largest cruise association and is dedicated to the promotion and growth of the cruise industry. CLIA is composed of 24 of the major cruise lines serving North America. A statement by CLIA reports that despite the economic recession of 2008/2009, the cruise industry is growing strongly. Its figures show that approximately 13.445 million guests sailed on CLIA member cruises in 2009 and forecasts a total of 14.3 million passengers in 2010, representing a 6.4 per cent growth. This means that the economic impact of the cruise industry is considerable. In 2008, direct spending in goods and services by CLIA cruise lines and their passengers totalled $19.07 billion.

The growth in the supply of the cruise industry continues apace. In 2009, CLIA members introduced 14 new ships at a total investment of $4.7 billion. In 2010, CLIA members invested an additional $6.5 billion with 12 new vessels. New additions to this fleet include:

- American Cruise Line's Independence, 101 passengers
- Avalon Waterways' Luminary, 138 passengers
- Avalon Waterways' Felicity, 138 passengers
- Celebrity Cruises' Celebrity Eclipse, 2850 passengers
- Costa Cruises' Costa Deliziosa, 2260 passengers
- Cunard Line's Queen Elizabeth, 2092 passengers
- Holland America Line's Nieuw Amsterdam, 2100 passengers
- MSC Cruises' MSC Magnifica, 2550 passengers
- Norwegian Cruise Line's Norwegian Epic, 4200 passengers
- Pearl Seas Cruises' Pearl Mist, 110 passengers
- Royal Caribbean International's Allure of the Seas, 5400 passengers
- Seabourn Cruise Line's Seabourn Sojourn, 450 passengers.

For the future CLIA member lines have 26 new ships on order between 2010 and 2012 which means an increase in capacity of 53,971 beds or 18 per cent of total.

Source: Adapted from CLIA Report http://www.cruising.org

Since the supply curve describes the relationship between supply and price, these other factors will affect the position of the supply curve and changes in these factors will cause the supply curve to shift its position to the left or to the right. Exhibit 3.6 describes the increase in the supply of cruise ships over recent years.

Prices of other goods supplied

Where a producer can use factors of production to supply a range of goods or services, an increase in the price of a particular product will cause the producer to redeploy resources towards that particular product and away from other ones. For example, the owners of a flexible sports hall will be able to increase the supply of badminton courts at the expense of short tennis, if demand changes. In the long run, a rise in the price of hotel rooms will cause owners of buildings and land to consider changing their use. Airlines are particularly able to adapt their routes and redeploy their aircraft as demand patterns change.

Changes in production costs

The main costs involved in production are labour costs, raw material costs and interest payments. A fall in these production costs will tend to stimulate supply shifting the supply curve to the right, whereas a rise in production costs will shift the supply curve to the left.

Technical improvements

Changes in technology will affect the supply of goods and services in the leisure and tourism sector. An example of this is aircraft design: the development of jumbo jets has had a considerable impact on the supply curve for air travel. The Airbus A380 represents a big technological leap forward here, extending the capacity of aircraft. Such developments mean that the supply curve has shifted to the right, signifying that more seats can now be supplied at the same price. Technology has had a large impact on the production of leisure goods such as mobile devices, televisions, personal computers, games, consoles and cameras. The supply curve for these goods has shifted persistently to the right over recent years, leading to a reduction in prices even after allowing for inflation.

Taxes and subsidies

The supply of goods and services is affected by indirect taxes such as sales taxes and also by subsidies. In the event of the imposition of taxes or subsidies, the price paid by the consumer is not the same as the price received by the supplier. For example, assume that the government imposes a $20 sales tax on hotel rooms. Where the price to the consumer is $200, the producer would now only receive $180. The whole supply curve will shift to the left since the supplier will now interpret every original price as being less $20. Table 3.5 shows the effects of the imposition of a tax on the original supply data. The effects of an imposition of a tax are illustrated in Figure 3.4. Notice that the supply curve has shifted to the left. In fact the vertical

Table 3.5 The effects of the imposition of a tax on supply

Price ($)	220	200	180	160	140	120	100
Original supply (per day $S0$)	4400	4000	3600	3200	2800	2400	2000
New supply (per day $S1$)	4000	3600	3200	2800	2400	2000	

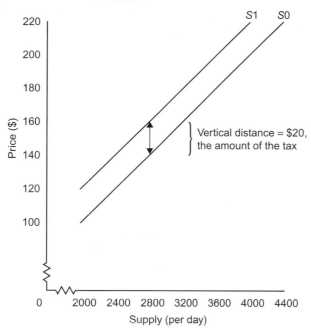

Figure 3.4 The effects of the imposition of a tax on supply.

distance between the old (S0) and the new (S1) supply curves represents the amount of the tax. Similarly, the effects of a subsidy will be to shift the supply curve to the right.

Other factors

There are various other factors which can influence the supply of leisure and tourism goods and services, including strikes, wars and the weather. The year 2010 was a particularly difficult year for airlines as their services were subject to severe and prolonged disruption from the volcanic ash cloud that drifted across much of Europe from Iceland.

EQUILIBRIUM PRICE

Equilibrium is a key concept in economics. It means a state of balance or the position towards which something will naturally move. Equilibrium price comes about from the interaction between the forces of demand and supply. There is only one price at which the quantity that consumers want to demand is equal to the quantity that producers want to supply. This is the equilibrium price. Figure 3.5 brings together the demand schedule from Table 3.1 and the supply schedule from Table 3.4. The equilibrium price in this case is $160, since this is where demand equals supply, both of which are 3200 units per day.

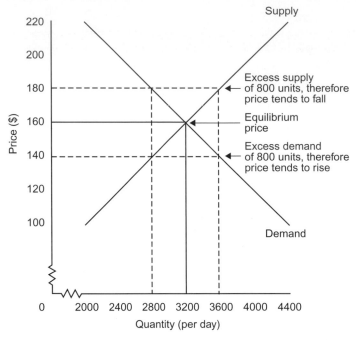

Figure 3.5 Equilibrium price in the market for four-star hotel rooms.

It can be demonstrated that this is the equilibrium by considering other possible prices. On the one hand, at higher prices, supply exceeds demand. In the example, at a price of $180 there is excess supply of 800 units a day. Excess supply will tend to cause the price to fall. On the other hand, at lower prices demand exceeds supply. At a price of $140 there is excess demand of 800 units a day. Excess demand causes the price to rise. Thus, the equilibrium price is at $160, since no other price is sustainable and market forces will prevail, causing price to change until the equilibrium is established.

CHANGES IN EQUILIBRIUM PRICE

Equilibrium does not mean that prices do not change. In fact, prices are constantly changing in markets to reflect changing conditions of demand and supply.

The effect of a change in demand

We have previously identified the factors that can cause the demand curve to shift its position. Table 3.6 reviews these factors, distinguishing what will cause the demand curve to shift to the right from that which will cause it to shift to the left.

In the example of four-star hotel rooms, a fall in the price of substitutes, for example five-star hotels, will cause the demand curve

Table 3.6 Shifts in the demand curve

Demand curve shifts to the left	Demand curve shifts to the right
Fall in income (normal goods)	Rise in income (normal goods)
Rise in income (inferior goods)	Fall in income (inferior goods)
Rise in price of complementary goods	Fall in price of complementary goods
Fall in price of substitutes	Rise in price of substitutes
Unfashionable	Fashionable
Less advertising	More advertising
Less leisure time	Increased leisure time
Fall in population	Rise in population

Table 3.7 A shift in demand for four-star hotel rooms

Price ($)	220	200	180	160	140	120	100
Original demand (per day $D0$)	2000	2400	2800	3200	3600	4000	4400
New demand (per day $D1$)		2000	2400	2800	3200	3600	4000
Supply (per day $S0$)	4400	4000	3600	3200	2800	2400	2000

to shift to the left from $D0$ to $D1$. The supply curve will remain unchanged at $S0$. This is illustrated in Table 3.7. Figure 3.6 shows the effect of this on equilibrium price. The original price of $160 will no longer be an equilibrium position since demand has now fallen to 2800 units a day at this price. There is now excess supply of 400 units per day, which will cause equilibrium price to fall until a new equilibrium is achieved at $150 where demand is equal to supply at 3000 units a day. Similarly, if the demand curve were to shift to the right as a result, for example, of an effective advertising campaign, the excess demand created at the original price would cause equilibrium price to rise.

The effect of a change in supply

The factors which cause a leftward or rightward shift in supply are reviewed in Table 3.8. In the example of four-star hotel rooms the effect of the imposition of a tax is shown in Table 3.9. A tax will cause the supply curve to shift to the left from $S0$ to $S1$, but the demand curve will remain unchanged at $D0$ as illustrated in Figure 3.7. The original price of $160 will no longer be in equilibrium since supply

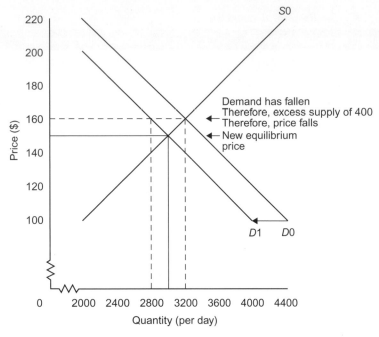

Figure 3.6 The effects on price of a shift in the demand curve.

Table 3.8 Shifts in the supply curve	
Supply curve shifts to the left	**Supply curve shifts to the right**
Rise in price of other goods that could be supplied by producer	Fall in price of other goods that could be supplied by producer
Rise in production costs	Fall in production costs
Effects of taxes	Effects of subsidies
Effects of strikes	Technical improvements

Table 3.9 Shifts in the supply of four-star hotel rooms							
Price ($)	220	200	180	160	140	120	100
Original demand (per day D0)	2000	2400	2800	3200	3600	4000	4400
New demand (per day S0)	4400	4000	3600	3200	2800	2400	2000
Supply (per day S1)		4000	3600	3200	2800	2400	2000

has now fallen to 2800 units a day at this price. There is now excess demand of 400 units per day, which will cause equilibrium price to rise until a new equilibrium is achieved at $170 where demand is equal to supply at 3000 units a day.

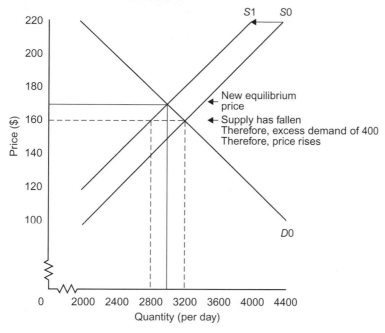

Figure 3.7 The effects on price of a shift in the supply curve.

Similarly, if the supply curve were to shift to the right as a result of an improvement in technology, for example, the excess supply created at the original price would cause equilibrium price to fall.

THE PRICE MECHANISM IN ACTION

Maximum prices and black markets

It is common in the leisure sector to interfere with free market pricing. The effects of this are particularly evident at prestige sports and music events where the capacity of the stadium is fixed as illustrated in Figure 3.8. The capacity of the Rugby Football Union (RFU) ground at Twickenham in the UK, for example, is about 70,000, and thus the supply curve (S) is fixed and vertical at this point. The demand curve for tickets is downward sloping (D). The RFU fixes a price (P0) which is considerably below the equilibrium price (P1). At the RFU official price there is considerable excess demand (a to b). Equilibrium is restored through the activities of ticket touts in the black market. Prices charged by touts rise and the effects of this can be shown by moving along the demand curve (b to c) until demand falls sufficiently to match supply. Exhibit 3.7 reports on how ticket touts are able to exploit the principles of elementary economics.

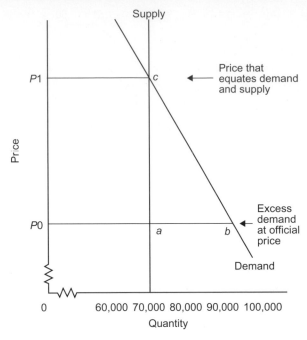

Figure 3.8 The effects of setting a maximum price below equilibrium price.

Exhibit 3.7 Ticket touts

The BBC has reported on research that claims ticket touts are selling tickets for major sports and music events on online auction sites with a typical profit of 59 per cent. A ticket tout is a person who buys up tickets for major events, generally at face value with a view of selling the tickets on at a profit where demand significantly outstrips supply. Touts traditionally operated by targeting fans outside concerts, matches and other events. However, they increasingly operate on the Internet with auction sites such as e-bay being popular outlets and where they can maximize their profit. Examples of ticket prices sold by touts include

- A pair of Paul McCartney tickets sold for £450 – some 235 per cent over face value.
- Two tickets for the V Festival sold for £430. The pair had a face value of £162.50.
- A £35 international rugby ticket selling for £85.

Source: Adapted from BBC News www.bbc.co.uk/news/10137075

REVIEW OF KEY TERMS

- Effective demand: demand backed by cash.
- *Ceteris paribus*: all other things remaining unchanged.
- Perfect market: many buyers and sellers, rational players, perfect knowledge, no interference.

- Normal good: demand rises as income rises (also called superior good).
- Inferior good: demand falls as income rises.
- Substitute: good that can replace good in question.
- Complement/joint demand: good that is used with the good in question.
- Equilibrium price: where demand equals supply.

Data Questions

Task 3.1 **Anyone for tennis?**

Recap Questions

1 If a local council decided to build *OB* tennis courts, what would happen if they decided to make these free?
2 If the council wished to create a market equilibrium, what price should they charge?
3 What problems arise from charging an equilibrium price?
4 How would the courts be allocated if they were provided free of charge? (see Figure 3.9)

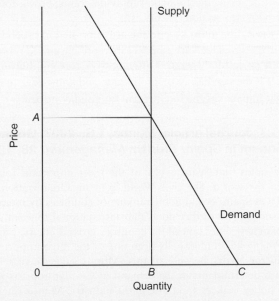

Figure 3.9 The demand and supply curves for tennis courts.

Task 3.2 **What am I bid for a week in the sun?**

The reporter for a TV holiday programme was looking pleased with himself as he sipped a cocktail on a Caribbean beach. He had managed to book a week in Cuba's winter sun for couple of hundred pounds, and he was keen to make a point. It was not long before his camera crew had

Task 3.2 **continued**

found a couple to gloat over. Gill and Tom had paid over £500 each for an identical holiday and they had booked several months before. Enter camera left a man who stole the show £110 – for 2 weeks. So how can the price of the same holiday go up and down like share prices and currencies?

The answer lies back in main tourism-generating countries where the late bookings section of one of the major tour operators resembles a share dealing room with banks of flickering screens. Here analysts change holiday prices several times a day. They are not alone – their competitors change their holiday prices every day too. Each uses the latest information on the other's prices to adjust their own prices to maximize profits. They get much of their information on competitors' prices through the Internet. When demand for their products is strong and supply is tight, the companies push up prices. However, faced with a half-empty plane departing in 2 days time, prices plummet as the tour operator teams try to get bums on seats that would otherwise earn nothing at all. One operator's team has developed some ground rules for pricing. These include the observbation that there is nothing like grey skies and rain at home to move prices up on the day.

Somehow in the face of all this Gill and Tom managed to keep their smiles fixed.

Source: The author.

Recap Questions

1 Illustrate, using demand and supply diagrams, how a tour operator's late bookings section sets prices.
2 Why is it difficult to keep to the prices printed in brochures?
3 How does a plane with empty seats represent market disequilibrium and how do tour operators attempt to restore equilibrium?
4 What is the significance of information and knowledge to market prices?
5 What impact has the Internet had on holiday prices?

Task 3.3 **Journal article: Munoz, T.G., 2007. German demand for tourism in Spain. *Tourism Management* 28, 12–22.**

Munoz notes that Spain is one of the most important tourism destinations in the world. She cites World Tourism Organization (WTO) data that places Spain second in the ranking of countries by international tourism earnings. She further notes that international tourism contributes to approximately 6 per cent of the country's gross domestic product (GDP).

Germany has traditionally been one of the most important sources of tourism for Spain. Because of this, Munoz suggests that knowledge of the main determinants of the demand of German tourists would be useful for policy makers and those in the industry. Munoz refers to previous studies where the most commonly tested explanatory variables for tourism demand are income, population, relative prices, exchange rates and transportation costs. Munoz bases her own research on a panel data set consisting of inbound German tourism in 17 Spanish destinations. Her results suggest that:

1 tourism demand in the previous period has an important effect on current tourism demand;
2 German tourism is very sensitive to prices;

3 the demand for tourism in Spain is a luxury for Germans;

4 tourism demand is highly dependent on the evolution of relative prices and cost of travel between Germany and the destination.

Recap Questions

1 List in two columns the factors described above which would tend to:
   (a) Shift the demand curve for tourism in Spain to the left.
   (b) Shift the demand curve for tourism in Spain to the right.

2 What do you think are the main factors that have affected German demand for tourism in Spain in the past 3 years?

3 Identify and explain the likely affects of German demand for tourism in Spain of:
   (a) A rise in oil prices.
   (b) A fall in the value of the Turkish lira.
   (c) A rise in unemployment in Germany.

4 How can the Spanish National Tourism Organization use economic theory to increase the amount of tourism to Spain?

MULTIPLE CHOICE

1 Which of the following will shift the demand curve for four-star hotel accommodation in New York to the right?
   (a) A rise in the value of the US dollar against other currencies.
   (b) A fall in incomes of consumers.
   (c) A successful advertising campaign.
   (d) A terrorist threat to New York.

2 Which of the following statements is not true?
   (a) As income increases the demand for inferior goods rises.
   (b) As income increases the demand for inferior goods falls.
   (c) As income increases the demand for normal or superior goods rises.
   (d) As income falls the demand for normal or superior goods falls.

3 Which of the following statements is not true?
   (a) The income consumption curve for inferior goods is upward sloping to the right.
   (b) The income consumption curve for inferior goods is downward sloping to the right.
   (c) A typically demand is inversely proportionate to price.
   (d) At the point of equilibrium, demand equals supply.

4 Which of the following is not true?
   (a) A rise in the price of air travel causes demand to fall.
   (b) A rise in the price of air travel causes a rise in the demand for train travel over similar routes.

(c) Where the price of air tickets is above equilibrium, supply will exceed demand.

(d) Air travel is an inferior good.

5 SNCF is the monopoly supplier of rail travel in France. This means that:

(a) The rail market in France is a perfect market.

(b) There are no perfect substitutes for a rail journey in France.

(c) Demand for rail travel in France rises as price rises.

(d) *Ceteris paribus* is not useful in analysing the market for French rail travel.

REVIEW QUESTIONS

1 Distinguish between the factors which cause a movement along a demand curve and those which cause a shift of the curve.

2 'An increase in the price of a good may arise from an increase in the price of its substitute, *ceteris paribus*'. Explain this statement.

3 Distinguish between a normal and an inferior good using examples from the leisure and tourism sector.

4 What is the likely effect of setting the maximum price of a good below its equilibrium price?

Websites of interest

Burj Al Arab Hotel, Dubai: http://www.jumeirah.com/en/hotels-and-resorts/destinations/dubai/burj-al-arab/

The Airbus A380: www.airbus.com/en/aircraftfamilies/a380/

Tourism Spain: www.spain.info

Where to Ski and Snowboard: www.wheretoskiandsnowboard.com

World Airline Awards: www.worldairlineawards.com

Cruise Lines International Association: http://www.cruising.org

Population Reference Bureau: www.prb.org

PART 2

Further Issues of Demand and Supply

Demand: time preference, elasticity and forecasting

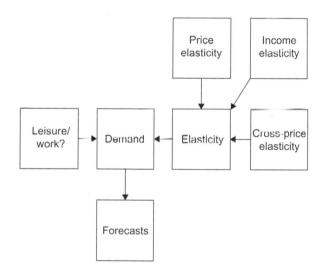

This chapter looks in more detail at demand. First it considers the choice between leisure and work and asks whether we are becoming a Leisure Society. Various concepts of demand elasticity are explained, and the importance of these concepts to the recreation, leisure and tourism sector examined. Finally the chapter considers some techniques of demand forecasting, their uses and shortcomings. By studying this chapter students will be able to:

- evaluate the work/leisure trade-off;
- evaluate the notion of a 'Leisure Society';
- understand and apply the concept of price elasticity of demand;
- understand and apply the concept of income elasticity of demand;
- understand and apply the concept of cross-price elasticity of demand;
- describe simple methods of demand forecasting;
- evaluate techniques of demand forecasting.

THE DEMAND FOR LEISURE

We approach the demand for leisure by assuming that consumers act rationally to maximize their satisfaction given a range of economic choices. Leisure time represents an element in the choice set available to consumers, and maximization of consumer satisfaction will therefore also involve choice about how much leisure time to take. Just as when choosing between other goods and services, consumers will consider the extra satisfaction they derive from leisure time against the price or cost of leisure time.

Consumers face the problem of limited time. There are only 24 hours in a day, and thus the most fundamental choice that consumers face is whether to devote their limited time to leisure or work. We can consider the cost or price of leisure time as its opportunity cost or what has to be given up in order to enjoy leisure time. The opportunity cost of leisure time can be thought of as earnings that are lost through not working. An interesting question is what will happen to the trade-off between work and leisure when income changes? Let us consider the case of an increase income. There are two potential effects of an increase in income on the demand for leisure time.

First, an increase in income means an increase in the opportunity cost of leisure time, in terms of greater loss of earnings per hour. In this case we may expect consumers to demand less leisure time. This is called the substitution effect. Consumers will tend to substitute work for leisure to reflect the increased opportunity cost of leisure. However, an increase in income will also result in consumers having more income and spending power. Leisure time can be classed as a 'normal service' and in common with other 'normal' goods and services, as income increases more will be demanded. This is called the income effect. So after an increase in income we are faced with two competing forces that relate to our new demand for leisure time. There are complex set of forces which will determine whether the income or substitution effect is greater. One possibility is that as income increases, consumers have the ability to get more satisfaction out of their leisure time, thus resulting in a strong income effect. The satisfaction derived from labour is also influenced by psychological and social factors. Some individuals may favour long leisure hours which they can happily fill with cheap or free activities such as reading, watching television, sleeping or walking. Other individuals may have a low boredom threshold and thus get less satisfaction from leisure time. Equally there are cultural influences at work. There appears to be a greater work ethic in countries such as Germany and Japan than in other countries, particularly those with warmer climates.

CHOICE OR RIGIDITY?

The extent to which choice can actually be exercised in the work/leisure trade-off depends on flexibility in the labour market. When choosing between most goods and services, consumers can readily vary the amounts consumed in response to changing relative prices. Consumers generally have less choice in their participation in labour markets. Many jobs have standardized hours where individuals cannot choose to add or subtract hours in response to changes in wages. However, workers can express their general preferences through trade unions and staff associations, and these may be taken into account in determining the overall work package of pay, hours and holiday benefits.

Some jobs offer flexibility in offering overtime provision, and some individuals may have extra employment in addition to their main job. In these cases individuals will be in a position to exercise more precisely their choice between work and leisure. Finally the unemployed are generally not acting out of choice but by lack of opportunity in their allocation of leisure time. However, there has been considerable debate regarding social security benefits and incentives to work. Right-wing economists argue that benefit levels are distorting the labour market so that some unemployed maximize their satisfaction by remaining unemployed rather than entering the labour market.

TRENDS IN WORK AND LEISURE: A LEISURE SOCIETY?

It was the French sociologist Joffre Dumazedier (1967) who wrote tantalizingly about the imminent arrival of the Leisure Society in the 1960s. Politicians warmed to this theme and in the UK, Prime Minister MacMillan reminded the British electorate that they would never had it so good. Landmarks of the emerging Leisure Society may be glimpsed in subsequent years. The 1970s witnessed the release of Ian Drury's *Sex and Drugs and Rock and Roll*, Disneyland conquered Europe and Japan in the 1990s and opened and in 1994 Sony launched the Playstation. Ibiza (Spain), Cancun (Mexico) and the beaches of Southern Thailand seem to have hosted non-stop parties for most of the last decade and Dennis Tito became the first Space Tourist in 2001 and recently five-star hotels have been topped by seven-star arrivals such as the Burj Al Arab in Dubai. So are we having it even better? Have we become a Leisure Society?

Certainly in the developed world the opportunities for leisure have never been better, fuelled by rising incomes, technological advances and a dazzling array of new products. Only a fraction of our income is needed to fulfil basic needs of food, clothing and shelter, and much of our rising income is devoted to leisure spending. Almost every household now possesses a television and computer – all considered luxury items in the 1960s. Labour-saving devices such as washing machines, Hoovers and dishwashers increase our leisure time. So what do we do in our non-working time? Our homes are populated with even more sophisticated leisure devices – TVs, PCs, mobile devices and increasingly more than one of each. Outside the home we walk, play sports, go to cinemas, clubs, gyms, attractions, restaurants and bars and we shop. We travel further abroad and more frequently. International tourist arrivals reached 600 million in 2000 and are predicted to rise to 1500 million by 2020. Indeed the growth of tourism is such that it now claims to be the world's biggest industry. Other discernible trends include the influence of particular interest groups (witness the importance of the Homo-Euro in Sitges, Spain), the strength of the over-40s leisure markets and the displacement of traditional industries by leisure. On Sundays churches are increasingly deserted in favour of shopping malls. IKEA, the MacDonald's Golden Arches and the Spires of the Magic Kingdom of Disneyland all trumpet leisure as our new religion.

But there are several paradoxes surrounding the development of a Leisure Society. The first concerns leisure as a social activity. We have equipped our homes for more comfortable and more sophisticated entertainment with videos, DVDs, widescreen TVs, cable, digital and surround-sound. Yet, despite this, cinema attendance has grown steadily in recent years. It seems we still like the spectacle of the cinema and the atmosphere created by a larger audience. The cinema at least provides an opportunity for social interaction in leisure. But there are also signs of a retreat from leisure as a social activity to that of a solitary one. This is symbolized in a book called *Bowling Alone* where Robert Putnam (2000) describes the individual who now goes bowling alone, rather than with friends.

Plate 4 Porters in Nepal. *Source: The author.*

A Leisure Society also suggests leisure for all. Certainly there are more opportunities than ever for mass consumption of leisure, but herein lie other problems. First, there is that of involuntary leisure. Unemployment has remained obstinately high in many parts of Europe. This means that a significant group of people have large swathes of leisure time, but insufficient income to participate in what has become an increasingly marketized activity, and this creates a frustrated leisure class. Second, for large populations in many parts of the world, working conditions are harsh, pay is low and paid holidays are uncommon. Plate 4 illustrates porters in action in Nepal. Each porter carries the rucksacks of two to three tourists in the Himalayan mountain range. Not only is the work hard for modest pay but some porters are not equipped with high-altitude clothing (note the flip-flops in the picture). In some cases they have lost toes through frostbite.

The phrase 'money rich, time poor' has become a popular mantra for those in employment and suggests that achieving a perfect state of leisure may be illusive. The evidence portrays a mixed picture here. Research in the UK suggests that British people have decreased their working hours by 2 hours 40 minutes per week since the 1950s, representing a modest gain of 7 extra weekly hours of leisure over the century. The average holiday entitlement of EU manual workers is 4–5 weeks a year. The European Work Directive has capped the working week at 35 hours for most employees. Perhaps the division here is between the Mediterranean and Anglo Saxon traditions since for the latter Juliet Schor (1992) pointed up an unexpected decline of leisure in the book *The Overworked American*. In the USA, annual holidays rarely exceed 2 weeks. In the UK, a survey by the Chartered Institute of Personnel and Development found that over one-fifth of employees are working more than 48 hours a week and 56 per cent of these said the balance between their work and personal life was weighted too much towards their job. This gives rise to contrasting effects. In the UK, the term TINS (Two Incomes No Sex) pithily describes those couples who are too exhausted by work for sex. On the other hand in France and Spain a new architecture of leisure emerges. Bridges are formed by adding leave days to public holidays to form extended weekends, and some French workers have constructed ambitious viaducts to take most of May off. Unsurprisingly a study by the French Employment Ministry found that 59 per cent of workers felt their daily lives had improved as a result of the shorter hours.

In terms of working patterns the other significant feature is the steady increase of working women. The upside of this is the concomitant increase in disposable income available for leisure purchases by women (and a notable result of this, in the UK at least, is a marked increase in female alcohol consumption). However, the amounts of time women have available for leisure depends largely on their ability to reduce their historical burden of unpaid housework activities.

Another intriguing paradox exists between the terms leisure and leisurely. Bertrand Russell wrote *In Praise of Idleness and Other Essays* (1932), an essay in favour of the 4 hour working day. In contrast, Staffan Linder's (1970) *The Harried Leisure Class* provided an insight into what might frustrate the opportunities for greater leisure. He noted that as earnings per hour increase workers are faced with a notional increase in the cost of not working. Hence rational individuals will be tempted to reallocate time towards paid work or at least increase the intensity of their leisure consumption. A stark choice arises between less leisure and unleisurely leisure, and our growing obsession with fast food is surely the paradigm example of the latter.

A further paradox in leisure is that of individualism versus massification. There are strong forces at work leading to the latter and the homogenization of leisure. Global brands such as Nike, Holiday Inn and Sony are strengthening their grip on their markets and lessening our exposure to global cultural differences. Equally, a particular view of culture is transmitted through the cinema where films from the USA account for a majority of box-office receipts in the EU. Package holidays still sell in their million by offering low prices based on economies of scale. In his book *The McDonaldization of Society*, Ritzer (1993) describes the spread of the principles of fast food production. In leisure, MacDonald's itself, as well as Disneylands and shopping malls, illustrate this process at work with an emphasis on predictable experiences and calculable and efficient production techniques. Against this the French theorist Bourdieu (1984) stresses the importance of individualism or 'distinction' where leisure enables the individual to construct a distinctive lifestyle and to assert individuality in a modern society. So we face the paradox of searching for difference and distinctiveness in a world of increasing similarity.

We are surrounded by the symbols and signals of a Leisure Society. Our economic circumstances surely permit us to live in a Leisure Society. That we do not always fully claim our leisure or feel the full pleasure of it is due partly to personal and partly to political choices. It is the latter which must cause some worry. Perhaps as leisure has displaced religion it has also become the new opium of the people. Where we used to work and pray we now work and play. This leaves insufficient time for participation in the politics of leisure and decisions about what kind of Leisure Society we want to create. For despite the obvious richness, diversity and accessibility of leisure experiences available, we do not appear to be a Society at Leisure. Time seems ever more at a premium. We are not a calm or contemplative society. Rather we are a frenetic society that not only still works remarkably hard but now plays hard too.

PRICE ELASTICITY OF DEMAND

Price elasticity of demand measures the responsiveness of demand to a change in price. This relationship can be expressed as a formula, and Exhibit 4.1 shows a worked example for calculating price elasticity of demand.

$$\frac{\text{Percentage change in quantity demanded}}{\text{Percentage change in price}}$$

Where demand is inelastic it means that demand is unresponsive to a change in price, whereas elastic demand is more sensitive to price changes.

The range of possible outcomes is summarized in Figure 4.1.

Exhibit 4.1 Price elasticity of demand: a worked example

When the price of four-star hotel rooms rose from $160 to $180, demand fell from 3200 to 2800 rooms per week. Calculate elasticity of demand.

1 To calculate percentage change in quantity demand, divide the change in demand ($\Delta Q = 400$) by the original demand ($D0 = 3200$) and multiply by 100
2 $400/(3200 \times 100) = 12.5$
3 To calculate percentage change in price, divide the change in price ($\Delta P = 20$) by the original price ($P0 = 160$) and multiply by 100
4 $20/(160 \times 100) = 12.5$
5 Elasticity of demand $= 12.5/12.5 = 1$

Numerical value	Graph	Explanation	Term
0	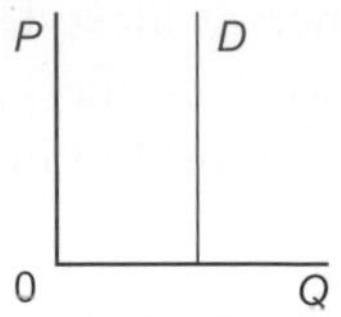	Demand is unresponsive to a change in price	Perfectly inelastic
> 0 < 1	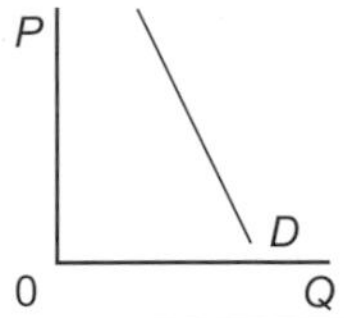	Demand changes by a smaller proportion than price	Inelastic
1	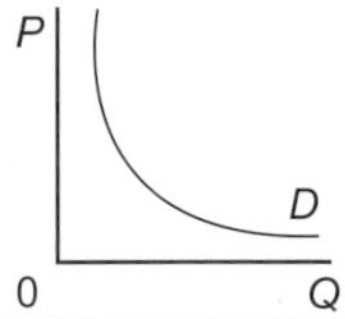	Demand changes by the same proportion as price	Unit elasticity
> 1 < ∞	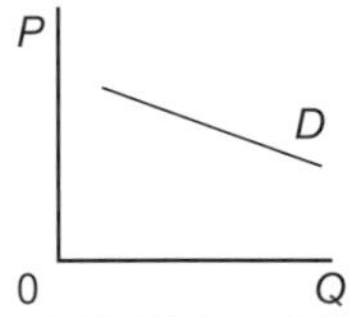	Demand changes by a larger proportion than price	Elastic
∞	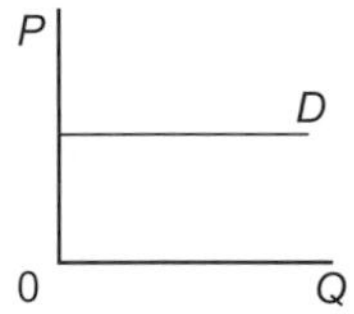	Any increase in price causes demand to fall to zero	Perfectly elastic

Figure 4.1 Elasticity of demand.

It should be noted that, since a rise in the price of a good causes a fall in demand, the figure calculated for price elasticity of demand will always be negative. Economists generally ignore the minus sign. Note that the demand curve, which has elasticity of demand of 1 throughout its length, is a rectangular hyperbola.

Factors affecting price elasticity of demand

The following are the main factors which influence price elasticity of demand:

- necessity of good or service
- number of substitutes
- addictiveness
- price and usefulness
- time period
- consumer awareness.

Necessity of good or service

Goods and services which are necessities generally have a lower price elasticity of demand than goods which are luxuries.

Number of substitutes

Goods and services which are provided in conditions of near monopoly tend to have inelastic demand, since the consumer cannot shop elsewhere should the prices increase. Competition in a market makes demand more elastic.

Addictiveness

Goods such as cigarettes which are addictive tend to have inelastic demand.

Price and usefulness

Cheap and very useful goods and services tend to have inelastic demand since an increase in a low price will have little impact on consumers' purchasing power.

Time period

Demand elasticity generally increases, and more time is allowed to elapse between the change in price and the measurement of the change in demand. This is because consumers may not be able to change their plans in the short run. For example, many holidaymakers book holidays 6 months in advance. Thus a fall in the value of the US dollar might have limited effect on the demand for US holidays in the short run since consumers have committed holiday plans. It may not be until the next year that the full effects of such a devaluation on demand can be measured.

Consumer awareness

Package holidays represent a bundle of complementary goods and services which are bought by consumers and consumers may be attracted to the bottom-line price of a holiday. Consumers may be unaware of destination prices. For this reason, elasticity of demand for services such as ski passes may be inelastic for UK holidaymakers due to lack of information. It should also be noted that the rise of the Internet provides consumers with better knowledge about prices and is therefore likely to lead to demand becoming more price sensitive (elastic).

Elasticity of demand and total revenue

The concept of price elasticity of demand is useful for firms to forecast the effects of price changes on total revenue received from selling goods and services, as well as for governments wishing to maximize their tax receipts.

Total revenue is defined as:

Total revenue = Price × Quantity sold

Consider a rise in the price of a good by 10 per cent. If demand is elastic, quantity sold will fall by more than 10 per cent and thus total revenue will fall. However, if demand is inelastic, it will fall by less than 10 per cent and thus total revenue will rise. Similarly, a fall in the price of a good will lead to a rise in total revenue in the case of elastic demand and a fall in total revenue where demand is inelastic. Exhibit 4.2 illustrates the application of these principles to tourism in New Zealand. Here relatively moderate price elasticity of demand means that New Zealand tourism is not very sensitive to changes in prices. Tourism revenues are likely to remain resilient in the face of price rises, for example those that might be caused by high oil prices or Emissions Trading Schemes (ETS). Equally heavy discounting of prices is unlikely to be a successful policy in terms of increasing overall tourism revenues.

Several other studies have been made into price elasticity of demand in the leisure and tourism sector of the economy. For example, Boviard et al. (1984) researched elasticity values for National Trust sites in the UK. Time-series analysis was used and changes in visitor numbers were compared with changes in admission prices, with account being taken of other factors such as changes in the weather,

Exhibit 4.2 Demand elasticity estimates for New Zealand tourism

Schiff and Becken (2010) estimated demand elasticities for New Zealand tourism for 16 different international visitor segments using time-series data. Their findings showed that overall price elasticities of tourist arrivals and demand are moderate (with the exception of the Asian markets). The authors point out some of the implications of this for policy. They note, for example, that lack of price sensitivity means that New Zealand as a destination is not put at particular risk of tourism revenue declines from increases in prices. The authors further note that this means that tourism is likely to remain strong even in the face of possible global oil price shocks or increased prices that might result from or the introduction of an ETS. Schiff and Becken also note that the low elasticities in some of the key markets has implications for discounting and that current trends for lower prices will not necessarily lead to higher overall revenues. They note that Australian tourists, in particular, are not likely to change their behaviour in response to cheaper on the ground products.

Source: Adapted from Schiff and Becken (2010) http://www.sciencedirect.com/ science?_ob=ArticleURL&_udi=B6V9R-505G29B-1&_user=6269266&_coverDate= 05%2F26%2F2010&_rdoc=1&_fmt=high&_orig=search&_origin=search&_sort=d&_ docanchor=&view=c&_searchStrId=1462229390&_rerunOrigin=scholar.google&_ acct=C000047720&_version=1&_urlVersion=0&_userid=6269266&md5=3dcfc09a3f10cf 3cc059d3f5f0845857&searchtype=a

travel costs, unemployment and inflation. Using data from 1970 to 1980, estimates for price elasticity varied from 0.25 at Wallington to 1.05 at Hidcote, but with most results lying in the inelastic range.

INCOME ELASTICITY OF DEMAND

Income elasticity of demand measures the responsiveness of demand to a change in income. This relationship can be expressed as a formula:

Percentage change in quantity demanded
Percentage change in income

Calculation of income elasticity of demand enables an organization to determine whether its goods and services are normal or inferior.

Normal or superior goods are defined as goods whose demand increases as income increases. Therefore their income elasticity of demand is positive ($+/+ = +$). The higher the number, the more an increase in income will stimulate demand. Inferior goods are defined as goods whose demand falls as income rises. Therefore their income elasticity of demand is negative ($-/+ = -$).

Knowledge of income elasticity of demand is useful in predicting future demand in the leisure and tourism sector. For example, Song et al. (2000) undertook an empirical study of outbound tourism demand in the UK. Their results show that the long-run income elasticities for the destinations studied range from 1.70 to 3.90 with an average of 2.367. These estimates of income elasticities imply that overseas holidays are highly income elastic. In other words, demand for outbound tourism should continue to grow with economic growth. The study also considered own-price elasticities and found that the demand for UK outbound tourism is relatively own-price inelastic.

Knowledge of income elasticity of demand also helps to explain some merger and take-over activity as organizations in industries with low or negative income elasticity of demand attempt to benefit from economic growth by expanding into industries with high-positive income elasticity of demand. Such industries show market growth as the economy expands.

CROSS-PRICE ELASTICITY OF DEMAND

Cross-price elasticity of demand measures the responsiveness of demand for one good to a change in the price of another good. This relationship can be expressed as a formula:

Percentage change in quantity demanded of good A
Percentage change in price of good B

Cross-price elasticity of demand measures the relationship between different goods and services. It therefore reveals whether goods are substitutes, complements or unrelated. An increase in price of good B will lead to an increase in demand for good A if the two goods are substitutes. Thus substitute goods have a positive cross-price elasticity of demand $(+/+ = +)$. For goods which are complements or in joint demand, an increase in the price of good B will lead to a fall in demand for a complementary good, good A. Therefore complementary goods have negative cross-price elasticity of demand $(-/+ = -)$. An increase in the price of good B will have no effect on the demand for an unrelated good, good A. Unrelated goods have cross-price elasticity of demand of zero $(0/+ = 0)$.

Canina et al. (2003) undertook a study to quantify the effects of gasoline price increases on hotel room demand in the USA. Their analysis was based on data from 1988 to 2000. They found that each 1 per cent increase in gasoline prices is associated with a 1.74 per cent decrease in lodging demand. In other words, there is a negative cross-price elasticity of demand between gasoline prices and lodging demand which can therefore be seen as complementary items. However, they noted that changes in gasoline price changes do not affect all industry segments equally. The segments that feel the greatest effects of gasoline price increases are full-service mid-market properties and highway and suburban hotels. High-end hotels seem to be immune to the negative effects of fuel price increases.

DEMAND FORECASTING

The supply of leisure goods and services cannot generally be changed without some planning and in particular the supply of capital goods such as aircraft requires long planning cycles. Similarly, tour operations require considerable planning to book airport slots and hotel accommodation. Equally, leisure and tourism services are highly perishable. It is not possible to keep stocks of unsold hotel rooms, aircraft and theatre seats, or squash courts. Whilst the supply of some leisure goods, such as golf balls and tennis rackets, can be more readily changed, and stocks of unsold goods held over, there is clearly a need for forecasting of demand for leisure and tourism goods and services.

Exhibit 4.3 reports on forecasts from the Boeing Corporation for aircraft demand.

Methods for forecasting demand (Frechtling, 2001) include:

* naive forecasting
* qualitative forecasts
* time-series extrapolation
* surveys
* Delphi technique
* models.

Exhibit 4.3 Aircraft set for take off

The Boeing Corporation, manufacturers of airplanes, released its 20-year forecast for new commercial aircraft in which the following major points were made:

- 2010 was a year of falling air traffic demand.
- Passenger traffic will rise 5.3% annually led by emerging markets especially those of China, India and Southeast Asia.
- By 2029 the global airline fleet will expand by around 64% to 30,900 aircraft from 18,890 in 2010.
- This is driven by the proliferation of low-cost airlines and emerging markets such as China.
- About 47% of this growth will be for narrow-body planes.
- About 45% of growth will be for wide-body planes.
- Particular opportunities exist in the Asia-Pacific region for narrow-body planes.
- Traffic for the Asia-Pacific region is forecast to grow on average by 7.1% per anum.
- Traffic for the North American region is forecast to grow on average by 2.8% per anum.
- The Asia-Pacific region will be the world's most important aerospace marketplace within 20 years.
- Forecasts are based on an assumption that the global economy will grow by an average of 3.2% per anum.

Source: Adapted from Boeing Forecasts as reported in e-turbo news www.eturbonews. com/17284/boeing-forecasts-64-global-airline-fleet-expansion-2029

Naive forecasts

Naive forecasting makes simple assumptions about the future. At its simplest, naive forecasting assumes that the future level of demand will be the same as the current level. Naive forecasting may also introduce a fixed percentage by which demand is assumed to increase, for example, 3 per cent per annum.

Qualitative forecasts

Qualitative forecasts consider the range of factors which influence the demand for a good or service, as discussed in Chapter 3. These factors are then ranked in order of importance, and each of them is in turn analysed to reveal future trends. Although statistical data may be consulted at this stage, no attempt is made to construct a mathematical formula to describe precise relationships between demand and its determinants. Such forecasts rely on a large measure of common sense and are likely to be couched in general terms such as 'small increase in demand' or 'no change in demand envisaged'.

Table 4.1 Time series of sales of a product				
Year	**Q1**	**Q2**	**Q3**	**Q4**	**Total**
1	112	205	319	421	1057
2	124	220	350	460	1154
3	90	245	383	503	1221
4	138	267	412	548	1365
5	160	285	450	595	1490

Note: Q1, Q2, etc. = year quarters.

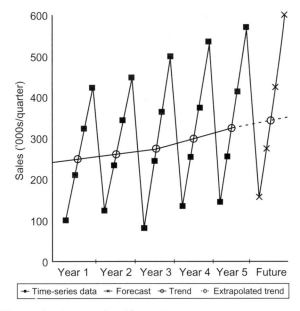

Figure 4.2 Time-series data, trend and forecast.

Time-series analysis

A time series is a set of data collected regularly over a period of time. An example of such data is given in Table 4.1.

First, this data can be seen to exhibit seasonal features. Sales of this product rise within each year to a peak in the fourth quarter and drop back sharply in the first quarter of the next year. Second, there seems to be a trend. The figures for each quarter and the yearly totals nearly all display an upward movement. Third, the figure for the first quarter in year 3 does not fit in with the rest of the data and appears as an unusual figure. This may well have been caused by a random variation such as a strike or war or natural disaster.

Forecasting using time-series data first averages seasonal and random variations from the data, to reveal the underlying pattern or trend. The trend can then be used to predict future data, for general yearly totals and adjusted to indicate future seasonal totals. This is illustrated in Figure 4.2 and is a process known as extrapolation.

Time-series forecasting is useful in predicting future seasonal demand and adjusting supply to anticipate seasonal fluctuations. This is particularly important in the leisure and tourism sector where demand tends to be very seasonal (tennis equipment in early summer, leisure centre use after work and at weekends, and holiday demand).

However, care must be taken in using time-series data. Planning ski holiday capacity using time-series data may be useful in predicting market growth, but seasonal fluctuations due to school holidays are not best predicted from past events (which would give the average date) but by looking to see when Easter falls to find the precise date. Equally it is random events that can cause significant changes in the demand for ski holidays. Clearly snowfall and exchange rates are two key factors that cannot be forecast using time-series analysis. It is important therefore that time-series analysis should be used as part of a package of forecasting techniques.

Surveys

Surveys may be carried out by the organization itself or contracted out to a specialist market research organization. Alternatively use may be made of published forecasts constructed using surveys. Surveys can be useful ways of forecasting demand for new or revised products where no time-series data exist. However, survey results are only as valid as their underlying methodology; so care must be taken to ensure that the sample used for the survey is a true reflection of an organization's potential customers, and is of a large enough size to be valid. Additionally, a pilot survey needs to be conducted and analysed to iron out any problems of interpretation of words or leading questions. In fact, surveys turn out to be more useful for testing ideas such as advertising campaigns or design, where respondents are asked to choose between real and concrete alternatives. Hypothetical questions are generally used in demand forecasting, and respondents' answers may not necessarily reflect what they would actually do if they had to spend money.

Delphi technique

The Delphi technique is a method of forecasting which attempts to harness expert opinion on the subject. Questionnaires are used to discover opinions of experts in a particular field. The results of the forecasts are then fed back to the participants with the aim of reaching a consensus view of the group.

Modelling

More complex forecasting methods attempt to describe accurately the relationship between demand for a product and the factors determining that demand. They consider a number of variables, and use statistical techniques of correlation and regression analysis to test relationships and construct formulae. Some include econometric techniques which forecast key economic variables such as growth rates, interest rates and inflation rates to construct a comprehensive model which relates general economic conditions to the factors affecting demand for a particular product to the demand forecasts for that product.

Problems with forecasts

There are several problems which arise from using forecasts. First, the forecasts are only as good as the assumptions of the model being used. For example, the assumption that the past is a good guide to the future limits the validity of extrapolation using time-series analysis. However, there are equally questionable assumptions included in some very complex models. It is important to know what these assumptions are so that should any of these assumptions prove to be incorrect, forecasts can be re-evaluated. The major problem, however, is the unpredictability of economic trends and outside events such as wars or strikes or disasters. For example, the events of 11 September 2001 undermined the accuracy of many forecasts and caused severe financial problems to those who had relied on overly optimistic predictions of future levels of demand. This does not mean that forecasts are useless, but that those who use them should be constantly monitoring their operating environment to detect any factors which will upset the forecasts they are using.

REVIEW OF KEY TERMS

- Income effect: change in demand caused by change in income.
- Substitution effect: change in demand caused by change in relative prices.
- Price elasticity of demand: the responsiveness of demand to a change in price.
- Inelastic demand: demand is unresponsive to a change in price.
- Elastic demand: demand is responsive to a change in price.
- Income elasticity of demand: the responsiveness of demand to a change in income.
- Cross-price elasticity of demand: the responsiveness of demand for one good to a change in the price of another good.
- Time series: a set of data collected regularly over a period of time.
- Seasonal variation: regular pattern of demand changes apparent at different times of year.

- Extrapolation: extending time-series data into the future based on trend.
- Delphi technique: finding consensus view of experts.

Source: The author, from news cuttings.

Data Questions

Task 4.1 **Teleworking**

An office worker who works for 48 weeks a year and has a 90 minute journey to and from work clocks up some alarming statistics. An average of 720 hours each year are spent on commuting. That is 30 whole days. Over the last decade, commuting has reached new heights, largely because of high inner-city house prices and motorways. Cheaper house prices in out-of-city locations, together with the development of a comprehensive network of motorways, have encouraged people to increase their time spent on commuting and to cast a wider net in search of well-paid employment. It may be, though, that we are nearing the peak of commuting. The technological revolution in the office means that the possibility for people to work from home is becoming a reality. Why spend a fortune in time and money sending people to the office, when the office can be sent to the people? The fax, digitalization of information, the telephone network, PCs, modems and videoconferencing are all enabling the spread of teleworking. Meanwhile, environmental concerns have encouraged the government to increase taxes to curb the use of car journeys.

Many companies are experimenting with teleworking schemes. This has resulted in the creation of a new class of full-time and part-time teleworkers. Telecoms companies are major potential benefactors of increased teleworking, since teleworking means more use of data links. However, many telecoms organizations also use the scheme itself. Telephone number enquiries' operators can now work at home where they have databases with telephone numbers installed on PCs and calls rerouted. To the customer there is no apparent change in service.

The choice for workers looks fairly straightforward. It has been estimated that the overall benefit to a $25,000-a-year employee who is able to work at home for 4 days a week and cut commuting to 1 day a week is of the order of $7080 a year. This is calculated mainly in terms of increased leisure time priced at $6335. To these benefits employees can add more flexibility in terms of house location and hours worked and less commuting stress. On the other hand, some psychologists have pointed out the important functions that a place of work may fulfil, particularly pointing to the friendship factor, and the benefits of a physical separation of work and home. A key question posed by the release of commuting time is how it will be spent. Will people choose to use it as leisure time or might they instead seek to increase their earnings by working more hours?

Recap Questions

1 Economic theory assumes that people act rationally and maximize their total satisfaction. Explain this proposition and discuss whether people who spend 30 days a year commuting fulfil these assumptions.

Task 4.1 **continued**

2 'For individuals, the advantages of teleworking are usually believed to have more to do with quality of life than with economics'. Can economic theory consider the quality of life?

3 The value of the extra leisure time made available to the employee cited above is $6335.
  (a) How might this calculation be made?
  (b) What factors will determine what the person will do with the extra leisure time?

4 If the benefit to individuals of teleworking is so clear, why do not more people telework?

5 How might teleworking affect the leisure sector?

Task 4.2 Journal Article: Li, G., Wong, K.K.F., Song, H., Witt, S.F., 2006. Tourism demand forecasting: a time varying parameter error correction model. *Journal of Travel Research* 45, 175.

In this article Dr Gang Li and his co-researchers present elasticity of demand data for tourists from the UK to the destinations of France, Greece, Italy, Portugal and Spain (Table 4.2).

Table 4.2 Elasticity of demand data for tourists from the UK to the destinations of France, Greece, Italy, Portugal and Spain

Generating market	Destination	Measurement data	Income elasticity	Price elasticity
UK	France	Expenditure	2.817	−1.163
UK	Greece	Expenditure	1.834	−1.959
UK	Italy	Expenditure	1.935	−1.184
UK	Portugal	Expenditure	1.779	−0.161
UK	Spain	Expenditure	2.22	−1.23

Recap Questions

1 Classify UK tourism income elasticity of demand in these destinations as inferior/normal.

2 Classify UK tourism price elasticity of demand in these destinations as elastic/inelastic

3 Comment on these findings.

4 What implications do these figures have for policy makers and tourist organizations in the destination countries?

5 Devise a method of estimating price and income elasticity of demand for cinema attendance, explaining any problems foreseen.

Task 4.3 Air Traffic Forecasts for Europe

A report by EUROCONTROL presents Long-Term Forecast of Instrument Flight Rules (IFR) traffic in Europe to 2030 (see Table 4.3).

Data Questions

Table 4.3 Summary of forecast for the ESRA

	IFR movements ('000s)						Average annual growth						AAGR 2030/ 2007	Traffic Multiple 2030/ 2007
	2006	2007	2014	2020	2025	2030	2006	2007	2014	2020/ 2015	2025/ 2021	2030/ 2026		
A: Global Growth	.	.	14,119	17,532	19,890	22,086	.	.	5.2%	3.8%	2.6%	2.1%	3.5%	2.2
B: Business as Usual	.	.	12,930	15,553	17 763	19,549	.	.	3.9%	3.1%	2.7%	1.9%	3.0%	2.0
C: Regulation & Growth	9,439	9,916	12,930	14,955	16,724	18,170	3.9%	5.1%	3.9%	2.5%	2.3%	1.7%	2.7%	1.8
D: Fragmenting World	.	.	11,773	13,460	15,062	16,507	.	.	2.5%	2.2%	2.3%	1.8%	2.2%	1.7

Note: ESRA = Eurocontrol Statistical Reference Area.

Source: Based on EUROCONTROL Long-Term Forecast (http://www.eurocontrol.int/statfor).

Task 4.3 continued

The forecast uses four scenarios to capture the possible futures for the aviation industry. The four scenarios are:

- Scenario A: Global Growth: Strong economic growth in an increasingly globalized economy, with technology used successfully to mitigate the effects of challenges such as the environment and security.
- Scenario B: Business as Usual: Moderate economic growth and little change from the status quo, that is, trends continue as currently observed.
- Scenario C: Regulation & Growth: Moderate economic growth, but with stronger regulation to address growing environmental challenges for aviation and for Europe more generally.
- Scenario D: Fragmenting World: A world with increasing tensions between regions, with knock-on effects of weaker economies, reduced trade and less long-haul travel.

Recap Questions

1 What additional information would you like before trusting these estimates?
2 What factors would be taken into account in preparing demand forecasts for the air transport industry?
3 Which organizations will use these forecasts, and how?
4 Which of the four scenarios do you think is the most plausible?

MULTIPLE CHOICE

1 Which of the following statements is always true?
(a) An increase in wages increases the opportunity cost of leisure.
(b) An increase in wages will cause workers to work less.
(c) US workers have longer holidays than European workers.
(d) All of the above.

2 When the price of a leisure good rose by 10 per cent demand remained the same. Which of the following best describes the price elasticity of demand for this good?
(a) Perfectly elastic.
(b) Perfectly inelastic.
(c) Unit elasticity.
(d) Neither elastic nor inelastic.

3 Which of the following will cause the demand for air travel to destination x to be more inelastic?
(a) Punctuality of service.
(b) Consumer awareness of the prices of competitors.
(c) The absence of close competition.
(d) x representing a long-haul destination.

4   Which of the following statements is true?
   (a) Normal goods have positive income elasticity of demand.
   (b) An increase in price will cause total revenue to rise when demand is elastic.
   (c) Income elasticity of demand for foreign travel tends to be negative.
   (d) An elastic demand curve generally has a steep gradient.

5   The Delphi technique for forecasting involves:
   (a) Time-series analysis.
   (b) Regression analysis.
   (c) Extrapolation.
   (d) Asking expert opinion.

REVIEW QUESTIONS

1   What degree of income elasticity of demand would you expect for summer holiday breaks to an exotic destination?

2   What cross-price elasticity of demand would you expect to find between:
   (a) Price of dollars/holidays in the USA?
   (b) Holidays in Spain/holidays in Greece?
   (c) Sony games consoles/Sony games cartridges?

3   What is meant by extrapolation?

Websites of interest

Boeing Corporation: www.boeing.com
Eurocontrol: www.eurocontrol.int/statfor

CHAPTER

5

Supply and costs

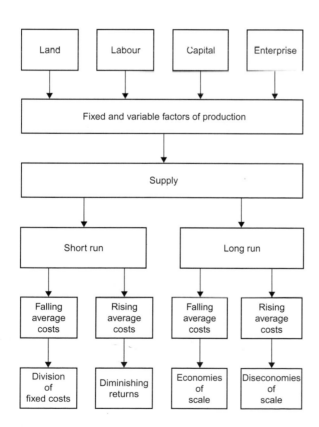

Objectives and learning outcomes

Some airlines provide 'Shuttle' services which operate on a turn-up-and-fly principle, so their operations divisions have to be able to provide a flexible service in order to meet sudden changes in demand. Air traffic control routes across Europe and hotel accommodation on the other hand are fairly inflexible – they are sometimes unable to cope with sudden surges in demand and this can lead to supply problems in peak times of the year. This chapter looks behind the supply curve at issues such as these. It investigates how easily the supply of leisure and tourism products is able to respond to changes in demand, using the concept of elasticity. It also considers how an organization's costs respond to changes in output and distinguishes between private costs and social or external costs.

By studying this chapter students will be able to:

- understand and utilize the concept of elasticity of supply;
- identify the factors of production;
- distinguish between fixed and variable factors of production;
- analyse the relationship between costs and output in the short and long run;
- establish the relationship between costs and the supply curve;
- understand the reasons for economies of scale;
- identify methods and rationale for growth;
- distinguish between social and private costs.

PRICE ELASTICITY OF SUPPLY

Elasticity of supply measures the responsiveness of supply to a change in price. This relationship may be expressed as a formula:

$$\frac{\text{Percentage change in quantity supplied}}{\text{Percentage change in price}}$$

Exhibit 5.1 shows a worked example of how to calculate elasticity of supply.

Where supply is inelastic it means that supply cannot easily be changed, whereas elastic supply is more flexible. The range of possible outcomes is summarized in Figure 5.1.

Note that any straight line supply curve passing through the origin has supply elasticity of 1.

Exhibit 5.1 A worked example

When the price of four-star hotel rooms rose from $160 to 180, supply rose from 3200 to 3600 rooms per week. Calculate the elasticity of supply.

1   To calculate percentage change in quantity supplied, divide the change in supply ($\Delta Q = 400$) by the original supply ($S0 = 3200$) and multiply by 100.
    $= 400/(3200 \times 100) = 12.5$.
2   To calculate percentage change in price, divide the change in price ($\Delta P = 20$) by the original price ($P0 = 160$) and multiply by 100.
    $= 20/(160 \times 100) = 12.5$.
3   Elasticity of supply $= 12.5/12.5 = 1$.

Numerical value	Graph	Explanation	Term
0		Supply is unresponsive to a change in price	Perfectly inelastic
$> 0 < 1$		Supply changes by a smaller proportion than price	Inelastic
1		Supply changes by the same proportion as price	Unit elasticity
$> 1 < \infty$		Supply changes by a larger proportion than price	Elastic
∞		Suppliers can supply any amount at the current price but none if price falls	Perfectly elastic

Figure 5.1 Elasticity of supply.

Factors affecting price elasticity of supply

The following are the main factors which influence price elasticity of supply:

- time period
- availability of stocks

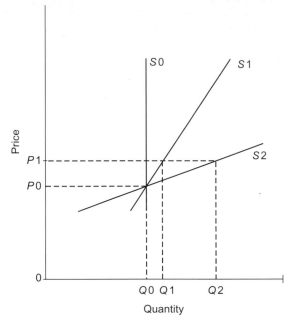

Figure 5.2 The effects of time period on elasticity of supply.

- spare capacity
- flexibility of capacity/resource mobility.

Time period

Generally the longer the time period allowed, the easier it is for supply to be changed. This is illustrated in Figure 5.2.

In the immediate time scale, it is difficult to change supply and thus supply is relatively inelastic, and a change in price of $P0$ to $P1$ results in supply being unchanged at $Q0$ on curve $S0$. In the short run, it may be possible to divert production or capacity from another use and thus supply becomes more elastic. This is shown by supply curve $S1$, where a rise in price from $P0$ to $P1$ results in a small rise in supply from $Q0$ to $Q1$. In the long run, it is possible to vary fixed factors of production (e.g. build more factories or invest in more capacity). Supply is thus more elastic during this time period, as shown by curve $S2$, where a rise in price from $P0$ to $P1$ results in a rise in supply from $Q0$ to $Q2$. For example, if there is a sudden increase in demand for air travel from Paris to Lyon due to a rail strike, airlines will not be able to provide more supply. If the increase in demand is sustained airlines could lease extra planes or transfer them from other less well-used routes to increase supply in the short run. In the long run, new planes could be purchased to provide increased supply.

Availability of stocks

For manufactured goods, the availability of stocks of goods in warehouses will enable supply to be more flexible and more elastic.

'Just-in-time' methods of production are geared towards enabling manufacturing to be more sensitive to market needs without recourse to large stocks. However, for some leisure services (e.g. theatres and hotels), it is impossible to keep standby stocks and so supply is inelastic in the short run.

Spare capacity

The existence of spare capacity either in terms of service capacity or manufacturing capacity will make supply more elastic. Examples here include airlines that have spare aircraft available for deployment.

Flexibility of capacity/resource mobility

Flexibility of capacity means that resources can easily be shifted from provision of one good or service to another. Flexible sports halls, for example, enable capacity to be shifted from one leisure service to another to respond to changes in demand and thus make supply more elastic. Flexibility of the labour force is also a key factor here, and many organizations train staff to be multi-skilled to enable them to shift from one task to another when temporary bottlenecks arise. In contrast, changing the supply of specialist goods or services may require the use of specialist skills or machines. These may be difficult or expensive to hire in the short period and hence will tend to make supply inelastic. For example, the training period for pilots is lengthy and this can make supply of air travel inelastic in the short period.

Significance of price elasticity of supply to leisure sector

The supply of some tourist attractions is totally inelastic. For example, there is only one tomb of Chairman Mao in Beijing, there is only one Sistine Chapel and there is only one home of Sir Winston Churchill at Chartwell in the UK. It is clearly not possible to replicate these sites as it is for other popular attractions such as Disney World.

Considerable thought therefore has to be given to managing such sites. The market could establish an equilibrium if prices were allowed to fluctuate, but the heritage aspect of such sites generally precludes such a solution since they are generally meant to be universally accessible. Inevitably, then, there is excess demand for these sites at the given price and this problem is managed differently at each site. At Mao's tomb, capacity is raised substantially by having the queue divided into two to pass each side of Mao's body. White-gloved attendants furiously wave people by and thus queuing is kept to a minimum despite free admission. At the Sistine Chapel large queues do form, but they are accommodated in an imaginative way by making the detour, through the Vatican museum, to the

Sistine Chapel progressively more and more circuitous. The problem of inelastic supply and excess demand at Chartwell is addressed by issuing timed tickets to visitors.

In general terms, price elasticity of supply determines the extent to which a rise in demand will cause either a change in price or shortage. Tour operators generally have relatively fixed capacity in ski resorts and thus the supply curve is inelastic. When demand rises, for example, during school holiday periods, supply is unable to expand to meet the increased demand and so price rise considerably.

SUPPLY AND COSTS

Leisure and tourism outputs

We need to distinguish between different forms of output in the leisure and tourism sector. Where manufacturing of a product takes place, for example in the production of sports clothing, then output is measured in terms of physical product. Where the provision of a service takes place, output is measured in terms of capacity.

Leisure and tourism inputs

Inputs (or factors of production) are classified in economics under the following general headings.

- *Land*: This includes natural resources such as minerals and land itself and can be divided into renewable and non-renewable resources (see Chapter 16).
- *Labour*: This includes skilled and unskilled human effort.
- *Capital*: This includes buildings, machines and tools.
- *Enterprise*: This is the factor which brings together the other factors of production to produce goods and services.

For example, a soccer club such as Arsenal FC needs a plot of land. Arsenal's new Emirates Stadium occupies 27 acres of prime inner city land (although this is quite modest compared with the 100-acre Manchester United site and the 130-acre Wembley complex). Additionally, it required capital to develop the land (mainly the provision of a stadium and facilities). Its labour force would include skilled employees such as players and accountants and less-skilled stewards and catering staff. But without enterprise, none of these factors of production would be brought together in this way. Enterprise is offered through the club's directors.

In tourism, land is a significant resource for some destinations (e.g. beaches for Tobago and Thailand and Coral for diving in the Red Sea). For other destinations, cultural capital is a key attraction (e.g. museums and historical buildings). Williamson and Hirsch (1996) discuss the process of tourism development in Koh Samui, Thailand and the form that this took, in particular, the building of bungalows. It examines the changing control over factors of production and the importance of land, labour and capital in bungalow development.

Factors of production are further classified as:

- fixed factors
- variable factors.

Fixed factors of production are defined as those factors which cannot be easily varied in the short run. Examples of fixed factors of production in the provision of leisure and tourism services include the actual buildings of theatres and hotels, whilst factories and complex machinery are examples in leisure manufacturing. Variable factors of production on the other hand can be changed in the short run and include unskilled labour, energy (e.g. electricity, gas and oil) and readily available raw materials. The existence of fixed and variable factors of production means that changes in output will be achieved by different means in the short and long run.

Production

Entrepreneurs bring together factors of production in order to supply goods and services in the market and maximize their profits. There are generally several possible ways to produce a given level of output or to provide a service. Profit maximization implies cost minimization and thus entrepreneurs will seek to combine inputs to produce the least-cost method of production. Input prices themselves are constantly changing to reflect changing conditions in their markets. As input prices change, entrepreneurs will adapt production methods to maintain lowest costs, substituting where possible factors of production which are rising in price with cheaper ones. For example, in travel retailing (as in most areas) there is a long-term move to substitute capital for labour. In this case, the Internet is increasingly used for bookings instead of the telephone or high street travel agent.

Short-run costs

Fixed costs

The existence of fixed factors of production means that the costs associated with that factor will also be fixed in the short run. Such costs are sometimes called indirect costs or overheads since they have to be paid irrespective of the level of production. So, for example, whether a plane flies to New York empty or full, its fixed costs or overheads are the same. Exhibit 5.2 illustrates fixed costs for art galleries.

Exhibit 5.2 High fixed costs for art galleries

The demand for art fluctuates according to the state of the economy. When economic growth is strong, galleries can be full of buyers, but these soon disappear when economic times are hard. During a recent downturn in the economy one commentator reported that 'buyers had gone into hibernation' and many art galleries were forced out of business.

A major factor in this is the high fixed costs that galleries face which can be easily accommodated when sales are strong. But the point about fixed costs is that they cannot be changed in the short term. If demand falls suddenly they can force a gallery into bankruptcy since they must still be paid even when there are few or no customers. Galleries are located in prime locations and so their major fixed costs are rent and property taxes. In addition, galleries typically produce three or four catalogues a year with a typical cost of US$10,000 per edition.

Source: The author, based on article from The Independent.

Variable costs

Variable costs are those costs which vary directly with output. They are sometimes called direct costs. For the production of leisure goods they would include raw materials, energy and unskilled labour costs, but for the provision of services such as air transport they are proportionately small and would include such items as meals and passenger handling charges.

Total costs

Total costs are defined as total fixed costs plus total variable costs. This distinction is an important one when deciding whether to continue to operate facilities out of season. A firm which is not covering its costs is making a loss and in the long term will go out of business. However, in the short run a firm which is covering its variable costs and making some contribution to its fixed costs may stay in business. This is because it has to pay for its fixed costs anyway in the short run and thus some contribution to their costs is better than none at all.

Average costs

Average Costs (ACs) (or unit costs, or cost per item) are defined as total costs divided by output.

Marginal costs

Marginal Costs (MCs) are defined as the cost of supplying one extra unit of output.

Relationship between output and costs in the short run (production)

Figure 5.3 shows a typical short-run average cost(s) curve for the production of goods in the short run. If a manufacturer has planned

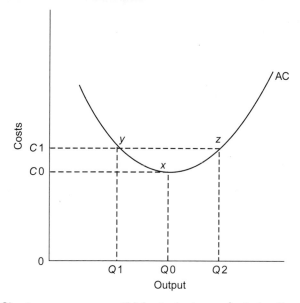

Figure 5.3 Short-run average cost(s) for typical manufacturing firm.

for a level of output $0Q0$, then $0C0$ represents the average cost(s) of production. These will represent the least-cost method of production and combination of factors of production since profit maximization is assumed. However, if the level of output should subsequently be changed in the short run, then by definition only variable factors of production can be changed and fixed factors remain constant. average cost(s) will therefore rise as the mix of inputs resulting in the least-cost method of production cannot be maintained.

Consider first a fall in output to $0Q1$. average cost(s) will rise to $0C1$. This is because the fixed costs will now be borne by a smaller level of output. For example, if a UK football premier division team is relegated to a lower division it is likely to see its match attendance fall – but it will still have to pay its stadium costs so its average cost(s) per spectator will rise. Similarly, if output rises to $0Q2$, average cost(s) rises to $0C1$ the fixed factors of production become overcrowded and production less efficient. This is related to the law of eventual diminishing returns.

Relationship between output and costs in the short run (services)

The provision of services often involves different cost relationships from the provision of goods. For a hotel, a theme park or a theatre, for example, fixed costs represent a large proportion of costs in the short run. marginal cost(s) for extra visitors to a theme park or a theatre are negligible up to the capacity level. Figure 5.4 illustrates typical cost curves for the provision of a service with high fixed costs. Notice that the average cost(s) curve falls all the way to short-run capacity and that for much of its range the marginal cost(s)is low and

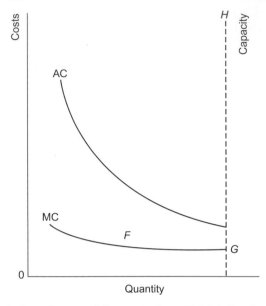

Figure 5.4 Costs for a firm providing a service with high fixed costs.

constant. The existence of low or sometimes zero marginal cost(s) explains some marketing activity for the service sector. Theatres sell standby seats to students at low prices but students still have to pay full prices for ice creams.

Long-run costs

In the long run, all factors of production are variable and so organizations are not faced with the problems of fixed factors or diminishing returns. Output can be satisfied by the most suitable combination of factors of production. Figure 5.5 illustrates three possible ways in which average cost(s) of production may vary with output in the long run. For the long-run average cost (LRAC) curve 1, ACs fall for the entire range as output rises, illustrating economies of scale. In the case of LRAC2, the curve flattens out after point A when constant returns to scale are achieved. For the curve LRAC3, ACs begin to rise again after point A where diseconomies of scale begin to set in. For Arsenal Football Club, the move from its stadium at Highbury with a capacity of only 38,000 to its new Emirates stadium with a capacity of 60,000 resulted in significant economies of scale – particularly economies of increased dimensions.

Internal economies of scale

Economies of scale arise from increases in the size of an organization and can be summarized as follows:

- financial
- buying and selling

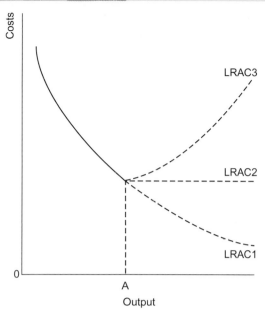

Figure 5.5 Long-run average cost.

- managerial/specialization
- technical
- economies of increased dimensions
- risk bearing.

Financial

Large organizations tend to have bigger assets. When they borrow money, they often raise large amounts and these two factors lead to financial economies. Borrowing from banks is likely to be at preferential rates of interest reflecting the security offered by large organizations and the amount borrowed. Additionally, larger organizations have the option of raising funds directly from capital markets by, for example, a rights issue of shares which can be an economical method of financing large projects.

Buying and selling

Buying and selling economies arise from buying and selling in bulk. On the buying side this leads to bulk purchase discounts, and on the selling side costs such as advertising are spread out over a large number of sales.

Managerial/specialization

As firms grow, the potential for managerial and specialization economies becomes greater. The proprietor of an independent travel agency, for example, will have to act across a range of managerial functions and may lack specialist knowledge. Large travel agency chains, however, will have the scope for employing experts in functional areas such as accounting, marketing and personnel.

Technical

Technical economies are also possible as firms grow. These relate in particular to the utilization of complex and expensive technology and machinery. A large hotel may employ a computerized reservations and accounting system since the cost per guest per year will be relatively insignificant. A small boarding house, however, may have insufficient business to justify the capital outlay.

Economies of increased dimensions

Economies of increased dimensions are well illustrated by the example of jumbo jets. Although these have the capacity of perhaps three conventional jets, they do not cost 3 times as much to buy or to staff or to run. Thus, the cost per seat of a jumbo jet is less than that in a conventional jet. Economies of increased dimension mean that costs rise proportionately less than increases in built capacity. Exhibit 5.3 illustrates economies of scale at work in the airline industry with the introduction of the Airbus A380 which is illustrated in Plate 5.

Risk bearing

Risk-bearing economies derive from the ability of large organizations to weather setbacks. This arises from two factors. First, many large organizations have diversified interests and thus a fall in demand in one area can be compensated for by business elsewhere. Second, large organizations with substantial assets are able to sustain short-term losses from their reserves.

External economies of scale

External economies of scale result not from the size of an organization but from the concentration of similar organizations in a particular location. For example, hotels in a particular resort benefit from resort as well as their own advertising, and may attract visitors on the strength of complementary attractions supplied by neighbouring organizations. Another example is that of Dive companies in the Red Sea resorts. The existence of so many companies in a defined area brings benefits to each individual company. These include the existence of a pool of skilled labour (e.g. instructors), the provision of specialist supplies (e.g. dive ships and oxygen suppliers) and the availability of specialist support (e.g. decompression chambers).

Exhibit 5.3 The Airbus A380: facts and figures

- The Airbus A380 is the world's first full-length double-deck airliner.
- It is manufactured by the European manufacturer, Airbus Industries.
- It made its first commercial flight in October 2007 with Singapore Airlines flying from Singapore to Sydney.
- It has a cabin floor space of $478.1\,m^2$ which is almost 50 per cent more than its closest rival the Boeing 747-400.
- Its seating configurations are 525 in a typical three-class configuration or up to 853 people in its all-economy class configuration.
- Air Austral ordered the Airbus in a single-class configuration for its service between La Reunion in the Indian Ocean and Paris, France with an 840-passenger capacity.
- Although it can carry 35 per cent more passengers than its competitor, the A380 burns 12 per cent less fuel per seat.
- Cost reductions also arise from reduction in flight numbers and the need for fewer take-off slots.

Source: Airbus S.A.S. http://www.airbus.com/en/aircraftfamilies/a380/

Additionally, the area becomes known for its diving facilities and this offers marketing benefits.

Diseconomies of scale

Internal diseconomies

The main reason for the occurrence of diseconomies of scale is managerial capacity. For some organizations, it becomes difficult to manage efficiently beyond a certain size and problems of control, delegation and communications arise. These may become significant enough to outweigh economies of scale generated in other ways. Diseconomies of scale may also arise from growth due to mergers when the two firms find that there is insufficient fit between themselves in terms of systems of management or organizational culture.

External diseconomies

The negative side of concentration of organizations in a particular area can be overcrowding and the associated congestion and pollution costs.

How firms grow?

The main methods by which firms grow are by:

- internal growth
- mergers and takeovers.

Plate 5 The Airbus A380.

Internal growth is often a slow process and firms can accelerate their growth by mergers and takeovers. The difference between these is that mergers are a joint agreement for two organizations to join together whereas a takeover does not necessarily have the agreement of the target firm. It is also useful to identify different types of integration:

- vertical integration
- horizontal integration
- conglomerate merger.

Vertical integration

This occurs when a firm takes over or merges with another firm in the same industry but at a different stage of production. It is termed backward integration when the merger is in the direction of suppliers, and forward integration when it is towards the consumer. Many tour operators demonstrate vertically integrated organizations with ownership of airlines and distribution chains.

The key motive in forward vertical integration is in ensuring a market for an operator's product. This may be offensive – selling your product at the expense of your rivals – or defensive – making sure your rivals do not monopolize retail outlets and thus block the selling of your product. Backward integration gives your organization control over suppliers, and means that you have better control over quality. In each case integration can add to profits.

Horizontal integration

This occurs when a firm merges with another firm in the same industry and at the same stage. For example:

- *2007*: Merger between tour operators TUI Tourism and First Choice to form TUI Travel.
- *2010:* PartyGaming and Bwin announce a merger of their online gambling companies to create the world's biggest in online gambling company.
- *2010*: BA announced a merger with Iberia.

Economies of scale are a prime motive for horizontal integration. For example, advertising costs per holiday fall and bulk purchase discounts can be maximized. Market share and market domination are also key motives. Horizontal acquisition can also occur in purchasing firms operating in complementary areas. The interest of the TUI Travel in companies such as Exodus (a specialist cycling and walking company) and Crystal (a ski company) is to extend its portfolio beyond the sun markets. There is also scope for cost savings through rationalization of activity and the closing down of sites which duplicate work (TUI Tourism and First Choice merger). Horizontal integration also buys into an existing market (e.g. BA merger with Iberia) and acquires an extended customer base and can be an effective way of reducing competition. Another argument made in support of mergers is the potential for service improvement. In a study of the lodging industry, Canina (2001) found that the equity markets view lodging mergers and acquisitions in a favourable light. For a sample of 41 acquisitions from 1982 to 1999, the stock price reaction was significantly positive for both the acquiring firms and their targets. This finding stands in contrast to the results for the overall market, where fewer than half of all mergers add value in terms of equity prices suggesting that the scale economies predicted for mergers may be less than often supposed.

Diversification

A conglomerate merger or diversification occurs when a firm takes over another firm in a completely different industry. The motives for such activity may include first a desire to spread risks. Second, growth prospects in a particular industry may be poor, reflecting a low or negative income elasticity of demand. In such circumstances, diversification into an industry with high-income elasticity of demand may generate faster growth. Third, it may be possible to get benefits of synergy, where the benefits of two firms joining exceed the benefits of remaining separate. For example, Time Warner is the world's leading media and entertainment company, whose businesses include filmed entertainment, interactive services, television networks, cable systems, publishing and music. Its interests span media and communications:

- Time Inc
- Time Warner Cable.

as well as entertainment and networks:

- Home Box Office
- Turner Broadcasting System
- Warner Bros. Entertainment.

A recent study examined a sample of Chinese tourism companies from 2001 to 2007 to determine the impacts of diversification on their financial performance. Its findings showed that in general a diversification strategy improves the performance of tourism companies. However, further analysis revealed that whilst this finding applies particularly to attraction-operating companies, diversification does not enhance the financial performance for hotel companies.

Declutter

A problem that may occur from diversification is that an organization may lose sight of its aims and objectives and find strategic management difficult. Under such circumstances 'decluttering' may take place, whereby an organization disposes of its fringe activities and concentrates on its core business. For example, the UK conglomerate Whitbread, the company behind Premier Inn and Costa Coffee brands embarked upon a period of declutter selling off:

- UK brand franchises for Marriott hotels and two chains, TGI Friday and Pizza Hut;
- David Lloyd Leisure rackets clubs and gyms;
- the majority of the group's pub restaurant holdings.

Social and private costs

Private costs of production are those costs which an organization has to pay for its inputs. They are also known as accounting costs since they appear in an organization's accounts. However, the production of many goods and services may result in side effects. Violent videos may, for example, result in more violent and antisocial behaviour. A nightclub may result in noise pollution. These are classed as external or social costs. They do not appear in an organization's accounts and do not affect its profitability although they may well affect the well-being of society at large. These issues are discussed more fully in later chapters.

REVIEW OF KEY TERMS

- Price elasticity of supply: responsiveness of supply to a change in price.
- Factors of production: land, labour, capital and enterprise.
- Fixed factor: one that cannot be varied in the short run.
- Variable factor: one that can be varied in the short run.
- Average cost: total cost divided by output.
- Marginal cost: the cost of producing one extra unit of output.
- Vertical integration: merger at different stage within same industry.
- Horizontal integration: merger at same stage in same industry.
- Conglomerate merger: merger into different industry.
- Private costs: costs which a firm has to pay.
- Social costs: costs which result from output but which accrue to society.

Data Questions

Task 5.1 **Journal article: Palmera, A., Mathelb, V., 2010. Causes and cons evelopment.** *Tourism Management* **31 (6), 925–935.**

Palmera and Mathelb undertook a qualitative and quantitative study of holiday home owners at a ski resort in France. The resort chosen was Valmeinier which is located at the southern end of the Alps close to the Italian border. The resort covers a total area of 5500 hectares and four skiing areas are spread out from heights of 1500–2600 m. The authors were interested to investigate the fact that many owners of holiday homes in tourist resorts choose not to rent out their property when they are not making personal use of it. This phenomenon results in underutilization of tourist resort capacity, typified by the problem of 'empty beds'.

Eighty-six respondents participated in the research which the authors considered to be a good representation of all property owners in the resort. The authors found that the personal use of holiday home properties was low but furthermore that 40 per cent of owners had never rented out their property. Their analysis of the data collected in their study resulted in on four themes emerging that explained this reluctance to rent out. The themes were as follows:

- *Fears about the social habits of renters*: Here the authors report on the 'significance which owners attached to their properties, and it became evident that owners had invested emotions in their properties and used their property to augment their personal identity. Fear of strangers using their property was a demotivator for renting out a property'.

Task 5.1 **continued**

- *Issues of freedom and flexibility in use of their property*: The research found that 'the ability to visit their property at any time without having to fit around prearranged rental agreements appeared to be an important factor deterring participants from renting out their property'.
- *Life course changes which affected renting/non-renting decisions*: Palmera and Mathelb noted here that as the owners 'became more affluent, or approached retirement, their financial needs became less, and their availability of leisure time to use the apartment for personal use became greater'.
- *Financial issues*: Here the authors report that 'for the majority of people (55.8%), return on investment was seen as important' and that this was especially important for younger owners with mortgages to pay off.

Recap Questions

1 Explain what factors influence the capacity of a ski resort.
2 How does room capacity relate to elasticity of supply in a ski resort?
3 From the understanding provided by Palmera and Mathelb explain how holiday home owners might be persuaded to add their properties to the supply of accommodation in Valmeinier.
4 What are MCs and what are the MCs for holiday home owners of letting out their properties?

Task 5.2 **Come fly with me**

Merger activity in the airline business has included the following major tie-ups:

- Delta Airlines and Northwest Airlines (USA)
- United Airlines and Continental Airlines (USA)
- Southwest Airlines and Air Tran Airlines (USA)
- BA (UK) and Iberia (Spain).

Commentaries on these mergers include the following:
Delta Airlines and Northwest Airlines:

- The merged Delta Airlines and Northwest Airlines operate under the Delta Airlines name.
- According to Richard Anderson, Delta CEO, 'Delta and Northwest are a perfect fit'.
- The merger will create a better global route system.
- Its combined fleet comprises around 800 aircraft with approximately 75,000 employees.
- A key member of the SkyTeam alliance.
- Greater financial stability.

United Airlines and Continental Airlines:

- The new airline to be owned by United Continental Holdings, Inc.
- The merger was a $3.2 billion all-stock merger.
- The new airline is the world's largest carrier measured by revenues.
- It overtakes Delta Airlines, which claimed top position in 2008 after merging with Northwest Airlines.

- It flies approximately 5800 flights a day to 371 destinations.
- The merger expects to capitalize on synergies of about $1 billion of which about $400 million should come from costs savings.
- A key member of the Star Alliance.

Southwest Airlines and Air Tran Airlines (USA):

- Southwest Airlines announced plans to buy Air Tran Airlines for $1.4 billion.
- A key motive for the merger is to obtain a larger market share.
- Southwest would be able to schedule more flights in and out of major airports such as La Guardia in New York and Logan Airport in Boston and operate from Atlanta's Hartfield-Jackson International Airport – the largest hub in the USA.

British Airways and Iberia:

- The merger creates the world's third biggest airline.
- The combined airline operates 419 aircraft flying to 205 separate destinations.
- The merger needed approval by the European Commission.
- Synergies were expected to save the two airlines $594 million in costs each year.
- Both airlines retain their unique brand identity.
- Key players in the Oneworld alliance.

Recap Questions

1 Distinguish between horizontal and vertical integration. What type of merger is illustrated by these cases?
2 What economic factors explain the increase in merger activity and concentration of airline ownership in this sector?
3 Discuss the relationship between fixed, variable and MCs for the airline sector.
4 What other major merger activity has there been in the airline sector?
5 What are the major advantages of mergers in the airline sector?
6 Are there any drawbacks or limits to mergers in this sector?

Task 5.3 **Small luxury hotels and economies of scale**

The combination of small hotels and economies of scale seem to present a paradox since the very idea of economies of scale is that they are achieved by size. Small luxury hotels on the other hand suggest the opposite of economies with special attention to items such as standards of service, uniqueness, high quality food and wine and particular attention paid to luxury and comfort. All these things point to rising rather than falling costs.

But economies of scale is the very thing on offer from the 'Small Luxury Hotels of the World' group. On its website that is designed to attract more members to the group it claims:

Becoming part of SMALL LUXURY HOTELS OF THE WORLD™ enables you to benefit from the economies of scale typical of large hotel chains while preserving your independence and exclusivity.

Amongst the benefits the group offers are membership of a brand which boasts over 500 hotels in more than 70 countries and a strong

Task 5.3 continued

brand awareness in key source markets. Hotels marketing themselves as part of this group include:

- *The Dorset Square Hotel*: An English townhouse style in London, UK.
- *The Banke Hotel*: A flamboyant interior design in the Opera quarter in Paris, France.
- *The Hoteldorf Grüner Baum*: Situated in a unique traditional spa village in Bad Gastein, Austria.

Recap Questions

1 Define the term economies of scale.
2 Explain how each of the following economies of scale might be achieved in the hotel sector and which are likely to be achieved by membership of the 'Small Luxury Hotels of the World' group:
   (a) financial
   (b) buying and selling
   (c) managerial/specialization
   (d) technical
   (e) economies of increased dimensions
   (f) risk bearing.
3 Explain the relationship between MCs and last-minute price deals at hotels.

MULTIPLE CHOICE

1 Which of the following is not a factor of production?
   (a) Land.
   (b) Labour.
   (c) Wages.
   (d) Capital.

2 When price increases by 10 per cent supply increases by 20 per cent. Which of the following is true?
   (a) Supply is elastic.
   (b) Supply is inelastic.
   (c) Elasticity of supply is 0.5.
   (d) Marginal cost(s) doubles.

3 Which of the following is false?
   (a) average cost(s) is total cost divided by output.
   (b) Fixed costs cannot be altered in the short run.
   (c) 'Economies of scale' means that total costs fall as output rises.
   (d) The takeover of the airline Go by its rival easyJet is an example of horizontal integration.

4 A U-shaped LRAC curve demonstrates:
   (a) Economies of scale followed by diseconomies of scale.
   (b) Diseconomies of scale followed by economies of scale.

(c) Falling sales followed by rising sales.

(d) External economies of scale followed by internal economies of scale.

5 Which of the following is an example of a financial economy of scale?

(a) Delta Airlines is able to borrow money more cheaply than smaller airlines.

(b) Delta Airlines is able to buy aviation fuel cheaper than smaller airlines.

(c) Delta Airlines has bigger profits than smaller airlines.

(d) Delta Airlines operates jumbo jets.

REVIEW QUESTIONS

1 Why an organization's average cost(s) of production rise as output rises in the short run, but fall in the long run?

2 What is the marginal cost(s) of selling an empty seat on a scheduled flight?

3 Distinguish between private costs and social costs in the provision of air travel.

4 How elastic is the supply of:

(a) Hotel rooms?

(b) Theatre seats?

(c) Package holidays?

5 Distinguish between vertical and horizontal integration.

6 Distinguish between fixed costs, variable costs, the short and long run.

Websites of interest

Arsenal Football Club: www.arsenal.com

TUI Travel: www.tuitravelplc.com

British Airways: www.ba.com

Iberia: www.iberia.com

Time Warner: www.timewarner.com

Whitbread: www.whitbread.co.uk

Delta Airlines: www.Delta.com

United Continental Holdings, Inc: www.unitedcontinentalholdings.com

Small Luxury Hotels of the World: http://www.slh.com

PART 3

Markets in Practice

CHAPTER 6

Market structure and pricing

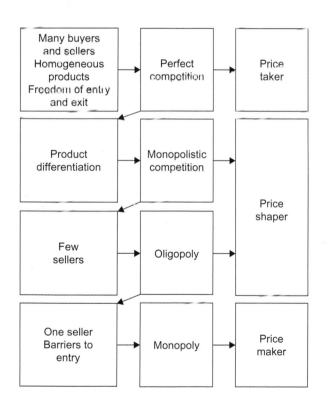

Many buyers and sellers Homogeneous products Freedom of entry and exit	Perfect competition	Price taker
Product differentiation	Monopolistic competition	
Few sellers	Oligopoly	Price shaper
One seller Barriers to entry	Monopoly	Price maker

In the real world it is often difficult to relate prices to the simple demand and supply analysis presented in Chapter 3. For example, we find leisure centres and fitness centres offering similar services at vastly different prices. It has been said that an airline running a jumbo jet carrying 350 passengers will charge 100 different prices. A simple T-shirt can cost as little as $3. Print the word 'Billabong' or 'Versace' on it and its price can rise to more than $50. Some shops have as many sale and offer days as normal trading days. This chapter investigates how prices are determined in the real world.

By studying this chapter, students will be able to:

- understand how and why firms come to be price takers, price makers or price shapers;
- analyse the pricing strategies that result from different market situations.

PRICING IN THE PRIVATE SECTOR

Private sector organizations which seek to maximize profits will attempt to minimize their costs and maximize their revenue. Revenue is composed of price multiplied by quantity sold, and the price that an organization can charge for its product depends largely on the type of market within which it is operating.

PRICE TAKERS

Perfect competition

At one extreme, economic theory describes the model of perfect competition. In this model there are many buyers, many sellers, identical products, freedom of entry and exit in the market and perfect knowledge about prices and products in the market. Firms which operate in this type of market have to accept the market price. This is because any attempt to increase their own price over and above market price will lead to consumers purchasing identical goods or services from competitor firms. This is illustrated in Figure 6.1.

Figure 6.1A shows the market demand curve DM, the market supply curve SM and the equilibrium price $P0$. Figure 6.1B shows the demand curve faced by an individual firm, DF. Note that it is

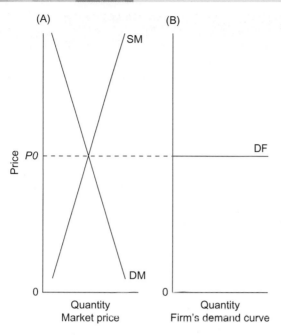

Figure 6.1 (A) The market and (B) the firm under perfect competition.

perfectly elastic. This is derived from the conditions of perfect competition. Consumers with perfect knowledge about other prices will buy an identical product from one of the other many sellers if an individual firm attempts to raise prices above the prevailing market rate. What level of profits do firms earn in such markets? They earn normal profits. Normal profit is defined as that level of return which is just sufficient incentive for a firm to remain in its present business. Any excess profits will lead new firms into the industry and this extra supply will drive prices down to the level where normal profits are restored.

It is interesting to note that consumer ignorance (i.e. lack of perfect knowledge) about other prices means that perfect competition is less prevalent than it might be. For example, in the UK Amazon sells top 50 CDs for as little as £6.99. Regular retailers (e.g. HMV) charge £9.99 for an identical product. Despite this HMV still manages healthy sales of its more expensive CDs. However, it is likely that increasing use of the Internet will lead consumers to better knowledge of prices of competing goods, thus promoting more competition and lower prices.

Whilst free market prices and normal profits are good for consumers, profit-maximizing producers will aim to increase and protect profits. Thus there are few examples in the real world of price takers, and if firms are not in the fortunate position of being price makers, they will generally take steps to become price shapers. They may achieve this by introducing imperfections into the market.

PRICE MAKERS

At the other extreme from perfect competition, some firms exist in conditions of monopoly or near-monopoly and thus have considerable control over prices.

Monopoly pricing

A monopoly is literally defined as one seller, and monopoly power is maintained by ensuring that barriers to entry into the industry are maintained. In the case of one seller the firm's demand curve is the same as the industry demand curve. Because of this, the monopolist is in a position to be a price maker.

There are examples of near-monopolies in the leisure and tourism sector. For example, there are only two car ferry services to the Isle of Wight (an island off the South coast of the UK) and these operate on different routes, thus giving each operator some control over price. Unique tourist attractions also have some degree of monopoly power. There is no similar attraction to the London Eye in the UK, although to some extent the main visitor attractions in London all compete with each other. Manchester United Football Club, like many other sporting clubs, is unique. Table 6.1 shows typical demand data for a unique attraction. It demonstrates the trade-off that a monopoly producer faces – it can raise prices but as it does

Price (£)	Quantity demanded (visitors/hour)	Total revenue[a]	Marginal revenue[b]
10	0	0	
9	10	90	9
8	20	160	7
7	30	210	5
6	40	240	3
5	50	250	1
4	60	240	−1
3	70	210	3
2	80	160	−5
1	90	90	−7
0	100	0	−9

Table 6.1 Monopoly attraction demand data

[a]Total revenue: price × quantity sold.
[b]Marginal revenue: the extra revenue gained from attracting one extra customer ($\Delta TR \div \Delta Q$), where TR = total revenue and Q = quantity.

so demand falls (but does not disappear as would be the case under perfect competition). So the question that arises for a monopolist is what is the best price to charge? The answer is that price that will maximize total revenue.

The price that maximizes total revenue for this organization is one of £5 when total revenue of £250 per hour is generated. This is illustrated in Figure 6.2. In Figure 6.2A, D represents the firm's demand curve using the data from Table 6.1. In Figure 6.2B, TR represents the firm's total revenue curve. This is found by multiplying quantity sold at each price. Price £5 generates total revenue of

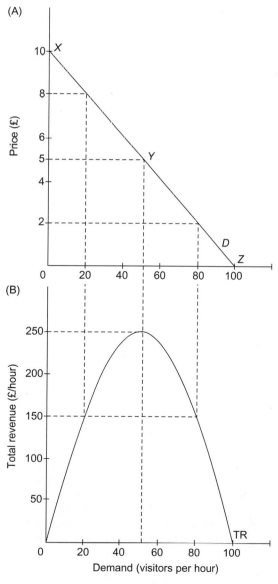

Figure 6.2 (A) Demand and (B) revenue-maximizing price for monopolist.

£250 per hour, whilst a higher price of £8 or a lower price of £2 causes total revenue to fall to £160.

This confirms the relationship between changes in price, changes in total revenue and elasticity of demand discussed in Chapter 4. Where demand is inelastic, a rise in price will cause an increase in total revenue. Where demand is elastic, a rise in price will cause a fall in total revenue. Profit maximization therefore occurs where demand elasticity is −1. In Figure 6.2 the demand curve is elastic in the range X to Y, inelastic in the range Y to Z and has unit elasticity at point Y.

To summarize, monopolists can choose a price resulting in high profits, without fear of loss of market share to competitors. The actual price chosen will reflect both demand conditions and the firm's cost conditions. Exhibit 6.1 shows how top UK football clubs can exploit their market position but how difficult market conditions can reduce their monopoly power.

Price-discriminating monopolist/yield management

Some firms sell the same goods or services at different prices to different groups of people. For example, BA return fares from London to New York (2011) are: £5474 (first class), £2184 (club class), £937 (premium economy), £1238 (flexible economy), £356 (restricted economy), £123.80 (staff 10 per cent standby) and £0 + tax (staff yearly free standby/holders of airmiles or frequent-flyer miles).

Exhibit 6.1 Chelsea fans: sold out

Price increases for season tickets at Chelsea Football Club for the 1998–1999 season were in some cases as high as 47 per cent as against inflation of around 2.5 per cent in the UK economy. This meant that the cheapest season ticket for supporters rose to £525, while the most expensive rose to £1250.

Top premier clubs find themselves in monopoly positions. Stadiums are full to capacity and price increases do not lead fans to choose alternative products elsewhere. Nearby Fulham or Arsenal do not offer alternative football for Chelsea fans in the way that different brands of beer can be seen as substitutes.

However, conditions of a deep economic recession mean that even near-monopoly organizations have to consider their pricing strategies more carefully. For the 2010–2011 season Chelsea Football Club announced that their season ticket prices would rise for the first time since July 2005. The increases, which follow a 4-year price freeze, saw the cheapest season ticket in the family stand priced at £550 and the most expensive excluding hospitality a West Upper Stand ticket priced at £1210. This means that between 1998 and 2010 the cheapest season ticket rose in price by only £25 whilst the most expensive fell by £40.

Source: Adapted from The Guardian *and* FootballTadeDirectory.com *by the author.*

In fact, BA is not a monopolist since there is much competition on this route. It should also be recognized that the fare differential for club and first-class passengers is not strictly price discrimination since these represent different services with different costs. But since all economy-class passengers receive an identical service, why should BA charge different prices and why do passengers accept different prices? The answer is that by price discrimination companies can increase their profits by charging different prices according to how much different market segments are prepared to pay.

The conditions for price discrimination to take place are as follows:

- The product cannot be resold. If this were not the case, customers buying at the low price would sell to customers at the high price and the system would break down. Services therefore provide good conditions for price discrimination.
- There must be market imperfections (otherwise firms would all compete to the lowest price).
- The seller must be able to identify different market segments with different demand elasticities (e.g. age groups and different times of use).

Figure 6.3 illustrates a typical demand curve for economy-class travel. If a single price of £500 is charged as in Figure 6.3A, then 250 seats are sold and total revenue is £125,000. Figure 6.3B shows a situation in which three prices are charged. One hundred seats are sold at £800, the next 150 seats are sold at £500 and the next 150 seats are sold at £200, producing a total revenue of £185,000, an increase of £60,000 over the single price situation.

Airlines must consider the behaviour of costs when price discriminating. Once the decision has been taken to run a scheduled service, marginal costs are low up until the aircraft capacity, when there is a sudden large jump. Airlines are able to discriminate by applying travel restrictions to differently priced tickets. So, for example, full-fare economy tickets are fully refundable and flights may be changed at no cost. Cheaper tickets are non-refundable and have advance purchase and travel duration restrictions.

Yield management is a sophisticated form of price discrimination. Hamzaee and Vasigh (1997) discuss a model for establishing the optimal allocation of available seats to different classes of airfare. Computer technology is able to identify patterns of demand for a particular product and compare it with its supply. A request for a hotel reservation or an airline ticket will result in the system suggesting a price that will maximize the yield for a particular flight or day's reservations. So for budget airlines, for example, seats on a Friday or Sunday night or in school holidays tend to be expensive whilst a seat to the same destination on a Tuesday morning would be much

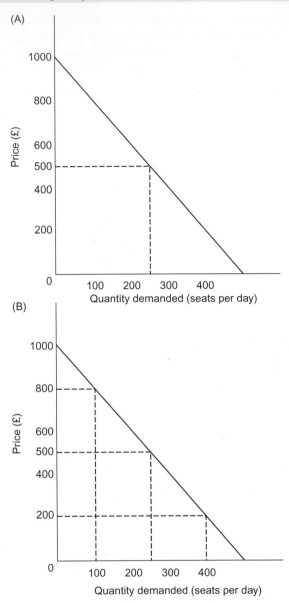

Figure 6.3 (A) Single price and (B) price discrimination.

cheaper. Exhibit 6.2 shows how orchestras are hoping to exploit this system to maximize revenue at concerts.

PRICE SHAPERS

Whilst firms operating under conditions of perfect competition are price takers and those operating under conditions of monopoly are price makers, firms operating in markets between these two extremes

Exhibit 6.2 Orchestras conduct research into pricing

Managers from an airline and a Premier League football club offered advice to help Britain's symphony and chamber orchestras increase their profits from selling concert tickets. A marketing manager for the airline easyJet and the marketing manager for Everton Football Club offered advice at an annual conference of the Association of British Orchestras, which represents 60 orchestras across the country.

The idea is to exploit 'yield management' techniques (Plate 6). This is a favourite device of no-frills airlines whose tickets become more expensive as departure dates approach. Transferring the idea to concerts could mean that concert-goers who book their tickets in advance might pay £10 for the best seat while those who buy nearer the day of the concert could pay up to £30.

The director of communications at the City of Birmingham Symphony Orchestra said: 'At present we do not have the ability to track demand and make prices elastic as it peaks and falls. I know the Chicago Symphony has a marketing director who comes from the airline industry and they have been experimenting with this. I think it is a really interesting concept.'

Source: Adapted from The Guardian Newspaper *by the author.*

Plate 6 Virgin Blue: ticket prices determined by yield management system.
Source: The author.

can exert some influence on price. Such firms are called price shapers. The two main market types which will be examined are:

- oligopoly pricing
- monopolistic competition.

Oligopoly pricing

An oligopoly is a market dominated by a few large firms. An example of this is the cross-channel (UK to France) travel market.

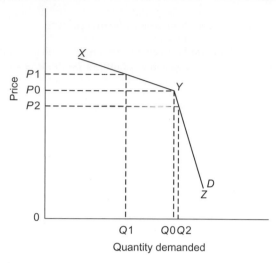

Figure 6.4 The kinked demand curve.

Aguiló et al. (2003) examined the prices of package holidays to the Balearic Islands, Spain, one of the Mediterranean's leading tourist destinations, offered by a sample of 24 German and 20 UK tour operators studied in 2000. They concluded that tour operators' strategies and price structures are characteristic of an oligopolistic market. Oligopoly makes pricing policy more difficult to analyse since firms are interdependent, but not to the extent as in the perfectly competitive model. The actions of firm *A* may cause reaction by firms *B* and *C*, leading firm *A* to reassess its pricing policy and thus perpetuating a chain of action and reaction. For these reasons firms operating in oligopolistic markets often face a kinked demand curve. This is illustrated in Figure 6.4.

Consider the demand curve *D*, which might illustrate the demand curve for a cross-channel car ferry firm. The prevailing price is *P*0. Notice that the demand curve is elastic in the range *X* to *Y*. This is because, if a firm decides to increase its price, for example from *P*0 to *P*1, it will lose customers to its competitors and demand will fall sharply from *Q*0 to *Q*1 and the firm will suffer a fall in total revenue. On the other hand, if it should decide to reduce its price from *P*0 to *P*2, it is likely that its competitors will match the reduction in price to protect their market share, and there will be only a small increase in demand from *Q*0 to *Q*2, resulting in a fall in the firm's revenue. Thus the demand curve is inelastic in the range *Y* to *Z*, and the demand curve is kinked at point *Y*. In this situation it is clearly not in the interests of individual firms to cut prices, and thus such markets tend to be characterized by price rigidities. Marketing and competition under oligopoly conditions are often based around:

- advertising
- free gifts and offers
- quality of service or value added

- follow-the-leader pricing – pricing is based on the decisions of the largest firm
- informal price agreements
- price wars occasionally break out if one firm thinks it can effectively undercut the opposition.

Braun and Soskin (1999) investigated the transformation of the Florida (USA) theme park industry during the 1990s. Here Anheuser Busch carried out a series of acquisitions to complete a successful horizontal merger of the three major competitors to the market leader Walt Disney World. Busch then mobilized its financial resources to match Disney's $10 billion investment programme. Next the entry of Universal Studios with its considerable financial investment deterred other entrants to the market. Finally, aggressive pricing strategies consolidated the market share and drove out smaller competitors. In the 1980s, Walt Disney World operated like a dominant firm. The other firms matched Walt Disney World with a lag. However, the authors concluded that the late 1990s illustrate behaviour characteristic of an interdependent oligopoly. Price increases have been tempered, relative prices have converged and prices have become more stable.

Monopolistic competition

This is a common type of market structure, exhibiting some features of perfect competition and some features of monopoly. The competitive features are freedom of entry and exit and the existence of a large number of firms. However, firms which are operating in essentially competitive environments may attempt to create market imperfections in order to have more control over pricing, market share and profits.

It is competition from other sellers with homogeneous products that forces market prices down, and thus firms will often concentrate on these two issues in order to exert more market power. The more inelastic a firm is able to make its demand curve, the more influence it will have on price, and thus firms will attempt to minimize competition by:

- product differentiation
- acquisitions and mergers
- cost and price leadership.

Product differentiation

This entails an organization in making its product different from those of its competitors and exploiting unique selling points (USPs). The rationale for product differentiation is to make the demand for a good or service less elastic, giving the producer more scope to increase prices and/or sales and profits. There are a number of routes to product differentiation.

The first is by advertising. One of the aims of persuasive advertising is to create and increase brand loyalty even if there are no major differences between a firm's product and that of its competitors. The second route to product differentiation is through adding value to a good or service. This may include, for example, making improvements to a good or service or adding value somewhere along the value chain. The value chain can be thought of as all the interconnecting activities that make up the whole consumer experience of a good or service. Table 6.2 demonstrates aspects of the value chain for Singapore Airlines' business class where it is able to differentiate its product at all parts of its value chain.

Exhibit 6.3 shows how Accor Hospitality brings product differentiation to its hotels. The point of adding value and differentiating

Table 6.2 Value chain for Singapore Airlines' business class

Pre-sales	Pre-check-in	Check-in	Flight	Arrival	Post-flight
Advertising	Valet parking	Dedicated check-in	Dedicated cabin	Rapid transit arranged to city centre	Frequent-flyer awards
		Express security/ passport route	Luxury meal		Complaints procedure
			Seat size		
		Dedicated lounge	Increased staff ratio		

Exhibit 6.3 Accor Hospitality

Accor Hospitality is a global hotel operator. It has over 40 years of experience, operates in over 100 countries with 4000 hotels and around 500,000 beds. It has developed a market strategy to cover all the key market segments. These include:

- *Luxury:* Sofitel
- *Upscale:* Pullman, MGallery
- *Midscale:* Novotel, Mercure, Suitehotel, Adagio
- *Economy:* Ibis, All seasons
- *Budget:* Etap, Hotel, Formule 1, hotelF1 and Motel 6.

The characteristics of each of these segments are as follows:

Luxury and upscale: These hotels have an emphasis on unique, non-standardized offers with a commitment to exceptional service.
Midscale and economy: These brands offer quality accommodation at competitive local value.
Budget: These hotels are functional and cheap. Low prices are possible from an offer of standardized offering in clean but basic accommodation in sub prime locations.

Source: The author.

product is that it enables firms to charge a premium price but still retain customers.

Acquisitions and mergers

These are discussed in detail in Chapter 5, but they are an important consideration in pricing strategy as they can:

- reduce competition (and thus reduce downward pressure on prices);
- lead to economies of scale (which can underpin price leadership strategies).

Cost and price leadership

Another key strategic move to increase market share and profitability is through cost and price leadership. Cost leadership involves cutting costs through the supply chain – squeezing margins from suppliers, and economizing where possible in the production of goods or provision of services by stripping out unnecessary frills. The aim of cost leadership may be to increase margins, but this is unlikely to be achieved since consumers are likely to resist lower quality of goods or services without any compensation in price.

Equally it is difficult to maintain cost leadership since other firms will attempt to achieve similar cost reductions. However, where cost leadership is translated into low prices, it may be possible to increase market share. This can then lead to the creation of a virtuous circle where increased market share leads to economies of scale which enable lower costs and thus lower prices to be maintained ahead of rival firms. The no-frills airlines again provide good examples here. Virgin Blue (Australia), for example, has been competing strongly with the Australian flag carrier Qantas. Similarly, the UK low-cost airline Ryanair now carries more passengers than BA.

Figure 6.5 provides a summary of the main differences between different market types.

Type of market	Number of firms	Entry barriers	Product differentiation	Firm's demand	Control over price
Perfect competition	Many	None	No	Perfectly elastic	None
Monopolistic competition	Many	None	Yes	Elastic	Limited
Oligopoly	Few	Some	Yes	Kinked demand	Some
Monopoly	One	Total	Unnecessary	Inelastic	Considerable

Figure 6.5 Market structure

PRICING IN THE PUBLIC SECTOR

Prices of public sector goods and services will depend upon the market situation which prevails in a particular industry as well as the objectives set for a particular organization. These might be:

- profit maximization
- break-even pricing
- social cost/benefit pricing.

Profit maximization

In the case where public sector organizations have profit-maximizing aims, its pricing policy will follow the pattern set out earlier in this chapter. However, public sector organizations are rarely allowed to exploit a monopoly situation if they have one.

Break-even pricing

Break-even pricing aims at a price which is just sufficient to cover production costs rather than one which might take advantage of market imperfections and maximize profit. In this case price will be set to produce a total revenue which covers total costs.

Social cost/benefit pricing

Where the aim of public provision is to take fuller account of public costs and benefits, the supply will be subsidized to produce a price either lower than market price (partial subsidy) or at zero price (total subsidy). More detailed analysis of this can be found in Chapter 7.

PRICING AND THE MACROECONOMY

The condition of the economy at large also has an influence on a firms' pricing policy. If the demand in the economy is growing quickly there may be temporary shortages of supply in the economy and firms will take advantage of boom conditions to increase prices and profits. Similarly, during a recession, there may well be overcapacity in the economy and demand may be static or falling. These conditions will force firms to have much more competitive pricing policies to attract consumers.

REVIEW OF KEY TERMS

- Price taker: a firm in a perfectly competitive market which cannot directly influence price.
- Price maker: a firm in a monopoly market which sets its desired price.
- Price shaper: a firm in an oligopoly or imperfectly competitive market which may seek to influence price.
- Perfect competition: many buyers and sellers, homogeneous products, freedom of entry and exit to market.
- Monopoly: one seller, barriers to entry.
- Oligopoly: a small number of powerful sellers.
- Monopolistic competition: many buyers and sellers, freedom of entry and exit, products differentiated.
- Product differentiation: real or notional differences between products of competing firms.
- Price discrimination: selling the same product at different prices to different market segments.

Data Questions

Task 6.1 **Ups and downs of cross-Channel prices**

The English Channel is the name of the sea between the southern coast of England and the North Coast of France. Its narrowest point is between the English port of Dover and the French port of Calais, and this for a long period of time was the main route chosen by UK holiday-makers heading for France and further afield in Europe. The market was dominated for years by a few ferry companies and notorious for high ticket prices, but in 1994 a major new competitor entered the market in the form of the Channel tunnel. The story below charts the changes in the competitive environment on the cross-Channel route.

1994: The Channel tunnel opens and the fares for Le Shuttle, the train that will ferry motorists and their cars under the Channel, have been set higher than expected. They range from £125 return for a car-load in winter to a peak price of £310. Most are a little higher than the equivalent ferry fare.

There was an almost audible sigh of relief from the Channel ports as Christopher Garnett, Eurotunnel's commercial director, outlined the structure; at least the tunnel was not trying to undercut the ferries. Asked by the *Independent on Sunday* whether Eurotunnel would respond if the ferries cut their fares, Mr Garnett said: 'We would not be following. We're not going to get involved with price wars. We're not going to get involved in discounting.' Richard Hannah, an analyst with UBS and a close follower of Eurotunnel, is sceptical: 'I'm convinced there will have to be a price war because of the excess capacity created by the tunnel.' He said fares would have to come down sharply to generate the extra volumes needed to meet Eurotunnel's ambitious revenue targets. 'Even if Eurotunnel captured the entire existing cross-Channel business from the

Task 6.1 **continued**

ferry companies, it would still not generate enough revenues even to cover its costs.' He argued that Eurotunnel had to create a fresh wave of demand for cross-Channel travel, and it could only do that by cutting prices.

Mr Garnett sees Le Shuttle's advantages over ferries as speed, convenience and reliability. But the other unknown quantity in the calculation is the response of the ferry companies and the ports. According to Chairman, Mr Dunlop, P&O has spent £400 million over the past 5 years modernizing its fleet. 'We've revolutionized the ferry industry in the last five years, creating an attractive product.' Certainly its newer vessels, such as the *Pride of Dover* and the *Pride of Calais*, are a far cry from the shabby, vomit-smelling, beer-soaked, cramped, crowded tubs that used to ply their trade across the Channel. 'The ferry crossing is now part of the holiday', said Mr Dunlop.

Source: Adapted from the Independent on Sunday, 16 January 1994.

1999: No one pays £310 to cross the channel any more. The opening of Eurotunnel gave rise to a period of intense competition and the 'Channel war' was a consumer's dream. The competition has seen the merger between the two ferry companies, P&O and Stena, but even so there continue to be good deals.

- Le Shuttle: A 35-minute crossing. A 5-day return costs £95 per car with four departures an hour during the day and three an hour at night. Few facilities but weatherproof.
- Sally Line: Ferry from Ramsgate to Ostend, from £25 for a car and two passengers. Smorgasbord restaurant, cafeteria facilities and a supervised crèche.
- P&O Stena Line: Car and passengers £95 for a 5-day return and £159 for a standard return. Restaurants, games arcade, cinema and club class available.
- Hoverspeed: Standard return on the Hovercraft for a car and passengers is £158. Crossing time is 35 minutes. Same price but 50-minute crossing on SeaCat.

2002: Prices seem to have crept back up again. The following are for a return car journey from Dover to Calais in summer 2002:

- P&O Stena Line from Dover to Calais: £234.
- SeaFrance from Dover to Calais: £209.
- Eurotunnel from Folkestone to Calais: £237.
- Hovercraft from Dover to Calais: £278.

2003: The European commission launches a surprise investigation into cross-Channel ferry and rail prices and raided the offices of P&O and Eurotunnel in its hunt to uncover supporting evidence. The commission said that it suspected an illegal price-fixing cartel was in operation and that it was acting on complaints from British consumers, Amelia Torres, a commission spokeswoman said: 'Many consumers are concerned about the market and the commercial practices of firms who operate cross-Channel services and we have to take those concerns very seriously. We have a duty to investigate.'

The Dover–Calais ferry route is thought to be the busiest route in the world. It is dominated by the Anglo-French firm Eurotunnel which has a 50 per cent market share. P&O has about 25 per cent, SeaFrance 15 per cent and Hoverspeed and Norfolk Line account for the rest.

Source: Adapted from The Guardian, 4 September 2003.

2011: The following prices for summer 2011 reflect a new economic and competitive environment for cross-Channel operators. A weak economy, still suffering from the effects of a recession, and sustained competition from low-cost airlines which means that many tourists prefer to fly direct to a destination and hire a car, means that prices on cross-Channel routes have softened.

- Norfolkline – Dover to Dunkerque – Crossing time 120 minutes: £48.00;
- SeaFrance – Dover to Calais – Crossing time 70 minutes: £93.00;
- P&O – Dover to Calais – Crossing time 90 minutes: £95.00;
- Eurotunnel – Folkestone to Calais – Crossing time 35 minutes: £137.00.

Recap Questions

1 What degree of competition exists in the cross-Channel market?
2 Explain why the Channel Tunnel's initial strategy was not price based.
3 What elements of product differentiation strategy are illustrated and what is the logic of these?
4 What have been the key factors affecting price in the cross-Channel market between 1994 and 2011? Explain this using economic theory and diagrams.
5 What pricing strategies would you recommend to P&O Stena Line to maximize revenue?
6 What is the economics behind price fixing?

Task 6.2 **Researching prices and markets**

Conduct local research in one of the following areas:
1 Air travel suppliers and prices.
2 Hotel accommodation suppliers and prices.
3 Restaurant suppliers and prices.
4 Package holiday suppliers and prices.
5 Cinema suppliers and prices.
6 Other leisure markets in your locality.

Your research should concentrate on a specific product or service (e.g. return airfare from Auckland to New York) and identify the main suppliers, prices and product differences.

Recap Questions

1 Identify the market conditions which operate in your chosen market.
2 Account for the patterns of pricing which emerge from your research.
3 To what extent and why does your chosen market deviate from the model of perfect competition?
4 Is there any evidence of price discrimination or price leadership in your chosen market?
   If so, explain the reasons and consequences.
   If not, explain the reasons and consequences.
5 Compare and contrast your results with those of obtained in a different market.

6

Task 6.3 Journal article: Shaw, S., Lu, F., Chen, J., Zhou, C., 2009. China's airline consolidation and its effects on domestic airline networks and competition. Journal of Transport Geography 17 (4), 293–305.

In this article the authors reflect on the fact that there has been fast growth and major reforms in the past three decades in air transportation in China. They note China's transformation from a centrally planned economy to a market economy and suggest that an interesting question is whether experience in China is similar to the experiences of airline industry liberalization that have occurred in other countries. Shaw et al. point to the United States Airline Deregulation Act in 1978 as a key catalyst towards a more global movement towards liberalization of airlines.

The article outlines four significant phases of development in civil aviation following the founding of the People's Republic of China in 1949:

- The first phase identified is that of 1949–1978 which was a period of a carefully regulated environment. The Civil Aviation Administration of China (CAAC) was set up under military control. Control extended to all aspects of aviation including fares, schedules, routes market entry and exit. This was a period of no market competition.
- The second phase identified is that of 1978–1987 with the introduction of economic reforms. Here a key aim was to move the air transport sector towards profit-seeking goals. Importantly here the military was removed from control of the CAAC in 1980 but the CAAC continued in it regulatory role for the air transport industry. However, in 1985 private sector airlines were allowed to enter the market.
- The third phase spans the period 1987–2002. In 1987 the administrative and the operational roles of the CAAC were separated and between 1987 and 1991 six state-owned airlines (Air China, China Eastern Airlines, China Southern Airlines, China Southwest Airlines, China Northwest Airlines and China Northern Airlines) were established and encouraged to make and retain profits.
- The fourth phase commenced in 2002 and heralded a period of CAAC-led airline consolidation. Three major airline groups were formed around Air China, China Eastern Airlines and China Southern Airlines.

The article concludes that China employed a reform programme in which the state remains a strong influence on the airline industry. This, it is noted, was different from the free market liberalization approach implemented in the USA. Of particular note is that the CAAC pursued a goal of creating three major airlines of roughly equal size and tried to orchestrate minimal direct competition between them. In contrast, airline deregulation in the USA followed a strong free market philosophy with minimal state intervention and maximum competition.

Recap Questions

1 What kind of market type for airlines is evident:
   (a) In China and how has the market changed?
   (b) In the country in which you are studying?
2 Are airlines price makers or price takers? Use diagrams to explain your answers.

3 What are the likely consequences of each of the four phases described in the article for fares and service quality?

4 Distinguish between oligopoly, monopoly and competition using examples from the global airline industry.

5 Investigate recent merger activity amongst major airlines: How is market structure and pricing affected by this?

6 On what basis do airlines set fares?

MULTIPLE CHOICE

1 The demand curve for a firm under perfect competition is as follows:

(a) Perfectly inelastic.

(b) Upward sloping.

(c) Perfectly elastic.

(d) Of unit elasticity.

2 The kinked demand curve is a typical feature of the following:

(a) Public sector markets.

(b) Oligopoly.

(c) Perfect competition.

(d) Monopoly.

3 Which of the following is not a feature of perfect competition?

(a) Barriers to entry for firms.

(b) Perfect knowledge of products.

(c) Identical products.

(d) Many sellers.

4 Which of the following is found under monopolistic competition but not under perfect competition?

(a) Product differentiation.

(b) Many buyers.

(c) Freedom of entry for firms.

(d) Many sellers.

5 Which of the following is not true?

(a) Under price discrimination firms are able to increase their revenue in comparison to charging a single price.

(b) Yield management systems charge differing prices according to predicted demand levels.

(c) An oligopoly is a market dominated by a few large firms.

(d) A private sector monopoly will operate break-even pricing.

REVIEW QUESTIONS

1 What kind of market structures do the following operate in:
 (a) Package tour operators?
 (b) London five-star hotels?
 (c) Destinations?
 (d) McDonalds?

2 Explain the elasticity of demand of a kinked demand curve.

3 Why will a monopolist choose not to produce in the inelastic range of its demand curve?

4 Why are there so few examples of perfectly competitive markets?

5 Under what circumstances is price leadership likely to lead to increased profits?

Websites of interest

British Airways: www.ba.com

Amazon: www.amazon.com

Accor Hospitality: www.accorhotels.com

Virgin Blue: www.virginblue.com.au

Ryanair: www.ryanair.com

P&O Ferries: www.poferries.com

Eurotunnel: www.eurotunnel.com

Air China: www.airchina.com

China Eastern Airlines: www.flychinaeastern.com

CHAPTER

Market intervention

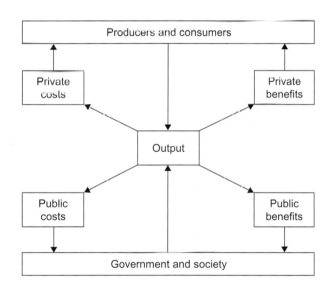

Objectives and learning outcomes

The price mechanism as described in Chapter 3 seems to offer a simple yet effective system of signalling consumer demands to producers. It is often contrasted with systems of state planning – particularly as practised in former communist Eastern Europe. Many commentators noted that the Berlin Wall was built to stop people escaping from Eastern Europe to Western Europe, not the other way round. The economic landscape of Eastern Europe was characterized by queues for goods and services, empty shops, shoddy goods and service sector workers who exhibited indifference to their customers. For example, Burns (1998) discusses some of the problems associated with developing a modern tourism industry in Romania. He finds that the main problem confronting tourism is the lack of a market ethos, and a prevailing view that service is demeaning to the server and concludes that a new customer-focussed service sector needs to be developed. Free market economies, on the other hand, boast shops full of attractive consumer goods, few queues and a world of slick advertising and attention to service quality.

However, critical analysis of the market mechanism raises issues of concern. Sex tourists signal an effective demand for prostitution which suppliers satisfy for profit as demonstrated in Exhibit 7.1. Similarly, the demand for snuff, and child pornography videos, and for addictive drugs is met by the operation of market forces. The market has also created the tower blocks of Benidorm.

The objectives of this chapter are first to examine whether leisure and tourism provision should be left to the free market, and second to consider reasons for, and forms of, market intervention.

By studying this chapter, students will be able to:

- evaluate the benefits of the free market;
- evaluate the problems of the free market;
- understand the methods of market intervention;
- justify market intervention;
- understand recent developments in public sector provision.

Exhibit 7.1 Brazil is overtaking Thailand as sex tourism destination

A BBC documentary has recently focussed on the growing problem of sex tourism in Brazil. The documentary reports on the particular issue of child prostitution. Its presenter explains how he encountered groups of young girls on the street corners of Recife and how one girl appearing to be about 13 years of age approached him and offered him sex for US$5. Another young girl, also about 13 years of age, tells him how she generally has more than 10 clients a night each paying her 10 reais for her services. The programme cites UNICEF data that estimates that there are around 250,000 child prostitutes in Brazil.

The rise in child prostitution is fuelled by a number of factors. On the demand side the British charity Happy Child International reports on increasing numbers of international tourists who travel to the north-east of Brazil for the specific intent of sex tourism. 'Love motels' which hire rooms by the hour are part of the infrastructure. On the supply side many of the girls live in poverty in favelas (shanty towns) and prostitution is a way to earn money to buy foods for their families. They then come under the control of pimps who may threaten them with violence and introduce them to drugs to exercise power and control over them.

Source: Adapted from http://www.bbc.co.uk

THE FREE MARKET

The benefits of free markets

Adam Smith wrote in *The Wealth of Nations* of the main benefits of the free market (Smith, 2003). He drew attention to the fact that people exercising choice in the market in pursuit of their own self-interest led to the best economic outcome for society as a whole. The concept that 'the market knows best' was also a central plank of the economic philosophy of the Thatcher (UK) and Reagan (USA) administrations of the 1980s. Indeed, Mrs Thatcher's economic minister summed up this thinking as: 'The business of government is not the government of business.' The post-1980 period has seen free market economics gain favour in much of Europe and Australia. More significantly it witnessed the collapse of communism in Soviet Russia and its replacement with economies in transition (from central planning to free markets).

In particular, free markets have the potential to deliver:

- economic efficiency
- allocative efficiency
- consumer sovereignty
- economic growth.

Economic efficiency

Economic efficiency means having the maximum output for the minimum input. Profit maximization and competition between firms both result in firms choosing least-cost methods of production and economizing on inputs, as well as using the best technological mix of inputs. This is because profit maximization is achieved by the twin track routes of revenue maximization and cost minimization. Exhibit 7.2 illustrates how competition in the market place and rising fuel costs stimulate organizations such as airlines into a drive for economic efficiency.

Exhibit 7.2 Competition and costs drive airline fuel efficiency

An article in the US *Wall Street Journal* recently reviewed the fuel efficiency of major US airlines. It found that the three worst major US carriers for fuel efficiency were the three biggest:

- Delta
- American
- United Airlines.

The best US airlines in terms of fuel economy were found to be:

- Alaska Airlines
- jetBlue Airways
- Continental Airlines.

The survey was based on figures from the Department of Transportation. Interestingly, economies of scale do not necessarily apply when it comes to fuel consumption. For example, the Airbus A380 jumbo jet when fitted out with a 500 seats configuration averages around 65 miles per (US) gallon per seat. However, the smaller Airbus plane, the A320, in its configuration of 150 seats, averages around 77 miles per gallon per seat.

Fuel efficiency is affected by factors such as the age of the aircraft and its engines, the length of the flight, the speed of the flight and the weight of the aircraft and the article explains how and why Alaska achieved its position as most fuel efficient US airline.

The why is simple – the spike in oil prices caused all airlines to review their fuel efficiency.

The how included the following steps:

- Retiring its fuel-inefficient MD80 planes.
- Concentrating its fleet on Boeing 737s and reducing the average age of the fleet.
- Adding vertical fins to its fleet's wing tips. These 'Winglets' improve aerodynamics and so fuel efficiency.
- Reducing plane weight by, for example, the installation of smaller water tanks on its planes.
- Ensuring that auxiliary electrical power is promptly plugged into arriving flights which allows faster shut down of engines.
- Using its 'Required Navigation Performance' route planning that enables shorter routings and carefully controlled ascents and descents.

Source: Adapted from The Wall Street Journal, *http://europe.wsj.com/home-page*

Allocative efficiency

Allocative efficiency is related to the concept of Pareto optimality and means that it is not possible to reallocate resources, for example, by producing more of one thing and less of another, without making somebody worse off. It results first from economic efficiency and second from consumers maximizing their own satisfaction and implies maximum output from given inputs and maximum consumer satisfaction from that output.

Consumer sovereignty

Consumer sovereignty means that consumers are able to exercise power in the marketplace. It implies that production will be driven by consumer demand rather than by government decisions. In a free market system, firms which survive and grow will be those which make profits by being sensitive to consumer demand.

Economic growth

Economic growth will be encouraged by the free market since those firms which are the most profitable will survive and flourish. Under conditions of competition, firms will compete to increase productivity and thus in the market system resources will be allocated away from unprofitable and inefficient firms towards those which are profitable and efficient, thus generating economic growth.

In summary, under a competitive free market system consumers will get the goods and services they want at the lowest possible prices.

Criticisms of the market solution

Criticisms of the free market focus on the following:

- the inappropriateness of the perfect market assumption
- reservations about consumer sovereignty
- externalities
- public goods
- realities of economic growth
- equity.

Perfect market assumption

For free markets to deliver economic and allocative efficiency, perfect markets as outlined in Chapter 3 are assumed, that is many buyers and sellers, homogeneous products, perfect knowledge, freedom of entry and exit in markets and no government interference. The existence of market imperfections will reduce the efficiency of the free market system. The Thatcher (UK) and Reagan (USA) administrations in fact devoted considerable legislation to the removal of market imperfections, particularly in the labour markets. However, in practice markets are far from perfect. Omerod (1994, p. 48) pointed out that the competitive equilibrium model is 'a travesty of reality. The world does not consist, for example, of an enormous number of small firms, none of which have any degree of control over the market in which it is operating.' Instead, many markets are dominated by a few suppliers, and considerable product differentiation occurs by producers attempting to make their goods or services different from the competition in order to minimize price competition. These factors mean that consumers may not get the benefits of lowest prices afforded by perfect markets.

Consumer sovereignty

There are a number of factors at work in market economics that undermine the concept of consumer sovereignty. The first is lack of information. In the complex world of competing goods and services – particularly for technical products – consumers may not have enough information about the range of goods available and may find it difficult to make comparisons beyond the superficial. Second, consumers are subject to persuasive advertising from producers, the aim of which is to interfere with the consumers' exercise of free choice.

Externalities, merit and demerit goods

It is also evident that free markets fail in their signalling function in some areas. For example, there are some missing markets. There is no market for the ozone layer. There is no market for peace and quiet. There is no market for views and landscapes. It is therefore difficult for people to register their preferences in these areas. Equally markets do not always consider the full range of costs and benefits associated with production, or consumption of certain goods and services. The selling of alcohol is associated with the private benefit of feeling happy but has the unwanted public cost of fighting and accidents. Missing markets and externalities are closely linked. Consider a plan for a development of holiday apartments on a piece of farmland adjacent to the sea. In a free market situation the developer will have to consider the costs of the land, materials and labour. However, the development will clearly have an impact on the landscape, the view and the tranquillity of the area. But no one owns these rights, so there is no market in them and there is no price associated with the using up of them to develop the site. In this case there is a clear difference between the private costs of development and the public or social costs of development.

In Figure 7.1, MPC is the marginal private costs of the development. This shows the additional private costs of supplying extra units and represents the supply curve, S. The demand curve, D, shows the quantity demanded at different prices and the marginal private benefit (MPB). In this case it is assumed that there are no external benefits to consumption and thus this curve also represents the marginal social benefit (MSB). A market equilibrium price is achieved at price $P0$ and the development will go ahead with a quantity of $Q0$.

However, MXC represents marginal external costs, that is the costs in terms of amenities lost such as views and tranquillity. Adding MXC to MPC gives the marginal social cost curve (MSC). In this case it can be seen that the external costs are such that no equilibrium is achieved in the market, since the marginal social cost curves exceed

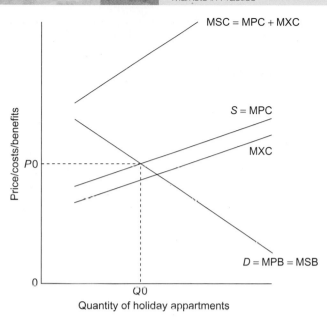

Figure 7.1 External costs and private costs: different equilibrium solutions.

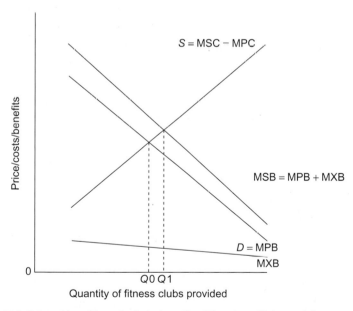

Figure 7.2 External benefits and private benefits: different equilibrium solutions.

the marginal social benefits at all prices. Thus we can see that the free market overproduces goods and services which have significant external costs.

A similar argument may be deployed to demonstrate that the free market under-produces goods and services which provide external benefits to society over and above the private benefits enjoyed by the consumer. In Figure 7.2, MPB is derived from the use of fitness clubs and represents the demand curve, D. S is the supply curve which

Exhibit 7.3 KPMG says tax breaks could boost health clubs sector

The consulting company KPMG has reported that the introduction of US style tax breaks in the UK could provide a useful boost to the private health club industry.

In the USA, the federal government encourages businesses to subsidize worker's exercise regimes by letting companies claim the contributions as income tax deductions. The International Health, Racquet & Sportsclub Association (IHRSA) has consistently lobbied the government to offer tax breaks to fitness clubs.

KPMG feels that similar tax measures in the UK could help boost membership at private health and fitness sectors. It reported 'A tax break for employees in the UK could be just the tonic to restore the health of the sector. Robust and increasing demand for private health clubs is firmly rooted in personal health. It is not a fashion fad, health club membership is considered by many to be a non-discretionary expenditure.'

Source: Adapted from Health Club Management.

shows the quantity supplied at different prices and the marginal private costs. In this case it is assumed that there are no external costs to provision and thus this curve also represents the marginal social cost curve. A market equilibrium quantity is achieved at $Q0$. MXB, however, represents external benefits, that is the benefits to the community at large of the use of fitness clubs which might include a fitter and more productive workforce, less costs to the health service and a reduction in petty juvenile crime. Adding MXB to MPB gives the MSB curve. In this case it can be seen that the equilibrium quantity rises to $Q1$. Exhibit 7.3 demonstrates industry moves to capture tax breaks for the fitness industry.

Goods which include substantial external costs are sometimes termed demerit goods. A demerit good is one which the government feels that people will over-consume and which therefore ought to be banned or taxed. Goods which include substantial social benefits are sometimes termed merit goods. A merit good is one which the government feels that people will under-consume and which therefore ought to be provided free or subsidized. Coalter (1998) examines the centrality of the merit good rationale to the public provision of leisure, suggesting that the leisure studies' defence of recreational welfare and leisure needs is not wholly coherent.

Public goods

The market has an incentive to produce private goods or services because it can charge for them and make profits. It is very difficult to charge consumers for public goods and services and thus they are not provided in free markets. A public good is defined as a good or service which has features of non-rivalry and non-excludability and as a result would not be provided by the free market. Signposts to tourist attractions are an example of a public good since:

- they are non-excludable (you cannot exclude people who do not want to pay for them from seeing them); this is sometimes referred to as the free-rider problem;
- consumption is non-rival (if I use the sign it does not prevent anyone else from using it – unlike a tennis court).

Sable and Kling (2001) describe the 'double public good' model that can be applied to cultural heritage. They argue that social welfare is modelled on both public and private benefits of households' production of individual heritage experience. This in turn depends on the stock of historic assets (a public good) and access effort (a private good). The public benefit of private experience arises from 'shared experience' that fosters cultural identity and social understandings. They thus demonstrate the public good (i.e. merit aspects) of the public good (i.e. non-excludable) aspects of heritage.

Economic growth

There is considerable debate as to whether the free market left alone will provide the fastest route to economic growth. It is true that the free market provides a kind of Darwinian natural selection process where profitable industries survive and unprofitable ones perish. However, the free market is also subject to economic upswings and downswings and does not include any inbuilt tendency to promote sustainable growth.

Equity

Consumer sovereignty only exists for those who have the spending power to influence the market. Those with insufficient purchasing power to influence a market do not exercise any power over supply decisions. Therefore, production in unregulated free markets may favour the rich at the expense of the poor.

MARKET INTERVENTION

The following forms of market intervention are often proposed in order to address the problems inherent in a pure free market economy:

- central planning
- control of monopolies and mergers
- laws, planning controls and permits
- taxes and subsidies
- public provision.

Methods and benefits of market intervention

Central planning

The most drastic solution to market failures is the adoption of state or central planning of production. In this model, production decisions are made by state planning teams rather than in response to consumer demand and profitability. This is the main way in which resources were traditionally allocated in China and Cuba; although both countries are increasingly liberating their markets.

Control of monopolies and mergers

One of the aims of monopolies and mergers legislation is to protect the consumer from the disadvantages of the monopolization of an industry by a single firm. The key disadvantages are higher prices and the reduction in choice that may result from concentration of ownership in an industry. The key aspects of monopolies and mergers legislation are firstly the power to prevent mergers that could lead to market domination that is against the consumer interest and secondly to investigate firms where monopoly conditions appear to conflict with consumer interests.

One way to measure the degree of monopoly in an industry is to examine the concentration ratio. Thus the four-firm concentration ratio shows the market share achieved by the largest four companies. In the US airline industry before the Continental Airlines and United Airlines merger in 2010 the four-firm concentration ratio was 54.9 per cent. This rose to 62.6 per cent after the merger indicating a heightened degree of market imperfection and potential monopoly power.

The UK's monopoly prevention legislation was built around a number of pieces of key legislation, although much of its controls now operate under EU directives. Its original national legislation included:

- *1948 UK Monopolies and Restrictive Practices Act*: This set up the Monopolies and Restrictive Practices Commission which could investigate any industry referred to it that had a market share of more than 30 per cent, and investigate whether the public interest was being served.
- *1956 UK Restrictive Trade Practices Act*: This banned formal restrictive practices (e.g. price agreements between firms) that were not in the public interest.
- *1965 UK Monopolies and Mergers Act*: This instigated a name change to the Monopolies and Mergers Commission and allowed examination of proposed mergers that might create a monopoly. Such mergers could be blocked.
- *1973 UK Fair Trading Act*: This reduced the definition of monopoly to 25 per cent of market share.

- *1980 UK Competition Act*: This widened the terms of reference of the Monopolies and Mergers Commission to include public corporations.

The EU has strict controls over monopolies that extend across all its member states. These include:

- *European Union Article 85*: This bans agreements and restrictive practices which prevent, restrict or distort competition within the EU and affect trade between member states.

- *European Union Article 86*: This prohibits a firm from abusing a dominant position in the EU which affects competition and trade between member states.

- *1990 European Union Merger Control Regulation*: This gave the European Union Commission (as opposed to national government regulators) responsibility for control over large-scale mergers which have a significant EU dimension. The European Commission is able to fine firms up to 10 per cent of their turnover if they are found to be in contravention of Articles 85 or 86.

Examples of proposed mergers which had to be cleared by the European Commission include:

- the BA/Iberia merger
- the TUI Tourism/First Choice merger.

The main elements of the anti-trust (monopolies and mergers) legislation in the USA are the:

- Sherman Act (1890)
- Clayton Act (1914)
- The Federal Trade Commission.

The Sherman Act has two main components. Section 1 forbids trade restraints that hurt competition and section 2 aims to curtail monopolization. The Clayton Act specifies actions that are illegal including price discrimination that hurts competition and exclusive dealing. The Federal Trade Commission enforces anti-trust legislation which examines the markets and investigates anti-competitive behaviour. In the USA, Eckard (2001) examined the creation of the first professional athletic labour market restriction in 1879. Here, professional baseball club owners agreed that each could reserve five players whom the others would not sign without permission, justifying the action by claiming that it was in the 'public interest'. Eckard found a lack of support for the public interest arguments proffered by owners and concludes that the more likely motive for the reserve rule was collusion to exploit the power of the clubs.

In Australia it is the Competition and Consumer Commission (ACCC), an independent statutory authority, that administers legislation and informs government policy relating to competition and

Plate 7 Holidaymakers relaxing on a car ferry: Bargain fares or restrictive practices?
Source: The author.

anti-trust law. It promotes competition and fair trade for the benefit of consumers, businesses and the community. The key pieces of anti-trust legislation are:

- the Trade Practices Act 1974
- the Prices Surveillance Act 1983.

Exhibit 7.4 reports on the Australian Competition and Consumer Commission (ACCC) verdict on an application by Air New Zealand and Air Canada to enter into a Cooperation Agreement.

There are also arguments for allowing large, potentially monopoly firms to prosper. These include competition with other large firms in the global markets, the ability to engage in expensive research and

Exhibit 7.4 ACCC denies authorization to Air New Zealand
and Air Canada's proposed Cooperation Agreement

The Australian Competition and Consumer Commission has denied
authorization to Air New Zealand and Air Canada to enter into a Cooperation
Agreement. Under the agreement, the airlines would share the revenue from
Air Canada's direct Sydney Vancouver route and Air New Zealand's direct
Auckland-Vancouver route, and would jointly promote the flights.

The statement from the ACCC contained the following observations:

- The ACCC is concerned that the agreement would reduce competition
  between Air New Zealand's indirect flights and Air Canada's Australia-
  Canada direct flights, since Air New Zealand will receive revenue from
  the direct flights.
- The ACCC can authorize such an agreement where it meets a public
  benefit test but the ACCC considers that the test has not been met here.
- The ACCC considers it is important to ensure effective competition
  in aviation markets to continue delivering choice and lower fares to
  consumers.
- On balance, the ACCC considers that the public benefits of the
  Cooperation Agreement are not likely to outweigh the public detriments.

Source: Adapted from The Australian Competition and Consumer Commission,
www.accc.gov.au

development and the fact that competition is difficult where a natural monopoly exists. The latter is particularly true for firms that
depend on an infrastructure that cannot feasibly be duplicated – for
example, a rail network.

Laws, planning controls and permits

Governments use laws, planning controls and permits to prevent the
free market from operation in certain areas. For example, licensing
laws limit the hours that licensed premises may open and who may
be served with alcohol. Betting and gaming are regulated by the law.
Similarly, some goods and services are banned outright. For example,
possession of a whole range of drugs is illegal. Interestingly, legislat-
ing against something is not sufficient to prevent a market emerging
and so black markets have arisen for the supply of drugs. However,
because of the risk involved in supplying drugs, the market price
reflects considerable profit. Planning control affects new buildings
and change of use and is generally the function of local or state government. Without planning controls there would be a considerable
erosion of the countryside and loss of areas of outstanding natural
beauty by new building projects.

Taxes and subsidies

Taxes and subsidies may be used to encourage the consumption
of merit goods and discourage the consumption of demerit goods.

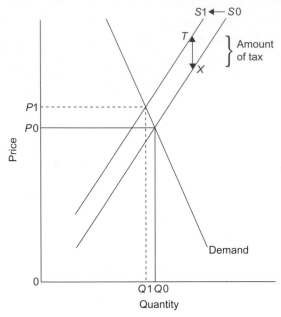

Figure 7.3 The effects of imposition of a tax on the market for cigarettes.

Cigarette smoking, for example, is subject to large taxes although it is not entirely clear whether the main purpose of taxation is to collect revenue, or to cut consumption.

The effect on the market is illustrated in Figure 7.3. Originally, equilibrium price is established at $P0$ where demand equals supply at $Q0$. The effects of the imposition of a tax of TX is to shift the supply curve to the left, the vertical distance between the two supply curves representing the amount of the tax. Equilibrium price rises to $P1$ and cigarette consumption has been reduced to $Q1$. Notice that the demand curve has been drawn to reflect the relative demand inelasticity for cigarettes and thus the effect of a tax on quantity bought and sold is relatively modest.

If it were possible to measure marginal external costs of provision of a good or service, it would be possible to restore an optimum level of output in a market by the imposition of a tax. This is illustrated in Figure 7.4. The equilibrium price is at $P0$ with an equilibrium quantity of $Q0$. However, the existence of external costs MXC establishes the MSC curve to the left of the supply curve S, which only reflects marginal private costs. This would suggest an optimal price of $P1$ and quantity of $Q1$, but since the marginal external costs are purely national and do not actually affect the supply curve, overproduction of $Q0$–$Q1$ occurs. This could be remedied by the imposition of a tax which would shift the supply curve to STX and result in an equilibrium quantity of $Q1$.

Taking another example, a tax on airlines could be used to reduce the amount of noise pollution. But the use of taxation for this purpose demonstrates a flaw in this approach. Whilst the problem would be

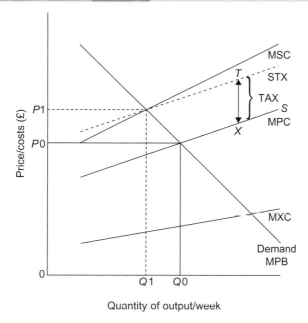

Figure 7.4 The use of taxation to restore optimal provision of goods with externalities.

addressed from an overall perspective (i.e. output would be adjusted to where MSB equals MSC), it would be the government that benefits from the tax and not those who are directly affected by the noise.

Similarly, where there are significant marginal social benefits involved in the supply of a good or service, a subsidy could be used to ensure that the market equilibrium occurred where marginal social cost curve equal marginal social benefits, rather than where marginal private benefits equal marginal private costs. This is the economic justification for the subsidy of arts and recreation and such a policy results in more provision than would result from free market activity alone.

Public provision

Public provision consists of supply through public corporations and local government ownership. The rationale for public ownership has included a mixture of political and economic aims. In the leisure and tourism sector in the UK the British Airports Authority and BA were both privatized, although around the world there are still many examples of nationalized airlines, Air India and the rail system in France being prime examples. There are many examples of public sector broadcasting in evidence and O'Hagan and Jennings (2003) examined the key issues in the debate in Europe over public sector broadcasting. They considered the arguments for public sector broadcasting under five headings, namely diversity, democracy/equality, network externalities, innovation and investment and public broadcasting as 'insurance'. At a local level arts centres and leisure centres are often publicly owned.

Economic arguments for public ownership have included first:

- economies of scale
- rationalization
- avoidance of competitive costs.

These arguments all stem from government ownership of a whole industry. The resulting size of operation leads to economies of scale where bulk purchasing can result in considerable cost reductions. Rationalization – making processes and products uniform and cutting waste – is also then possible, and competitive costs such as advertising can be eliminated. These arguments were powerful reasons for maintaining state monopolies in rail transport.

The second group of arguments in support of public ownership includes:

- control of monopoly power and excess prices
- consideration of externalities
- provision of merit and public goods
- employment provision.

Under private ownership monopoly industries are able to charge high prices in the absence of competition, and profit maximization will encourage such industries to do so. State ownership enables non-profit-maximizing pricing strategies to be adopted. Price may be set, for example, to ensure that the industry breaks even to protect consumers from excess prices. In the case of an industry supplying merit goods or public goods, price may be set below market price where marginal social cost curve equals marginal social benefit. Such a pricing strategy would involve the industry making an accounting loss (since total private revenue would be less than total private costs) and thus require government subsidy. The use of public sector industries to provide employment would also be based on wider economic considerations, including social costs and benefits, rather than the narrow considerations of private costs and benefits. Exhibit 7.5 illustrates public preferences for leisure facilities offered by the City of Auckland, NZ. It shows which facilities the public would like to see under private ownership, which should be public funded and which should have mixed funding.

Problems of market intervention

Resource allocation in disequilibrium

Where goods and services are provided free of charge – changing the guard at Buckingham Palace, roads and children's playgrounds, for example – price is not able to bring demand and supply into equilibrium. The problem of excess demand often arises and therefore allocation of goods and services occurs in some other way. Queuing,

Exhibit 7.5 Spectrum of public support for leisure, Auckland, NZ.

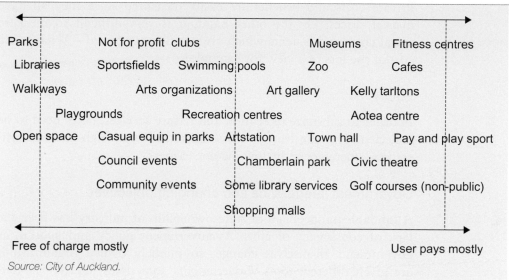

Parks
Not for profit clubs
Museums
Fitness centres

Libraries
Sportsfields   Swimming pools
Zoo
Cafes

Walkways
Arts organizations
Art gallery
Kelly tarltons

Playgrounds
Recreation centres
Aotea centre

Open space
Casual equip in parks   Artstation
Town hall
Pay and play sport

Council events
Chamberlain park
Civic theatre

Community events
Some library services   Golf courses (non-public)

Shopping malls

Free of charge mostly
User pays mostly

Source: City of Auckland.

first come first served, and ability to push through to the front of crowds are all methods in which goods and services may then be allocated in the absence of an effective market.

Public ownership: efficiency and culture

The profit motive engenders an organizational culture of efficiency and customer service. A criticism of public ownership is that lack of incentive leads to waste and poor service.

Side effects of subsidies and taxes

The provision of subsidies to industry has to be paid for. Subsidies are financed from increasing taxes or from reducing government spending elsewhere, or from government borrowing. Increasing the level of taxes can cause problems since it may reduce incentives in the economy. Similarly, it is rarely prudent to pay for current expenditure by borrowing since this merely postpones the raising of taxes to a future generation.

Loss of consumer sovereignty

In the extreme case of total state planning, consumer sovereignty is replaced by decision-making by state officials, often leading to a mismatch between what consumers want and what the state provides. Government subsidies or ownership also reduce consumer sovereignty. Consumers' spending power is reduced by taxes, and government then makes decisions about how taxes will be spent. A key question here is whether the government is well qualified to choose, for example, what art should be produced.

Measurement of external costs and benefits

Private costs and benefits are easily measured since they all have market prices. On the other hand, it is very difficult to measure social costs and benefits which are not directly priced – What is the cost of the loss of a view for example?

Equity

In order to subsidize recreation and leisure services, taxes need to be collected. This can lead to cross-subsidization of high-income earners (e.g. opera goers) by low-income earners.

Government interference and changing objectives

A fundamental problem of state ownership of industry has been the lack of consistency of aims. As government policy and, indeed, as governments themselves change, so publicly owned organizations are given different aims. Governments sometimes interfere in purchasing decisions for political reasons. Public corporations are also hypersensitive to the condition of the general economy. Governments may interfere with public sector pay to control inflation, and investment funds may suddenly disappear when public sector borrowing becomes too high.

Trends in public sector provision

Central planning

This has been abandoned by Eastern bloc countries and the two remaining significant examples of this – Cuba and China – are allowing the free market an increasing role in their economies. This has been long established in China and even Cuba is allowing the free market more emphasis in the economy.

Privatization

Since the 1980s, the scale of public ownership has been drastically reduced. Government-owned companies have been privatized, their shares floated on the stock exchange and their aims have become those of profit maximization. Examples include Lufthansa in Germany and the railways in the UK. Those organizations remaining in the public sector have been subject to greater accountability. Exhibit 7.6 demonstrates an example of privatization in Russia.

Service standards

These defined the rights, complaints procedures and compensation provision for customers.

Exhibit 7.6 Privatization of leisure in Russia

In the late 1990s the city government of Moscow extended its privatization programme by putting 200 hotels up for sale for an expected price of about $1 billion. The portfolio on offer was a mixed one. It included the five-star National near to Red Square but also a number in a poor state of repair which required substantial refurbishment and in some cases reconstruction. The city had already been actively promoting joint ventures with foreign companies and at this time had an equity stake in at least 80 hotels and restaurants.

The privatization was subjected to two conditions. First, the freeholds of the hotels, some of which are on prime sites would not be sold, but instead renewable leases of up to 49 years would be offered. Second, the city would retain a 25 per cent interest in the joint stock companies that are sold.

The main advantages to the city of Moscow were an immediate income from the asset sales and the inflow of foreign investment that is needed to bring the hotels up to international standards. Transfers of management expertise would also be beneficial as would be the spreading of a service culture mentality from incoming multinational firms such as Hilton International and Marriott. Hotel management would be freed of the bureaucracy of local government ownership and control and uncertainties about finance and policy.

However, in the longer term, income would be lost to the city and profits of many cases would be repatriated to foreign multinational organizations. Employment prospects appeared to be mixed. Efficiency requirements meant a loss of jobs and some jobs would be taken by foreign employees. However, the long-term development of the hotels would probably provide new jobs in the future. In terms of state planning, another small part of the economy would be lost to city control. Pricing policy, employment levels and the future development of these hotels would all be transferred to the free market.

Source: The author, from press cuttings.

Performance targets and indicators

Public sector organizations are increasingly required to define their provision in terms of measurable outcomes. These outcomes are often subject to interorganizational comparison – 'league tables' and targets for improvement from year to year.

Contracting out

Where local or national government takes responsibility for the provision of leisure (and other) services there are two main ways of doing this. First the government authority can provide the service directly creating its own service departments and directly employing labour and owning facilities. Another possibility is by contracting out of such services. Here the government authority determines service standards and then invites private sector organizations to bid for contracts to provide these service levels by competitive bidding.

Robinson and Taylor (2003) report on the results of a project from Sport England, which establishes performance indicators and national benchmarks for performance by local authority sports halls and swimming pools in England.

REVIEW OF KEY TERMS

- Consumer sovereignty: goods and services produced according to consumer demand.
- Economic efficiency: maximum output from minimum input.
- Allocative efficiency: maximum output from given inputs and maximum consumer satisfaction from that output.
- Externalities: costs or benefits which have social significance.
- Merit goods: goods with external benefits.
- Demerit goods: goods with external disbenefits.
- Public goods: goods which are non-excludable and non-rival.
- Concentration ratio: percentage of market share held by top companies.

 Data Questions

Task 7.1 **The art of the Ann Arbor City budget by Tom Gantert**

The debate in Ann Arbor (a US city), where firefighters are being laid off due to a multimillion dollar budget deficit, is over an $850,000 piece of art.

That is how much the city has agreed to pay German artist Herbert Dreiseitl for a three-piece water sculpture that would go in front of the new police and courts building right by the City Hall.

The city has the money to do it because in 2007, it agreed to set aside for public art one per cent of money that went into capital improvement projects that were $100,000 or larger. Most capital projects involve streets, sewers and water.

Ann Arbor City Council member Stephen Kunselman, a Democrat, opposed the art deal. 'I think it is incredibly insensitive', Kunselman said. 'It is insensitive to the staff and their morale. It is insensitive to the community. There are people out there struggling financially, and here we are spending a large amount of money on a piece of art.'

Kunselman said the city is also eliminating the solid waste coordinator from the budget, which oversees trash pickup, and hiring an art coordinator.

City Administrator Roger Fraser wrote in an e-mail that the solid waste coordinator position was eliminated as a cost-cutting measure because the solid waste millage had decreased. Fraser wrote that the art coordinator position would be paid for by the public art fund.

Fraser noted that the public art dollars did not come from the city's general fund, which is used to pay salaries and benefits, and that less than $6000 of the art money came from the general fund.

The art projects also must have a 'thematic connection' to the source of funding, Fraser wrote. The $850,000 art project is water-themed, because the money came from storm water funds.

But some critics say that a city creative enough to fund art from storm water projects should be able to find money to cover essential city services.

'That's the classic argument', said Glenn Thompson, an Ann Arbor resident and longtime critic of city spending. 'But the city has become very, very good at shuffling money in and out of the general fund when they want. These people are very good at putting it in and out of the general fund when they wish.'

Michael LaFaive, the director of the Mackinac Center for Public Policy's Morey Fiscal Policy Initiative, said non-essential services are being funded throughout the state.

'Administrators cry poverty while lavishing money on the beautiful people', LaFaive said. 'The threat to dismiss firefighters often comes while officials protect golf courses, wave pools and art. No city can cry poverty while it defends recreation and aesthetics such as art.'

LaFaive said administrators get creative with budgets to fund pet projects.

'It doesn't mean officials can't find ways to redirect the money', LaFaive said. 'It appears on the surface that they are redefining what a capital improvement is, by designing a sculpture instead of true municipal infrastructure projects such as roads and bridges.'

Source: ©The Mackinac Center for Public Policy (USA) (www.mackinac.org) reproduced with kind permission.

Recap Questions

1 Evaluate the case for and against subsidizing the arts under the following headings:
   (a) opportunity cost,
   (b) tax burden and borrowing,
   (c) merit goods and externalities,
   (d) consumer sovereignty,
   (e) equity.
2 Do you think that the city of Ann Arbor should use public funds to purchase this piece of art?
3 Construct a graph to justify the subsidy of merit goods.
4 What recreation and leisure activities are currently subsidized in the country in which you are studying. What are the arguments for spreading or reducing such a subsidy?

Task 7.2 **European Commission prohibits acquisition of Aer Lingus by Ryanair**

The following are the highlights of the European Commission 2007 judgment on this case:

- On 27 June 2007 The European Commission prohibited the proposed takeover by Ryanair of Aer Lingus.
- It based its decision on EU Merger Regulations.

Task 7.2 continued

- The Commission analysed the competitive effects of the proposed merger on the basis of the competitive situation on individual routes. Its evidence included:
  - questionnaires sent to competing scheduled airlines, charter airlines, airports, corporate customers, slot coordination authorities, civil aviation authorities and transport authorities;
  - econometric submissions from Ryanair, Aer Lingus and other third parties;
  - regression analysis to identify the level of competitive constraints exercised between Ryanair and Aer Lingus and by their competitors;
  - price correlation analysis for individual airport pairs and city pairs;
  - a customer survey at Dublin Airport.
- Its judgment cited the following reasons:
  - The acquisition would combine the two leading airlines that operate from Ireland.
  - These airlines currently compete vigorously against each other.
  - The merger would harm consumers by removing this competition.
  - The merger would create a monopoly or a dominant position on 35 routes operated by both airlines.
  - The merger would reduce choice.
  - The merger would probably lead to higher prices for passengers using the affected routes to and from Ireland.
  - There exist significant barriers to entry to individual routes to/from Ireland (and in particular Dublin) for competitors of Ryanair and Aer Lingus including the strong position of Ryanair and Aer Lingus in Ireland, their recognized brands and Ryanair's history of aggressive competition against new entrants.
  - The Commission's investigation and market test of remedies offered by Ryanair demonstrated that these remedies were inadequate to remove the competition concerns.

  The Commission therefore concluded that the concentration would significantly impede effective competition within the European Economic Area or a substantial part of it and was incompatible with the common market.

  In 2010 Ryanair was unsuccessful in its appeal against the decision:

- The EU General Court dismissed Ryanair's appeal against its decision of June 2007 (case T-342/07).
- The Court acknowledged the Commission's very detailed and careful analysis of the competitive effects and the proposed remedies.
- The Court confirmed the Commission's analysis that the proposed merger would have significantly impeded competition on 35 routes to and from Ireland.

Recap Questions

1 What are the general principles of EU/UK/US and Australian anti-trust (monopoly) laws?

2 Why did the European Commission prohibit the Ryanair/Aer Lingus merger?

3 What was the evidence collected to support the European Commission's judgment?

4   Are there any potential drawbacks of the European Commission's decision?

5   Given that Ryanair is known for its cheap fares do you think the European Commission's decision was a good one?

Task 7.3 Journal article: Grinols, E., Mustard, D., 2006. Casinos, crime, and community costs. Review of Economics and Statistics 88 (1), 28–45

Do casinos cause an increase in crime? This was the question that prompted this research project in the USA. The theoretical basis of Grinols and Mustard's article included a number of factors which may either reduce or increase crime following the introduction of casinos.

Taking the crime-reduction factors first the authors suggest two possible arguments:

- First, casinos may provide better job opportunities for low-skilled workers leading to a reduction in crime.
- Second, the expansion of casinos may lead to economic development effects and this general raising of economic activity gambling might reduce crime.

Grinols and Mustard also set out five arguments whereby casinos may lead to an increase in crime:

- First, casinos may drain the local economy of resources and so harm economic development.
- Second, casinos may lead to increased possibilities for criminal proceeds which might result in more crime.
- Third, pathological gambling may increase with the spread of casinos and this can lead to more crime to feed the gambling habit.
- Fourth, criminals may be attracted to regions with casinos bringing more crime with them.
- Fifth, casinos may cause changes in the local population characteristics whereby they become more likely to commit crimes.

With a clear rationale for their research provided by various theoretical viewpoints, Grinols and Mustard undertook an exhaustive research project to analyse the relationship between casinos and crime. Their research covered a significant number of regions in the USA and considered a variety of control variables in a project that collected data over a period of several years. Using the data obtained the authors constructed a model of model crime rates.

Their model found that crime had fallen in both casino and non-casino counties during the period they researched. However, the authors also found that crime rates dropped by 12 per cent more in non-casino counties compared to in casino counties. The authors therefore concluded that there are higher crime rates in casino counties and that these are caused by the presence of casinos.

The research also found that whilst there is little or no effect of casinos on crime for the first 2 or 3 years after the opening of a casino, by the fourth and fifth years most forms of crime begin to increase. Grinols and Mustard then combined their estimates of crime effects with estimated costs of these crimes to arrive at estimated cost of crime by casinos.

These were calculated as $75 per adult in US casino-hosting counties.

Task 7.3 **continued**

Recap Questions

1 What is:
   (a) a demerit good?
   (b) a merit good?
2 Is gambling a merit or demerit good? Explain your answer.
3 Should governments control gambling? Why?
4 One method of government control of goods and services that have negative economic consequences is by state ownership. Assess the economic arguments for public ownership of casinos.
5 What other steps might government take to control gambling?

MULTIPLE CHOICE

1 A merit good is one that:
   (a) People should be rewarded with for good behaviour.
   (b) Is non-excludable.
   (c) Has external benefits.
   (d) Improves consumer sovereignty.

2 The free market tends to:
   (a) Overproduce merit goods.
   (b) Under-produce merit goods.
   (c) Produce goods and services inefficiently.
   (d) Limit consumer sovereignty.

3 Which of the following is *not* an approach to preventing the abuse of monopoly power?
   (a) Anti-trust laws.
   (b) Public ownership.
   (c) Subsidies.
   (d) Evaluation of mergers.

4 Which of the following is *not* true of public goods?
   (a) A public swimming pool is an example of one.
   (b) They are non-excludable.
   (c) Consumption of them is non-rival.
   (d) They tend not to be produced in a free market.

5 Which of the following is *not* true of demerit goods?
   (a) Cigarettes are an example of them.
   (b) They incur social as well as private costs.
   (c) They tend to be overproduced by the free market.
   (d) They are often subject to taxation.

REVIEW QUESTIONS

1 Why might leaving provision of the arts entirely to the private
   sector lead to sub optimal resource allocation? Use a diagram to
   show how provision of a public subsidy to the arts might restore
   optimal allocation and explain why achieving this aim might be
   difficult in practice.
2 Should children's playgrounds be provided free of charge?
3 Should opera be subsidized?
4 Should football admission be subsidized?
5 Should local authorities provide arts centres and what should
   their pricing policy be?
6 What problems arise from providing merit goods additional to
   those provided in the market?

Websites of interest

UK Office of Fair Trading: www.oft.gov.uk/
UK Monopolies and Mergers Commission: www.mmc.gov.uk/
The Wall Street Journal: http://europe.wsj.com/home-page
The Mackinac Center for Public Policy (USA): www.mackinac.org
The Australian Competition and Consumer Council: www.accc.gov.au

PART 4

The External Operating Environment

C H A P T E R **8**

The competitive, technological, political and sociocultural environment

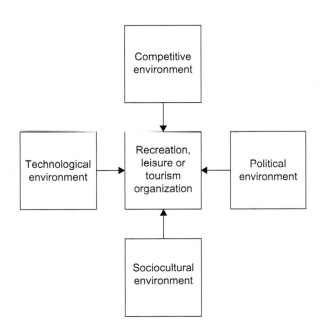

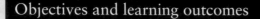
Objectives and learning outcomes

The environment in which organizations operate is often now characterized by the four 'D's:

- Difficult
- Dangerous
- Dynamic
- Diverse.

In other words, the environment is constantly changing. It is this constant change that makes environment scanning important for recreation, leisure, tourism and other organizations. Organizations that remain static in a dynamic environment experience strategic drift and are likely to fail. Figure 8.1 illustrates the concept of strategic drift which can explain such failure.

Between period $t0$ and $t1$, the operating environment is static, and the organization illustrated makes no policy change, so that by the end of the period, at $t1$, organizational policy at B is in tune with the environment at A. However, the period $t1–t2$ represents a period of dynamic change in the operating environment. The organization, however, undertakes only marginal policy change so that by the end of the period it is experiencing strategic drift, represented by the distance CD.

Chapters 8 and 9 analyse the nature of the operating environment. This chapter considers the competitive, technological, political and sociocultural environments. Chapter 9 considers the economic environment. These environments are often referred to using the acronym C-PEST (competitive, political, economic, sociocultural and technical) environment and their analysis enables comprehensive opportunities and threats analysis to be undertaken. A framework for this is provided at the end of Chapter 9.

By studying this chapter, students will be able to describe and analyse an organization's:

- competitive environment;
- technological environment;
- political environment;
- sociocultural environment.

THE COMPETITIVE ENVIRONMENT

In his book *Competitive Strategy*, Porter (1980) proposed the following model ('the five forces') for investigating the competitive environment:

- the threat of entrants
- the power of suppliers

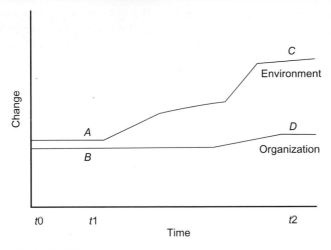

Figure 8.1 Strategic drift.

- the power of consumers
- the threat of substitutes
- competitive rivalry.

Exhibit 8.1 reports on the strategic impact of the Internet on the travel and tourism industry using Porter's five forces analysis (Buhalis & Zoge, 2007).

The threat of entrants

The threat of new entrants into an industry will have a significant effect on a recreation, leisure or tourism organization. New entrants may stimulate more price competition or more investment in product differentiation as they attempt to win market share and profits and existing firms seek to defend market share and profits. Chapter 6 analysed these effects of competition on pricing policy and strategy.

The extent of the threat of new entrants will depend upon barriers to entry such as:

- economies of scale
- capital and experience barriers to entry
- advertising barriers to entry
- availability of distribution channels (vertical integration)
- anticipated entry wars
- natural monopoly conditions
- brand proliferation barriers.

Clearly barriers to entry will represent a hurdle to be surmounted for organizations wishing to enter an industry or defences to be maintained and strengthened in the case of established organizations.

Exhibit 8.1 Journal article

Buhalis, D., Zoge, M., 2007. The strategic impact of the Internet on the tourism industry. *Information and Communication Technologies in Tourism*, 481–492.

In this article the authors examine the impact of the Internet on the structure of the tourism industry and its operational and strategic practices. Buhalis and Zoge use *Porter's Five Forces* analysis to analyse the competitive position of the key sectors and players in the industry. Their research showed a dramatic increase in *competitive rivalry* and that the *bargaining power of suppliers* (principals) and buyers (consumers) has been strengthened as the Internet has allowed direct communication between them often cutting out the power and influence of intermediaries.

More specifically the authors note:

As far as the threat of *new entrants* is concerned, the Internet had an effect on *entry barriers* as it altered economies of scale and the amount of capital required for competing in the industry. *Rivalry* among existing competitors was also affected as technology and the Internet affected differentiation and cost structures as well as switching costs (Porter, 1985). Changes also appeared to the *bargaining power of buyers* as the Internet introduced a much higher degree of transparency and lower switching costs. Similarly, a shift in the bargaining power of suppliers has been noticed, as the Internet provided alternatives and reduced the need to buy only from few powerful sellers. Finally, the emergence of the Internet affected substitution as *"it influences both the relative value/price and switching costs of substitutes"* (Porter, 1985).

Note: Italic format added by author.

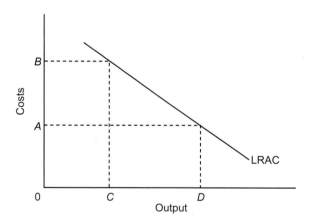

Figure 8.2 Economy of scale barriers to entry.

Economies of scale

Economies of scale, discussed in more detail in Chapter 5, result in reductions of average costs of production as the scale of production increases. Figure 8.2 illustrates the Long-run average cost (LRAC) curve of an organization experiencing economies of scale.

An established organization producing at level of output $0D$ will experience significant economies of scale with LRACs at $0A$. A new entrant to the industry will initially produce a low level of output, for example at $0C$, and lack of scale economies will result in high average costs of $0B$. The established organization can therefore often out-compete the new entrant by passing these lower costs on in the form of lower prices or by using higher profit margins to finance more added value of the product.

Capital and experience barriers to entry

For some areas of business the capital costs of entry are fairly modest. This is true, for example, for dance and fitness classes, small hotels and guesthouses and for tour guiding. Entry into such areas is thus relatively easy. On the other hand, there are substantial capital costs in entering the airline or theme park industry and thus entry barriers are stronger in such industries.

Similarly, an experience curve can be envisaged for the supply of complex goods and services. Experience means that organizations learn how to do things better. Established firms, having travelled along their experience curve, develop expertise that delivers lower costs and better service. On the other hand, potential entrants will find themselves disadvantaged by being at the start of their experience curve.

Advertising barriers to entry

Advertising may be used to create an artificial barrier to entry. Successful brands can be underpinned by extensive advertising which makes it difficult for newcomers to break into the market. For example, extensive advertising on larger brands has the effect of minimizing the threat of new entrants because they find it difficult to establish their brand.

Availability of distribution channels

Entry into some markets may be prevented or limited by access to distribution channels. There are many examples of this in the leisure and tourism sector. Many airlines would like to expand their operations into some of the key global airports but are unable to do so because take-off and landing slots are either unavailable or at inconvenient times. Some airlines (particularly the established traditional 'legacy carriers') are able to maintain market power because of their allocation and ownership of slots (often called 'grandfather rights'). Potential new entrants to the airline business have to surmount a formidable hurdle in gaining access to take-off and landing slots at major airports. These landing rights give established airlines a big advantage over potential rivals. For example, there are around half

Exhibit 8.2 Ryanair condemns EU airport slots protectionism

Ryanair, Europe's largest low-fares airline...condemned the EU's proposal to waive the 'use it or lose it' rule in relation to airport slots as high-fare airlines continue to reduce capacity at slot-controlled airports. The Commission's proposal would mean that it would no longer be mandatory for these airlines to operate and use their slots in order to retain them and could prevent Ryanair, the only airline increasing its traffic in Europe, from using them.

Reacting to the EU's proposal, Ryanair's Deputy Chief Executive, Michael Cawley said:

This is protectionism of the worst type and will lead to further state and EU support for inefficient, high cost airlines which don't have the cost base to support growth or even the maintenance of existing services. The Commission's proposal will ensure that these inefficient, high cost airlines can hold on to valuable slots at slot coordinated airports without using them and essentially block any plans by Ryanair to grow at these airports. This is bad for aviation, airports and, above all, consumers as it reverses Europe back to its old regulated ways in aviation when inefficient, monopolistic, state run airlines blocked more efficient operators from competing on a level playing field.

Ryanair is set to grow by 9 million passengers this year, much of which will be at slot coordinated airports. Our path to reduce fares and increase passenger traffic should not be blocked by the inefficient, high fares airlines aided and abetted by the EU Commission's misguided decision to allow them to hold on to slots without operating them.

We call on the EU Parliament and the EU governments to reject this protectionist proposal from the Commission and allow free access to unused slot times at all airports throughout Europe so that the most efficient operator can prevail and customers can enjoy the guaranteed lowest fares.

Source: Ryanair Press Release www.ryanair.com/en/news

a million slots at Heathrow, the world's busiest airport, and British Airways owns the rights to a large percentage of these.

Exhibit 8.2 registers the frustration of Ryanair over the ability of airlines to keep their slots even if they are not using them. Ryanair is a highly successful Irish-owned low-cost airline but it feels that its lack of fair access to airport slots means that it suffers unfair competition from those airlines with substantial slots accumulated through grandfather rights.

One of the motives for vertical integration in an industry may be to discriminate against other suppliers by ownership of distribution channels, as discussed in Chapter 5. Thus, TUI Travel's ownership of the Thomson travel agency chain and Internet retail site may represent a strategy to prevent competitors from increasing their market share by preferential retail selling of the group's own products. Ownership of distribution channels has led to similar debates about fair access to markets in the film and cinema, and satellite television industries.

Exhibit 8.3 Price wars in US airspace: Spirit Airlines versus Northwest Airlines

At the time of this case Spirit Airlines was a regional airline operating between a small number of cities in the USA whilst Northwest Airlines was a major international airline operating services all around the world. In 1996, Northwest Airlines and Spirit Airlines engaged in a price war on two domestic US routes between Detroit and Philadelphia as well as between Detroit and Boston. The period witnessed a sudden and dramatic reduction of fares and a sudden increase in capacity on these routes and the following details some of the changes on the route between Detroit and Philadelphia:

- Prior to December 1995 Northwest offered a lowest unrestricted fare of $355 and a lowest restricted fare of $125.
- In December 1995 Spirit started operating on the route with a lowest restricted fare of $49.
- In June 1996 Spirit introduced a second daily flight.
- Following this Northwest introduced a lowest published fare of $49.
- Northwest added another daily flight to the route.
- Subsequently Spirit's load factors fell and its operations on the route became unprofitable.
- This lead to Spirit withdrawing its flights.
- After this Northwest increased its fares again and reduced capacity.

Although initially the lower fares were introduced by Spirit, during the period of intense price wars Spirit protested that:

1. Northwest's fares were calculated to be predatory.
2. Northwest's predatory fares would lead to Spirit's exit from operating on these routes.
3. Northwest's fares would rise again to previous levels once Spirit had been driven from the market.

Based on 'Predatory Pricing in the Airline Industry: Spirit Airlines v. Northwest Airlines' by K. Elzinga and D. Millshttp://www.virginia.edu/economics/Workshops/papers/mills/Kwoka-White%20Spirit%20Airlines%20Chapter.pdf

Anticipated entry wars

Where entry into a market is likely to precipitate a strong reaction from established organizations, potential new entrants may be dissuaded from market entry. The example of the Laker SkyTrain in the 1970s is still a potent one. The arrival of this new service on UK/US air routes introduced substantially lower fares. This led to price wars from British and American carriers that were so intense that Laker Airways went out of business. The established companies had the financial muscle to cut prices deeper and for longer than Laker, and once Laker Airways had gone out of business, fares were allowed to rise again.

Exhibit 8.3 illustrates aspects of an entry price war in the USA between Northwest Airlines and Spirit Airlines which attempted to operate new services on Northwest's routes.

Natural monopoly conditions

A natural monopoly exists where it is not technically feasible or desirable to have many competing services. For example, it is only feasible to have one rail network or fixed telephone line network, and for smaller destinations one airport. Organizations operating in natural monopolies generally are less exposed to the threat of new entrants.

Brand proliferation barriers

Brand proliferation occurs when producers flood the market with a range of brands, often advertised strongly, in order to capture a large proportion of shelf-space and consumer awareness. One of the motives for this can be to make it difficult for new brands to enter a multibrand market as their possible share of the market is likely to be diminished by such practices.

The power of suppliers

Supplier power is another important aspect of the competitive environment. Suppliers of an organization's inputs have a key impact on prices and quality, and the greater the power of suppliers, the lower margins will be for the 'supplied to' organization. Supplier power is increased by the degree of monopoly or oligopoly in the supplying industry, and whether there are high costs of switching suppliers. Because of this airport operators are often able to exert considerable supplier power when negotiating with airlines. Supplier power is diminished where the organization buying inputs has large purchasing power.

In some cases, backward vertical integration is a route to avoiding supplier power by the take-over of the supplying organization. TUI and Thomas Cook each own their own airlines and this means that these organizations can dictate the level of service and its price. The latter is particularly important when demand is buoyant and airlines find their bargaining position enhanced.

The power of buyers

Where the buyer is a monopsonist (single buyer) or a near monopsonist, considerable power can be exerted over the selling organization. For example, in Spanish resorts where hoteliers have become dependent upon one or two UK tour operators, room rates are negotiated with very slim margins for the hoteliers. Indeed Exhibit 8.4 shows an example where a large tour operator has required a cut in prices charged by hotels.

Exhibit 8.4 Major tour operator puts pressure on hotel bills

Thomas Cook is one of the only two major tour operators in the UK following recent rationalizations and liquidations. In 2007, four separate tour operators became just two as Thomas Cook merged with MyTravel and TUI merged with First Choice whilst XL went out of business in 2008. This has led to a significant concentration of market power.

One recent example of the exercise of this demonstrates the extent of *buyer power* when Thomas Cook took the decision to demand a 5 per cent discount from the hotel suppliers it uses in Spain, Portugal, Greece and other popular holiday destinations.

An article in *The Guardian* newspaper reported the reactions of those affected by the move: It quotes Hotrec, the European umbrella trade body for hotels, restaurants and cafes, which condemned Thomas Cook's actions as 'unfair, unwarranted and amounting to a breach of contracts'. Hotrec also disclosed that Thomas Cook had used threats to withdraw future business in order to pressure hoteliers into accepting a reduction in contracted prices.

The Guardian also reported the reaction from The Spanish Confederation of Hotels and Tourism (Cehat) which said that Thomas Cook's actions 'unilaterally break contract terms and represents a dangerous precedent for the Spanish hotel industry…we will provide legal advice for all the affected hoteliers with the aim of recovering the owed and unpaid amounts'.

The move is made possible by the imbalance between the huge buying power of Tour Operators such as Thomas Cook and the dependency that many hotels and hotel groups have on getting business from these big companies. For them there is now little choice when it comes to obtaining the mass bookings they depend on.

Source: Adapted from The Guardian *newspaper http://www.guardian.co.uk/business/ 2010/nov/01/thomas-cook-refuses-pay-hotel-bill*

Competition between suppliers is a key factor that increases buyer power. This is evident for air travel where there is intense competition on routes, for example, London–New York fares are very competitive, but where a route is served by a single operator price per kilometre flown increases sharply.

The level of buyer knowledge is another important factor. In order to exercise buyer power, customers need information about goods and services on offer and prices of competitors. In some areas of recreation, leisure and tourism this is difficult. However, the increasing use of the Internet offers consumers better knowledge in making price comparisons. The limitation to this, however, is the time cost of making comprehensive price comparisons.

Finally, the overall state of the market is important in determining the relative balance of buyer and supplier power. When the economy is growing strongly, there may be shortages of supply and supplier power becomes stronger. In conditions of recession there is often a shortage of customers and buyer power increases. This is also reflected in the example discussed in Exhibit 8.4.

The threat of substitutes

Substitutes can take several forms. First, a new product or service may make a current one obsolete. Word processors and MP3 players have made the typewriter and the CD obsolete. Second, a substitute may result in a new product or service competing closely with existing ones. Third, to some extent all goods and services compete for consumers' limited incomes and thus new products even in distant markets may have some impact on a variety of unrelated organizations.

Organizations faced with the threat of substitutes may react in several ways. These include:

- price leadership strategies
- differentiation strategies
- withdrawal or diversification strategies
- creating switching costs to prevent loss of customers.

The degree of competitive rivalry

Competitive rivalry within an industry is increased by the threat of new entrants and the threat of substitutes, but it is also influenced by current conditions in the industry. These include:

- whether competitors can cross-subsidize
- degree of market leadership and number of competitors
- changes in capacity
- high storage costs/perishability.

Cross-subsidization occurs where an organization uses profits from one sector of its business to subsidize prices in another sector particularly where new competition is emerging. This can lead to intense competition in the markets for some goods and services. The motive behind cross-subsidization is to win market share by low prices, and to make life difficult for new entrants to a market.

The degree of market leadership and number of competitors also influences competitive rivalry. Clearly, monopoly or near monopoly supply means little competitive rivalry. Oligopoly conditions can lead to competitive rivalry, but since, as Chapter 6 explains, rivalry reduces profits all round, organizations may choose to follow the lead of the dominant firms in such circumstances. Competitive conditions of supply are likely to lead to a state of constant rivalry. Firms may attempt to insulate themselves from such rivalry by differentiating their product from other products.

Where the supply of a good or service is subject to large increases in capacity, competitive rivalry is likely to become more intense. For example, the opening of the channel tunnel between the UK and

France led to a sudden increase in the capacity for cross-channel traffic and was followed by an intense period of competitive rivalry.

Some goods and services have high storage costs or are highly perishable. Aircraft seats, hotel rooms, hire cars and theatre seats are highly perishable. There is always the prospect of intense last-minute competition to sell such services, but in reality competition here is carefully orchestrated so that an organization's main market is not disrupted. For example, tour operators want to encourage advance bookings at brochure prices and therefore do not make big advertising capital over the last-minute bargains that can be obtained.

THE TECHNOLOGICAL ENVIRONMENT

Technological change offers two key opportunities for leisure and tourism organizations. First, it can lead to cost reductions. The LRAC curve is constructed on the assumption that technology remains constant, and thus improved production technology will cause the LRAC curve of an organization to fall as illustrated in Figure 8.3. LRAC1 represents the original LRAC curve. The use of improved production technology enables the curve to shift downwards to LRAC2. Average costs of producing level of output 0C now fall from 0A to 0B.

Second, technology can provide new products and markets. Both of these routes can lead to an improvement in an organization's competitive edge and can be the basis of price-based or differentiation strategies.

However, technological change also poses threats where existing products become obsolete in the face of new developments. Technological change is being delivered mainly at present by the increased processing power of computers and hand-held devices, the provision of high-capacity fixed and wireless data links, the fall in price of hardware and software and a virtuous circle of increased consumer uptake leading to further developments in software and

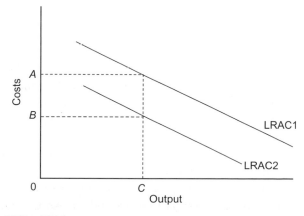

Figure 8.3 Shifting LRAC curve.

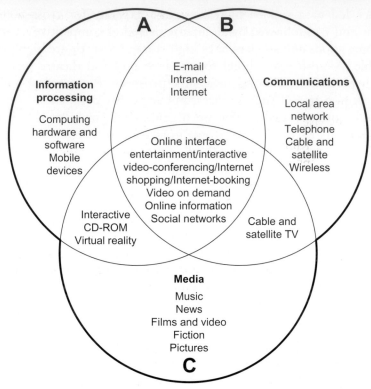

Figure 8.4 Multimedia.

applications. Silicon chip developments lead to faster data processing. Fibreoptics, digital and wireless technologies mean that data can be quickly transmitted globally at low cost, and these hardware developments mean that software of ever-increasing sophistication can be developed.

Multimedia continues to be a key driver of technological change and its components are illustrated in Figure 8.4. Thus at a simple level an organization's computer network on its own can perform word processing, accounting and other functions (circle A). Linked to other computers, it can enable communications to take place inside the organization through its Intranet and it can communicate with the world outside through the Internet. For example, here it can access reservation systems, provide marketing and booking systems and access e-mail and Internet conferencing (circles A + B).

Linked to other media, at the simplest level text, images and video clips can be incorporated into software programs (circles A + C). At the most sophisticated level virtual reality can be set up. Linking personal computers (PCs) and media sources through data links provides access to the whole repertoire of computer applications (circles A + B + C). This includes, for example, downloading of music, books, video on demand, Internet shopping and social networks. Home booking allows access to central reservation and booking systems from home, with the possibility of video clips of resorts and hotels.

But perhaps the most potent recent development in technology has been the rapid uptake of mobile devices led by the i-phone. Here, many of the connections previously only possible on a PC or laptop are now accessible on mobile devices.

The key drivers to multimedia technology include the falling price and rapidly increasing specification of PCs, the development of smart phones and the falling price and increasing availability of home broadband and wireless Internet connections along with their greater bandwidth.

Technological impacts may be analysed in the following areas:

- hospitality
- tourism
- leisure and recreation.

Hospitality

Technological developments include the following. First, links into central reservation systems are important so that hotels can capture reservations generated from distant terminals. Previously consumers used travel agents to access one of the central reservation systems to book air travel, car hire and accommodation, and access to these systems represented an important marketing tool. However, increasingly consumers and suppliers are bypassing retailers and seeking direct bookings via the Internet, so a user-friendly real-time Internet booking system is important for hotels and restaurants. Specialist Internet providers such as *lastminute.com* and *rooms.com* specialize in selling rooms. Smartphones are able to direct consumers to local restaurants based on their current location. At the same time technology is providing an important new dimension in terms of customer feedback. Customers can see the ratings of restaurants they wish to visit and *Tripadvisor.com* has become a must for those who wish to book their own rooms and avoid bad experiences of previous guests.

Second, there has been considerable progress in accounting packages. In management accounting, yield management packages are an important tool enabling hotels to maximize revenue by adjusting rates to best-fit changing market conditions. Yield management packages are able to compare likely demand with actual demand and capacity and suggest rates accordingly. In financial accounting, packages enable financial reporting to take place speedily and efficiently. Check-in time can be minimized by using credit-card readers to automate registration and issue a high-technology key which can even be a credit card itself. High-technology keys reduce the possibility of theft since codes may be changed frequently at minimal cost. It is possible for a reservation system to use its database to provide personalized services such as provision of a particular newspaper.

Exhibit 8.5 Hi-tech hotels are revolutionizing budget accommodation in France – Rob Davidson

You are driving through France and decide to stop for the night. The question is: how do you break your journey without breaking the bank? The answer is the budget hotel where a clean, quiet room for up to three people sharing costs from £15 a night.

How are overheads kept so low? Most cost trimming is achieved by reducing services to a bare minimum. Hi-tech, manpower-saving devices also help to cut costs. A good example is automatic check-ins, which are placed at entrances for use when reception areas are unattended. La Réception Automatique works like a cash machine: you insert a credit card and 'converse' with the facility (in French, English or German) about the room you want, how long you plan to stay and whether you want breakfast. The machine then debits your card and issues a key and room number.

French technology is also applied in the automatic cleaning systems installed in the showers and lavatories of the hotels. Every time the facility is used, a powerful spray of a water–disinfectant mix ensures that it is left spotless for the next user.

The labour-saving devices and basic services mean that budget hotels can be run by just two people plus cleaning staff.

Source: The Independent.

Computerized reservation systems (CRS) can also reduce check-out time to a minimum.

Other computer-assisted management systems range from energy management systems to conference management systems and computer-intelligent buildings. A computer-intelligent building means that most of the functions of the building are computer-assisted, and so, for example, room cleaning schedules can be computer-generated from the information from guests' smart keys, payrolling can be generated from reading employees' time sheets which themselves are based on electronic monitoring, and a wide range of on-screen services are available in rooms.

It is also vital for top hotels to ensure that their provision matches their customers' technology aspirations. This may include Plasma television screens, wireless connectivity and sophisticated music systems.

Exhibit 8.5 and Plate 8 show how technology has been used at the budget end of the hotel industry. Here its prime aim is to cut costs, enabling some French hotels to pursue an effective price-based strategy. The conference industry illustrates possible opportunities and threats posed by new technology. A recent study found that a significant proportion of hotel room sales was made to conference delegates, and there has been growth in the number of centres with capacities for in excess of 1000 delegates. However, some firms are increasingly turning to video-conferencing as a way of reducing travel and hospitality costs, and saving expensive executive time.

Plate 8 Réception Automatique, Hôtel Première Classe, France. *Source: The author.*

Some hotels are responding to this challenge and have introduced video-conferencing in their key conference venues. However, with the growth of multimedia technologies it is possible that more conferencing will in future be office or home based, utilizing PCs. Here, the growth of Skype which offers free video links is notable. The implications these moves would be a shift in conference spending away from airlines, hotels and local hospitality providers towards the providers of data links and other hardware and software companies.

Travel and tourism

Technological changes in transportation are likely to be extensions of existing technologies in the form of larger jumbo jets and faster trains for travel. Notable developments here include the two-deck Airbus

Exhibit 8.6 Virgin Galactic

If you log onto Virgin Galactic at http://www.virgingalactic.com you can click on to the bookings page where you will find the following information:

'Book your place in space now and join around 340 Virgin Galactic astronauts who will venture into space'.

'Tickets cost $200,000 and deposits start from $20,000. If you are interested in discussing your reservation with us directly please fill in the booking form...and we will be in touch as soon as possible to answer any questions you may have. Or you can contact one of our Accredited Space Agents around the world. They have been specially selected and trained by us to handle all aspects of your spaceflight reservation'.

A380. Additionally, some shortages of air space may be relieved by using information technology to create smaller air tunnels than the existing air corridors. So one of the key impacts of technology in this sector will be continually to open up the borders of the possible for travel as well as reducing travel time and cost. The flight of the first space tourist – Denis Tito – demonstrated possibilities for the future which are now being developed by Virgin Galactic. Indeed it is now possible to book for space flights as can be seen from Exhibit 8.6.

Buhalis and Law (2008) offered a comprehensive review of developments in e-tourism. Their review article included some of the following key observations which are summarized by Tribe (2010):

- The Internet has increased consumers choices.
- Information and communication technology (ICT) offers cheap, convenient, immediate and portable access to information, reservation and purchase.
- The Internet provides a channel for consumers complain about poor service (so called Electronic Word of Mouth).
- Web 2.0 and Travel 2.0 technologies extend the benefits of social networking and virtual communities to the tourism industry. For example TripAdvisor (www.tripadvisor.com) offers a communal pooling of reviews and ratings of hotels. It therefore offers a participatory and democratic system of updated and independent advice.
- 'Wiki' technologies will enable the creation of more collaborative and community websites. It is a technology that allows accessible and open creation and editing of interlinked Web pages using a simple text editor embedded in the website.
- The Internet allows suppliers to collect data on customers allowing profiling and therefore customization of offers and personalized recommendations.
- Wireless and mobile networks are increasingly important in ICT.
- Multimedia can be deployed as a powerful aspect of ICT in tourism where photos, graphics and videos are incorporated into

Internet sites to provide a more realistic image of services and destinations.

- Dynamic packaging, where for example airlines up-sell car hire, insurance and hotels, offers a significant opportunity for developing new markets.
- Interactivity, for example the use of virtual environments, offers the possibilities for visitor immersion in potential destinations.
- The sophistication and widespread adoption of mobile phones offer new opportunities. Smartphones that incorporate Internet access and global positioning systems (GPSs) enable tourists to access ICT services without any spatial constraints. Downloadable applications (Applications and Widgets) enable location-based services (LBS) to be accessed. These include locating persons, provision of routes, searching for local restaurants, shops, hotels or sights, and the provision of information about travelling conditions, such as traffic and air-departure-related data and weather.
- WiMAX technology can offer wireless broadband access over a 40-km radius as an improvement on cable and DSL. WiMAX is capable of providing Internet broadband wireless access to entire destinations and extending Internet access to tourists away from their usual network providers.
- The Internet is changing the competitive environment of the tourism industry by opening access to distribution channels, reducing barriers to entry, reducing switching costs, enabling greater consumer knowledge about prices and services, stimulating competition and generating production efficiencies.

Leisure and recreation

The multimedia revolution offers the prospect of sophisticated home-based leisure and enhancement of attractions away from home. The reduction in price and wider availability of broadband for home use are likely to accelerate changes that are already in the pipeline. In home, video on demand has led to the demise of the video rental store. Digitized movies can be stored in distant databases which can be accessed via a menu and decoding system using broadband. Interactive games which started life on floppy disks swiftly moved through CD-ROM and DVD-ROM technology to Internet-based platforms where players can interact wherever they are based.

Currently, an interesting development computer applications is virtual reality. Virtual reality is an extension of the technology of the flight simulator. It enables participants to enter a computer-generated three-dimensional environment and interact with the environment. Perhaps, the best example of this is Second Life which refers to the virtual world created and accessed on the Internet. Users create

Avatars which can be customized in any way and through these they are able to explore the second life world (called the grid) and interact with other Avatars as well as creating homes and trading.

The Wii is Nintendo's new-generation home-based games console where headsets, data gloves, data suits and other interactive devices are the passport to a variety of virtual worlds where participants can take part in a number of different games and stories. Virtual reality also affects leisure away from home. Sega has developed theme parks in Japan with interactive attractions which will let people shoot and steer their way through adventures. Disney utilizes virtual reality in its heritage theme park in Washington, DC so that visitors can experience life as a civil war soldier or as a slave. The future interpretation of heritage may well rely less on exhibits in glass cases and more on participation and interaction with virtual artefacts and virtual historical figures.

In recreation, technological developments in design and materials mean a constant upgrading of sports equipment ensuring a healthy market for replacement goods. A similar situation arises in the music sector. Changing technologies for recorded music means that consumers often have bought the same music several times – on vinyl, tape, CD and MP3. However the huge growth in downloading music from the Internet has been a continuing threat and opportunity for companies in this sector with the i-tunes store and Amazon being notable beneficiaries. The ways that consumers use newspapers and books are also undergoing a transformation. Many newspapers have an online edition and are searching for ways to collect revenue for such services. The introduction of e-books and e-book readers such as Amazon's Kindle mean that users can download books from anywhere in the world through 3G access to the Kindle bookstore. The improvement in quality and rapid fall in costs of digital photography meant that Eastman Kodak's traditional film and developing market has completely collapsed.

THE POLITICAL ENVIRONMENT

The political environment is shaped by those with political power or with the ability to influence events, and Veal (2002) offered a comprehensive examination of policy in relation to leisure and tourism. A key player in this is the party in government for the immediate period until the next election in the case of democratically elected governments. Longer term political trends are clearly difficult to predict since they depend largely upon which political party wins the next election. Although opinion polls give some indication of current party popularity they are likely to change considerably by the pre-election period and in any case do not have a good record of accuracy.

The government itself will be subject to its own operating environment and thus policy will be shaped by the economy, international relations and interest group activity. In addition, radical political groupings which operate outside of mainstream politics – such as Al Qaeda – can play a significant role in the political environment.

Given the range of possible directions of policy, scenario planning is likely to be used by organizations wishing to incorporate the political environment into their strategic planning. This involves analysing the impact of a range of possible political outcomes on an organization. Sources of information on changes in the political environment include:

- government reports
- party manifestos
- other interest groups
- changes in the law.

Government reports

Government reports and initiatives are a useful guide to policy. They set out detailed points which can affect specific organizations and give clues about the general direction of government policy. The following are examples of reports affecting the recreation, leisure and tourism sector.

The President's Council on Fitness, Sport and Nutrition (PCFSN) (USA)

The PCFSN's mission is to engage, educate and empower all Americans across the lifespan to adopt a healthy lifestyle that includes regular physical activity and good nutrition. The Council plays a key role in the development of the administration's programmatic priorities, outreach and awareness efforts to improve the health and quality of life for all Americans. Among the Council's charges are to:

- Expand national interest in and awareness of the benefits of regular physical activity, fitness, sports participation and good nutrition;
- Stimulate and enhance coordination of programs within and among the private and public sectors that promote physical activity, fitness, sports participation and good nutrition;
- Expand availability of quality information and guidance regarding physical activity, fitness, sports participation and good nutrition; and
- Target all Americans, with particular emphasis on children and adolescents, as well as populations or communities in which specific risks or disparities in participation in, access to, or knowledge about the benefits of physical activity, fitness, sports participation and good nutrition have been identified.

Source: www.fitness.gov

Low-Pay Commission report on minimum wage (UK, 1998)

One of the manifesto commitments of the UK Labour Government, elected to power in 1997, was the introduction of a statutory minimum wage. Recreation, leisure and tourism is an industry where the introduction of a minimum wage has a significant effect since low wages are characteristic across much of the sector. Over a long period there have been two key interest groups fighting the battle for the minimum wage. On the one hand, the trade union movement has long supported a minimum wage since many of its members or potential members stand to gain by it. Opposed to this have been industrial groups such as the Confederation of British Industry (CBI). It was the responsibility of the Low-Pay Commission to recommend a figure for the minimum wage. The eventual recommendation was for £3.60 an hour in 1999, rising to £3.70 in 2000. This represented a compromise between the Trade Union Congress (TUC), which lobbied strongly for a rate of more than £4.00 an hour, and the CBI submission which favoured a lower rate of £3.20.

The national long-term tourism strategy (Australia, 2009)

This strategy document sets out the key aims and objectives for the Australian tourism industry which include:

- Positioning for long-term growth by stimulating consumer demand and securing jobs.
- Developing leadership that will drive the national tourism agenda.
- Developing a research and development agenda that will inform industry and government.
- Facilitating investment and regulatory reform.
- Supporting labour and skills development that will support tourism industry needs.
- Responding to challenges including those of climate change and other external shocks.
- Ensuring product quality and service delivery commensurate with Australia's positioning as a high-value destination.
- Strengthening competitiveness with industry and product development that make the most of Australia's unique attributes.
- Measuring our performance that will track progress and support strategic priorities.

Sources: adapted from http://www.ret.gov.au/tourism/Documents/ tmc/DRET%20Tourism%20Strategy.pdf

Party manifestos

These identify policies which political parties will follow if elected to government. They are generally available in the period preceding

Table 8.1	Age characteristics		
Life stage	**Characteristics**	**Leisure income**	**Leisure time**
Child	Leisure decisions generally taken by parent	Low	High
Single	High propensity for leisure pursuits and travel. Independence asserted, budget travel popular, social aspects sought	Medium	Medium
Partnered	High leisure and tourism propensities underpinned by high income and free time	High	Medium
Full nest	Children become key preoccupation. Leisure and tourism must meet children's requirements. Costs per person important	Medium	Low
Empty nest	Children have left home. Opportunities for leisure and tourism increase. Exotic destinations and meaning of life sought	High	Medium
Old age	May lack partner, may suffer from infirmity. Safer leisure and travel pursuits sought, package holidays popular	Low	High

of home-improvement leisure activities such as DIY and gardening. Television still exerts a big influence on people's lives and 98 per cent of households have television sets. The total hours of television viewing have changed very little over the last 10 years. However, there is a marked division between social classes in their viewing habits. By 2009, 78 per cent of women and 83 per cent of men lived in households that have access to a car and the extension of the motorway network has extended the distance that can be reached within 3 hours of home. Out-of-town shopping and browsing has become a key leisure pursuit. Visitor attractions have benefited from increased mobility, and some parts of the countryside are becoming overwhelmed by their urban visitors.

Culture refers to the dominant beliefs, values and attitudes of society or a sub-grouping in society. Changing beliefs, values and attitudes affect the way in which people perceive, demand and use leisure and tourism products, for example:

- The mass availability of visual and music media has led to a large upward revision of what is ordinary. This leads to an ever-desperate search for the extraordinary in leisure and tourism pursuits.

- Culture is organic. For example, materialism has replaced religion; feminism has made inroads into sexism; hedonism has become a dominant form of social behaviour. Leisure and tourism accommodate these changes with Sunday betting, women-only swimming sessions and sex tourism in Bangkok.
- The population is becoming less culturally homogeneous and more culturally fragmented. Subcultures have particular leisure and tourism demands.
- Advertising is promoting leisure and tourism fantasies.
- Crime is increasing, as is fear of crime.
- Women have become more significant in leisure and tourism provision.

Exhibit 8.8 looks at some of the generational theories related to The Silent Generation, Baby Boomers and Generations X, Y and Z and the implications for tourism.

REVIEW OF KEY TERMS

- Environment scanning: monitoring of operating environment.
- Strategic drift: failure of business strategy to keep abreast of environment change.
- Operating environment: competitive and PEST environment.
- PEST: political, economic, sociocultural and technical environment.
- Barriers to entry: factors making entry into industry difficult.
- Monopsonist: single buyer.
- Cross-subsidization: using profits from one division to subsidize prices in another division.
- Fibreoptics: high-capacity data transmission lines using optical fibre rather than copper wire.
- CRS: computerized reservation system.
- Multimedia: combination of media sources (e.g. video), computing and communications.
- Computer-intelligent building: building use monitored and controlled by computer (e.g. security, temperature, staff location and room use).
- Digitalization: transforming images and sound to digital code for ease of storage and transmission.
- Internet provider: company which provides Internet access to PC user.

Exhibit 8.8 Generations X, Y and others

The Silent Generation, Baby Boomers and Generations X, Y and Z are all cohorts of generations who are often distinguished between in terms of different attributes. The approximate years of birth of these cohorts are as follows:

The Silent Generation	1929–1945
Baby Boomers	1946–1964
Generation X	1965–1981
Generation Y	1982–2003
Generation Z	2003–

The Silent Generation refers to the cohort that was born during the Great Depression and World War II. Its characteristics include being quite serious, conventional, and sometimes with confused morals and for women especially a desire for marriage and a family. The Baby Boomers saw a marked rise in prosperity in relation to this previous cohort and witnessed the mass communications era of the television and especially a loosening of morals and standards of public and private behaviour. This was also an era of liberalization and exploration in the arts but also one of stable jobs. Generation X is characterized by more variety, individualism, hedonism and freedom. Generation Y grew up in a somewhat different world than that of Generation X as neoliberal ideologies spread across the world. Generation Z is sometimes called the 'net generation' or 'wired generation' with easy familiarity with and adoption of communications and media technologies such as the Internet, Google, instant and text messaging, MP3 formats, mobile phones, Facebook and pocket devices.

Benckendorff et al. (2010) offer a comprehensive analysis of Generation Y in their book *Tourism and Generation Y* and identify the following travel characteristics of this cohort:

- They travel more often.
- They explore more destinations.
- They spend more on travel.
- They book more over the Internet.
- They are experience hungry.
- They are information hungry.
- They are intrepid travellers.
- They get a lot out of their travel.

- Broadband: wide bandwidth providing faster data transmission for the Internet (cf. narrowband).
- Political power: the ability to influence events.
- Scenario planning: developing plans to cope with different views of future.
- Crude birth rate: number of births per thousand population.
- Ageing population: average age of population increasing.

Data Questions

Task 8.1 **Skywars**

1995: A 14-day advanced purchase excursion fare (APEX) return flight between London Heathrow and Glasgow costs £138. It is about the same distance as Los Angeles–San Francisco which costs only £51. That is not the worst comparison. Stansted to Aberdeen is the same distance as Chicago to Kansas but at £192 costs 3 times as much. Why? Some of the difference lies in costs. It costs more to run an airline in the UK than in the USA. But the main difference must lie in the competitive environment. People's Express, the now-defunct US carrier, started the ball rolling with its $49 New York–Miami fare. These new carriers offer no frills but low fares. You might have to lug your own bags to the far side of the runway (cheap aircraft parking), pack your own sandwiches and fly a propeller museum piece, but you will not have to dig too deep into your pocket. Competition in Britain's domestic air travel market is much more limited. Since the collapse of Dan-Air in 1992 there are only three major players: BA, British Midland and Air UK. A major problem for potential entrants is the UK's crowded skies and airports. There are few slots available for competitors at London.

1999: London to Glasgow from £68 return (British Midland and easyJet) and London to Inverness from £68 return (easyJet). 'Frills included' boasts British Midland in a swipe at its low-cost rival easyJet. Suddenly the UK skies are criss-crossed with competing airlines – KLM UK, Ryanair, Debonair, BA, easyJet, Go, Virgin Express and British Midland. They are still airborne despite doubts that they could ever start up or that they would not last. But although passenger numbers are booming profits are not. The new entrants have mainly logged losses. Sir Michael Bishop, Managing Director of British Midland, predicts that not all the current airlines can survive. He points to cut-throat competition which has forced prices down to uneconomic levels, unsustainable losses being borne by some airlines and rising airport charges. He also notes that few of the budget airlines that have been started in the USA have survived bankruptcy or take-over. Several factors have helped the new airlines to gain a competitive advantage over their older-established competitors. For example, some of the new entrants managed to secure cheap use of secondary airports such as Stansted, but these are now coming up for renegotiation, and slots at main airports remain heavily oversubscribed. Their cost-cutting 'no frills' have been undermined by the established carriers competing on price but maintaining frills. Sir Michael sums up the prospects saying: 'There will be some natural consolidation at some stage. The same thing has happened in the USA, where there was a huge initial launch of low-cost airlines but then many disappeared. Five went bust last year'. He singled out Debonair as a likely victim.

1999: Debonair goes out of business.

2001: Air Asia commences operations from Kuala Lumpur International Airport.

2003: The great Ryanair seat sale: Fly for just 1 penny plus taxes.

2004: The future holiday forum publishes its report on predications for the travel industry. These include that 'within two decades a long weekend in New York will cost just £50 and a week in Australia could be as little as £99'.

2006: The first dedicated budget terminal in Asia is opened in Kuala Lumpur International Airport and is the new home for AirAsia.

2009: AirAsia is voted the world's best low-cost airline.

2010: AirAsia again voted the world's best low-cost airline.

2010: AirAsia achieved a world record by selling more than 500,000 seats in 24 hours!

2010: AirAsia's growth and size is demonstrated by its workforce (almost 7500 employees), fleet (92 aircraft) and operations (more than 65 destinations).

2011: Fly AirAsia London to Kuala Lumpur for £240 including tax.

Source: The author from cuttings (1995, 1999, 2004, 2010).

Recap Questions

1 Analyse the changes in the competitive environment of air travel using Porter's five forces analysis.

2 Examine the possible responses of legacy carriers (e.g. British Airways, Air Malaysia) to new low-cost entrants (e.g. Ryanair, AirAsia) under the following headings:

   (a) Price leadership strategies

   (b) Differentiation strategies

   (c) Withdrawal or diversification strategies

   (d) Creation of switching costs.

3 How have new entrants managed to penetrate the entry barriers found in the airline business?

4 Evaluate the future of the competitive environment of air travel.

Task 8.2 (Inter)netting the market

1994: If you need to buy a book you will have to visit a bookshop (e.g. W.H. Smith in the UK) or telephone one that does mail order.

1995: Amazon.com started the Internet market in book sales.

1997: Amazon becomes the third largest bookseller in the USA, as sales reach $148 million.

1998: W.H. Smith (UK) acquires for £9.4 million bookshop.co.uk, Europe's largest online retail site, selling more than 1.4 million book titles and 50,000 CDs, videos and computer games. This is seen by analysts as a defensive/offensive move against Amazon as well as a way to capture a growing market. In 1997, Internet sales in the UK were worth about £200,000 and are forecast to increase to £800,000 by 2000.

2002: In just 8 years, Jeff Bezos has made Amazon the world's leading online sales operation – it is even showing a profit.

2004: W.H. Smith issued a severe profits warning. Beverley Hodson, the Managing Director of the retail business, is leaving immediately, after the alert on profits wiped almost 20 per cent of the company's stock market value.

Analysts say that the growth of online sales is not necessarily at the expense of high-street booksellers – but rather that it is generating extra sales. The reasons for this are several. First, online bookstores offer substantial discounts which can be as high as 40 per cent. Second, interactive screens entice potential purchasers with lists of bestsellers, recommendations tailored to personal interests, reviews of books extracts and interviews with the authors.

Online selling costs are cheaper not only because of cheaper premises costs and lower staff costs but also because of minimal stock costs – Internet bookstores only take the stock when a customer has ordered a

Task 8.2 **continued**

book. The publishing houses are already moving towards smaller print runs and this could lead eventually printing on demand which would further reduce costs of returns and holding stocks.

However, despite all these benefits Internet bookstores are slow to move into profits: in 1997, Amazon reported losses of $28.6 million and only moved into profit in 2002.

2010: Amazon sells its Kindle e-book reader for around $200. For this customers get a device on which they can read e-books. These can be downloaded across the 3G network anywhere in the world from a large catalogue of titles.

Recap Questions

1 Account for the differences in fortunes between Amazon and W.H. Smith.
2 What are the benefits of physical, online and e-sales to consumers and retailers?
3 Conduct an opportunities and threats analysis on a named bookseller that operates high-street outlets.
4 Evaluate the impact of online and e-sales elsewhere in the leisure and tourism sector.

Task 8.3 **Grey expectations**

Whilst global greening is still in its infancy, global greying gathers momentum.

Almost everywhere in the world, from Japan to Taiwan, in Singapore, Western Europe and the USA, populations are getting older. In the western European Organization of Economic Co-operation and Development (OECD) countries, the population of over-65s will grow from a figure of 50 million in 1990 to over 70 million by 2030 – a rise of 40 per cent. With the number of people of working age falling there will be only roughly three workers per retiree compared with five at present. Within these countries, the effects of ageing will be felt most acutely in Germany, with ageing in the UK being more moderate. Since these predictions can be made with some certainty, we ought to look to the possible consequences: tax and benefit systems may need reviewing. Savings and investment patterns may alter. There will certainly be changes in demand. The market research group Mintel has identified 'third-age consumers' as a significant and distinctive market for leisure, holidays and health care. Another commentator, Ms Frankie Cadwell of a New York advertising firm, Cadwell Davies Partners, expresses surprise that European companies have been much slower to address the needs of this market than their US counterparts. Her firm specializes in selling to the over-50s.

Finally, older populations may be less innovative, more conservative and have a less adaptive labour force. If this is so, there may be some shift in competitive advantage towards those newly industrializing economies where the average age is lower, such as China, Brazil and India.

Source: The author from news cuttings.

Recap Questions

1 To what extent is it true that population trends can be predicted with certainty?

2 'Economists predict that demographic restructuring could alter patterns of consumption, production, employment, savings, investment and innovation'. Use these headings to predict how a named recreation, leisure or tourism organization might be affected by demographic change.

3 Why might ageing lead to a competitive disadvantage, and which countries are likely to be affected by this?

MULTIPLE CHOICE

1 Which of the following is not one of Porter's five competitive forces?
(a) The power of suppliers.
(b) The power of buyers.
(c) The power of buyers.
(d) The power of negotiators.

2 Which of the following does not represent a barrier to entry for new firms in an industry?
(a) Perfect competition.
(b) Natural monopoly conditions.
(c) Economies of scale.
(d) Capital requirements.

3 Which of the following is not true?
(a) An ageing population can be caused when the birth rate exceeds the death rate.
(b) Italy has an ageing population.
(c) An ageing population tends to be more conservative and less risk-taking.
(d) Ageing populations are typical in less economically developed countries.

4 Which of the following is not generally true of left-wing governments?
(a) They favour minimum wage legislation.
(b) They favour minimal state interference.
(c) They wish to reduce inequality of income.
(d) They wish to provide a comprehensive welfare state.

5 Which of the following statements is not true?
(a) Technological advances tend to reduce an organization's LRAC curve.
(b) Technological advances can bring opportunities and threats for leisure organizations.
(c) Airport operators often have strong supplier power.
(d) Horizontal integration can secure distribution channels.

REVIEW QUESTIONS

1 How does strategic drift occur?

2 Which sectors of the recreation, leisure and tourism industry are currently secure from new entrants?

3 Where is supplier power high in the leisure and tourism industry?

4 What are barriers to entry? Identify entry barriers for airlines and hotels.

5 What factors tend to create a high degree of competitive rivalry?

6 What effects might minimum wage legislation have on the leisure and tourism sector?

7 What is an ageing population? Why is the population in some countries ageing? What are the consequences of this for leisure and tourism organizations?

8 How are changes in lifestyles and attitudes affecting leisure and tourism?

9 Is home-based recreation an opportunity or a threat?

Websites of interest

British Airways: www.ba.com

TUI Travel: www.tuitravelplc.com

Delta Airlines: www.Delta.com

Lastminute.com: www.Lastminute.com

Trip Advisor: www.tripadvisor.com

Virgin Galactic: www.virgingalactic.com

The President's Council on Fitness, Sport and Nutrition: www.fitness.gov

Tourism Concern: www.tourismconcern.org.uk

AirAsia: www.airasia.com

Thomas Cook: www.thomascook.com

Geohive (population data): www.Geohive.com

The economic environment

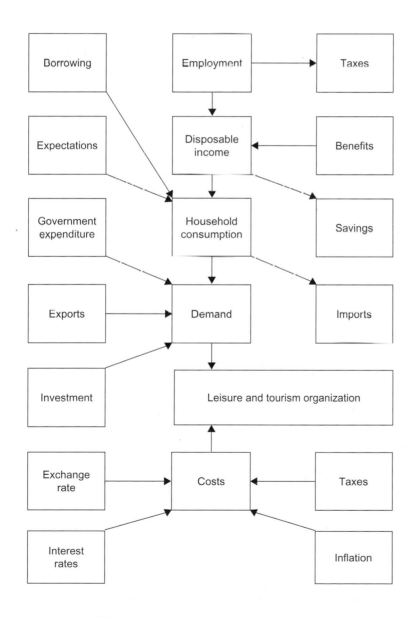

Objectives and learning outcomes

National economies are characterized by upswings and downswings. The UK, for example, witnessed the boom years of the mid-1980s – characterized by rising profits – as well as the profound recession of the early 1990s – characterized by rising bankruptcies. The period 1994–2007 saw the UK economy performing well, witnessing an unusually stable period of modest economic growth. So much so that the Economics Minister (and later Prime Minister) Gordon Brown declared 'an end to boom and bust'. Then in 2008 the UK, like many Western Economies (especially in Europe and the USA), was hit by the financial crisis and these economies suffered acute recessions. The UK economy suffered negative growth between 2008 and 2010. On the other hand, the economy of China has demonstrated rapid economic growth (often up to 15 per cent per annum). It escaped the 2008 financial crisis with continued growth (albeit at a lower level). The Australian economy (largely helped by its south-east Asian neighbour economies) also escaped the global recession of 2008. At the same time, the Japanese economy has languished in a prolonged period of stagnation.

Figure 9.1 charts the path of the UK economy over recent years. It is clearly important for organizations to monitor their economic environment carefully. Managers who read the rapid growth of the UK economy between points *A* and *B* as being normal and sustainable may well have instigated optimistic and expansionary strategic plans. These plans may have proved ruinous as the economy nose-dived between points *B* and *C*. This squeezed organizations as each recession caused a fall in demand and sales revenue.

Exhibit 9.1 illustrates the effects of changes in the economy on recreation, leisure and tourism attractions in the UK and Ireland. This chapter considers the variables in the economy that affect leisure and tourism organizations and the causes of changes in these variables. It also peers tentatively into the future and summarizes the features of an opportunities and threats analysis.

By studying this chapter, students will be able to:

- identify the key variables in the economy which affect leisure and tourism organizations;
- identify and utilize information sources;
- analyse the impact of changes in economic variables on leisure and tourism organizations;
- explain the interrelationship between key economic variables;
- understand and analyse the causes of change in the economic environment;
- appreciate the use of CGE modelling;
- understand and evaluate government economic policy and the significance of the budget;
- understand the global economic environment;
- utilize economic forecasts with due caution;
- conduct an opportunities and threats analysis.

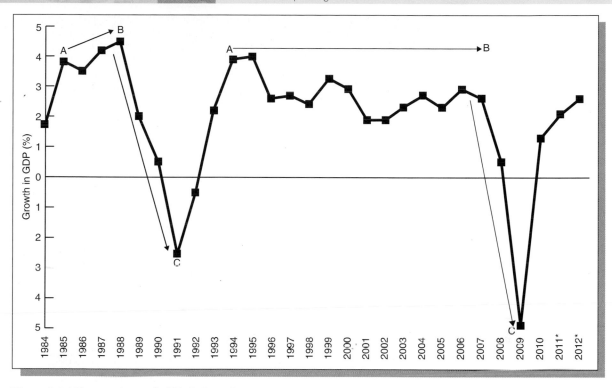

Figure 9.1 UK economic growth. '*' indicates estimate. *Source: Office for National Statistics, Economic Trends.*

Exhibit 9.1 Leisure ups and downs

1991: The Tower of London and other leading attractions are suffering in the recession, the English Tourist Board reported. The tower was visited by 1.9 million people last year (1991), 16 per cent fewer than in 1990.

Source: The Independent (10 August 1992).

1991: Tussauds Group (a major UK leisure group) had a tough trading year. The Gulf War and the recession affected visits to tourist attractions and the spending of those who did visit was less than 1990 levels. For the group as a whole, attendances were therefore lower than in the previous year, and profits down 44 per cent to £8 million.

Source: Pearson PLC: Annual Report (1991).

1993: Attendances, turnover and operating profits of the Tussauds Group reached new heights in 1993. Operating profits reached £14.1 million, an increase of 34 per cent. Attendances at Alton towers reached an all time high and there were improved attendances at Madame Tussauds in London. With continuing improvement in the UK economy, trading prospects for 1994 and beyond are encouraging.

Source: Pearson Group Annual Report (1993).

1999: In the UK, bookings for winter 1998–1999 are currently 6 per cent ahead of the previous year. To date the overall bookings taken in the UK for the next summer is 5 per cent ahead of the position achieved at the same time last year.

Source: Airtours Annual Report (1999).

Exhibit 9.1 continued

2001: London continues to be one of the most popular cities for overseas tourists with 11.5 million visitors in 2001, although there was a drop of 13 per cent between 2000 and 2001, and a 15 per cent drop in overseas visitor spending. The weak global economy and the effect of the Foot and Mouth outbreak were partially responsible, but there was also the impact of the September 11 terrorist attacks.

Source: National Statistics website: www.statistics.gov.uk

2002: Last year (2002) was a good year for the (UK) leisure industry, seeing the strongest growth – 4.8 per cent in real terms reaching £187billion in value – since 1998. ... Household demand has been very strong in the UK despite slowing growth in the GDP and reduced share prices. In this sense the UK economy stands out from other industrial economies, except for the USA and France.

Source: Gratton and Kokolakakis (2003).

2002–2007: Overall the (UK) leisure economy will grow by 15 per cent in real terms over the period 2002–2007.

Source: Gratton and Kokolakakis (2003).

2009: Aer Lingus suffers losses of almost 93 million euros in the first 6 months of 2009. The outlook was described as being 'extremely challenging' with the expectation that any recovery in the Irish economy will take until 2011 at the earliest.

Source: TravelMole (www.travelmole.com), 2009.

2010: Travel at lowest level for almost a decade: Britons took fewer trips last year than at any time since 2001 and spend on overseas travel was less than in 2005, according to a new report from market intelligence provider Key Note.

Source: TravelMole (www.travelmole.com), 2010.

WHAT ARE THE KEY VARIABLES?

The economic environment affects organizations in the leisure and tourism sector in two main ways. First changes in the economic environment can affect the demand for an organization's products and second changes may affect an organization's costs. Additionally background factors such as share and property prices may affect organizations. These three areas will be discussed in turn.

THE ECONOMIC ENVIRONMENT AND DEMAND

The key macroeconomic factors affecting demand for recreation leisure and tourism industries are:

- household consumption
- export and import demand

Plate 9 What economic factors are keeping the tourists at home? *Source. The author.*

Table 9.1 US Changes in real GDP and Household Consumption				
	2006	**2007**	**2008**	**2009**
Real GDP	2.4	2.3	−2.8	0.2
Consumption	3.3	1.8	−1.9	0.2
Source: US Treasury Office of Economic Policy (http://www.ustreas.gov).				

- government expenditure
- investment.

Household consumption

Household consumption (or spending) can be defined as the total expenditure on goods and services for immediate consumption. Thus the level of household consumption is a key element in determining the demand for goods and services in the leisure and tourism sector. Table 9.1 shows changes in real GDP and household consumption in the USA 2006–2009. Notice that the recession can be seen clearly in the data. GDP (a measure of the value of output produced in the economy) fell by 2.8 per cent in 2008. The fact that the whole economy shrank meant that households had less money to spend and household consumption also fell by 1.9 per cent. However, care needs to be taken in interpreting household consumption statistics.

Household consumption can be measured at current prices (sometimes referred to as 'money household consumption') or at constant prices (sometimes referred to as 'real household consumption'). An organization basing its business planning Household Consumption at current prices data might draw false and overly optimistic conclusions about the state of the economy. This is because household consumption at current prices includes the effects of inflation on household consumption. However, household consumption at constant prices has had the inflationary element removed and is therefore a more useful guide:

Real household consumption
= money household consumption − inflation

To understand fully the movements in household consumption we need to consider its determinants. The main determinants of household consumption include:

- real household's disposable income
- employment and wages
- taxes and benefits
- borrowing and savings and interest rates
- expectations.

Real household's disposable income

The main determinant of consumers' expenditure is the amount of income earned. Figures for national income can be an important source here, but real household's disposable income provides a more useful guide. To understand real household's disposable income we need to consider the meaning of the terms 'real' and 'disposable'. First, we are generally more interested in real income rather than money income since the former has had the effects of inflation removed. Therefore:

Real income = money income − inflation

Second, disposable income can be defined as the amount of income left after deduction of direct taxes (such as income tax and national insurance contributions), and the addition of state benefits (such as child benefit and unemployment benefit). In other words, it is the amount of income available for spending:

Real household's disposable income
= real household's income − taxes + benefits

Table 9.2 records recent data for per capita real household's disposable income for selected countries in the EU. Notice that this is per capita (or per person) data meaning that each county's total household disposable income has been divided by the number or

Table 9.2 Real adjusted gross disposable income of households per capita (selected EU countries, euros)

Country	2006	2007	2008	2009
Czech Republic	12,276	13,332	13,533	13,527
Hungary	11,408	11,385	11,542	10,990
Netherlands	20,359	21,632	21,591	21,492
Estonia	9,541	10,782	11,079	10,983
All EU	18,216	18,976	19,292	18,967

Source: Eurostat (www.epp.eurostat.ec.europa.eu).

Table 9.3 Unemployment in OECD countries

Country	2007	2008	2009	2010*
Australia	484,392	482,514	648,790	646,472
Iceland	4,150	5,525	13,075	na
US	7,077,667	8,924,250	14,264,580	14,843,000
UK	1,622,500	1,754,833	2,365,167	2,421,000
Japan	2,568,333	2,650,000	3,355,833	3,290,000
Spain	1,835,167	2,600,083	4,151,000	4,800,000
Ireland	101,250	141,583	259,000	297,000

Source: OECD (http://stats.oecd.org).
na, not available.
*Estimate.

persons in the population of the country. Again the data shows the effect of the recession where the data for the EU as a whole as well as the countries of the Czech Republic, Hungary, The Netherlands and Estonia shows a decline in 2009.

Employment and wages

The change in the income component of real household's income is determined by the level of employment and the amount of wages and salaries earned. As the level of employment in the economy grows, so generally does the level of income. Conversely a rise in unemployment is likely to cause a fall in incomes and spending power. Table 9.3 shows recent fluctuations in the level of unemployment in some of the OECD countries. It can be seen that unemployment levels rose in all of the countries in this table between 2007 and 2010, reflecting the effects of the global recession on many national economies. Some countries were particularly hit by the recession and these include Iceland, Spain and Ireland where unemployment trebled or nearly trebled. These high levels of unemployment depress levels of income and this in turn feeds into lower levels of household consumption and less sales. The level of unemployment has several effects on firms in the recreation, leisure and tourism sector. High unemployment has a detrimental effect on household spending and confidence. Ironically, it provides individuals with more leisure time, but with reduced spending power to enter leisure markets. Even those who have kept their jobs often face wage freezes or reductions in times of severe economic crises.

Taxes and benefits

Changes in taxes and benefits can cause significant changes to the disposable element of disposable income. For example, deductions for income tax in the UK start at 0 per cent with most people paying 25–40 per cent of income, rising to 50 per cent for top earners. Table 9.4 illustrates differing rates of income tax from around the world ranging from 0 per cent in Monaco to 59 per cent in Denmark. On the other hand, most countries also operate systems of benefits which can add to disposable income. These may include tax credits for low-income earners, and credits for dependent children. It is not surprising that Denmark has some of the best levels of social welfare in the world.

In addition to household disposable income, the amount consumers actually spend depends on the following factors:

- borrowing, saving and interest rates
- expectations.

Table 9.4 Taxation rates, 2011			
Country	**Income tax**		
	Corporate rate (%)	**Personal rate (%)**	**Sales tax (%)**
Australia	30	17–45	10 (GST)
China	25	5–45	17
Denmark	25	38–59	25
Hong Kong	16.5	2–17	–
Monaco	33.33	0	19.6
Russia	20	13	18
Saudi Arabia	20	20	–
Singapore	17	3.5–20	7 (GST)
Spain	30	24–43	18
UK	28	0–50	17.5
USA	15–35	15–35	–

Source: Worldwide Tax (www.worldwide-tax.com).

Borrowing, saving and interest rates

Borrowing enables households to spend in excess of their current disposable income. The level of borrowing depends on several factors including the ease of obtaining credit, future income and interest rates. Many organizations offer in-house credit facilities in order to increase the demand for their products.

Interest rates have an important effect on household consumption. In general, lower interest rates tend to stimulate household consumption for two reasons. First, at lower interest rates borrowing becomes cheaper and thus more credit is taken out. At the same time households with mortgages (loans to buy houses) find their monthly repayments falling thus leaving more money available for spending. Second, low interest rates make savings less attractive and savings may tend to fall. During the run up to the 2007 financial crisis credit became easier to obtain in many countries. This was particularly so in the USA with the explosion of so-called sub prime mortgages. On the other hand, the period following the banking crisis after 2007 saw a sudden reversal in credit availability and the arrival of the so-called credit crunch. Exhibit 9.2 describes this process. Of course the credit crunch becomes another factor in causing economic activity to rapidly slow

Exhibit 9.2 From credit ease to credit squeeze

From sub prime

Rising property prices in many parts of the world led to a frenzy of property demand as purchasers sought to get rich quick and a frenzy of supply as banks sought to profit from the demand for home loans. As prices increased some banks reduced their previously strict lending criteria and moved from a cautious and conservative approach to loans to a more liberal and even reckless approach. They lent not only very high proportions of asset values in loans (sometimes more than 100 per cent) but also to people who were more risky in terms of income levels and job stability. Good commissions for banks added to this credit explosion and property prices continued to rise. Sub prime loans were also offered at initial rates below the main bank rate but were contacted to reset to higher rates of interest after a couple of years.

To credit crunch

Of course when low-income borrowers were faced with higher rates they were unable to repay their loans and this led to a rising number of repossessions. This was an important factor in causing house prices to fall. Falling prices and loan defaults turned these loans into 'toxic assets' as the loan values started to exceed the underlying asset values (properties) and the loans were increasingly subject to default. This caused a liquidity crisis in banks (they started to run out of money) (especially in America) which quickly spread to the UK and beyond (especially to Iceland) through the globalized system of banks. The banking system suddenly turned from one of easy credit to one where it suddenly became very difficult to borrow money. The credit crunch had arrived.

Table 9.5 UK bank base rate

Year (October)	Base rate (%)	Year (October)	Base rate (%)	Year (October)	Base rate (%)
1987	9.50	1996	6.00	2005	4.50
1988	12.00	1997	7.00	2006	4.75
1989	15.00	1998	7.25	2007	5.75
1990	14.00	1999	5.25	2008	4.50
1991	10.50	2000	6.00	2009	0.50
1992	8.00	2001	4.50	2010	0.50
1993	6.00	2002	4.00		
1994	5.75	2003	3.50		
1995	6.75	2004	4.75		

Source: Adapted from National Statistics (www.statistics.gov.uk).

down thus fuelling the recession. The level of savings is also affected by culture, habit and income.

Table 9.5 illustrates changes in interest rates. This table goes back to 1987 because it is important to show that interest rates can be very volatile. It can be seen that interest rates peaked at 15 per cent in 1989 and troughed at 0.5 per cent in 2009. In each case these unusual interest rates were set by the government to try to influence household consumption. In 1989 the Bank of England was trying to reduce household consumption because of high inflation in the economy. In 2009 the Bank of England was trying to stimulate household consumption to avoid a prolonged recession.

The term 'interest rates' can be misleading since there are many interest rates in the economy. The bank base rate which is quoted in Table 9.5 is the rate to which many other interest rates are referenced. Taking 1993 as an example, bank base rate was 6.0 per cent. Rates paid to savers in building society ordinary share accounts would be around 2 per cent. Mortgage rates would be around 8 per cent, whilst interest charges on credit cards would be about 23 per cent. A change in the bank base rate will trigger a change in the whole structure of interest rates. The reasons behind changes in interest rates are discussed later in this chapter.

Expectations

Expectations (or business confidence) refers to the degree of optimism or pessimism with which consumers and business people view the future. Expectations have a profound effect on the economy because they tend to deliver self-fulfilling prophecies. When consumers feel optimistic about the economy they tend to spend more and they thus

Exhibit 9.3 Changing expectations

1994: The most pessimistic level of confidence since April 1990 was revealed by a Gallup survey conducted in March.

1994: 42 per cent of those questioned felt that their financial position would deteriorate over the next year.

Source: The author, from Gallup data.

1998: The Dun & Bradstreet survey on business confidence questioned 1400 finance and managing directors in June. It showed business confidence has hit its lowest level since the end of the last recession. Senior analyst Mr Philip Mellor said: 'As more firms expect further increases in interest rates, so gloom has spread from exporters into the domestic economy. For the first time in years the survey has shown a severe drop in confidence among the service, retail and wholesale sectors.'

Source: The author, from Dun & Bradstreet survey.

2004: According to a survey by the Woolwich bank millions of people still believe that the housing boom will continue. The Woolwich found that 53 per cent of people expect house prices to increase significantly in 2004. Of that number, 34 per cent believe they will rise by up to 10 per cent, while the rest expect an increase of more than 10 per cent.

Source: The author, from Woolwich survey.

2010: Gallup's Economic Confidence Index found 48 per cent of Americans rated current economic conditions as 'poor' and think economic conditions are 'getting worse'.

Source:http://www.gallup.com

cause the economy to grow. Conversely, when they feel pessimistic about the economy they tend to spend less and thus they may prolong the recession that is causing their pessimism. Expectations tend to be influenced by recent experience, by the mass media, by asset prices (particularly property prices) and by the level of unemployment. Measuring expectations is often done by way of surveys, as illustrated in Exhibit 9.3.

Export and import demand

Not all of household consumption results in demand for the goods and services of domestic firms. Some household consumption is spent on imports and so this expenditure is lost to the domestic economy. For the recreation, leisure and tourism sector this can be a significant amount. The demand for imports is affected by overseas costs, quality and uniqueness and the exchange rate. On the other hand, some demand for the goods and services of domestic firms arises from overseas customers in the form of exports. Exports generate additional expenditure to domestic economies. The demand for exports

Exhibit 9.4 Japan and the tiger economies in recession

The economies of south-east and far-east Asia managed to avoid the worst of the global downturn in 2008 but 10 years earlier the world's economic prospects were reversed: In 1998 Japan and the tiger economies of Asia, for years the envy of the world, finally saw their economies suffer major downturns.

The domino effect was started when Thailand devalued its currency in 1997 and, one by one, neighbouring countries and trading partners dragged one another down. By 1998 Japan, the world's second largest economy, was in recession. Elsewhere, Russia defaulted on its debts and Brazil suffered a major devaluation in its currency.

The effects of this on the leisure and tourism industry were mixed. In the countries suffering from recession, domestic demand for leisure and tourism diminished considerably as real disposable incomes fell. For some countries, currency devaluations caused an increase in the inflow of tourists who were able to obtain better value for money. Leisure and tourism outside of these countries was affected mainly by the Japanese recession. Japan traditionally was a high-spending country on tourism abroad. So destinations that were previously dependent on visitors from Japan were affected.

More serious consequences would have resulted if the economic effects of economic problems in Asia, Russia and South America had spread and caused a simultaneous recession in Europe and the USA. The leisure and tourism industries would have been early casualties of such a global recession.

Source: The author.

is similarly affected by relative costs, quality and uniqueness, the exchange rate and the prosperity of overseas economies. Exhibit 9.4 illustrates a period of economic recession which centred on Japan and the 'tiger economies' of Asia in the late 1990s which had impacts for example on tourist destinations that are dependent on Japanese tourists.

Uniqueness in terms of cultural heritage, nature, landscape or climate can be important in determining tourism demand to various countries. Similarly low production costs and a favourable exchange rate mean that China, Thailand and Vietnam are significant suppliers of leisure goods such as PCs, laptops, games, mobile devices, cameras and sports equipment.

Government expenditure

Leisure and tourism organizations which are sensitive to changes in government expenditure are those which depend upon government for their income. Examples of these include arts organizations such

Exhibit 9.5 German museum victim of recession

As in many parts of the world the global recession has hit the port of Hamburg in Germany. The economic crisis has caused a fall of 6 billion euros in tax revenue for Germany's biggest port whose wealth relies on global trade. This has prompted Hamburg's mayor Christoph Ahlhaus to make savings of 510 million euros a year in the city's expenditure. High on the list of casualties is the cultural leisure sector where the city is reducing funding for the arts forcing theatres into crises, closing a museum and making libraries reduce their opening hours.

Hamburg's principal theatre is the Deutsches Schauspielhaus. It has had 1.22 million euros cut from its 2011–2012 budget and is likely to have to close its youth-theatre project and shut many of its workshops. Hamburg's main museum is also affected. The Altonaer Museum focuses on regional cultural history. But the museum has been identified for closure in order to save around 3.45 million euros in government spending.

Torkild Hinrichsen, the director of the museum commented:
'It will be the first time since World War II that a museum of this size has been closed in Germany.'

as museums, community sports organizations and national and local tourist marketing organizations. The level and detail of government expenditure tend to reflect two things. These are the state of government finance and the political party in power.

When government finances are in deficit it is often 'soft' areas of expenditure such as the arts that are cut in order to reduce public spending. This is because it is very difficult to reduce core areas of government spending such as education and social security. A change in government can also change the economic fortunes of leisure organizations that are dependent on government subsidy. Right-wing governments generally attempt to reduce public spending, whilst left-wing governments are more likely to support leisure organizations that bring benefits to the community. Exhibit 9.5 shows a typical example of how national and state governments around the world, faced with substantial budget cuts, have reduced expenditure on publicly funded leisure programmes.

Investment

Some organizations do not supply goods and services to consumers, but specialize in supplying capital goods to other firms. Thus the aircraft manufacturer Boeing, selling to airlines and tour operators, finds demand for its products is sensitive to the level of investment in the economy. This in turn is affected by demand for goods and services as well as interest rates which have an impact on investment funding costs.

THE ECONOMIC ENVIRONMENT AND COSTS

The key macroeconomic factors affecting costs of recreation, leisure and tourism goods and services are:

- interest rates
- inflation
- the exchange rate
- indirect taxes.

The effects of changes in interest rates have been discussed earlier with reference to household consumption. However, interest rates also affect firms' costs, particularly those with significant borrowings.

Inflation can be defined as a general rise in the level of prices in an economy. Leisure organizations operating in high inflation economies will face regular increases in their input prices – particularly labour and raw material costs.

The exchange rate is the price of the domestic currency in terms of foreign currencies. Where imports form a substantial component of a good or service, changes in the exchange rate can have an effect on production costs. A fall in the exchange rate of the US dollar against foreign currencies will make imports into the USA more expensive. This would affect retailers of recreation and leisure equipment and clothing much of which is imported from the Far East.

Indirect taxes are taxes paid indirectly to the government. They are paid first to a third party – generally a retailer. In the USA, sales tax and in the European Community, value-added tax (VAT) are each examples of indirect taxes (see Table 9.4). Any increase in indirect taxes will generally cause an increase in prices. Exhibit 9.6 records the introduction of new taxes on air travel. There is considerable protest from the airline industry over these taxes. In particular they argued that, since surface transport is not subject to such a tax, it may cause a loss of passengers. This is particularly likely on routes such as London to Paris, where the rail service Eurostar offers a close substitute to air travel. Additionally UK airlines operating out of Heathrow London argue that the UK taxes will mean that business is lost to competing hubs such as Schipol in The Netherlands where air taxes have been abolished.

MODELLING LEISURE AND TOURISM

I–O models

I–O tables are used to create a set of accounts that show the industries that make up the economy. They show how these industries are linked together through purchase and sales activity. They show for each

Exhibit 9.6 Taxes take off on air travel

2004: The UK Government introduced a new tax, air passenger duty (APD), at £5 for short-haul flights and £20 for long-haul flights.

2008: Air Passenger Tax introduced in the Netherlands.

2009: The Netherlands scraps its Air Passenger Tax.

2009: Ireland introduces an airport tax.

2010: The UK Government introduced a new banding system to relate the tax more closely to distance travelled (based on the distance from London to the capital city of a destination) as well as the class of travel. Under these rules APD for economy-class travellers will increase from £10 to £11 per passenger on short-haul flights, from £40 to £45 on medium-haul flights, from £40 to £50 on extended-haul flights and from £40 to £55 on long-haul flights. Prices for passengers in premium-economy cabins will rise by up to a further £30.

2011: Germany introduces a tax on air travel.

industry from which other industries purchases are made from and sales are made to. They therefore provide a picture of the complex relationships that exist between different industries in the economy and help identify complex supply chains. I–O tables are organized in matrix form. The columns of each matrix show the inputs required by each industry from other industries and the rows show the sales of output from each industry to other industries. I–O models can be used by tourism and leisure economists amongst other things to show how changes in economic variables impact on different industries in the economy through supply chains.

CGE models

CGE modelling has become increasingly popular as a way of predicting the effects of changes in economic variables on the tourism sector as well as the impacts of tourism on employment, GDP, exports, etc. It involves describing the relationships between economic variables as a series of solvable, linked mathematical equations. CGE models are constructed as a series of interlinked sectors – production, consumption, trade and government – each with their own formulae and behavioural characteristics. Once established the model can be expressed as a computer programme and used to examine a variety of scenarios such as:

- changes in the exchange rate;
- the introduction of a tourism tax;
- changes in interest rates;
- the impacts of tourism expenditure on employment;

Table 9.6 Characteristic of economic cycles

	Upswing/boom	Downswing/recession
Unemployment	Falling	Rising
Profits	Rising	Falling
Household spending	Rising	Falling
Consumer borrowing	Rising	Falling
Imports	Rising	Falling
Inflation	Rising	Falling
Expectations	Optimistic	Pessimistic
Economic growth	High	Low/negative
Can lead to ...	Hyper-inflation	Recession

- the effects of crises (e.g. 9/11) on tourism (Blake & Sinclair, 2003);
- changes in visitor numbers;
- impacts of tourism on poverty reduction;
- the effects of government policy changes;
- the introduction of carbon taxes.

ECONOMIC CYCLES AND GOVERNMENT POLICY

Economic cycles

The economic environment is rarely stable. Rather, as indicated in Figure 9.1, economies are subject to economic cycles demonstrating upswings and downswings in economic activity. Sometimes the downswings are prolonged causing deep recessions such as the great depression of the 1920s, the Japanese recession of the late 1990s and the near-global recession of 2008. Equally the upswings may cause an economy to become overheated causing high or hyper-inflation and an unsustainable boom in imports. Table 9.6 summarizes the key characteristics of upswings and downswings.

The economist John Maynard Keynes (1883–1946) was important in bringing an understanding to the analysis of economic cycles. First, he analysed their causes. In particular he demonstrated the circular flow of income around economies. The circular flow of income is illustrated in Figure 9.2. Here the economy is divided into *households* and *firms*. Households provide firms with *factors of production* (especially labour) in return for *factor incomes*. This income is

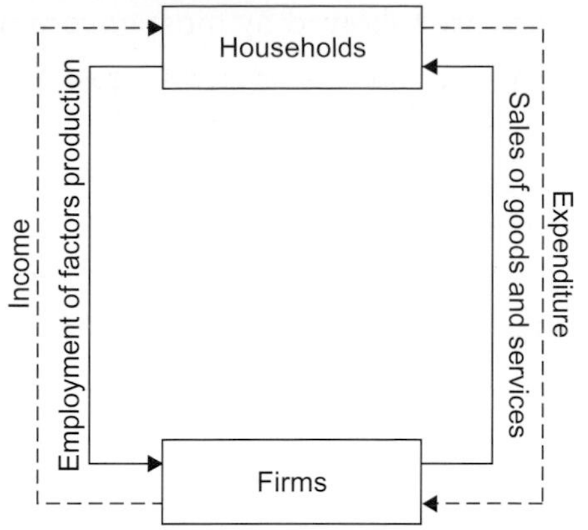

Figure 9.2 The circular flow of national income and expenditure.

used on *expenditure* on *goods and services* produced by firms. The dotted line represents *money flows* and the solid line represents *physical flows*. This diagram can show, for example, how a downswing could occur. If unemployment rose, households would have less income and their expenditure would fall. This would mean less demand for goods and services so firms would cut back production and employ less factors of production causing unemployment to rise further and the cycle to repeat in a downward direction.

Second, he argued that there is no reason that economies should be naturally stable in a virtuous state of growth or that full employment was the norm. Instead, he showed how economies might get stuck in a recession with persistent and high levels of unemployment. Third, he showed how governments could intervene in the economy with a view of making economic cycles less pronounced and attempting to generate full employment.

Much of the period after 1940 has been characterized by government attempts to manage the macroeconomy. Crudely speaking in Keynesian terms the government would attempt to stimulate the economy to offset a slump and to cool-down the economy to counter a boom. It would do this by adjusting its own spending and attempting to influence household spending. However, Keynesian policies were criticized in the 1970s with the onset of stagflation (high inflation and high unemployment). Opponents of Keynesianism argued against government intervention arguing instead that only a return to free markets (less trade union power, lower taxes, more competition and less state ownership) could deliver economic growth without inflation.

Government economic policy

It is impossible to understand changes in the external economic environment without consideration of the government's role in the economy. This in turn can be understood in terms of aims and policies.

The following aims are followed by most governments:

- low inflation
- low unemployment
- balance between government spending and income over the medium term (balanced budget)
- balance between overseas earnings and expenditure (balanced trade)
- economic growth.

However, different governments have different priorities among these objectives. Right-wing (Conservative/Republican) governments, for example, put control of inflation and a balanced budget at the top of the list. Left-wing (Labour, Liberal and Democrat) governments generally have full employment as their top priority. It must also be recognized that these aims are sometimes conflicting (in particular full employment often goes hand in hand with higher inflation). Also, as elections occur, policy aims are often distorted towards short-term reductions in taxation.

Economic policy refers to a set of measures designed to affect the economy. Classic Keynesian policies can be divided into:

- *Fiscal policy*: This uses changes in the level of taxation or government spending to influence the economy.
- *Monetary policy*: This uses changes in interest rates, and thus the cost of borrowing, to influence the economy.

A Keynesian recipe for managing a recession would utilize each of these. Fiscal policy would be expansionary with a reduction in taxes (to stimulate household expenditure) and an increase in government spending. Monetary policy would reduce interest rates to stimulate spending. However, an increase in spending and a reduction in taxes meant that the government budget would fall into deficit which could cause other economic problems – particularly inflation.

Economic environment and government policy 1985 – present: the case of the UK

An analysis of the UK economic environment over the past two decades gives a useful insight into the cyclical nature of the economy showing changes in key economic indicators as well as government tactics to manage the economy.

Table 9.7 shows changes in the main indicators for the UK economy since 1986, and four distinct phases can be identified.

1986–1988: boom

It can be seen that the UK economy grew strongly in the period 1986–1988, and unemployment which was at a high level of over 3 million fell. This was despite the fact that monetary policy was generally quite

Table 9.7 The UK economy: selected indicators

	1986	1988	1990	1992	1994	1996	1998	2000	2002	2004	2006	2008	2010
Growth (%)	3.6	4.5	0.6	−0.5	3.9	2.6	2.7	2.3	2.4	2.7	2.9	0.5	1.3
Inflation (%)	3.4	4.9	9.5	3.9	2.5	2.4	1.5	3.0	1.7	3.0	3.2	4.0	3.2
Current balance (£ billion)	−3.6	−19.8	−22.2	−13.0	−6.7	−7.0	−20.9	−19.5	−19.0	−24.9	−44.9	−23.7	−36.0
Unemployment (million)	3.2	2.4	1.6	2.7	2.5	2.1	1.8	1.6	1.5	1.6	1.7	1.7	2.4
Rate of interest (%)	13	13	14	7.0	6.25	6.0	6.0	5.8	3.9	4.75	4.75	4.5	0.5
Government borrowing (£ billion)	−0.8	−0.35	−11.6	−40.5	−47.3	−32.4	−0.84	13.9	−20.1	−41.8	−35.3	−68.5	−180.1
£/$	1.5	1.8	1.8	1.8	1.5	1.6	1.6	1.5	1.5	1.9	2.0	1.5	1.6
£/€	1.5	1.5	1.4	1.3	1.3	1.2	1.5	1.6	1.6	1.5	1.5	1.5	1.2

Source: Adapted from Office for National Statistics, Economic Trends, Barclays Bank Review.
Notes: Rate of interest: 3-month interbank. (−) = borrowing requirement, (+) = repayment.

tight during this period. The purpose of tight monetary policy and high interest rates was to suppress inflation. The rationale behind this policy was first that high interest rates reduced consumer demand by making credit expensive, and second that import prices were kept low as high interest rates stimulated the demand for sterling and kept the exchange rate high. However, the government reduced interest rates in 1987 and also relaxed fiscal policy. The 1987 budget cut the basic rate of income tax to 27 per cent and the 1988 budget made a further cut in income tax to 25 per cent and scrapped higher rates of income tax from 60 to 40 per cent. The result of this loosening of monetary and fiscal policy was that economic growth became unsustainable. By 1989 inflation had risen rapidly to nearly 8 per cent, and the UK's overseas trading account showed a deficit of £26 billion.

1989–1992: bust

The rapid deterioration in inflation and foreign currency earnings meant that the government had to apply the brakes to the economy. Monetary policy was designated for this task, and interest rates were progressively increased to 15 per cent in 1989. The government used the famous phrase, 'if it's not hurting it's not working' to explain the policy. What this meant was that interest rates were going to be used by the government to slow down household consumption – mainly by making credit expensive – and that rates would continue to rise until household consumption was curbed.

Eventually the government's policy did work, but perhaps too successfully, since the economy slowed down and went into reverse, economic growth being a negative figure for both 1991 and 1992. As the recession took hold, unemployment rose quickly to reach 2.8 million by 1993. During this period government policy got into a mess. The recession, and the consequent rise in unemployment, meant less tax receipts for the government and more spending on state benefits. Thus the public sector net cash requirement increased sharply and the government had to borrow £37 billion in 1992. The high government borrowing meant that it was difficult to stimulate the economy by reducing taxes. At the same time, the government had taken sterling (£) into the exchange rate mechanism (ERM) of the European monetary system. Monetary policy was used to maintain sterling's agreed rate of exchange against European currencies. High interest rates were used to make sterling an attractive currency and thus maintain its value. Thus the recession was prolonged by high interest rates, and tax cuts could not be used to stimulate consumer spending because of high government borrowing.

1992–1994: a lucky escape

Despite all the government's efforts (interest rates were raised from 10 to 15 per cent in one day), sterling was forced to leave the ERM in September 1992. This enabled the government to relax its monetary policy and interest rates were lowered in a series of moves via 10.5 per cent in 1991 to 7 per cent in 1992. This allowed the economy to recover, led by a rise in household consumption. However, government borrowing was still high, reflecting the effects of the recession in reducing government tax income and increasing benefit payments and in 1993 the government had to borrow £46 billion. The budgets of 1993 and 1994 thus contained a series of measures to increase taxes to reduce government borrowing. They also maintained tight control on government expenditure.

1994–2007: Sustainable growth?

The period between 1994 and 2007 was a period of modest economic growth and stability in the British economy. Unusually there have been no significant crises in any of the main economic indicators. The economy entered a period of low inflation. The economic policy of the incoming Labour government in 1997 was to keep to existing public spending plans and to set up an independent monetary policy committee of the Bank of England whose task is to use interest rates to keep inflation at 2.5 per cent. This led to rises in interest rates in 1997 and 1998. The 1998 rises coincided with worries about a world recession and caused alarm amongst some policy analysts. But rates were reduced rapidly again in 1999 as inflation steadied. So throughout this period the economic picture was one of:

- low inflation
- falling unemployment
- modest economic growth
- low interest rates
- modest government budget deficit.

This period also saw some serious oil price spikes as world demand sometimes outstripped oil supplies.

2007–2010: back to bust – the financial crisis and near-global recession

The year 2007 can be added to the list of significant economic crises which include the Great Depression (1929–1935) and the Asian Economic Crisis of 1997–1998. The 13-year period prior to 2007 was a time of relative economic stability. For example, the UK and US economies were enjoying 2–4 per cent per year growth, China's economy often grew at 14 per cent per year. But by 2007, an unsustainable set of economic conditions were developing. Property price inflation was particularly evident, fuelled by overly optimistic expectations and cheap and easy availability of loans – especially sub prime loans in the USA. But the property boom faltered in the USA (as those who were on sub prime loans were moved to higher rates and defaulted on their debt) and so was soon followed by banking crises in Freddie Mac and Fanny Mae, the Northern Rock and Lehman Bros.

A domino effect occurred and the root cause of the subsequent economic crisis is easy to trace. The causes can be attributed to:

- *Overpriced assets – particularly property prices:* Property prices increased sharply in the period prior to 2007.
- *Market madness and unrealistic optimism:* Capitalist markets sometimes get overheated. Because property prices continued to rise, people wanted to buy more and more property to benefit from property inflation. This caused an unsustainable speculative bubble.
- *Deregulation of the banks:* Banks had moved from a system of strong regulation by governments to a 'light touch' regulation. The rules about how much banks could lend and the type of assets they must keep in order to be able to meet demands for cash were relaxed.
- *A change in banking culture from the conservative to the risky:* A new generation of bankers focussed on growth and profits rather than liquidity and stability. Short-term pay incentives and commissions for selling loans overshadowed long-term sustainability in the banking sector.
- *Sub prime loans:* Rising property prices were seen as the norm rather than an exception. Banks competed strongly with each other to sell more loans. 'Sub prime' loans became a popular way to sell more loans. They were sold at initial rates that were lower than prime (central bank) rates of interest as an opening inducement. Banks were also less careful about the credentials of borrowers.
- *Property crash:* It did not take much to reverse the unsustainably high prices of property. Borrowers had overstretched themselves. In particular those on sub prime rates were being moved to market rates of interest. Many could not afford these higher rates and defaulted.
- *Bad debt and toxic assets:* Banks were left with bad debt – a combination of loan defaults and insufficient asset values (as property prices fell) to cover bad debt. Some banks became bankrupt.
- *Globalization:* International connectivity enabled the crisis to spread quickly and globally.

The economic crisis caused a run on the banks. There was a serious run on the Northern Rock Bank (UK) and Lehman Brothers (USA) went bust. Share prices dropped on stock exchanges worldwide. Economic activity froze up when the credit crunch hit as banks were desperately trying to restore their assets and reduce liabilities. Two quarters of falling output in 2008 confirmed the arrival of a recession in both the UK and the USA, together with mass unemployment and a feel-bad factor. On the other hand, the period witnessed falling oil prices and exchange rate adjustments.

However, perhaps the recession was not as bad as it might have been. Governments were quick to introduce policies to prevent a more catastrophic depression on the scale of 1929. In the UK the government introduced short- and long-term economic measures: short-term measures included a stabilization and stimulus package:

- An emergency nationalization/part nationalization programme of banks in the USA, UK and elsewhere.
- A reduction of interest rates in the UK to 0.5 per cent.
- A temporary reduction in sales tax from 17.5 per cent to 15 per cent.
- 'Quantitative easing' whereby the Bank of England makes extra funds available to the banking system.

But as a result of the bank rescue package and the negative effect of the recession on government spending and tax revenues in the UK, government debt soared to £160 billion in 2010. So the government introduced long-term measure to address this unsustainable deficit which included:

- An increase in sales tax to 20 per cent.
- A 2-year pay freeze for public sector workers.
- A comprehensive spending review with cuts of £81 billion in government spending.

The recession had mainly similar effects in the USA and elsewhere in the world but put considerable strain on the Eurozone as its heavily indebted countries – the so-called PIGS group – Portugal, Italy (and Ireland), Greece and Spain fought to reduce their substantial government deficits. However, other parts of the world, notably South America, Asia and Australasia managed to avoid the global recession.

THE FUTURE

An eminent professor of economics, the Lord Maurice Peston of Mile End, cautioned against blind faith in economic forecasting, suggesting that random typing of a monkey at a keyboard would result in equally useful forecasts as those produced by complex mathematical models. However, economic forecasts are an essential part of business planning, but must be used with extreme caution, and the assumptions upon which they are made must be constantly monitored. Many forecasts now include a pessimistic outlook, an optimistic outlook and a middle range forecast.

Table 9.8 Opportunities and threats analysis

Environment	Opportunities	Threats
Competitive		
Threat of entrants		
Power of buyers		
Power of suppliers		
Threat of substitutes		
Competitive rivalry		
PEST		
Political		
Economic		
Sociocultural		
Technological		

OPPORTUNITIES AND THREATS ANALYSIS

An opportunities and threats analysis examines an organization's operating environment. The operating environment can be audited using the framework established in this and the previous chapter and this is illustrated in Table 9.8.

Once the key opportunities and threats have been established for an organization, its strategic plan can be updated to show how opportunities can be exploited and threats can be countered.

REVIEW OF KEY TERMS

- Real household consumption: money household consumption − inflation.
- Disposable income: income − direct taxes + government benefits.
- Recession: two consecutive quarters of falling output.
- Public sector net cash requirement: government spending − taxes.
- GDP: total value of output of an economy in a year.
- Economic cycle: up and down movement of economic activity.
- Fiscal policy: use of tax and government spending levels to influence the economy.
- Monetary policy: use of interest rates to influence the economy.

Data Questions

Task 9.1 **Journal article: Brent Ritchie, J.R., Molinar, C., Frechtling, D., 2010. Impacts of the world recession and economic crisis on tourism: North America. Journal of Travel Research 49 (1), 5–15**

This article investigates the impact of the economic crisis of 2008–2009 on the tourism industry of North America. It draws its research data for Canada from Statistics Canada and information bulletins from the Canadian Tourism Commission. Research on for Mexico uses official reports prepared by government agencies. Information on the USA was mainly extracted from the US Travel and Tourism Satellite Account system of the US Bureau of Economic Analysis. In comparing the three regions the authors find that whilst tourism in Canada and the USA was affected by the economic crisis, tourism in Mexico has been affected more by the swine flu pandemic, exchange rates and weather conditions than by the economic crisis itself and that for tourism in the USA the events of 9/11 had a much greater impact than the economic crisis.

More specifically the authors make the following observations:

- *Canada:* 'Leisure travel intentions, in particular, have taken a dramatic tumble. In brief, the declining economic prospects have taken a toll on Canadians' future travel plans. Survey data from late 2008 from the CTRI (Canadian Tourism Commission information) indicate that only 39.1% of Canadians plan to take a winter holiday – down from 47.5% a year earlier' (p. 8).

- *Mexico:* 'the current global economic recession has certainly had an impact on the tourism sector of the Mexican economy, although moderate. This moderate impact is basically reflected in the reduced tourist expenditures, job losses in the sector, and a reduced number of passengers on cruises and border excursionists...' (pp. 10–11).

- *USA:* 'Travel demand [for the U.S.] during the current recession is down at twice the rate of the GDP decline ... travel prices have fallen ... tourism industry employment directly related to tourism demand has fallen...' (p. 13).

Recap Questions

1 To what extent was the economic crisis of 2008–2009 a 'world recession'?
2 Identify the main effects of the economic crisis of 2008–2009 on tourism in Canada, the USA and Mexico.
3 Why did the economic crisis of 2008–2009 affect Canada, the USA and Mexico unevenly?
4 What policies might the governments of Canada, the USA and Mexico adopt to counter the effects of the recession?
5 What is the current state of the US economy? Explain any changes from the economic crisis of 2008–2009.
6 What is GDP and why does it decline in a recession?
7 What is the definition of a recession?

Data Questions

Task 9.2 **Impacts of the economic crisis (2008/2009)**

1 United Nations World Tourism Organization predictions
 (a) International tourism to stagnate or even decline slightly throughout 2009.
 (b) Amongst those most affected are the Americas and Europe as most of their source markets are already in, or entering, recession. In Asia and the Pacific the industry is expected to grow however at a slower rate than in previous years. Africa and the Middle East find themselves in a similar situation.

2 Effects on transport
 (a) Emirates Airline slows expansion during 2009 – a year seen as one of consolidation.
 (b) Virgin Atlantic is responding to a drop in demand for air travel by cutting 600 jobs.
 (c) Ryanair has been hit with a third quarter loss of €102 million, compared to a profit of €35 million in the same period a year earlier.
 (d) BA releases February passenger statistics showing a 20.2 per cent decrease in premium traffic and a 5.5 per cent fall in non-premium traffic.
 (e) Cathay Pacific posted a loss of HK$8.56 billion.
 (f) IATA figures paint bleak picture for airline industry. Industry is 'drowning in red ink', says IATA chief executive.

3 Effects on destinations
 (a) The number of people visiting tourist attractions in Amsterdam in November dropped by 13.3 per cent, says Lodewijk Asscher, Amsterdam's deputy mayor of economic affairs.
 (b) 12 per cent fewer British and American visitors came to Amsterdam via Schipol airport in November.

4 Effects on operators
 (a) Sales for the hotel breaks division, which includes Superbreak, is 10 per cent below last year.

5 Effects on hospitality
 (a) DLA Piper 2009 Europe Hospitality Outlook Report has published its findings which include:
  (i) The majority of UK hotel executives are predicting hotel chain bankruptcies in the next 12 months. Respondents cited two main reasons for their level of pessimism – the inability to raise capital in the current market and the struggling European economy.
  (ii) The poll also found that almost three quarters of respondents are witnessing a significant reduction in business travel.
 (b) A poll of 170 business travel buyers commissioned in London at the Business Travel Show revealed two fifths are downgrading accommodation.

6 How is tourism responding?
 (a) Virgin launches a seat sale with flights to New York from £279 return.
 (b) Virgin Atlantic introduce a pay freeze for staff.
 (c) Emirates announces increase reward scheme points.

(d) Bmibaby switches away from cities: beach resorts are more popular as demand for impulsive city breaks weakens.

(e) Royal Caribbean (cruises) is able to maintain booking levels but at 'significantly' lower prices.

(f) Kuoni imposes group-wide job cuts and CEO Peter Rothwell outlines a 3-year plan including strengthening electronic distribution.

(g) Dynamic packaging becomes more important and Ryanair secures a new accommodation supplier in a deal which sees 57,000 hotels available via airline's website.

(h) Moves to more upselling on websites including insurance, car hire and accommodation.

7 Broad lessons

(a) Existing strategies are often torn up in the crisis with a new focus on consolidation and tactical withdrawal.

(b) Bankruptcies inevitable.

(c) Much more selective discounting offered as there is an expectation of good deals from customers.

(d) Capacity management becomes important.

(e) Cost management is paramount.

(f) Important to understand the crisis. It offers a variety of opportunities and threats (e.g. exchange rate benefits) and should not be seen as homogeneous economic crisis.

Source: TravelMole (www.travelmole.com).

Recap Questions

1 To what extent is the economic crisis a global phenomenon?

2 What are the main impacts of the economic crisis on the leisure industries?

3 In what ways have leisure organizations sought to contain the negative effects of the economic crisis?

4 Explain how the economic crisis 'offers a variety of opportunities and threats and should not be seen as homogeneous economic crisis'.

Task 9.3 **Scenario planning**

Organizations increasingly use the method of scenario planning to anticipate changes in the external environment. This enables them to plan considered responses.

Recap Questions

1 Choose two firms in the leisure and tourism sector and analyse how they might be affected by the following scenarios:
   (a) A rise in interest rates.
   (b) A fall in unemployment.
   (c) A fall in the exchange rate.
   (d) A rise in inflation.

2 Which two of these represent the most likely scenario for the next 2 years? Explain your reasoning.

MULTIPLE CHOICE

1   Which of the following is unlikely to cause a fall in household consumption?
    (a) A rise in unemployment.
    (b) An increase in interest rates.
    (c) Pessimistic expectations about the economy.
    (d) A fall in income tax.

2   Which of the following is true of real household's disposable income?
    (a) It equals real household's income − direct taxes + benefits.
    (b) It equals real household's income − benefits + direct taxes.
    (c) It is directly determined by the level of real exports.
    (d) It equals real household's income − borrowing + savings.

3   Generally an increase in interest rates will
    (a) Reduce savings.
    (b) Increase consumption.
    (c) Decrease consumption.
    (d) Reduce an organization's costs.

4   Which of the following is unlikely during an economic boom or upswing?
    (a) Unemployment is falling.
    (b) Household consumption is rising.
    (c) Imports are falling.
    (d) Expectations are optimistic.

5   Which of the following is false?

    (a) Fiscal policy involves changes to interest rates.
    (b) Real income: money income − inflation.
    (c) Keynesian policy seeks to stimulate the economy during a downswing.
    (d) Public sector net cash requirement will rise if taxes fall and government spending rises.

REVIEW QUESTIONS

1   Households' consumption at current prices rises from £100 billion in year 1 to £110 billion in year 2. Over the same period inflation is 10 per cent. What is the level of households' consumption at constant (year 1) prices in year 2?

2   What is the definition and what are the characteristics of a recession?

3   What is the definition and what are the characteristics of a recovery?

4   Distinguish between fiscal and monetary policy.

5   What type of fiscal and monetary policy could be used to stimulate the economy in a recession?

6   What is the relationship between public sector borrowing, taxation and government revenue?

7   What is the economic outlook for:

(a) China?

(b) USA?

(c) Australia?

(d) The EU?

8   Explain the significance of the following to a named leisure or tourism sector organization:

(a) Interest rates.

(b) Exchange rates.

(c) Real disposable income.

(d) Expectations.

Websites of Interest

TravelMole: www.travelmole.com

USA Statistics: www.usa.gov

Global economic outlook: www.merrilllynch.com

Organization for Economic Development and Cooperation Statistics: www.oecd.org

European Union Statistics: http://europa.eu.int

Australian Bureau of statistics: www.abs.gov.au

Brazil Statistics www.ibge.gov.br

Canada Statistics: www.statcan.ca

New Zealand Statistics: www.stats.govt.nz

UK Office for National Statistics http://www.statistics.gov.uk

US Treasury Office of Economic Policy: www.ustreas.gov

Eurostat: http://epp.eurostat.ec.europa.eu

Worldwide Tax: www.worldwide-tax.com

PART **5**

Investment

C H A P T E R **10**

Investment in the private sector

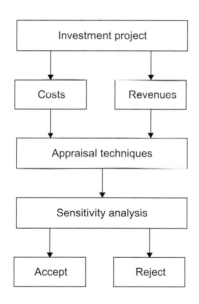

Objectives and learning outcomes

With hindsight, it is not difficult to analyse the factors that have made some private sector investment projects in the recreation, leisure and tourism sector such successes and others such dismal failures. The failures include airlines such as Swissair whilst successes include projects as diverse as films (*Lord of the Rings*), visitor attractions (LegoLand, Denmark; Port Aventura, Spain) and electronic devices (i-phone, i-player, i-pad).

However, at the planning stage, it is much more difficult to forecast the success of investments, largely because of the uncertainty surrounding the future. This chapter seeks to define the meaning of investment, consider how potential investment projects are appraised and stress the shortcomings of quantitative techniques.

By studying this chapter, students will be able to:

* define and distinguish between different types of investment;
* analyse the factors which affect an investment decision;
* utilize techniques for investment appraisal;
* understand the uncertainty surrounding investment appraisal;
* analyse the effects of investment on the economy;
* evaluate government policy with regard to investment.

DEFINITION AND EXAMPLES

In general usage people use the term 'investment' to include bank and building society deposits and the purchase of stocks and shares. Economists are more specific in their use of the term. Investment may be defined as expenditure on capital goods and working capital. Capital goods can be contrasted with consumer goods. The latter are produced because of the direct satisfaction they yield (e.g. food, magazines and clothes), whilst the former are produced because they improve efficiency of production.

Fixed capital goods consist of buildings, plant and machinery, and in the leisure and tourism sector examples include hotel buildings (see Plate 10), computer reservation and booking systems, aircraft and golf-ball making machinery. The total expenditure on such items is recorded as 'gross domestic fixed capital formation' in government statistics.

Working capital consists of stocks of raw materials, semi-manufactured goods and manufactured goods which have not yet been sold. Manufacturers monitor stocks of unsold products closely and these tend to be the key signals in a market economy to reduce or increase production. Working capital is an essential part of

Plate 10 Investment in new Beachside Luxury Accommodation, Vietnam.

Table 10.1 Private new capital expenditure (Australia) (chain volume measures) (AUS$ million)

	Buildings and structures	Equipment, plant and machinery	Total
2006–2007	39,753	48,660	88,267
2007–2008	44,284	54,539	98,671
2008–2009	55,519	57,602	113,121
2009–2010	52,531	57,069	109,600

Source: Australian Bureau of Statistics.

production, although 'just-in-time' production techniques have reduced the need for large stocks of raw materials and components to be held in factories. Expenditure on these items is recorded in government statistics as 'increase in stocks and work in progress'.

Table 10.1 shows recent changes in private new capital expenditure for Australia. This refers to the total amount of investment in new private sector capital goods. Sometimes a distinction is made between 'gross' and 'net' investment. The term 'gross' means that it covers all capital investment including the replacement of worn-out machines. The term 'net' would cover only investment over and above the replacement of worn-out machines:

Net investment = gross investment − depreciation

Table 10.1 shows a considerable fall in investment from 2008 to 2009. Some important factors affecting the level of investment include:

- households' consumption
- expectations
- amount of spare capacity
- interest rates.

Therefore, changes in the above factors should be examined for an explanation of the fall in investment in 2008 that is evident from Table 10.1. In fact, three factors contributed to the fall in investment. Interest rates were quite stable and had little effect on households' consumption or the cost of borrowing for investment projects. But the global recession meant that suppliers were left with spare capacity in the form of empty planes, unused accommodation and idle machinery and thus there was little need for additional or replacement investment. Finally, as the global recession deepened, people's expectations became more pessimistic and investment depends on optimistic expectations about future levels of income and expenditure.

Lowering interest rates is often suggested as an appropriate government policy to stimulate investment. However, it should be noted that lower interest rates will not necessarily, single-handedly, stimulate investment demand in a recession since there may already be spare capacity in an organization and expectations may remain pessimistic.

Table 10.1 presents data for private new capital expenditure using chain volume measures. This means that the data has been adjusted for inflation and is similar to what is sometimes referred to as 'real' rather than 'money' data.

FACTORS AFFECTING INVESTMENT

Investment in the private sector is undertaken to increase profitability. Since we assume that the motive of private sector organizations is the maximization of profits, such organizations will seek to invest in those projects which yield the highest return. Investment projects will incur planning, construction and running costs and yield revenue when in operation. Thus, the profitability of an investment project can be analysed by investigating its costs and revenue.

Exhibit 10.1 illustrates that a key barrier to tourism investment in Cuba by foreign firms has been the prohibition of land ownership on the island enforced by the communist government.

Cost of investment

The main costs of an investment will be:

- planning costs
- costs of capital goods

Exhibit 10.1 Foreign investment in tourism to be allowed in Cuba

The Revolution of 1959 saw a demise of Golf in Cuba and in 2010 there was only one 18-hole golf course in the whole of the island. But recently the government announced plans to allow foreigners to invest in marinas, golf courses and other land projects to help develop Cuba's tourism industry. This represents a profound change in policy as previously the government prohibited foreign ownership of land or business assets.

The tourism Minister Manuel Marrero said it was important to attract more affluent tourists to the island and exploit the tourism potential of regions that are undeveloped.

The Communist government has developed plans to grant foreigners medium- to long-term leases of land associated with investment in tourism, especially golf courses, marinas and complementary tourist investments. A number of foreign investment firms have proposed building golf courses and complexes which include luxury sea front accommodation.

Source: Adapted from the BBC (www.bbc.com)

- cost of financing investment
- running costs of the investment.

Planning costs

The planning costs of an investment include consultancy costs for technical feasibility, market research, competitor scanning, financial appraisal and overall project planning. For large-scale projects, planning costs can be considerable and add to the overall project timetable. The BAA made a substantial investment in a new passenger terminal – terminal 5 – at London Heathrow Airport. Table 10.2 shows the original timetable for the project as envisaged in 1992. It can be seen that the planning, consultation and enquiry phase represents an equivalent 5-year period to the construction phase, doubling the project timetable to 10 years. In the event this timetable underestimated the planning stages of the project and the UK government did not give the go ahead until 2001–four years later than expected. This added significantly to the costs of the project which are discussed in Exhibit 10.2. Indeed, the terminal did not actually open until 2008. Additionally, BAA wished to build a new runway (R3) at London Heathrow and accumulated substantial planning, land purchase and legal costs before the project was rejected by the new coalition government in 2010.

Costs of capital goods

The capital costs of an investment are the costs of buildings, plant and machinery. In some cases these are known costs, since there is

Table 10.2 Terminal 5 timetable

Year	Projected stage
1992	Local consultations
1992	Submission of planning application
1994	Start of public planning inquiry
1995	End of public planning inquiry
1997	Government decision expected
	Subject to planning approval being granted
1997	Start of construction
2001	Completion of phase 1 construction
2002	Opening of phase 1
2016	Terminal reaches maximum capacity

Source: BAA (1992).

Exhibit 10.2 High costs of terminal failure

1999: If things had gone according to plan, BAA's Terminal 5 (T5) would by now be a busy construction site of cranes, half-completed buildings and road links. The fact that the site is still occupied by a sewerage work demonstrates how far the project has slipped behind schedule. The year 2001 was to have seen the completion of phase 1 of the project, but it will now be the year when the government gives its final decision on whether the project is allowed to go ahead. This will push back the opening of phase 1 from 2002 to 2006, if the project is allowed. The main delay to the project has been the public enquiry which in the event has taken 3 years to hear the evidence of the BAA, local authorities, environmental campaigners and other interest groups. The overall project has an estimated cost of €2.6 billion. But the delays to the project mean that the planning and preparation costs, which have to be paid even if the project is eventually rejected, have now reached €360 million. These costs have been needed to pay for legal teams at the public enquiry, design costs of the building and the cost of land purchase.

2001: On 20 November 2001, the Government announced its decision to approve the building of Heathrow's Terminal 5 after a planning process which has cost nearly $120 million over 14 years. The cost of this process has been met mostly by BAA and BA, the two main proponents of the Terminal's development. The new terminal is expected to be completed in 2007 and project itself will cost around $3 billion.

2008: Terminal 5 opens.

Source: The author, from press reports and briefings (1999, 2004, 2008).

---

a market in commonly purchased capital goods such as computer systems, vehicles and standard buildings. For more complex investments, capital costs can only be estimated in the planning stage and for large construction projects, estimates of costs are notoriously unreliable. The original estimate for building and equipping the Channel Tunnel was £5 billion but by 1993 the figure had been revised to £10 billion. Such escalations in costs are typical of large construction projects. In the case of the Channel Tunnel, factors such as price increases in materials, increased wages, unforeseen technical difficulties in boring the tunnel, specification changes to improve safety and legal disputes over costs between Eurotunnel and the construction company Trans-Manche Link (TML) all added to the increased costs.

Cost of financing investment

Finance for investment projects may be found internally out of a company's profits, or externally from the capital markets, for example, through banks or share issues.

External funding by loans carries costs in terms of interest rates that have to be paid for the duration of a loan. These interest rates may be fixed or variable. External funding by a share issue incurs issue costs but the costs of funding (i.e. the dividend payments to shareholders) are then tied into future profits.

It might appear that internally generated funds do not carry any special costs, since a company does not have to pay interest on its own funds. However, there is an opportunity cost of using internal funds. That is, the cost in terms of other uses to which the funds could have been put. A company could put funds on deposit in the money markets and gain interest on such deposits. Thus, even where internal funds are used for investment, a notional interest rate will be used to represent their opportunity cost. In general, higher interest rates will act as a disincentive to investment.

Running costs of the investment

The running costs of an investment will include all the other costs of operating the project. These include labour costs, maintenance costs and raw material costs. New technology which reduces running and production costs can be an important cause of investment.

Revenue from investment

Total revenue from sales resulting from an investment project can be calculated by multiplying the selling price by the quantity sold, and thus the main factors affecting the revenue obtained from an investment are:

- price of output
- quantity of output sold
- other factors.

Price of output

The price of the output of an investment project will largely depend on demand and the competition in the market under consideration. This is discussed fully in Chapter 6, and in general the less competition, the more power a supplier will have to set price. Where a monopoly or near-monopoly exists, price can be producer determined (but quantity sold will reflect demand). However, potential competitors will move quickly to produce near substitutes where possible, particularly if a premium price is being charged. Where a few producers exist in a market (oligopoly or monopolistic competition), the impact of a new entrant will change the actions of those already in the market and thus lead to unpredictability. In a perfectly competitive market, prices will be driven down to reflect the lowest average costs in the industry. Thus, although a company may have market intelligence about current prices in the market where its investment is to take place, any estimate of prices in future years is likely to be very uncertain. Channel Tunnel prices, for example, changed considerably between the planning stage and the present. This reflects the changing marketing strategies of competing ferry and airline companies.

Quantity of output sold

Quantity sold will be closely related to price charged. However, it will also be related to factors including consumers' income, competitive prices and advertising. Figure 10.1 shows forecasts of passenger demand for airports in the south-east of England. These were part of the feasibility study for London Heathrow's Terminal 5. Clearly

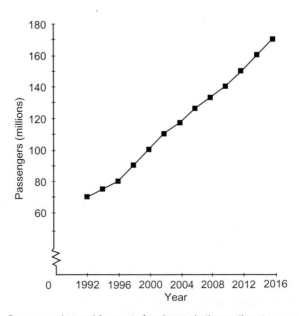

Figure 10.1 Passenger demand forecasts for airports in the southeast. *Source: BAA.*

there are a range of factors, for example, environmental pressures, taxes, fuel costs and other unforeseen shocks, which might cause the forecasts to be wrong.

The Tourism Forecasting Council (1998) developed the Tourist Accommodation Regional Demand, Investment and Supply (TARDIS) model. This is a tool to measure the interaction between the demand for and the supply of tourist accommodation to help determine the viability of proposed investment.

Other factors

Government policy may affect the revenue that derives from an investment project in several ways. First, government taxation policy may affect prices (sales taxes), or spending power (income tax) or profits (corporation tax). Second, government legislation may affect the demand for goods, and finally monopolies and mergers legislation may have an impact upon prices that can be charged.

Expectations play a key part in investment decisions. Expectations reflect views about how successful the economy will be in future years. Where investors have a pessimistic view about the future economy, they will generally defer investment decisions.

Property development is a prominent feature of much leisure and tourism investment. Whilst rental income is a part of the anticipated revenue from such developments, capital appreciation can also be an important factor. Thus, such developments are often sensitive to expectations about future prices of property.

Above all, the factors surrounding an investment decision are subject to a great deal of uncertainty. Few of the factors have known values. Current interest rates are known, and where an investment obtains funds at fixed rates, this provides a predictable element. However, where funds are obtained at variable interest rates, considerable uncertainty will exist. Similar uncertainty surrounds the final costs of complex capital projects, price of output and demand for the final good or service. These are all subject to changes in the C-PEST environments.

Knowles and Egan (2000) reviewed the impact of the combined effects of global recession and the terrorist attacks of 11 September 2001 on the international hotel industry. They argued that those hotel companies heavily dependant on the US market, particularly four- and five-star properties located in the major gateway cities, will see significant falls. First, in revenue per available room (revPAR) and second, in occupancy. From an investment point of view, Knowles and Egan argued that the major firms, which had announced significant expansion plans prior to September, are likely to be extremely cautious in their implementation. They also noted that a key factor that affects the international hotel industry is consumer confidence and that UK surveys during October 2001 recorded a decline in confidence, particularly with regard to peoples' willingness to travel.

APPRAISAL TECHNIQUES

Having identified the factors affecting the profitability of an investment, these can be used in a variety of quantitative methods to aid decision-making.

Investment appraisal reports may appear very authoritative, neatly summarizing projects in figures. However, in view of the uncertainties discussed in the previous section, care should be taken to examine the assumption on which appraisals are made. The main appraisal techniques are:

- payback method
- average rate of return
- net present value
- internal rate of return.

Payback method

This method compares investment projects by measuring the length of time it takes to repay the original investment from the revenues earned. It therefore favours projects which have the earliest payback. The key problems with this method are first that earnings that an investment may make after the payback period are not taken into account, and second revenues are not discounted so earnings within the payback period are given equal weight irrespective of the year they appear in. On the other hand, the sooner the payback, the less a project will be subject to uncertainties, and some companies may see speed of return as a priority over total return. Table 10.3 shows an example of this method and it can be seen that in this example the payback period is 3 years, when the cumulative cash flow reaches zero.

Average rate of return

This method calculates the total earnings from an investment and divides this by the number of years of the project's life. This figure is then expressed as a percentage of the capital costs of the project. For

Table 10.3 Payback method of investment appraisal (£ million)

Year	0	1	2	3	4
Costs	2.4	0.4	0.4	0.4	0.2
Revenue	0	1.0	1.2	1.4	1.4
Cash flow	−2.4	0.6	0.8	1.0	1.2
Cumulative cash flow	−2.4	−1.8	−1.0	0.0	1.2

example, if an investment project had a total cost of £100,000 and earned a total of £150,000 over 5 years, the annual earnings would be £10,000, which represents an annual average rate of return of £10,000/£100,000 or 10 per cent on the capital employed. This method also fails to discount future earnings.

Net present value

The net present value method takes into account the fact that future earnings have a lower value than current earnings. For example, £100 today could be invested at a rate of interest of 10 per cent to give £110 in a year's time. Working this backwards, £100 in a year's time is only worth £90.91 today at a rate of interest of 10 per cent. In other words, it has been discounted at a rate of 10 per cent to find its present discounted value (PDV). Discount tables exist to assist such calculations but there is also a formula for calculating PDV:

$$PDV = Rt/(1 + i)t$$

where R = return, t = year and i = rate of interest or discount rate (expressed as decimal).

Row 1 of Table 10.4 shows the net revenues of a project with an initial capital cost of £16 million in years 1–4, and row 2 shows these figures discounted to their present values using a discount rate of 10 per cent. The net unadjusted revenues sum to £19 million and thus the project appears to show a net surplus of £3 million. However, the net present value technique compares costs and revenues discounted to their net present values. The total net revenue falls to £14.55 million when discounted to present value, and the project shows the following net present value:

Costs at present value	£16.00 million
Revenue at present value	£14.55 million
Net present value	−£1.45 million

This negative figure indicates an unprofitable investment.

Table 10.4 Discounted cash flow method of investment appraisal (£ million)					
Year	**0**	**1**	**2**	**3**	**4**
Net revenue		2.0	5.0	6.0	6.0
PDV of net revenues		1.82	4.13	4.5	4.1

Note: Discount rate = 10 per cent.

Internal rate of return

The internal rate of return method also uses discounted cash flow. It calculates the discount rate that would equate the net present value of future earnings of an investment to its initial cost. This rate is called the internal rate of return. An investment will be profitable if its internal rate of return exceeds the rate of interest that has to be paid for borrowing funds for the investment, allowing a margin for risk. A feasibility study into a fixed channel link by Coopers and Lybrand and Setec Economie in 1979 concluded that the internal rate of return on the project would be between 11 and 18 per cent. When comparing investment projects, those with the highest internal rate of return will be selected.

CHANGES IN THE LEVEL OF INVESTMENT

Changes in the level of investment will be caused by changes in the costs and predicted revenues of investments. These factors are summarized in Table 10.5.

Falling investment can sometimes be attributed to high interest rates making the cost of borrowing funds to invest high, or to falling consumers' expenditure, or poor expectations about the economy in the medium term. Falling demand leaves production or service capacity underutilized and thus there is little need for new investment.

Table 10.5 Factors causing changes in investment

	Investment conditions	
	Good	Poor
Rate of interest	Low	High
Capital costs predictable?	Yes	No
Project duration	Short	Long
Price of output	Predictable	Uncertain
Market for product	Rising	Uncertain
Competition in proposed market	Limited	Competitive
Political stability	Stable	Unstable
Expectations about economy	Optimistic	Pessimistic
Sensitivity of project to shocks	Low	High
Spare capacity	Low	High

The accelerator principle

Investment activity in economies tends to be volatile, that is, subject to considerable fluctuations. One of the explanations of this is the accelerator principle.

When demand for consumer goods and services is relatively stable in an economy, much of the demand for capital goods will take the form of replacing worn-out plant and machinery. However, if demand for final goods rises and there is no spare capacity in an industry, then new machinery will have to be purchased. Thus, the demand for capital goods will significantly increase to include new machines as well as replacement machines.

Similarly, if the demand for final goods in an economy falls, firms will find they have overcapacity and too many machines. They will reduce the stock of machines to the new lower levels needed by not replacing worn-out machines, so the demand for capital goods will fall. Thus, a rise in the demand for final goods will cause an accelerated rise in the demand for capital goods, and a fall in the demand for final goods will cause an accelerated fall in the demand for capital goods. The accelerator theory helps to explain the sudden fall in investment in 2008 in response to a fall in consumer demand.

RISK AND SENSITIVITY ANALYSIS

Sensitivity analysis is a technique for incorporating risk assessment in investment appraisal. It works by highlighting the key assumptions upon which investment appraisal figures were based. For example, revenue forecasts for an investment might be based upon:

- sales of 100,000 units per year
- market growth of 3 per cent per year
- price of £3 per unit
- exchange rate of £1 = $1.5.

Sensitivity analysis would calculate the effects on an investment appraisal of changes in these assumptions. Such analysis would demonstrate the effects of, for example:

- sales of 80,000 units per year
- market growth of 1 per cent per year
- price of £2.50 per unit
- exchange rate of £1 = $1.75.

and thus illustrate a project's sensitivity to a variety of scenarios.

SOURCES OF FUNDS

The main sources of funds for private sector investment include:

- retained profits
- new share issues (see Chapter 2)
- loans
- government assistance (see Chapter 11).

The difference between large and small enterprises becomes apparent when considering alternative sources of finance. Generally, large organizations will have easier access to investment funds. Bank loans are likely to be at lower rates and access to equity finance via shareholders can reduce costs and risks of investment. Smaller organizations will generally find it more difficult and expensive to access investment funds. For example, Brooker (2002) argues that financing the smaller end of the hotel sector is made difficult by city attitudes and the capital intensity of the business in the UK. He considers the capital-intensive nature of the hotel industry and how various capital markets work in relation to the hotel sector. He argues that franchising can offer a route to securing investment funds for the small business.

GOVERNMENT POLICY

In general, right-wing governments interfere as little as possible in free markets, while left-wing governments are often prepared to offer financial assistance where a project provides employment in areas of high unemployment, or where there are wider community benefits.

REVIEW OF KEY TERMS

- Investment: expenditure on capital goods and working capital.
- Fixed capital: durable capital goods such as buildings and machinery.
- Working capital: finance of work in progress such as raw material stocks, partially finished and unsold goods.
- Net investment: gross investment − depreciation.
- Payback method: appraisal technique to see how quickly an investment repays its costs.
- Average rate of return: appraisal technique where the average annual returns are expressed as a percentage of the original capital costs.
- Net present value: appraisal technique where all future revenues are recalculated to their present value so that a comparison can be made with the project costs.

- Internal rate of return: the rate of return of a project on capital employed, calculated by finding the rate that discounts future earnings to equal the capital costs.
- Accelerator theory: explanation why changes in consumer demand lead to larger changes in demand for investment goods.
- Sensitivity analysis: investigation of sensitivity of an investment project to changes in forecasts.

Data Questions

Task 10.1 **The A380: superjumbo or white elephant?**

In Toulouse, France sits a vast 12-hectare factory that is to assemble the biggest airliner in history – the Airbus A380. By 2005 the first planes will be assembled with a capacity to produce around half a dozen a month.

The A380 is a double-decker superjumbo which can carry up to 550 people, compared with the 424 in Boeing's 747 and 365 seats in its 777. It represents a massive investment of $10.7 billion (excluding the factory buildings) and cannot but bring back memories of another major European aircraft collaboration – Concorde – which represented a massive loss-making exercise.

Airbus predicts that the project will break even when between 200 and 250 planes, at $260 million each, are sold. In 2003 Airbus had 103 orders from 10 customers, and about 100 further 'options'. But the project also contains some substantial downside risks:

1 The project has half its costs in euros and its revenues in dollars. Because of this Airbus has had to hedge ahead a massive $40 billion to cover currency movements.

2 Although Boeing – Airbus's main competitor – has no similar aircraft scheduled for production, it will probably compete very strongly on price to keep its orders for its existing range of planes.

3 Part of the projections include a total €1.5 billion worth of cuts to the company's €15 billion cost base.

4 Because break even for the A380 years away, its development must be funded through current revenues. Airbus has a target of 300 aircraft deliveries for 2003 and has said that a significant fall-off in deliveries – say to about 270 – would jeopardize revenues and the financing of the A380.

5 A falling market has intensified competition with Boeing.

6 The fallout of September 11, and the effects of the Iraq war on passenger numbers. Airbus believes the resumption of close to 5 per cent per annum air travel growth will resume after a period of uncertainty.

7 Boeing's 'spoiler' campaign in announcing the 747 (stretched to take 522 passengers) to take on the A380.

8 The future shape of air travel. If markets are fragmenting carriers may target regional airports direct rather than 'hubs' suiting the long range, lower capacity 777.

Task 10.1 **continued**

9 The massive growth of low-cost airlines focussed on short-haul traffic. Estimates are that low-cost airlines will account for 25 per cent of the market. Currently 8 of 10 low-cost airlines chose the Boeing 737 because of lower operating and maintenance costs.

Source: The author, from press cuttings (2004).

Recap Questions

1 What factors caused Concorde to be such a loss-making investment?
2 Identify the key costs and revenue factors affecting the A380 and analyse their likely impacts on its financial success.
3 Identify and analyse the key sensitivity factors affecting this project.
4 Explain using the accelerator principle why the demand for aircraft is so volatile.
5 Evaluate the success of the A380 project.

Task 10.2 **Journal article: Lashley, C., and Rowson, B., 2010. Lifestyle businesses: insights into Blackpool's hotel sector. International Journal of Hospitality Management 29, 511–519.**

'The vast majority of firms in the sector are micro-businesses employing 10 or fewer staff. Indeed many are so small as to employ no permanent staff at all. Those running these businesses are not classical entrepreneurs driven by a need to maximise profits and build a business empire. Many are best described as lifestyle entrepreneurs, their key motives are more associated with improving their quality of life. This paper reports on the owners of a significant sample of Blackpool hotels. The majority have sold a domestic property to buy the hotel. Few have any prior hotel experience, or small business experience, for that matter. The linkage between commercial and domestic provision of meals and accommodation convinced many of these interviewees that they had the skill sets required for hotel ownership and management. The paper also confirms earlier findings that a substantial minority withdraw from the hotel business in their first year. The lack of training in the business aspects of the hotel operation has serious implications for the quality of hotel operations in places like Blackpool, because a significant segment of hotel stock is being managed by these lifestyle entrepreneurs who are not primarily concerned with commercial objectives which prioritise service quality as a way of generating profits and growth.' (p. 511)

Recap Question

You and your partner are able to sell you current property and invest in a small guest house in Blackpool, a seaside resort in the UK, for the same amount of money. The guest house has eight double bedrooms. It is a bit run down. You currently work as a school teacher and your partner has been unemployed for a number of years. Outline the factors that would determine whether or not this is a good investment.

Task 10.3 **Merlin Entertainment**

Merlin Entertainment is a global leader in family leisure which operates 62 attractions in 13 countries and 3 continents. Its key brands include:

- Legoland
- SeaLife

- Alton Towers
- The Dungeons
- Madame Tussauds.

  Its recent and future investments include:

- the acquisition in 2010 of Cypress Gardens Theme Park and Botanical Gardens in Florida for conversion into a flagship Legoland Park in the world's largest tourist market;
- the opening of Madame Tussauds attractions in Bangkok and Vienna;
- the opening of a new Legoland park project in Malaysia.

  Merlin also identifies its principal risks and uncertainties as:

- loss of key personnel
- damage to its brands and offerings
- inability to secure new site and attraction developments
- environmental concerns
- the general economic environment
- competitive threats
- weather conditions
- interest rate risks
- credit risk
- liquidity risk
- foreign currency risk.

Source: Merlin Annual Report (http://www.merlinentertainments.biz/en/company/annual_report.aspx).

Recap Questions

1 What impact do you think current economic conditions have on Merlin's investment plans?
2 Explain the nature and the current status of the risks identified above to one of Merlin's key brands.
3 Identify the key costs and revenues associated with the Madame Tussauds Bangkok investment.
4 What might be the key sensitivity factors to consider in an investment appraisal of Madame Tussauds Bangkok?

MULTIPLE CHOICE

1 Net investment equals the following:
   (a) Gross investment plus depreciation.
   (b) Gross investment minus depreciation.
   (c) All investment in a given year.
   (d) Money investment minus inflation.
2 All other things remaining equal which of the following will cause an increase in investment?
   (a) A fall in interest rates.
   (b) A rise in interest rates.

(c) A fall in demand.

(d) Pessimistic expectations.

3 The accelerator principle explains the following:

(a) The positive relationship between investment and the rate of interest.

(b) The negative relationship between investment and the rate of interest.

(c) The relationship between gross and net investment.

(d) Fluctuations in the level of investment.

4 Which of the following is true?

(a) Net present value analysis translates future earnings to a lower present value.

(b) The average rate of return total earnings/the rate of interest.

(c) Payback method of investment includes credit cards and direct debits.

(d) All of the above.

5 Which of the following is false?

(a) An aeroplane is fixed capital.

(b) Stocks of goods represent working capital.

(c) The existence of spare capacity in an industry will stimulate new investment.

(d) Investment financed from retained profits is cost free.

REVIEW QUESTIONS

1 Distinguish between net investment and gross investment.

2 How important is the rate of interest in affecting the decision to invest in a project?

3 Distinguish between the short-term and long-term effects of investment to an economy.

4 Evaluate the payback method of investment appraisal.

5 What is a project's internal rate of return?

6 Distinguish between working capital and fixed capital.

7 Why is sensitivity analysis used?

Websites of interest

Australian Bureau of Statistics: www.abs.gov.au

British Airports Authority: www.baa.com

Airbus Industries: www.airbus.com

Merlin Entertainment: http://www.merlinentertainments.biz/en/homepage. aspx

CHAPTER **11**

Investment in the public sector

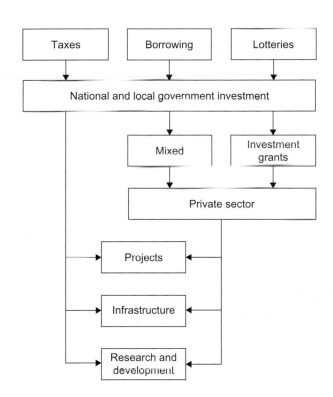

Objectives and·learning outcomes

Transport is essential to many recreation, leisure and tourism activities. Provision of transport infrastructure for example roads, railways and airports requires considerable investment expenditure. It is very noticeable around the world that different governments have different approaches to investment. Taking the railways as an example, France has a very sophisticated system of national rail. At the heart of its system is the Train à Grande Vitesse (TGV; high-speed train). In order to run the TGV new, straight track had to be laid – a massive investment and in France this has been undertaken by the government. The story in the UK is quite different. The railway system was privatized in the 1990s and has since suffered from under-investment and a poor record of safety or reliability.

Those who support public sector investment readily look to the failings of the UK privatized rail system to make their point. Opponents of public sector investment point to various symbols of policy failure as representing the worst aspects of public sector investment – consuming ever-increasing sums of taxpayers' money and never achieving viable commercial sales.

By studying this chapter, students will be able to:

- identify the sources of public sector investment;
- identify different types of public sector investment;
- describe different methods of public sector investment;
- appraise public sector investment projects;
- identify public sector incentives for private sector investment;
- understand private public partnership agreements;
- identify sources of funds for public sector investment.

SOURCES, TYPES, METHODS AND AIMS OF PUBLIC SECTOR INVESTMENT

Sources

Public sector investment can be financed from different sources. At the national level, government channels leisure and tourism investment through public corporations, quangos such as Sports Councils and government departments (e.g. the Department of Culture, Media and Sport in the UK). In Australia, the following government departments have responsibilities for public sector investment relevant to recreation, leisure and tourism:

- the Department of Infrastructure and Transport
- the Department of Energy, Resources and Tourism

- the Department of the Prime Minister and Cabinet
- the Department of Sustainability, Environment, Water, Population and Communities.

Local government is the other major source of public sector investment. For European countries, there is also a supranational level of government and here the EU is a key source of investment funds, particularly through the European Regional Development Fund.

Types

Public sector investment may also be classified according to type. First, public sector investment may be in buildings and land, for example, parks, leisure centres and museums. Second public sector investment includes plant and machinery such as playground apparatus, computerized booking systems and canal lock equipment. Third public sector investment may be made in infrastructure. Infrastructure, or social overhead capital, is the construction needed to support economic development, for example, roads, railways and airports, water and sewerage, power and telecommunications.

Public investment on infrastructure has been particularly high in China to accommodate and drive its fast expanding economy and Exhibit 11.1 reports on some key elements in China's recent public investment strategy for strategic infrastructure. Infrastructure

Exhibit 11.1 Key transport infrastructure projects in China 2006–2010

The following are the key transport infrastructure projects embarked upon in China during the period 2006–2010. These projects are part of a 5-year development plan.

- *Roads*: Fourteen motorways including a new highway from Beijing to Hong Kong and Macao.
- *Railways*: Six railways for the transportation of passengers including the track between Beijing and Shanghai; five intercity railways including the Beijing and Tianjin project; five railways upgraded including the link between Datong and Qinhuangdao.
- *Airports*: The expansion of 10 airports including those in Shanghai, Beijing and Guangzhou; the relocation of airports in Kunming and Hefei; and airports in north-eastern, central and western China to cater for flights on feeder lines.
- *Port*: Transit systems for the transportation of goods at 12 seaports including those in Shanghai, Dalian and Tianjin.
- *Shipping*: The upgrading of the deepwater channels at the mouth of the Yangtze River and the mouth of the Pearl River and strategic port construction along inland rivers.

Source: Xinhua News Agency (www.china.org.cn).

Exhibit 11.2 Research and development in the EU

"Knowledge lies at the heart of the European Union's Lisbon Strategy to become the 'most dynamic competitive knowledge-based economy in the world'. The 'knowledge triangle' – research, education and innovation – is a core factor in European efforts to meet the ambitious Lisbon goals. Numerous programmes, initiatives and support measures are carried out at EU level in support of knowledge.

The Seventh Framework Programme (FP7) bundles all research-related EU initiatives together under a common roof playing a crucial role in reaching the goals of growth, competitiveness and employment; along with a new Competitiveness and Innovation Framework Programme (CIP), Education and Training programmes, and Structural and Cohesion Funds for regional convergence and competitiveness. It is also a key pillar for the European Research Area (ERA).

The broad objectives of FP7 have been grouped into four categories: Cooperation, Ideas, People and Capacities. For each type of objective, there is a specific programme corresponding to the main areas of EU research policy. All specific programmes work together to promote and encourage the creation of European poles of (scientific) excellence." R&D projects in leisure and tourism which have been funded by EU funds include:

- ESCAPE – project to investigate pollution of coastal waters.
- A project to restore the stonework of European historic buildings by using laser techniques.
- TOURFOR – a project to use environmental management systems to limit environmental damage of tourism and recreation in forest areas.
- BRAIN – a project to develop mathematical models to improve soundproofing in aircraft cabins.

Source: European Commission Cordis (http://cordis.europa.eu/fp7/understand_en.html).

development is a key part of tourism destination development, as it has to precede specific project development such as hotels, leisure sites and restaurants. Finally public sector investment may be spent on research and development, and the EU has an ambitious programme to promote this across member states as illustrated in Exhibit 11.2.

Methods and aims

The main methods of public sector investment are first via projects which are wholly public sector-financed, second via projects which are jointly financed by the public and private sectors and finally via projects which are private sector investments but which are eligible for public sector investment incentive grants.

The aims of public sector investment include provision of goods and services which have significant public benefits, but which might not be profitable enough to attract private sector investment.

Exhibit 11.3 The Guggenheim Museum Bilbao

The new Guggenheim Museum was a central part of a strategic urban renewal scheme for Bilbao, a city in Northern Spain (in the Basque region). Bilbao had been dependent on steel and iron industries which had gone into decline and the city was suffering from high unemployment, industrial pollution and a spiral of decline. The urban renewal scheme planned to transform the city into a modern hub of clean industries (service, financial and high technology) strengthened also by significant tourist and cultural initiatives.

Bilbao Metropoli 30 was formed in 1989 as a public/private institution, in order to plan and execute the Bilbao urban renewal scheme The Guggenheim Museum came about as part of a collaboration between the Basque Administration and the Guggenheim Foundation. The Basque Administration had earmarked substantial funds (around $1.5 billion) for the urban renewal project. As part of this, it allocated $20 million to pay for the Guggenheim name and expertise, $100 million for the building, $50 million for acquisitions and $12 million per year to run it.

Source: Harvard Design School (http://www.gsd.harvard.edu/people/faculty/pollalis/cases/BilbaoG-CaseA.pdf).

O'Hagan and Jennings (2003) discussed some of the key issues in the current debate in Europe over Public Sector Broadcasting and examine the arguments for Public Sector Broadcasting. They find these to be classified under five headings, namely diversity, democracy/equality, network externalities, innovation and investment and public broadcasting as 'insurance'. They also examined the issues surrounding the licence fee as an instrument for funding Public Sector Broadcasting. These include the determination of the level of the fee, collection costs and evasion and the fairness of the instrument.

Public sector investment may also be focussed on projects aimed at the economic development or regeneration of a particular area. Exhibit 11.3 reports on the contribution of mixed public and private sector investment in the arts to the economy of Bilbao, a city in Northern Spain, that has been transformed from a declining iron and steel economy to a prosperous city of culture and high technology. Plaza and Haarich (2009) discuss the use of art museums for the reactivation (and/or diversification) of the economy of cities. They use the Tate Liverpool, the Guggenheim Museum Bilbao (GMB), the Tate Modern London, the Louvre-Lens (France), Pompidou-Metz (France), Guggenheim Hermitage (Lithuania) and Guggenheim Abu Dhabi (UAE) as examples. Casellas and Pallares-Barbera (2009) examine the urban and economic revitalization of a traditional industrial working-class neighbourhood of Barcelona into a knowledge-based economic district. They note the use of an assertive public policy stance led by Barcelona's city council and implemented by a quasi-public agency.

INVESTMENT APPRAISAL IN THE PUBLIC SECTOR

Cost–benefit analysis

Investment appraisal for private sector projects is relatively straight-forward as described in Chapter 10. If a project yields the required return on capital employed then the investment will go ahead. The different nature of the public sector makes investment appraisal more complex in this sector. Some parts of the public sector are run on private sector lines. In these cases an investment is required to earn a specified rate of return on capital employed and thus the investment decision is fairly clear-cut. However, many public sector investments are made for reasons of wider public benefits and thus private sector methods of appraisal are inappropriate. In such cases cost–benefit analysis provides a more useful method of project appraisal.

Cost–benefit analysis is described in detail in Chapter 17; however, its essential details are that all the costs and benefits of a project are identified and weighed up, including social as well as private ones. Table 11.1 shows an example of possible private and social costs and benefits for a canal restoration scheme. Private sector invest-ment appraisal of such a scheme would calculate the private costs of the project and the private benefits. These would be discounted to net present value (as explained in Chapter 10) and since the private costs would almost certainly exceed the private benefits, the invest-ment would not proceed. However, cost–benefit analysis would anal-yse the wider costs and benefits. Some extra costs such as noise and congestion associated with the construction phase might be identi-fied. Social benefits of the scheme would include lives saved through improved canal safety, greater public well-being caused by improved

Table 11.1 Cost–benefit analysis of canal restoration scheme

Costs	Benefits
Private costs	*Private benefits*
Construction costs of project, e.g. • Materials • Labour • Professional fees	Revenue from project, e.g. • Craft licences and charges • Fishing licences • Rentals from renovated buildings
Social costs	*Social benefits*
Inconvenience costs to local residents of construction	Drownings avoided through improved canal safety New jobs created by project Improved aesthetics of area

aesthetics from the project and the effects on the local economy of new industries and employment attracted to the area because of the project. The total figures would be subjected to discounting to calculate net present value, and it might well be the case that total public and private benefits would exceed costs. Thus, there may well be an argument for public sector investment in the project.

Newman et al. (2003) note that arts projects have become an important part of community development strategies but that project are expected to have positive and measurable impacts on local social capital. They show that funding organizations routinely demand evidence for this and that formal cost–benefit evaluations of projects are frequently a condition of investment. However, they further note that quantifying the impact of the arts in terms of 'social gain' presents considerable difficulties. These problems are not just methodological. They also raise the question of the extent to which creative processes can (or should) be managed and controlled. In other words cost–benefit accounting may be incompatible with the creative arts.

Pitegoff and Smith (2003) carried out an investigation into US State Destination Boards which have traditionally operated Welcome Centres at key vehicular entrance points to their states. These are often viewed as cost centres. However, they note that if visitors modify trips in the State as a result of their Welcome Centre experience so as to make an incremental economic contribution to the State, then what has been perceived as a cost centre may actually be a profit centre for the State. In other words, a wider public cost–benefit analysis rather than a strict accounting of the direct costs and revenues of the operation of these Welcome Centres can provide an economic argument for their continued existence.

Other factors affecting public investment

Whilst cost–benefit analysis is used for appraising some major public sector investment projects, its use is far from widespread. Public sector investment decisions are often determined by the priorities of the political party in power at a national or local level. Decisions will also be affected by interest group activity, and the general economic environment. In general, public sector investment is favoured and supported by political parties which are left of centre and where the economy is growing healthily and contributing to government tax revenues. For public investment decisions at a supranational level (e.g. in the EU) strategic considerations often outweigh national interests although of course there is often fierce national lobbying to promote the interests of individual nation states. Exhibit 11.4 describes the steps taken by the European Commission to improve transport links in Europe and some of the key projects under construction.

Exhibit 11.4   Trans-European networks

Transport infrastructure is fundamental for the mobility of the persons and goods and for the territorial cohesion of the European Union … Most of these transport infrastructures have been developed under national policy premises. In order establish a single, multimodal network that integrates land, sea and air transport networks throughout the Community, the European policymakers decided to establish the Trans-European transport network, allowing goods and people to circulate quickly and easily between Member States and assuring international connections.

Establishing an efficient trans-European transport network (TEN-T) is a key element in the relaunched Lisbon strategy for competitiveness and employment in Europe. If Europe is to fulfil its economic and social potential, it is essential to build the missing links and remove the bottlenecks in our transport infrastructure, as well as to ensure the sustainability of our transport networks into the future. Furthermore, it integrates environmental protection requirements with a view to promoting sustainable development.

In view of the growth in traffic between Member States, expected to double by 2020, the investment required to complete and modernise a true trans-European network in the enlarged EU amounts to some €500 billion from 2007 to 2020, out of which € 270 billion [is needed]for the priority axis and projects.

Priority projects include:

- The Berlin–Verona/Milan–Bologna–Napoli–Messina–Palermo rail link
- The south-west European high-speed rail link
- High-speed rail interoperability on the Iberian peninsula
- The Lyon–Trieste–Divača/Koper–Divača–Ljubljana–Budapest–Ukrainian border rail link
- The Paris–Strasbourg–Stuttgart–Wien–Bratislava rail link
- Motorways of the sea
- The European Rail Traffic Management System.

Source: European Commission (http://ec.europa.eu/transport/infrastructure/index_en.htm).

INVESTMENT INCENTIVES FOR TOURISM AND LEISURE PROJECTS

Most governments offer incentives to encourage private sector investment particularly:

- in areas of high unemployment;
- where there are clear social benefits offered by a scheme;
- where structural changes in the economy have led to geographic areas of economic decline (e.g. inner city decline, rural decline, and so on).

These incentives can include:

- matched funding
- tax relief

Exhibit 11.5 Public sector leisure investment initiatives in the UK

The following examples show support from a number of different public sector sources for leisure and tourism investment projects:

- Somerset District Council opened a visitor centre on the River Parrett at Langport with financial help from the Rural Development Corporation.
- Tourism in Thanet won funds from the European Regional Development Fund and the UK Government's Single Regeneration Budget to support investment in local hotels and attractions.
- The Imperial War Museum built a 6000-square-foot site in Manchester with a budget of £28.5 million. This is a mixed private sector/public sector initiative with £12.5 million coming from the private sector (Peel Holdings), £8.2 million from the European Regional Development Fund and £2.5 million each from English Partnerships, Trafford Council and the Imperial War Museum.
- The Manchester Museum, the Manchester City Art Gallery and the Manchester Museum of Science and Industry shared a £4.5-million grant from the European Regional Development Fund.

Source: The author.

- subsidized loans
- simplified planning procedures.

Exhibit 11.5 reports on public sector support for investment projects in recreation, leisure and tourism in the UK.

SOURCES OF FUNDS

Sources of funds for public investment include:

- operating profits, taxation and borrowing
- National Lotteries
- Public–Private Partnerships (PPPs).

Operating profits, taxation and borrowing

Operating profits are rare in public sector organizations since, as discussed in Chapter 2, they are run for motives other than profit. Thus, public sector investment is mainly financed from taxation receipts and government borrowing. This is a key reason why public sector investment is often under attack from opposition parties and from the government's own Treasury Department.

Because of the impact on public finances, the opportunity costs of public sector investment are immediately apparent. Thus, the opportunity cost of more public investment is higher taxes, or less government expenditure elsewhere, as illustrated in Figure 11.1. The circle

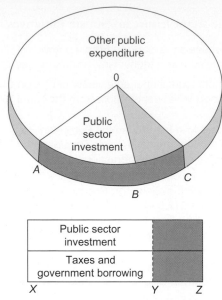

Figure 11.1 Opportunity cost of public sector investment.

represents total government spending and no increases in taxes or government borrowing are assumed. An increase in public sector investment from *A0B* to *A0C* can only be accommodated by a fall in other government expenditure of *B0C*. Alternatively, it is assumed below that other government expenditure remains unchanged. In this case, an increase in public sector investment from *XY* to *XZ* can only be financed through an increase in taxes or government borrowing of *YZ*.

Second, when the economy is performing badly, investment is often a target of government policy. If government borrowing is running too high, cutting social security payments or pensions has readily identifiable victims. Cutting investment generally results only in some improvement not taking place and therefore its consequences are more blurred.

National Lotteries

In some countries, National Lotteries offer significant income sources for public sector investment. For example, the first estimates for the costs of the Sydney Opera House (Plate 11) were $7 million. An appeal fund raised about $900,000 but the rest of the $102 million that the Opera House ended up costing came from the profits of a series of lotteries. The building was completely paid for by July 1975. Today the NSW Government contributes about 30 per cent of the annual cost of maintaining and operating the complex.

In the UK, whilst public spending has generally been squeezed by the Treasury, recreation, leisure and tourism are key beneficiaries of

Plate 11 Public Sector Investment: Sydney Opera House. *Source: The author.*

the National Lottery. Twenty-eight per cent of the lottery revenue goes to four major causes, three of which benefit leisure and tourism. These are:

- Health, Education, Environment, and charitable causes 50 per cent
- Sports 16.67 per cent
- Arts 16.67 per cent
- Heritage 16.67 per cent.

Projects in the arts which have benefited from the National Lottery include first, the South Bank arts complex in London where the National Theatre completed a major refurbishment of its foyer area with the help of lottery funds. Second, the lottery provided investment funds for the Tate Gallery's Bankside museum for modern art. The estimated cost of conversion of a disused power station in east London for this project was £80 million. The English National Opera also obtained funds to renovate the London Coliseum.

The Sports Council set up a lottery board to distribute its share of funds. Projects of between £5000 and £5 million can be considered for a grant of up to 65 per cent. Large projects include the new national stadium at Wembley and local council sports facilities.

The National Heritage memorial fund has responsibility for channelling funds into areas such as museum collections, historic buildings and monuments, landscapes, libraries and industrial heritage.

Other examples of contributions of lottery funding to leisure and tourism investment projects include:

- The Natural History Museum Earth Galleries (£6 million from Heritage Lottery Fund)

- National Trust renovation of Paul McCartney's Teenage Liverpool home (£47,500 from Heritage Lottery Fund)
- Redevelopment of Royal Naval Museum, Portsmouth (Heritage Lottery Fund)
- The National Space Science Centre, Leicester (£23 million from the Millennium Commission).

Public–private partnerships (PPP)

A PPP is where governments contract a private company to finance, design, construct, operate and maintain a project in return for future income. Projects include examples such as railways, leisure centres and concert halls. The finance for such schemes may involve investment companies or fund managers for insurance or pension bodies providing the initial investment in return for future revenue which may be generated through a variety of schemes that may include tolls, rentals or 'shadow payments' where the government pays a fee for each customer of the project. Through PPPs different combinations of public–private investment are possible. But the basic idea is that public payment for the project is not required up-front, but it is made as the project comes into use. Of course there is potential conflict in PPPs. The public sector is seeking a community benefit, better services and facilities delivered sooner at least cost to the community, whilst the private sector wants a profit. Long-term mutual benefit depends on how well the private sector manages the risk transferred to it and on the public sector's success in managing the contracts over the duration of the project.

THE PUBLIC SECTOR INVESTMENT DEBATE

Public investment has been subject to considerable debate and the arguments against public investment include the following:

1 The public sector is not a good interpreter of people's wants and thus often invests in 'white elephants'.
2 The public sector is not good at ensuring efficient use of funds and tends to allow waste.
3 Public sector investment causes an increase in taxation or public borrowing.
4 Public sector investment 'crowds out' private sector investment.

In the UK in the 1980s, the new neoliberal economic agenda of the Thatcher government removed a large slice of investment from the public sector through its privatization programme. It then concentrated its efforts on creating an 'enterprise economy' which it hoped would stimulate private sector investment by reducing income and corporation tax and making the labour market more flexible. The privatization of the public sector has been carried out with similar enthusiasm in parts of Europe – and of course particularly in ex-communist states.

However, many countries in the world still favour a substantial public sector and the arguments favouring public sector investment include the following:

1 There is insufficient incentive for the private sector to invest in public goods (see Chapter 7).
2 The private sector under invests in goods which have mainly social benefits.
3 The private sector may not be able to undertake the finance or risk for very large projects.
4 Public sector investment can help regenerate parts of the economy which have suffered from restructuring.
5 Public sector investments can generate jobs when unemployment is high.

Thus, where the market is used as the main determinant of investment, infrastructure projects with important public and merit angles will tend to be overlooked, despite the fact that the future capacity of the economy may depend on them. This has led to calls to distinguish between capital spending and current spending in government public sector accounts since the former will involve future benefits.

REVIEW OF KEY TERMS

- Infrastructure: construction needed to support economic development.
- Cost–benefit analysis: full analysis of public and private costs and benefits of project.
- City boosterism: investment in projects to regenerate city centres in economic decline.
- European Regional Development Fund: EU fund for projects and infrastructure to bring jobs to designated areas.
- Opportunity costs of public sector investment = alternative uses the funds could have been used for.
- PPPs: where governments contract a private company to finance, design, construct, operate and maintain a project in return for future income.

 **Data** Questions

Task 11.1 Journal Article: Plaza, B., 2010. Valuing museums as economic engines: Willingness to pay or discounting of cash-flows? Journal of Cultural Heritage 11, 155–162.

In this article the author notes that museums can have two objectives. These are not only cultural but can also include the generation of economic activity and creation of employment. With this in mind Plaza names a special category of museums as GLAMUR, that is, GLobal Art MUseums as Economic Re-activators. The author begins by defining the economic value of cultural heritage as 'the extent to which that heritage generates benefits for society', and the benefits to society are explained to be both market and non-market benefits.

The Guggenheim Museum Bibao (GMB) is seen by the author as an important case study to illustrate the impact of an internationally famous cultural attraction. The GMB was a key part of the regeneration strategy of Bilbao, a city in Northern Spain that had suffered a long period of industrial decline. But the GMB was a costly public project where the project costs totalled €166 million.

Plaza concludes her own study as follows:

While the GMB was a costly venture, the overall investments (not including the value of the permanent art collection) were recovered by the year 2005, as early as eight years after opening, whereas the overall investment (including the value of the permanent art collection) will be recovered by the year 2015 ... Results show that since the museum's opening, the city has received an average of 779,028 new yearly overnight stays and has created 985 new direct full-time jobs (indirect and induced not included). The GMB earns around Euros 28 million annually for the Basque treasury.

Her conclusions add weight to the GMB's own data. Here the economic impacts of the GMB were found in its annual impact study to generate direct expenditures in 2008 of €231,788,989 including contribution to the maintenance of about 4196 jobs. The specific sectors that have most benefited from the GMB effect are restaurants; bars and cafes; hotels and other accommodation; shops and stores; leisure activities such as cinemas, theatres, other museums and transport.

Recap Questions

1 What are GLAMUR attractions? Give examples.
2 Identify market and non-market benefits of investments in GLAMUR attractions. How can these be measured?
3 The GMB project costs about €166 million. Devise a simple spreadsheet to enable this project to be evaluated in terms of its economic viability. What difficulties arise from making such calculations?
4 What were the opportunity costs of investments in the GMB project?
5 What projects would you recommend for other cities/regions facing problems of industrial decline?

Task 11.2 Public spaces: Victorian heritage lost and found

1832: The Whig government conceives the idea of 'public walks'.
1837: Joseph Hume MP tables a parliamentary motion calling for the provision of open spaces to be financed from the public purse for the enjoyment of the public.

1840: The Arboretum in Rosehill, Derby, is opened to fanfares and fireworks. Joseph Strutt commends the park as offering local workers 'the opportunity of enjoying, with their families, exercise and recreation in the fresh air and in public walks and grounds'. The Arboretum is planted with 913 types of trees and shrubs and more than 100 types of rose. This is one of the first examples of a public park.

1979: Mrs Thatcher comes to power. Public sector spending cut.

1998: Patrick Weir of the *Guardian* surveys the sorry state of the park. He reports: 'The Lodge House, at the Rosehill Street entrance, serves bleak notice of what lies beyond: a crumbling, boarded up edifice, it would look more at home on a Hammer Horror set. Once in the park, signs of decay are all too evident. Public monuments are in disrepair, the bandstand is burned down, statues are missing and the centrepiece fountain is fenced off. Trees remain untrimmed, while graffiti, litter and dog dirt scar the environment. Gangs congregating at night render the park even less inviting'.

1999: Derby City Council awaits the result of a bid to the Heritage Lottery for £3 million. The council has made provision to access an initial £200,000 of lottery funds by providing £43,000 in matched funds, but it is not confident of finding the next tranche of £750,000 necessary to release the rest of the lottery's £3 million. Steve Jardine, of the DERBYES! Campaign, hopes that residents, local businesses and grant-providing trusts can help. He said: 'The council can't do everything'. People must be more proactive. It's a case of priorities and how much we value our parks. They are the lungs of the city, and, as recognized by the Victorians, areas where people can relax and play.

2002–2005: Arboretum Smiles Again Project. The bid was successful and with £3 million from Heritage Lottery, along with funding from the Council Single Regeneration Budget, European organization URBAN and the Derby and Derbyshire Economic Partnership (DDEP), the restoration project began in 2002. Over £5 million has been invested into the park to restore buildings and provide new facilities including play areas for toddlers and older children.

Source: The author based on article in The Guardian.

Recap Questions

1 What differing government attitudes to public sector investment does this article demonstrate?
2 What are the arguments for and against leaving provision of parks and gardens to the private sector?
3 Given the shortage of local council funds – suggest ways in which improvements in this park could be financed.
4 Explain the meaning of the terms *opportunity cost, crowding out, merit goods* and *public goods* in relation to this article.

Task 11.3 **Getting from A to B**

The London Underground, UK: In 2003, the London Underground began operating as a PPP. Under this scheme two private companies (Metronet and Tube Lines) were contracted to maintain infrastructure and rolling stock. London Underground itself would remain publicly owned. This PPP arrangement has not been very successful – Metronet went bust and there have been many costly disputes between London Underground and Tube Lines.

Task 11.3 **continued**

Skye bridge, UK: Skye bridge spans the sea between the Isle of Skye and the Scottish mainland and was built under the private finance initiative (PFI). Under this programme public schemes are funded by private money. A private sector consortia designed, built and financed the bridge and shouldered risks such as construction delays. In return the government entered into a contract to pay for yearly use of the bridge.

The Madrid–Seville high-speed train, Spain: The Spanish Ministry of Transport paid for the £450 billion construction costs of the high-speed train from Madrid to Seville which opened in 1992. It has been such a success that it later authorized the construction of the extension from Madrid to the French frontier to link with the TGV system.

US high-speed rail: In 2009, the House of Representatives voted $4 billion for high-speed rail projects, on top of the $8 billion that was part of the economic stimulus package. President Obama's administration is considering up to 10 high-speed rail networks in the Northeast, California, Texas, Florida and Wisconsin.

China high-speed rail: China plans to invest more than $1 trillion to develop more than 8000 miles of high-speed rail by 2020. Already, China runs the world's fastest high-speed train averaging 217 metres per hour. By 2012, China will have more miles of high-speed rail service than any other country.

The Haramain railway: Saudi Arabia's state-run Public Investment Fund (PIF) is providing interest-free loans to help finance a new railway project. The Haramain railway will connect Mecca with Medina and Jeddah and is due for completion by the end of 2012. The PIF will use revenue to finance the loans. The project hopes to ease the congestion during the Hajj and Umrah pilgrimages. The railway is forecast to transport around 3 million people a year.

Source: The author.

Recap Questions

1 What different types of investment are demonstrated in this article?
2 In each case what is the main determinant of the level of investment?
3 What are the benefits and drawbacks of investment in transport schemes under regimes of:
   – Private sector?
   – Private/public sector partnerships?
   – Public sector?
4 What factors would be taken into account in a cost–benefit analysis of the Madrid–Seville high-speed train?

MULTIPLE CHOICE

1 Which of the following is not a social benefit of a canal restoration scheme?

(a) Improved aesthetics.

(b) Revenue from boat licences.

  (c) New jobs created by the project.

  (d) Drownings avoided through improved safety.

2 Public sector investment is most appropriate where:

  (a) Social and private benefits exceed social and private costs.

  (b) Private benefits exceed private costs.

  (c) A project would not otherwise be undertaken.

  (d) A project has the support of local residents.

3 Under a PPP scheme:

  (a) The public sector partner provides the initial investment funds.

  (b) The private sector partner receives revenues for use of the facility.

  (c) Both the public and private partners will necessarily benefit.

  (d) Consumers are guaranteed low prices.

4 Which of the following statements is not true?

  (a) Public sector investment may 'crowd out' private sector investment.

  (b) Because the public sector is not a good interpreter of people's wants it often invests in 'white elephants'.

  (c) Public sector investment is inadvisable when unemployment is high.

  (d) The private sector may not be able to undertake the finance or risk for very large projects.

5 Which of these is not an opportunity cost of public investment?

  (a) Extra taxes paid by households.

  (b) Other possible government projects.

  (c) Interest paid on borrowings to finance the project.

  (d) Regeneration effects of the project.

REVIEW QUESTIONS

1 Under what circumstances would investment grants be available for the construction of a theme park?

2 What is cost–benefit analysis and why is it sometimes difficult to calculate?

3 Compare the sources of funds for public investment projects with sources available in the private sector.

4 What specific leisure and tourism projects might benefit from the National Lottery funding?

5 Compare the factors determining an investment decision in the public sector with those in the private sector.

Websites of interest

Department of Infrastructure and Transport (Australia):
www.infrastructure.gov.au

The National Lottery (UK): www.national-lottery.co.uk

The London Underground: www.tfl.gov.uk/tube/

The European Commission: http://cordis.europa.eu

PART **6**

Economic Impacts

C H A P T E R **12**

Income, employment and prices

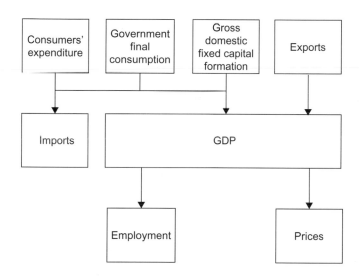

Objectives and learning outcomes

Chapter 9 looked at the effects of the economic environment on recreation, leisure and tourism organizations. The aim of this chapter is to examine the other side of this question, and ask how the leisure and tourism sector contributes to the general level of economic activity. In particular, it will examine the contribution of leisure and tourism to national output, national income and national expenditure, to the level of employment and consider the question of inflation. The issue of economic growth will be covered in Chapter 13, and the international impact of leisure and tourism will be addressed in Chapter 14.

By studying this chapter, students should be able to:

- distinguish between microeconomics and macroeconomics;
- measure the total level of economic activity in an economy;
- distinguish between changes in real and money gross national product (GNP);
- measure the contribution to GNP;
- understand the contribution to employment;
- understand the contribution to tax revenue;
- utilize simple economic models of the macroeconomy;
- understand and apply the multiplier principle;
- measure inflation in the recreation, leisure and tourism sector;
- interpret government policy in this area.

GNP AND THE LEVEL OF RECREATION, LEISURE AND TOURISM ACTIVITY

Macroeconomics

Chapters 2–7 dealt mainly with microeconomic issues. These were issues concerning the actions of individuals (demand) and firms (supply) and their interaction to determine prices in specific markets (e.g. the market for television sets and the market for air travel). Chapters 12–15 look mainly at macroeconomic issues. These are issues that affect the whole economy. Macroeconomics deals with aggregates. Thus, it adds together the spending of individuals to calculate consumers' expenditure or aggregate demand. It adds together the output of individual organizations to measure national output or product. Similarly, the general price level and rate of inflation are investigated rather than prices in individual markets.

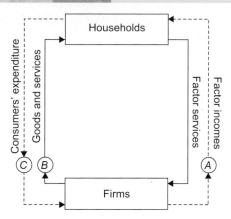

Figure 12.1 The circular flow of income.

A simple macroeconomic model

Figure 12.1 illustrates a simple model of the national economy. The economy is divided into two sectors, households and firms. Households own factors of production whilst firms utilize factors of production to produce goods and services. It is assumed in this initial model that all the output of firms is sold and all income is spent. Additionally, there is no government activity, no savings or investment and no international trade.

There are two flows in this system. First, 'real' flows are designated by unbroken lines. These represent the flow of factors of production (land, labour and capital) from households to firms, and the flow of goods and services, made from these factors of production, from firms to households. Second, 'money' flows are designated by broken lines. These represent factor rewards and payments for goods and services. For example, if a member of a household works for a firm it supplies the factor of labour and receives the reward of wages in payment. This payment can then be used to purchase goods and services from firms.

In this simple model of the economy firms buy factors of production to make goods and services, and households sell factors of production to buy goods and services.

Gross and net national income

The model can be used to illustrate the concept of national income. National income is a measure of the total level of economic activity which takes place in an economy over a year. In Figure 12.1, if the total flow of money at point A was measured over a year, this would represent the level of national income. The same picture can be viewed from different angles. The total value of goods and services passing point B over a year would represent national output or national product, and the total amount of expenditure passing point C over a year would represent national expenditure. This gives an important accounting identity:

National income = National product = National expenditure

The key rule in deciding how an item should be treated for national income calculation is whether it represents income earned by or output (or expenditure on that output) produced by, factors of production of the country under consideration. There are three methods of measuring GDP.

1   In the income method, incomes accruing to factors of production are added up.

2   In the expenditure method, the total spending on final output under different headings is measured. Some goods will be semi-finished or finished but not yet sold, so these are added as 'increase in stocks and works in progress'. Exported goods have been produced but not bought domestically so their value is added. Imports have been bought but not produced domestically, so their value is deducted. Finally, taxes artificially inflate prices and subsidies undervalue the underlying production costs, so these are deducted and added respectively to move from market prices to factor costs. An item for residual error is included. So, the formula for measuring GDP by the expenditure method is:

Consumers' expenditure
+ Government final consumption
+ Gross domestic fixed capital formation
+ Value of increase in stocks and works in progress
+ Exports of goods and services
− Imports of goods and services
− Residual error
= *GDP (at market prices)*
− Expenditure taxes
+ Subsidies
= *GDP (at factor cost).*

3   Under the output method the outputs of different sectors of the economy are valued, taking care to avoid double-counting.

From GDP to national income

GDP values the flow of goods and services produced domestically. But some income arises from investments and possessions owned abroad and thus an adjustment for net property income from abroad is made to GDP to calculate GNP. Finally, some investment spending occurs to replace worn-out machinery. Net national product (NNP) or national income deducts this amount (capital depreciation). These final calculations are summarized below:

GDP
+ Net property income from abroad
= GNP
− Capital consumption
= NNP (national income).

Real and money national income

When national income figures are compared over two different time periods, the effects of inflation can be misleading. Money national income or national income at current prices includes the effects of inflation. Real national income or national income at constant prices has had the effects of inflation removed.

Recreation, leisure and tourism contribution to GNP

Importance

Table 12.1 gives an indication of the importance of the leisure and tourism sector to the US economy. From the data, it can be seen that a significant proportion of expenditure in 2008 and 2009 was on leisure and tourism items. Table 12.1 also shows the difficulties in defining leisure and tourism and measuring its specific impacts on the national economy. The Department of Commerce data has three categories – recreational goods and vehicles, recreation services and foreign travel which are clear leisure and tourism categories. However, clearly some aspects of other categories such as 'food', 'beverages' and 'motoring' as well as other headings will include leisure expenditure. Care therefore needs to be exercised in interpreting the contribution of leisure and tourism to national income using Table 12.1 alone. Additionally, some leisure activity does not involve an activity which is bought and sold in the market. Neither informal sports games nor DIY labour are measured in GNP statistics because of this, although both result in services enjoyed and value added. Therefore, traditional GNP figures often undervalue the true contribution of recreation, leisure and tourism to national economies.

Satellite accounts

It has been seen that it is not always easy to isolate spending on recreation, leisure and tourism from other expenditure in national economic accounts. Taking tourism as an example, tourism is not an industry in the traditional sense. Traditional industries are classified according to the goods and services that they produce (e.g. restaurant and café meals). However, classifying a good or service as a tourism

Table 12.1 Personal consumption expenditures (USA) [billions of chained (2005) dollars]

	2008	2009
Personal consumption expenditures	**9265.0**	**9153.9**
Goods	**3180.3**	**3117.4**
Durable goods	**1136.4**	**1094.6**
Motor vehicles and parts	**348.2**	**324.0**
Furnishings and durable household equipment	**271.4**	**253.9**
Recreational goods and vehicles	**393.7**	**399.3**
Video, audio, photographic, and information processing equipment and media	255.4	271.1
Sporting equipment, supplies, guns and ammunition	61.3	59.7
Sports and recreational vehicles	43.6	40.1
Recreational books	33.1	32.9
Musical instruments	6.4	5.6
Other durable goods	**129.9**	**126.9**
...		
Educational books	8.4	7.7
Nondurable goods	**2041.2**	**2017.4**
Food and beverages purchased for off-premises consumption	**691.6**	**685.1**
Food and nonalcoholic beverages purchased for off-premises consumption	586.6	581.9
Alcoholic beverages purchased for off-premises consumption	104.6	102.7
Food produced and consumed on farms	0.4	0.5
Clothing and footwear	**341.7**	**326.8**
Gasoline and other energy goods	**282.0**	**285.5**
Motor vehicle fuels, lubricants and fluids	265.3	265.3
Fuel oil and other fuels	16.8	20.0
Other nondurable goods	**731.3**	**723.1**
...		
Recreational items	129.5	129.3
Household supplies	109.8	105.1
Personal care products	85.7	83.4
Tobacco	64.7	60.7
Magazines, newspapers and stationery	67.8	65.1
Net expenditures abroad by US residents	4.6	5.9
Services	**6082.3**	**6032.7**
Household consumption expenditures (for services)	**5816.1**	**5777.0**
Housing and utilities	**1638.6**	**1656.9**

(Continued)

Table 12.1 Continued

	2009	2009
Health care	**1410.0**	**1440.4**
Transportation services	**273.1**	**250.9**
Motor vehicle services	200.2	182.4
Motor vehicle maintenance and repair	141.4	131.3
Other motor vehicle services	59.0	51.2
Public transportation	72.9	68.5
Ground transportation	26.8	25.2
Air transportation	43.1	40.4
Water transportation	3.1	3.1
Recreation services	**350.0**	**341.8**
Membership clubs, sports centres, parks, theatres and museums	117.7	113.9
Audio–video, photographic and information processing equipment services	96.1	95.3
Gambling	101.4	99.4
Other recreational services	34.9	33.3
Food services and accommodations	**547.6**	**527.7**
Food services	472.1	456.5
Purchased meals and beverages	459.2	443.6
...		
Financial services and insurance	**770.9**	**743.0**
Other services	**826.5**	**817.0**
...		
Net foreign travel	−21.9	−16.5
Foreign travel by US residents	99.5	95.3
Less: expenditures in the USA by nonresidents	121.4	111.8
Final consumption expenditures of nonprofit institutions serving households	**267.3**	**256.0**

Source: U.S Department of Commerce http://www.bea.gov/national/nipaweb/TableView.asp?SelectedTable=71&Freq=Year&First Year=2008&LastYear=20090

good or service depends on the status of the customer (i.e. those restaurant and café meals consumed by tourists). Nearly all of the broad industry groups are involved to a greater or lesser extent in providing goods and services directly to tourists. While all the products that are produced and consumed in meeting tourism demand are counted in national economic accounts, the specific contribution of tourism is not readily apparent.

Because of this many countries now compile Tourism Satellite Accounts (TSA). Frechtling (2010) discusses TSA concepts, definitions and its structure as well as the five macroeconomic variables produced by this method. TSAs partition industries into tourism and non-tourism activities so that the direct contribution of tourism to the economy can be measured on a consistent basis with more traditional industries such as manufacturing, agriculture and retail trade. TSAs are generally prepared using tourism surveys to impute tourism values to broader economic activities. Typically, TSAs are compiled using a combination of visitors expenditure data from surveys conducted on tourists and industry data from national economic accounts. However, it should be noted that TSA estimates of tourism's value relates only to the direct impact of tourism. TSAs ignore tourism's indirect contribution to the economy (this is discussed later in this chapter under the heading 'Multiplier'). Examples in the literature of measurement of economics impacts include West and Gamage's (2001) article which uses an I–O model to assess the economic impacts of tourism on the economy of Victoria in Australia. Similarly, the Australian Bureau of Statistics (ABS, 2009) explains the steps needed to calculate Tourism Gross Value Added (TGVA), Tourism GDP and Tourism Employment.

Exhibit 12.1 describes the contribution of tourism to the economy of Australia based on figures from its TSA.

EMPLOYMENT

Tourism is an important contributor to employment in many economies and tourism-induced employment has been discussed by a number of researchers. For example, Riley et al. (2002) examine tourism employment in a holistic way. They consider behavioural and economic perspectives to address questions that are salient to manpower planning, education planning and tourism management. The demand for labour is a derived demand. Labour is demanded when a good or service is demanded. PricewaterhouseCoopers (2002) analysed hotel employment trends in the UK where they noted that following spectacular job gains in the UK in the mid- to late-1990s, during 2000 and 2001 UK hotel employment was hurt by a combination of factors that included foot-and-mouth disease and the global economic slowdown. The article confirmed that for hospitality sector hotel occupancy is the primary driving force behind hotel employment trends. Employment in the leisure and tourism sector is thus directly related to expenditure on goods and services offered by the sector. Figure 12.2 shows the possible outcomes of leisure and tourism spending.

Some expenditure will be on imported goods or services and will therefore create employment overseas. Domestic recreation, leisure and tourism goods and services will be supplied as a result of domestic

Exhibit 12.1   Tourism and the Australian economy

- Tourism is a significant factor in the Australian economy as it stimulates a wide range of industries.
- Tourism GDP is the total market value of Australian produced goods and services consumed by tourists after deducting the cost of goods and services used up in the process of production.
  - In 2009–10, direct tourism GDP increased 3.2 per cent … to $34 billion … Tourism's share of total GDP remained constant at 2.6 per cent.
  - Domestic tourism was responsible for 73 per cent of total direct tourism GDP.
  - International tourism was responsible for 27 per cent of total direct tourism GDP.
  - Over the period 1997–98 to 2009–10, direct tourism GDP increased [by] 85 per cent … an average annual growth rate of 5.2 per cent.
- TGVA measures the value of tourism gross output at factor prices (i.e. product taxes such as the GST are excluded) by all industries which supply tourism products. This measure also excludes the value of the inputs used in producing these tourism products.
  - In 2009–10, direct tourism GVA increased 3.2 per cent…to $31 billion.
  - The industries which accounted for the largest shares of TGVA were:
    - accommodation ($5.4 billion)
    - air, water and other transport ($4.6 billion)
    - cafes, restaurants and takeaway food services ($3.5 billion)
    - other retail trade ($3.9 billion)
    - education and training ($2.5 billion).

Source: Adapted from Australian Government Department of Resources, Energy and Tourism, Tourism Satellite Account 2009–2010, Summary of Key Results (http://www.ret. gov.au/tourism/Documents/Tourism%20Statistics/2009-10%20TSA%20summary%20 of%20key%20results%20web%20factsheet.pdf).

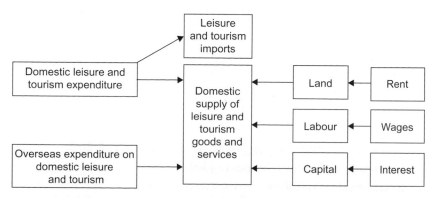

Figure 12.2   Demand for labour in leisure and tourism sector.

Table 12.2 Share of employment in the visitor economy in the UK	
Country	Per cent of total employment provided by the visitor economy
England	4.2
Scotland	5.3
Wales	6.3
Northern Ireland	3.0
UK Total	4.0
Source: Deloitte and Oxford Economics, 2010.	

expenditure and exports. The resulting derived demand for labour will also depend upon the price of labour relative to other factors of production and the possible technical mix of factors of production able to provide the goods or services. For example, if the price of labour rises, producers will attempt to use more machinery (capital) where this is technically possible. It is generally the case that the recreation, leisure and tourism share of total employment is higher than its share of industry gross value added. This is because this sector tends to be more labour intensive, on average, than other forms of economic activity.

Table 12.2 shows the relative importance of employment in what is called the visitor economy in the UK. It demonstrates an overall contribution to UK employment of about 4 per cent of the workforce. However, in some areas of the UK leisure and tourism is of particular significance and is one of the main sources of economic activity. For example, Deloitte and Oxford Economics (2010) found that approximately 31 per cent of the workforce of the rural area of the Isles of Scilly was employed in tourist industry and 21 per cent in the urban area of Kensington and Chelsea. Additionally, Thomas and Townsend (2001) examine evidence on tourism employment in the UK and find that the 1990s show major departures from patterns of change of the 1980s and from other sectors in the 1990s. In the 1990s they note that the tourism sector no longer seemed to exhibit the exceptionally rapid growth that had been almost an article of faith for those who build economic development strategies around tourism.

In Australia, there were about 500,500 persons in tourism-generated employment in 2009–2010, an increase of 1.4 per cent on the previous year, and the tourism share of total employed persons was 4.5 per cent. The distribution of tourism related employment was:

- Accommodation: 71,500
- Cafes, restaurants and takeaway food services: 128,200
- Air, water and other transport: 35,000
- Retail trade: 95,900
- Education and training: 32,800 (ABS, 2009).

Sector	2005	2006	2007	2008	2009
Services	22.023	22.256	22.411	22.574	22.140
Manufacturing	3.102	2.976	2.913	2.869	2.642

Table 12.3 Employees by sector, Great Britain (millions)

Source: UK Office of National Statistics, Annual Abstract.

It is more difficult to extract employment in leisure manufacturing from published data, as many of the industrial classifications used by governments include leisure and non-leisure items. Table 12.3 shows the employment totals for the services and manufacturers sectors in Great Britain. It shows a picture common in many post-industrial nations. Whilst employment in the services sector has grown in importance, manufacturing employment has shown a long-term decline. This is known as deindustrialization. This is caused by three factors. First, technological progress enables productivity increases in manufacturing and thus the ratio of labour input to output declines. Second, manufacturing has been subject to intense competition from low-labour cost countries such as China and Vietnam, so many manufactured goods are now imported. Third, as incomes increase expenditure on services increases by a greater proportion (services demonstrate high-income elasticity of demand). Although in many cases new service sector jobs have made up for job losses in manufactures, there are some concerns that wage levels for these emerging industries are less than those of the declining industries. Smeral (2003) discusses why in general, tourism grows faster than the economy as a whole. He notes structural changes in demand and the differentials between productivity in tourism and manufacturing. He also notes that the demand factor explains why tourism's income elasticity is above 1.

Wages

Wages in any particular labour market will be determined by the demand and supply of labour but will also be influenced by Trade Union activity and minimum wage legislation. In this regard, Waddoups (2001) has investigated the situation of a significant union presence in the hotel–casino industry in Las Vegas, Nevada, USA, juxtaposed to the near absence of union representation in Reno. Results of the analysis show a significantly higher incidence of poverty-level wages among hotel–casino workers in Reno compared to workers in similar occupations in Las Vegas. The supply of labour to some parts of the recreation leisure and tourism (e.g. hotels and catering) sector is largely unskilled and this exerts a downward pressure on wages. Similarly, more women than men are employed in this sector and the lower wages of the sector therefore reflect the lower wages paid to women than men in general.

Table 12.4 Average annual salaries, selected sectors, Australia (AUS$)

Sector	Salary
Accounting	81,936
Banking and Financial Services	92,900
Community, Sport and Leisure	62,064
Construction, Building and Architecture	109,295
Customer Service and Call Centre	54,135
Education and Training	65,625
Executive/Corporate Strategy	110,240
Hospitality, Travel and Tourism	53,929
Human Resources and Recruitment	91,242
Insurance and Superannuation	79,841
IT and Telecommunications	106,503
Manufacturing	82,701
Marketing	84,813
Medical and Healthcare	80,748
Mining, Oil and Gas	145,453
Property and Real Estate	83,400
Retail	61,750

Source: Adapted from MyCareer (http://content.mycareer.com.au/salary-centre).

This is illustrated in Table 12.4 which shows comparative annual salaries of selected industries in Australia. These figures should be viewed with some care as it is not always easy to classify jobs accurately to the leisure or tourism sector (e.g. does an accountant for a leisure organization appear under professional and business services or leisure?). However, the figures show that salaries in the hospitality, travel and tourism industries are significantly lower than those in other sectors. It is notable that the salary levels in the new service sector jobs are rarely as high as those in the old manufacturing sector jobs that they replace.

Workers in the hotel and catering sector are amongst the key beneficiaries of minimum wage legislation where it exists.

TAXATION

Recreation, leisure and tourism activities also offer an important stream of taxation revenue. There are a variety of forms of taxes that impact on these activities. These include general taxes and specific tourism taxes. General taxes include sales, income and profits

Plate 12 Tourism's contribution to tax revenue. *Source: The author.*

taxes and these are levied across the economy and naturally include leisure and tourism activities. Specific tourism taxes include departure taxes (Plate 12), entry taxes and accommodation taxes.

A World Travel and Tourism Council (WTTC, 2009) research report forecast that travel and tourism's global direct, indirect and personal tax contribution will exceed 10 per cent of total taxation revenues by 2020. This contribution is projected to grow to $1765.3 billion by 2010. Examples of specific taxes on the leisure and tourism sector include:

- The 5 per cent tax on luxury hotel rooms in New York (1990) (later removed).
- The 10 per cent bed tax on hotels in central Sydney (1997) (later removed).
- The Balearic Islands (Spain) tax on tourists staying in hotels or rented flats (2002) (later removed).

Exhibit 12.2 South Dakota's (USA) tourism tax

'The tourism or seasonal tax is an additional tax on certain lodging and amusement services that is imposed for tourism promotion. Beginning July 1, 2009 through June 30, 2011, the tourism tax rate will increase to 1.5%. Tourism tax applies to the gross receipts of:

- Hotels and Lodging Establishments
- Campgrounds
- Motor Vehicle Rentals
- Recreational Equipment Rentals
- Recreational Services
- Spectator Events
- Visitor Attractions
- Visitor-Intensive Businesses

The tourism tax on lodging establishments, campgrounds, motor vehicle rentals, recreational equipment rentals, recreational services, spectator events and visitor attractions applies year-round. The tourism tax on visitor-intensive businesses applies during the months of June, July, August, and September'.

Source: South Dakota Department of Revenue & Regulation (http://www.state.sd.us/drr2/businesstax/publications/taxfacts/tourism.pdf).

- The APD in the UK which has been progressively increased and varies according to flight length.
- The accommodation tax imposed in Rome between €1 and €3 per night (2011).
- The Maldives' Tourism Goods and Services Tax of 3.5 per cent on services supplied by the country's travel industry (2011).

Exhibit 12.2 details the scope and extent of South Dakota's (USA) Tourism Tax which is to be used to finance tourism promotion.

As well as providing revenue taxes may be used for macroeconomic management (see later in this chapter), for financing special projects and for discouraging consumption of goods and services which have negative externalities (see Chapters 7 and 17).

MULTIPLIERS

The analysis of data in the previous sections has looked at tourism, recreation and leisure contributions to national income and the economy at a single point in time. This is termed as 'static' analysis. However, consideration of Figure 12.1 shows that tourism and leisure expenditure, like any other form of expenditure, also has 'dynamic' or 'multiplier' (Archer, 1982) effects due to the circular flow of income and expenditure in the economy. The initial effects of expenditure will

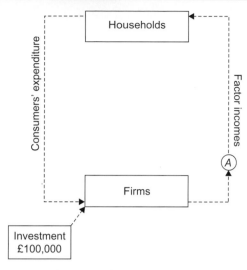

Figure 12.3 Investment and the circular flow of income.

generate income but there will be further effects as that income generates expenditure and so on.

Figure 12.3 illustrates the circular flow of income and expenditure derived from Figure 12.1. Assume now that there is an investment into this closed system of £100,000 on a new leisure complex. Firms will hire factors of production to the value of £100,000 and therefore national income, measured at point A, will rise by £100,000. However, the effects of the investment do not stop there. The workers who earned money from building the complex will spend their money in shops and bars and so on. Thus, the incomes of shop and bar owners will rise. They in turn will spend their incomes. In other words, a circular flow of income and expenditure will take place. The investment expenditure sets in motion a dynamic process, and the total extra income passing point A will exceed the initial £100,000. This is known as the multiplier effect.

In the closed system illustrated by Figure 12.3, the effect would be perpetual and infinite, with the extra expenditure circulating round and round the system. In the real world however there are points at which money can leave and enter the system. This is illustrated in Figure 12.4.

The key leakages or withdrawals from the economy are savings, imports and taxes. Savings represents funds retained by households and firms. Imports result in expenditure flowing overseas, and taxes represent money taken out of the circular flow of income by the government in the form of income tax, VAT and corporation tax, for example.

On the other hand, there are also injections or flows into the circular flow of income. These are investment, exports resulting in money from overseas entering the circular flow, and government spending including, for example, pensions and unemployment benefit. Clearly

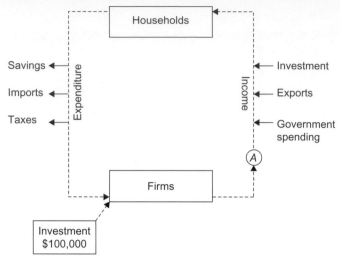

Figure 12.4 Circular flow with injections and leakages.

there are often strong relationships between specific leakages and injections. To keep the model simple, injections and leakages are located neatly around the system but in reality they occur in many different places.

The existence of leakages means that money is flowing out of the economy during each cycle. So, in the example of the £100,000 investment in a leisure complex, perhaps £10,000 might be saved by workers, £5000 spent on imported goods and £10,000 taken in taxation. Thus, the initial effect on national income measured at point *A* in Figure 12.4 is £100,000. Out of this, £25,000 will be lost in leakages from the economy, leaving £75,000 to recirculate, adding another £75,000 to national income at point *A*. This process then continues, but with each cycle becoming smaller. It should be seen that the size of the multiplier effect will depend upon the amount of the original injection under examination and the leakages from the economy.

The Keynesian multiplier

The Keynesian multiplier can now be formally analysed. The multiplier (*k*) shows the amount by which a change in expenditure (ΔEXP) in an economy leads to a change in national income (ΔY).

$$\Delta EXP \times k = \Delta Y$$

Thus, if an increase in investment on a leisure complex of £100,000 led to a final increase in national income of £400,000, then the multiplier would have a value of 4.

The multiplier can be illustrated by reference to Table 12.5 and Figure 12.5.

Table 12.5 Multiplier rounds

Round	ΔS	ΔT	ΔM	ΔEXP	ΔY
1				100,000	100,000
2	10,000	10,000	5000	75,000	75,000
3	7500	7500	3750	56,250	56,250
4	5625	5625	2812.50	42,187.50	42,187.50
5	4218.75	4218.75	2109.36	31,640.63	31,640.63
6	3164.06	3164.06	1582.03	23,730.47	23,730.47
7	2373.05	2373.05	1186.02	17,797.85	17,797.85
8	1779.76	1779.76	889.89	13,348.39	13,348.39
$9 - n$	...	...	...	...	...
Total				400,000	400,000

Rounds $9 - n$ represent the remaining multiplier rounds. S: savings; T, taxes; M, imports; EXP, expenditure; Y, income; Δ, change in.

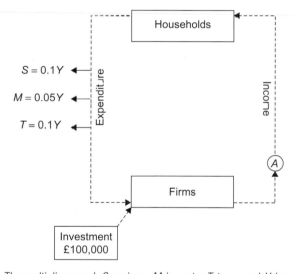

Figure 12.5 The multiplier round. *S*, savings; *M*, imports; *T*, taxes and *Y*, income.

Investment in the leisure complex of £100,000 is made and national income at point *A* is raised by £100,000. In round 2, leakages consist of £10,000 in savings, £10,000 in taxes and £5000 in imports, leaving £75,000 in domestic expenditure to recirculate round the circular flow. An extra £75,000 is therefore added to national income at point *A*. In round 3, leakages consist of £7500 in savings, £7500 in taxes and £3750 in imports, leaving £56,250 in domestic expenditure. This process continues, and the leakages reduce the value of extra domestic expenditure and national income at every round. In fact, the extra amounts of national income tend towards zero. If the additions to national income in column 6, for years $1 - n$ (where n is the year in which the effect has dwindled to near zero), were added up, they would sum to £400,000, thus giving a value for the multiplier of 4.

There is also a formula for calculating the multiplier:

k = 1/MPL

where MPL is the marginal propensity to leak (the proportion of extra income that leaks out of the economy).

MPL = MPS + MPM + MPT

where MPS is the marginal propensity to save (the proportion of extra income saved), MPM is the marginal propensity to spend on imports (the proportion of extra income spent on imports) and MPT is the marginal propensity to be taxed (the proportion of extra income taken in taxes).

In the earlier example, MPS = $0.1Y$, MPM = $0.05Y$ and MPT = $0.1Y$, where Y = income. Therefore:

k = 1/(0.1 + 0.05 + 0.1)
k = 1/0.25
k = 4

Tourism multipliers

Considerable research has been done into the impact of tourism and leisure expenditure using multiplier techniques. Salma (2002) explains the meaning of the indirect effects of tourism and measured these effects for the Australian economy and this is illustrated in Exhibit 12.3.

The aim of this approach is to assess the full impact of the sector on incomes, output and employment at national, regional and local levels. However, Leiper (1999) argues that many studies grossly overestimated tourism's contribution to employment in Australia. Impacts and multipliers are clearly an important issue for governments in assessing the contribution of such developments to economic activity. The main multipliers developed for impact analysis are:

- the output multiplier
- the income multiplier
- the employment multiplier
- the government revenue multiplier.

Taking the case of the tourism income multiplier (TIM), values vary according to leakages, as summarized in Table 12.6, and actual results include Canada (TIM = 2.5), UK (TIM = 1.8), Iceland (TIM = 0.6) and Edinburgh (TIM = 0.4).

Exhibit 12.3 Indicators of direct, indirect and total contribution of tourism to the economy of Australia

'The economic contribution of tourism has two elements: direct and indirect. The direct contribution is solely concerned with the immediate effect of expenditure made by visitors. For example, when a tourist uses a taxi service, the direct output effect includes only the service of the taxi driver and the direct employment effect includes the proportion of the driver's employment that is spent driving tourists.

The taxi driver, however, buys fuel from a petrol station, machinery parts from a garage, meals while on duty from a food outlet and so on. Petrol stations, garages and food outlets all hire staff and produce output to serve the taxi drivers, who in turn serve customers, some of whom are tourists. The food outlet in turn engages food manufacturers, electricity companies, delivery services and many other industries to provide the necessary inputs required to prepare the snacks it sells. Similarly, many industries are involved in supplying the necessary inputs to the petrol stations and the garages. The chain effects on output and jobs started by the initial taxi service demand of the tourist comprise what is termed tourism's indirect effects on output and employment'.

	Direct contribution	Indirect contribution	Total contribution
TGVA (AUS$ million)	26,284	26,772	53,056
Per cent	4.3	4.4	8.7
Tourism GDP ($ million)	31,814	27,287	59,101
Per cent	4.7	4.1	8.8
Tourism employment ('000 jobs)	551	397	948
Per cent	6.0	4.3	10.4

Source: Adapted from Salma (2002), Indirect Economic Contribution of Tourism to Australia (www.abs.gov.au).

Table 12.6 Multiplier and expenditure impacts

Value of multiplier	Leakages from the economy	Impact of expenditure on income
High	Low	High
Low	High	Low

Direct, indirect and induced effects

Discussion of the multiplier enables us to clarify the difference between the direct, indirect and induced effects of tourism expenditure.

- The direct effects of expenditure are those which accrue to the suppliers who supply tourists directly with goods and services (e.g. hotels, restaurants and so on).

Exhibit 12.4 Tourism impacts and the multiplier effect in the Philippines

- International tourist arrivals to the Philippines reached 3 million in 2007.
- This represents a growth of 72 per cent from 2001 level.
- The market declined by 3 per cent in 2009 due to the impact of the global recession.
- The market was predicted to recover in 2010 with 2.5 per cent growth compared to the 2009 value.
- International tourist receipts accounted for 23 per cent of Philippine service exports.
- The tourism industry generates 3,255,000 million jobs.
- Economists have calculated from input–output tables of the Philippines economy that tourism generates revenues of about 6 billion pesos from foreign visitors.
- The leading sectors that benefit from tourist expenditure are accommodation, food and beverage, guide tours, entertainment, local transport and shopping.
- The case of The Imperial Palace on Mactan Island illustrates the multiplier effects of tourism:
  - Capacity: 556 rooms.
  - Investment cost: 2.5 billion pesos.
  - Employment: 714 workers.
  - Indirect tourism expenditure includes about 5–7 million pesos for vegetables, fruits, pork, fish, seafood, eggs, chicken and other food items that Cebu and other nearby provinces can supply.

Source: Adapted from the Manila Bulletin (http://mb.com.ph/articles/259321/good-record-tourism).

- The indirect effects of expenditure result from supply chain activities that are needed to satisfy the initial direct expenditure, so for example restaurants need to purchase food, hotels need to employ labour and so on.
- The induced effect of tourism expenditure arises when the recipients of direct and indirect expenditure spend their extra incomes earned from this expenditure in the economy. This spending creates further incomes in the economy which in turn will be spent and it is this circular process that generates the multiplier effects.

Exhibit 12.4 discusses tourism impacts, direct, indirect and induced effects and multipliers in the Philippines.

LEISURE AND TOURISM INFLATION

Inflation can be defined as a rise in the general level of prices or a fall in the purchasing power of money. It is measured by the retail price index (RPI). If one country has a faster rate of inflation than

Table 12.7 Tourism price index (e.g. Kenyan Shillings)

Item	Weight (*W*)	2008			2009			2010		
		Price (*P*)	*P* × *W*		Price (*P*)	*P* × *W*		Price (*P*)	*P* × *W*	
Wine (25 cl)	0.4	200	80		220	88		250	100	
Beer (0.5 L)	4.0	190	760		195	780		200	800	
Three-course meal	11.6	800	9280		880	10,208		950	11,020	
...	...	...	...		...	...		...	...	
...	...	...	...		...	...		...	...	
Total			50,107			52,612			56,119	
Index multiple					0.0019957291					
Index			100			105			112	

Item = row 1, column 1; the dots in rows 5 and 6 denote the rest of the basket of goods.

that of other countries, it can cause a decline in international competitiveness. This is likely to affect firms producing leisure products for the export market, and countries which rely on tourism. It is less likely to affect firms in leisure services since customers rarely have the option to seek lower prices overseas for these.

Constructing a tourism destination price index

It is possible to construct a tourism destination price index (TDPI) using a similar methodology to that used to construct the general RPI. Table 12.7 gives an example of such an index. The steps are as follows (with rows and columns referring to Table 12.7):

- First, it is necessary to define the population for whom the index is intended. This might be a specific index for golfers or skiers.
- Next an expenditure survey must be conducted to establish the spending patterns of the target population, ensuring that a representative sample of the target population is surveyed.
- From this two important findings should emerge – first a 'basket of goods' (and services) that lists the items bought by tourists can be compiled (column 1) and second the relative importance of each item can be gauged from the expenditure survey and each item given a weighting accordingly. For example, if an expenditure survey in Kenya showed 10 times more beer to be consumed than wine, then beer would be assigned a weighting 10 times more than that for wine (column 2). Thus, if beer and wine both rose in price by 20 per cent, the effect of wine on the TDPI would be less than the beer effect.

Table 12.8 Tourism price index (exchange rate-adjusted)

	2008	2009	2010
Total (KES)	50,107	52,612	56,119
£1 = ? KES	112	120	125
Total (£s)	447.4	438.4	449.0
Index multiple		0.2235	
Index	100	97.98	100.35

KES = Kenyan Shilling.

- A survey of the prices of the basket of goods is then conducted (column 3).
- Expenditure on each item is determined by multiplying its price by its weighting (column 4).
- The total expenditure on the basket of goods is recorded (row 8).
- This amount is then converted to an index number with base 100, by using a multiplier (row 9), and this becomes the base year reading. (For example, if the expenditure total is £50, a multiplier of 2 is needed to convert the result to 100.)
- The basket of goods is priced at regular intervals (columns 5 and 7), with expenditure totals (row 8) being converted to an index number (row 10) using the multiplier established in the base year (row 9).

The index resulting from this exercise (Table 12.7) gives a picture of tourism inflation in the local currency. It is possible to adjust the index to reflect exchange rate conditions in different countries. Thus, whilst Table 12.7 measures tourism inflation for a Kenyan visitor to a Kenyan destination, Table 12.8 shows how the index can be adapted for a British visitor.

Table 12.8 uses the expenditure data from row 8 of Table 12.7. This is then converted to an equivalent in the currency under consideration (sterling in this example). A new index multiple is calculated to convert the raw expenditure figure to an index number with base 100. Comparison of the two tables shows the importance of considering exchange rate fluctuations when comparing prices between tourist destinations. In this case whilst Table 12.7 shows domestic inflation is pushing up prices in the local currency, Table 12.8 shows that for British visitors these price rises are largely offset by a fall in the value of the Kenyan Shilling.

It must be remembered that any tourism price index represents an average picture, and individuals will be affected differently according to their particular expenditure patterns. Care must also be exercised in the collecting of data. There must be consistency of sources,

Table 12.9 Big Mac prices (US$) for selected countries (2010)			
Norway	7.20	Singapore	3.08
Switzerland	6.19	Poland	2.60
Euro Area	4.33	Russia	2.33
Australia	3.84	Philippines	2.19
USA	3.73	Malaysia	2.19
Japan	3.67	Thailand	2.17
UK	3.48	China	1.95
Hungary	3.33	Hong Kong	1.90

Source: The Economist.

otherwise the index will be distorted by changes in prices which result, for example, by moving from a local store to a supermarket.

The Economist publishes an index each year which records the price of a Big Mac across a range of different countries. Since the Big Mac is a standardized product it can provide some indication of the price competitiveness of different destinations. However, since it is an American product it may provide something of a distorted picture of prices since products using more usual local ingredients may well be cheaper than Big Macs. Table 12.9 reproduces parts of the Big Mac index for 2010.

GOVERNMENT POLICY

Income and employment

Governments throughout the world see recreation, leisure and tourism as a source of employment, particularly where structural changes in the economy have led to job losses. Government policies to promote employment may include the following:

- *Demand management*: Where there is unemployment throughout the economy, some economists advocate government stimulation of aggregate demand so as to induce more production and thus employment. Aggregate demand may be stimulated through tax cuts, increased government spending and interest rate cuts. The major drawback to such a policy is its tendency to encourage inflation.
- *Export-led policies*: Overseas expenditure on leisure and tourism products can contribute to employment. Government policy here includes expenditure on overseas marketing to promote tourist demand for leisure, recreation and tourism services. A low-exchange rate also assists exports of services and leisure goods.

- *Project assistance*: The government also considers direct assistance with projects on an individual basis, particularly where a project can be shown to bring employment to areas of high unemployment (see Chapter 11). For example, there is considerable competition between countries over inducements offered to lure Disney Theme Parks. The EU also has a regional fund which can be a source of financial assistance.

Inflation

Governments of countries with comparatively high rates of inflation may utilize counter-inflationary policy. However, it is important first to diagnose the cause of inflation.

Causes of inflation

The causes of inflation can be divided into the categories of cost-push, demand-pull, monetary, taxation and expectations.

Cost-push inflation occurs when increased production costs are passed on as price rises. These can include, first, wage increases which outstrip productivity increases. Second, increased raw material prices can be important. If raw materials are imported, a fall in the exchange rate can increase their local currency price. Demand-pull inflation tends to occur when an economy is growing too fast. It arises because the aggregate demand in the economy exceeds the aggregate supply in the economy and therefore prices are bid up. For example, labour may become scarce, putting an upward pressure on wages.

Too rapid an increase in the money supply of an economy can cause an increase on consumer credit which can stimulate demand-pull inflation and accommodate cost-push inflation. Increases in indirect taxes such as sales taxes will have an effect on prices, whilst if people expect inflation to rise, they will often seek to protect their living standards by higher-wage demands. These of course will then cause the very inflation that people are seeking to avoid.

Counter-inflationary policy

Government counter-inflationary policy will affect the economic environment of leisure and tourism organizations. Cost-push inflation may be tackled by a high-exchange rate policy. Whilst this may be good for tackling inflation, it makes firms' exports less competitive. Wage rises may be tackled by government-imposed incomes policy to curb pay increases. This may cause a deterioration in industrial relations. Deflationary policy may be used to tackle demand-pull inflation. This may entail increasing interest rates to curb consumer borrowing or increased taxes to reduce consumer spending. Either way, whilst inflation may be tackled, firms will suffer a general contraction in demand.

High-interest rates are sometimes also used to curb overexpansion of the money supply by reducing the demand for borrowing. Indeed many Central Banks now set national interest rates at a level to control inflation.

REVIEW OF KEY TERMS

- Macroeconomics: the study of the national economy.
- National income: a measure of the total level of economic activity which takes place in an economy over a year.
- GDP: gross domestic product.
- GNP: gross national product.
- NNP: net national product (national income.
- Money national income: national income calculated at current prices.
- Real national income: national income calculated at constant prices (inflationary element removed).
- Tourism Income Multiplier: exaggerated effect of a change in tourism expenditure on an area's income.
- TDPI: tourism destination price index.
- Basket of goods: typical items bought by a defined group.
- Cost-push inflation: inflation caused by changes in input prices.
- Demand-pull inflation: inflation caused by excess of aggregate demand over aggregate supply.
- Demand management: government policy to influence total demand in an economy.

Data Questions

Task 12.1

Table 12.10 shows inflation rates for selected countries.

Table 12.10 Inflation rates (consumer prices annual change)

	2007	2008	2009	2010
Japan	0.0	1.4	−1.4	−1.4
UK	2.3	3.6	2.2	2.7
Turkey	8.8	10.4	6.3	9.7
Thailand	2.2	5.5	−0.8	3.2
USA	2.9	3.8	−1.3	2.1

Source: Adapted from IMF, World Economic Outlook.

Task 12.1 continued

Recap Questions

1 If entrance to Disneyland, Florida, costs $20 at the beginning of 2007 and its price has kept pace with inflation, what would a ticket cost at the beginning of 2008?

2 Why might the RPI for a country not be a good guide to tourism prices?

3 What other information would you seek before deciding on which countries might be good or bad value to visit?

4 Account for the differing rates of inflation between countries.

5 Describe and account for the possible causes of the different inflationary conditions in Japan and Turkey.

6 What likely consequences are there of inflation in Japan and Turkey?

7 Why did many countries see a fall in prices in 2009?

Task 12.2 **TSA – Fiji Islands**

- The first Fiji Tourism Satellite Account for 1995 brought together all the diverse aspects of tourism by providing a tourism dimension to the framework of the system of national accounts which makes it possible to separate and examine the demand and supply sides of tourism within this integrated system.

- It also accounts for the substantial spin-offs to the other economic sectors including agriculture, construction, transport and telecommunications industries.

- The development of TSA has been greatly influenced by the recognition that its implementation will serve to:
  - Increase and improve knowledge of tourism's importance relative to overall economic activity in the country.
  - Provide an instrument for designing more efficient policies relating to tourism and its employment aspects.
  - Create awareness among the various players directly and indirectly involved with tourism of the economic importance of this activity.

- The TSA focuses greatly on the direct impacts of tourism particularly the direct tourism demand, direct employment in tourism. compensation of tourism employees, gross fixed capital formation and the total net capital stock as well as the import leakage. It also covers the multiplier effects of tourism spending in the Fiji Islands.

- Analysis of import leakage indicated that the supply of tourism products requires three types of imports: (i) final goods and services, or directly consumable items such as foreign liquor, cigarettes; (ii) intermediate inputs or raw materials such as flour, meat, fuel; and (iii) capital goods and services such as machinery and equipment, busses and coaches. The total imports of goods and services purchased directly by tourists in 1995 was $122 million which is approximately 20% (Import leakage) of the total foreign exchange earnings.

- Multiplier analysis for the TSA assesses the initial spending which leads to several rounds of spending known as backward linkages or indirect impacts.

- Type I multiplier takes into account the direct and indirect effects while Type II multiplier is able to capture, in addition to direct and indirect impacts, the effects of incomes received by employees in the tourism industries which are known as induced effects.

- TSA used three types of multipliers namely output multipliers, employment multipliers and income multipliers. The tourism output multiplier (Type 1) applied to total tourism industries was 1.7 which means that each additional one dollar spending on tourism products created $1.7 worth of output in all industries.

- In relation to the employment effects, one additional employee in the tourism sector led to the creation of 1.95 of employment in the Fiji Islands.

- The direct and indirect employment opportunities created was 23,790 and when induced effects are taken into account, total employment created due to tourism in the Fiji Islands was 31,110.

- The TSA indicated that an income of one dollar from employment in the tourism industry could create $1.89 income throughout the economy.

Source: Extracted and adapted from Fiji Ministry of Tourism Press Release (http://www.tourism.gov.fj/press_release/Press%20Release%20-%20TSA95.pdf).

Recap Questions

1 Why are TSAs necessary?
2 How are TSAs compiled?
3 What are the benefits of compiling TSAs?
4 Distinguish between output multipliers, employment multipliers and income multipliers.
5 What factors affect the size of the multiplier in Fiji?
6 Distinguish between the direct, indirect and induced effects of tourism.

Task 12.3 **Consultant's report. Deloitte and Oxford Economics (2010).** *The Economic Contribution of the Visitor Economy: UK and the Nations.* **London: Visit Britain.**

Visit Britain commissioned Deloitte and Oxford Economics to report on the economic contribution of the visitor economy to the UK. Its main findings were:

- The visitor economy contributes about £52 billion in direct expenditure to the economy or 4 per cent of GDP.

- The visitor economy contributes about £63 billion in indirect expenditure to the economy through the subsequent effects of direct expenditure on the supply chain.

- The total direct and indirect economic impact of the visitor economy is around £115 billion or 8.9 per cent of GDP.

- The visitor economy directly supports around 1.36 million jobs or 4 per cent of total employment.

- The visitor economy is particularly important for the economic vitality of rural areas.

- The visitor economy offers particular opportunities for the provision of employment for women.

- The visitor economy encourages enterprise since small- and medium-sized businesses are able to enter the industry with relative ease.

- In the period to 2020 the visitor economy will be one of the best performing sectors in the economy directly contributing £87 billion (4.1 per cent of total) to GDP and generating 1.5 million jobs (4.6 per cent of total) by 2020.

Recap Questions

1 Explain the term direct expenditure with examples.
2 Explain the term indirect expenditure with examples.
3 What are the arguments for and against a tourism tax in the UK in the form of a hotel bed tax?
4 What steps could the government take to increase the economic impact of tourism in the UK?
5 What are the main factors that will determine the rate of growth of the visitor economy over the next 10 years?

MULTIPLE CHOICE

1 Which of the following is not true?
   (a) National income = national expenditure.
   (b) Real and money will be the same where there is no inflation.
   (c) Employment in the services sector is falling in most developed economies.
   (d) Minimum wages have little effect on those working in the hospitality industry.

2 TSAs:
   (a) Are useful because otherwise the contribution of tourism to GNP is underestimated.
   (b) Are necessary because the contribution of tourism to GNP is often overestimated.
   (c) Measure the contribution of space tourism to the economy.
   (d) Are needed to discount the effects of inflation on tourism's value to GNP.

3 A survey on a tourism destination found that for every £1 spent, 25 penny leaked out of the economy of the destination in the form of savings, taxes and imported goods. The value of the destination income multiplier would be:
   (a) 4.00.
   (b) 0.75.
   (c) 0.25.
   (d) 2.50.

4 Which of the following is classified as a leakage in the circular flow of income?
   (a) Savings.
   (b) Investment.

(c) Inflation.

(d) Exports.

5 Which of the following is not true?

(a) Cost-push inflation occurs when increased production costs are passed on as price rises.

(b) Inflation can be defined as a rise in the general level of prices.

(c) Inflation causes a rise in the purchasing power of money.

(d) Most Central Banks set interest rates to control the level of inflation.

REVIEW QUESTIONS

1 Distinguish between changes in money and real GNP.

2 What are the main leakages and injections into the circular flow of income?

3 What is meant by the TIM and what determines its size?

4 Outline the main steps involved in constructing a tourism price index.

5 What government policies have:

(a) Encouraged?

(b) Discouraged employment in the leisure and tourism sector?

6 Why is it difficult to measure the impact of recreation, leisure and tourism to the economy?

Websites of interest

Fiji Ministry of Tourism: www.tourism.gov.fj

Visit Britain: www.visitbritain.org

US Department of Commerce: //www.bea.gov

New Zealand statistics: www.stats.govt.nz/statsweb.nsf

Australian Bureau of Statistics: www.abs.gov.au

Canada statistics: www.statcan.gc.ca

International Monetary Fund: www.imf.org

C H A P T E R **13**

Economic development and regeneration

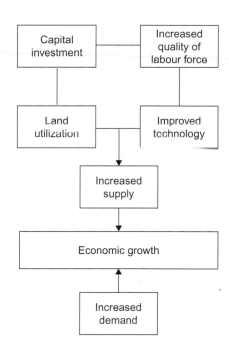

Objectives and learning outcomes

The objective of this chapter is to examine how recreation, leisure and tourism can contribute to the long-term growth of economies and to the regeneration of areas affected by structural change. First, general aspects of economic growth will be discussed. Second, case studies will demonstrate how leisure and tourism have contributed to economic growth in developed countries such as France, Japan and Spain. Third, the special problems of growth and development in less-developed countries will be examined. Case studies of China and Vietnam will be used to illustrate the role of leisure and tourism in such development. There is clearly much further scope for tourism development in less-developed countries. Fourth, the chapter will consider the issue of regeneration. Issues surrounding the costs of economic growth and development will be examined in Chapters 16 and 17.

By studying this chapter, students should be able to:

- define and explain economic growth;
- review critically the concept of economic growth;
- understand the determinants of economic growth;
- evaluate appropriate growth strategies for developed and developing countries;
- evaluate the role of the sector in regeneration strategies;
- evaluate the contribution of the sector to growth.

MEANING AND MEASUREMENT OF ECONOMIC GROWTH

Meaning and measurement

Economic growth is defined as the increase in real output per capita of a country. There are thus three elements involved in its measurement. First, the change in output of an economy needs to be measured. The most commonly used measure of output is GNP. However, as explained in Chapter 12, money GNP or GNP at current prices can overestimate changes in a country's output. This is because they include increases due to higher prices (inflation) as well as higher output. Therefore, real GNP figures (or chained data) are used to calculate growth. Second, the GNP figures need to be adapted to take account of increases in population. Dividing real GNP by the population gives real GNP per capita.

Figure 13.1 illustrates some comparative data for international growth rates. Caution should be used in interpreting this data since many economies were still suffering from the effects of the economic

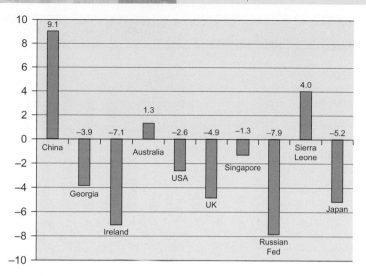

Figure 13.1 Growth rates (per cent change in real GDP) for selected countries, 2009.
Source: Adapted from World Bank *www.worldbank.org/data*

recession in 2009. Despite the recession it can be seen that the economy of China still exhibited remarkable growth of 9.1 per cent per annum, due largely to its economic reforms which have allowed foreign investment and private enterprise and its strong international competitiveness. Similarly, the Australian economy managed positive growth of 1.3 per cent, helped largely by its relationship with the Chinese economy. By contrast, a number of countries witnessed negative economic growth – meaning their output declined in 2009. These include two economies in transition (the Russian Federation and Georgia where economic reforms and the transition to the market economy still cause some economic problems) and also the mature economies of the UK, the USA and Japan. Ireland was hit particularly strongly by the recession with its economy shrinking by 7.1 per cent.

Problems of measurement

Figure 13.2 records per capita GNP data for various countries and demonstrates the huge international inequalities that are apparent. Burundi's GNP per capita at $150 in 2009 has barely increased from a figure of $140 in 1998. There is a huge gap between the data for Burundi and that of Switzerland which recorded GNP per capita of $65,430 in 2009. China of course has seen an impressive rise in GNP per capita from $750 in 1998 to $3650 in 2009. However, there are several problems involved in the measurement of GNP and thus economic growth. First, there are the problems associated with collecting national income data, as discussed in Chapter 12. Data collection is a particular problem in countries which do not have a highly developed statistical branch of government. Less-developed countries also have

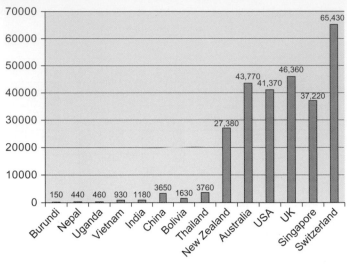

Figure 13.2 GNP per capita (US$), selected countries, 2009. *Source: Adapted from* World Bank *www.worldbank.org/data*

a bigger subsistence sector where goods and services are produced for self-consumption and therefore do not enter the market or appear on national income statistics. Second, in making international comparisons, country information measured in local currency is generally converted to dollar units. Thus, some apparent changes in growth may in fact stem from currency movements against the dollar. Third, over a period of time the labour force may work fewer hours in a week. GNP figures do not reflect this and they may therefore underestimate some aspects of economic improvement. Fourth, GNP per capita figures are an average. They may disguise the fact that there are large differences in incomes of the population or that some sectors of the community may actually be becoming poorer. Finally, economic activity which contributes to GNP has some unwanted side effects in the form of pollution. GNP information takes no account of these, a matter which is discussed more fully in Chapters 16 and 17.

Rationale for growth

The rationale for the pursuit of growth is that people become better off in an economic sense. There are more goods and services produced to meet people's material wants. This may result in some combination of more employment, more public services, less taxes, more leisure time or more consumption. How the benefits of growth are actually distributed depends on the workings of the economic system and government policy. In less-developed countries, the results of economic growth are generally much more profound, bringing social and environmental changes with material prosperity. Distribution of benefits is often less even. 'Those with land to sell, housing to rent, hotels to run, and labour, goods and services to sell favour it. The landless poor are generally less impressed'.

THE CAUSES OF ECONOMIC GROWTH

Economic growth is promoted by an increase in the quality or quantity of inputs into the economy. It can therefore be examined under the headings of land, labour, capital and technology.

Land

Different countries have not only differing amounts of land but also different types of land. Resources may include mineral and agricultural ones, and in the leisure and tourism sector, climate, scenery, coasts and countryside are important resources. It is by the exploitation of such resources that countries can use their comparative advantage against other possible tourist destinations. The success of the French tourism industry is largely dependent on the country's natural endowments which allow skiing and beach and countryside leisure developments. Similarly, specific land resources can be identified as attractions for other destinations, including:

- Nepal: Everest
- Caribbean: Coral reef, climate
- USA: Grand Canyon, Niagara Falls, Death Valley
- Kenya: game parks
- The Gambia: beaches and climate.

Labour

The labour force can be analysed in terms of its quantity and quality. The importance of the quantity of the labour force depends largely upon its relationship with other factors of production, land and capital. Where labour is a scarce factor of production, growth may be achieved by increasing the supply of labour, for example by encouraging immigration. However, in many economies labour is in over abundant supply. This means that the productivity of labour is low. This is particularly true in less-developed countries in the agricultural sector where land is overcrowded. On the other hand, the low wages that result from an abundant labour force can in some cases be a source of economic growth. Wages in China and Vietnam, for example, are very low by international standards, and this has partially accounted for the inflow of foreign investment and the growth of the Chinese and Vietnamese industrial sectors. The production

Exhibit 13.1 Egypt tourism workforce training

SRI International (originally the Stanford Research Institute but independent from Stanford University since 1970) has worked in partnership with the Federation of Egyptian Tourism Industries to deliver a comprehensive training programme to hotel industry workers across Egypt. The project was funded from USAID/Egypt. The project was delivered using the 'train-the-trainers' model.

Under this method, a group of trainers deliver training to supervisors. In turn, the supervisors then deliver training to next level workers. SRI International delivered the programme in conjunction with the American Hotel and Lodging Association-Educational Institute. In total, the project trained more than 10,000 workers in Egyptian two- to four-star hotels running over a period of 18 months.

Source: Adapted from http://csted.sri.com/projects/egypt-tourism-workforce-training

of leisure goods such as IT devices, audio equipment and toys is an important part of this industrial growth.

However, it is the quality of the labour force that is important in increasing productivity and improvements in quality stem from education and training programmes. Exhibit 13.1 illustrates steps being taken to improve the training of tourism workers in the hotel sector in Egypt using funding from United States Agency for International Development (USAID).

Capital

Capital, in the form of plant and machinery, results from investment and a distinction must be made between gross investment and net investment. Net investment refers just to investment which increases a nation's capital stock and therefore does not include replacement investment:

Net investment = Gross investment − Depreciation

Investment in new plant, machines and other capital enables labour productivity and GNP to rise. This can be an important source of economic growth for developing countries as labour moves from a relatively unmechanized agricultural sector to a mechanized industrial sector. The quality of investment is also an important issue. Investment in inappropriate machinery will have little effect on productivity and growth. Investment in infrastructure is important to develop industry in the leisure and tourism sector. This includes airports, ports and motorways, which allow access. Jamieson (2001) outlines eight key measures for creating a favourable atmosphere for investment in tourism infrastructure. These are:

1 Create a clear picture of the role of tourism in solving social, economic and environmental problems.
2 Creation of tourism investment information centres.
3 Encourage cooperation and integrated tourism development planning.
4 Creation of a positive investment climate.
5 Creation of special tourism investment zones.
6 Support human resource development.
7 Create opportunities for strategic product development.
8 Adopt innovative means of delivering quality infrastructure development.

A nation's cultural heritage includes investments made in previous generations and preserved for enjoyment today and therefore cultural capital is an important resource. For example, a third dimension to France's tourism attraction is its rich and well-preserved historical built environment. Other examples of cultural heritage capital include:

- China: the Great Wall and the Forbidden City
- Rome: the Sistine Chapel and the Coliseum
- Egypt: the Pyramids
- Peru: Macchu Picchu.

Technology

Improved technology can increase growth by reducing production costs and creating new products for the market. The leisure products industry has particularly benefited from new product technology with IT devices, MP3 players, cameras and the electronic games market. So R&D can be an important stimulus for economic growth. Exhibit 13.2 demonstrates the potential of technology to change the frontiers of tourism.

PROMOTING GROWTH

Growth-promotion policies tend to be split into those that require government intervention and those that rely on liberalizing the free market.

Intervention

Interventionists believe the government should play a key role in funding appropriate education and training, R&D and investing

Exhibit 13.2 Space tourism

1999: As the search for the exotic becomes more difficult on earth, attention has turned to space to satisfy the demands of the most adventurous tourists. Buzz Aldrin, a former Apollo astronaut, is one of a number of people employed to develop and promote space tourism.

A Japanese firm is developing plans for a hotel on the moon and a firm of architects, Wimberly Arson Tong and Goo are planning a hotel in space which is scheduled to be orbiting 200 miles above the earth by 2017.

A UK firm called Space Adventures are already accepting deposits for space flights. It is estimated that the flights will cost around £60,000, and a deposit of £4000 secures a place on the waiting list.

2001: A Soyuz U successfully launched Soyuz TM-32 carrying tourist Dennis Tito to the International Space Station (ISS) from Baikonur Cosmodrome, pad LC 1, at 0737 UTC (12:37 a.m. PDT) April 28. The Soyuz TM-32, flying on autopilot, docked with ISS at 1258 UTC (1:58 a.m. PDT) on April 30. Tito is reported to have paid US$20 million for his trip.

2010: 'Mojave, CA. Virgin Galactic, the US company developing the world's first commercial manned space flight system and tourism business, is delighted to announce the successful completion today of the first piloted free flight of SpaceShipTwo, named the VSS Enterprise. The spaceship was released from its mothership at an altitude of 45,000 ft'.

Source: The author (1999, 2001, 2011) from various sources including www.virgingalactic.com

in projects and infrastructure. They also note that the volatility of interest rates and exchange rates in the free market inhibits growth and so argue that government should manage the economy to provide a stable environment. Government intervention can also promote balanced growth where aggregate demand expands at a similar rate to aggregate supply, thereby avoiding the problems of inflation or unemployment associated with unbalanced growth.

Free market

The free market approach blames government intervention for lower growth. It is claimed that government spending programmes 'crowd out' funds, leaving less available and at higher interest rates for the private sector. Similarly, it is claimed that high taxes act as a disincentive for firms to invest. Supporters of market liberalization argue that profit is the best incentive for investment and that free trade and the actions of the price mechanism will ensure that investment and other resources are attracted to high-growth areas of the economy. Such policies are often referred to as 'supply side' policies. Supply side policies include:

● reducing government expenditure to release resources for the private sector;

Table 13.1	International tourism arrivals to Spain (millions)				
1990	1995	2000	2005	2008	2009
34.0	34.9	48.2	55.9	57.2	52.2

Source: Adapted from WTO statistics.

- reducing taxes to increase incentives;
- reducing trade union power to encourage flexible labour markets;
- reducing welfare payments to encourage individual enterprise;
- encouraging risk and entrepreneurship and privatization;
- encouraging competition through deregulation;
- reducing red tape.

LEISURE AND TOURISM DEVELOPMENT IN DEVELOPED COUNTRIES

The following case studies illustrate the role of different factors in the economic growth of Spain and Japan.

Leisure and tourism development in Spain

Leisure and tourism development has clearly made an important contribution to raising Spain's GNP per capita to levels approaching its EU partners. Table 13.1 shows the continued growth of international tourism for Spain (albeit with a recession-induced decline in 2009) to reach 57.2 million arrivals in 2008 earning US$61,628 million.

The rapid growth of Spain's tourism industry can be attributed to a number of causes. First, its natural resources – particularly of coastline, beaches and climate. However, many countries enjoy similar natural features but have not enjoyed such growth. It is Spain's proximity to the fast-growing economies of Western Europe that provided the demand, with tourists from the UK, Germany and France being the most numerous. Accessibility in terms of air transport and motorway developments has also played a part. In recent years, Spain has proved to be even more accessible as low-cost air travel has developed rapidly in its main supplier country – the UK. This has led to a trend towards taking more frequent breaks, establishing major cities as tourist destinations and contributing to the deseasonalization of tourism.

The success of tourism in Spain has itself stimulated investment. Earlier investment was often subsidized by overseas aid. For example, German investment in Gran Canaria was encouraged by the German government as a result of the 1968 Strauss Act which granted tax concessions for investments in underdeveloped countries.

To these factors must be added the low-wage costs which have enabled Spain to compete successfully with France and the active encouragement of government.

There is a government ministry with direct responsibility for tourism, the Ministry of Transport, Tourism and Communications, and tourism has been represented at ministerial level in Spain since 1951. Government has provided direct investment (e.g. in the *paradores* – the chain of state-run hotels often using renovated buildings of historical interest), as well as subsidies and infrastructure improvements (e.g. to develop ski resorts). The government also funds the Institute of Tourism of Spain which promotes Spain abroad. Since joining the EU in 1986, Spain has benefited from European Regional Development Fund grants for infrastructure, particularly for providing better road access in the northern coastal region.

Tourism has been an important driving element of Spanish economic growth, contributing more than 10 per cent of GDP annually. Foreign tourism brings with it significant foreign currency earnings making a strong contribution to the Spanish balance of payments. Payments related to outbound tourism (tourism carried out by Spaniards outside of Spain) are rising as Spain becomes a richer country and disposable incomes rise but the difference between tourism exports and imports shows a tourism credit balance for the Spanish economy, equivalent to about 4 per cent of the GDP. Tourism has also played an important role in the generation of employment in Spain since activities in tourism industries tend to be labour intensive. Here, the so-called 'characteristic' industries of tourism (hotels and other accommodations, restaurants, transport, travel agencies and so on) generate more than 1.5 million jobs, around 10 per cent of the Spanish total employment.

The main problems that have arisen from Spain's reliance on tourism are first its dependence on economic prosperity in countries such as the UK, Germany and France. Spain is highly dependent on spending by German and UK tourists, who account for around half of total visitors. Because of this the success of Spanish tourism is heavily dependent upon economic prosperity in these growth markets. The recession in the UK causing negative economic growth in 2008 and 2009 was an important contributory factor to the decline in visitor arrivals to Spain in that period from 57.2 million in 2008 to 52.2 million in 2009. However, one benefit of Spain's long-term economic growth has been a continued rise in the importance of domestic tourism which is an important factor in stabilizing demand in the sector.

Second, tourism employment tends to be low skilled and seasonal. Third, Spain's membership of the Euro means that it does not have the exchange rate flexibility of countries outside the Euro such as Turkey and Egypt. Fourth, Spain is increasingly facing strong competitive pressure from long haul destinations with cheap tourism price indices such as Thailand and Vietnam. Finally, the dash for tourism growth in the 1960s and 1970s caused environmental degradation which threatened the continued prosperity of some of the earlier resort developments. However, the government now takes a much stronger lead on environmental protection and there have been successful programmes to rescue resorts such as Benidorm, Torremolinos and Magaluf from earlier planning mistakes.

Balaguer and Cantavella-Jordá (2002) examined the role of tourism in Spain's long-run economic development. They confirmed a tourism-led growth hypothesis through cointegration and causality testing. The results of this indicated that during the three decades studied, economic growth in Spain was influenced by the persistent expansion of international tourism. They found that the increase of this activity has produced multiplier effects over time. External competitiveness is proved in the model to be a fundamental variable for Spanish economic growth. From their empirical analysis, the authors inferred that there is a positive effect on income that government policy may bring about – through ensuring adequacy of supply as well as by the promotion of tourist activity.

The sectors which particularly benefit from tourism include:

- accommodation
- the car rental market
- tourist attractions.

Leisure and tourism development in Japan

Japan's post-war economic development was largely driven by the export of manufactured goods based initially on competitive prices and product innovation. These exports included a comprehensive range of leisure goods. Indeed, it was the quality and innovative nature of much of these products that made them so successful. The product list includes recreational cars and motorcycles, jet-skis, audio and video equipment, sports equipment and musical instruments.

Following the wave of manufacturing investment there has been a movement towards investment in leisure projects. This was encouraged by the government with the passing of the Comprehensive Resort Region Provision Act in 1987 which provided tax relief and infrastructure support for resort construction projects. One of the aims of this was to create more balance in Japan's growth. Japanese economic growth has relied heavily on exports and these are subject to external factors such as overseas recessions and exchange rate movements. Investment in domestic leisure provision stimulates domestic demand and provides development in rural areas.

Projects have included golf courses, ski facilities, marinas and amusement parks along with hotel and infrastructure development. Ironically, Japanese workers have generally elected not to take the benefits of economic growth in increased leisure time. Their working year is around 200 hours more than in comparable industrialized countries. Japan's persistent surplus on the current account of its balance of payments accounts for two other important features in its leisure and tourism activities. First, Japan runs the world's biggest tourism account deficit, with tourism expenditure overseas exceeding tourism receipts by a significant amount. Second, Japan is very active in overseas investment. Some of this has involved aid to developing countries (e.g. loans for resort infrastructure in Thailand). The majority is in the form of private investment. It is estimated for example that Japanese companies own 150 golf courses overseas. In contrast to many developing countries, Japan has been able to build on its strong economic base. High GNP enabled high savings which can be used to finance more investment which further contributes to GNP.

However, the economic development of Japan subsequently encountered problems. Between 1960 and 1990 the Japanese economy had grown strongly. Its average growth rates averaged 10 per cent in the 1960s, 5 per cent in the 1970s and 4 per cent in the 1980s. It became one of the biggest economies in the world and this period led commentators to talk about 'the Japanese post-war economic miracle'. But during this period the Japanese economy also experienced rapidly rising stock and real estate prices which rose to unrealistic and unsustainable levels. This came to a head in the Tokyo Stock Exchange crash of 1990–1992 after which the economy demonstrated a prolonged period of readjustment. Growth in the 1990s averaged a very modest 1.5 per cent and the 'Period of the Economic Miracle' gave way to what was called the term 'Lost Decade'. The government made many attempts to stimulate the economy but it was not until 2005 that the economy finally entered into a period of recovery with GDP growth of 2.8 per cent.

It is interesting to note that whilst Japan was once the key exporter of high technology leisure products, the focus of production of these has shifted to China, Malaysia, Vietnam and other regional competitors.

ECONOMIC GROWTH IN DEVELOPING COUNTRIES

Stages of development

The World Bank classifies countries as advanced or emerging and developing economies.

Advanced economies

The World Bank classifies 33 economies as advanced ones. This group contains the following subgroups:

- Major advanced economies, often referred to as the Group of Seven (G7): these are the seven largest in terms of GDP – the USA, Japan, Germany, France, Italy, the UK and Canada.
- The Euro area (16 countries).
- The four newly industrialized Asian economies Hong Kong SAR, Taiwan, Korea and Singapore.
- Other advanced economies (e.g. Switzerland, New Zealand).

Emerging and developing economies

The group of emerging and developing countries (149 countries) includes all countries that are not classified as advanced economies. The regional groupings of emerging and developing economies are:

- Central and Eastern Europe (CEE)
- Commonwealth of Independent States (CIS)
- Developing Asia
- Middle East and North Africa (MENA)
- Sub-Saharan Africa (SSA)
- Western Hemisphere.

The emerging and developing countries are also classified according to two analytical criteria and into other groups.

- The first criterion, by source of export earnings, distinguishes between the categories of fuel, non-fuel and non-fuel primary products.
- The second criterion, focusses on debt distinguishing between net creditor, net debtor and the heavily indebted poor countries (HIPCs).

The major point of differentiation between advanced and emerging and developing countries is their GNP per head. There are a number of explanations for the low incomes of developing countries and several strategies for promoting economic growth. For some of these countries, promotion of the recreation, leisure and/or tourism will be an appropriate strategy.

Characteristics

The low standards of living enjoyed by developing countries are characterized not just by low per capita GNP but by a range of other indicators. These include high levels of mortality and low levels of literacy, medical care and food consumption. The economic circumstances of developing countries vary widely but barriers to economic growth in developing countries may include:

- *High population growth*: This may lead to overpopulation of land, the splitting of land into non-viable subunits and low labour productivity.
- *Low incomes*: This leads to low savings, leading to low investment, leading to low incomes (low rate of capital formation).
- *An undeveloped-financial sector*: This can mean that there is an absence of banks or a lack of trust in banks. Savings in this case are kept as cash or kind and not re-circulated into the economy as investment. This also means that access to cheap loans is difficult so that moneylenders are able to charge high rates of interest. This may mean that it is difficult to escape poverty or that cheap funds for investment in machinery is not available.
- *Absence of welfare system*: This can lead to overpopulation where children are seen as a financial insurance for old age.
- *Low levels of training and education*: This may be where there is a direct opportunity cost in lost agricultural labour where children stay on in school. Additionally, there is a shortage of state funding for education.
- *Existence of a large subsistence sector*: This can mean that taxation is difficult.
- Few resources.
- Dependence on low-value raw material exports.
- Employment centred on the agricultural sector of economy.
- Traditional (non-entrepreneurial) culture.
- Foreign currency shortages.
- Poor terms of trade (exports cheap, imports expensive).
- International debt.

Development strategies

Strategies to promote faster economic growth in developing countries generally involve investment in the agricultural, manufacturing or service sectors of the economy in order to improve labour productivity. This then raises the two key considerations for development. First, given the low rates of GNP per head, where will investment funds be obtained from? Second, what specific projects are most appropriate? The main sources of investment funds are:

- domestic savings (but these are often low because of low incomes)
- government investment funded through taxes or borrowing (but governments often have a low-tax base because of low incomes and subsistence economies and high-foreign debt repayments)

- private foreign investment
- overseas aid.

The main strategies for development include:

- import substitution (producing goods that are currently imported)
- export-led growth (producing goods and services where a local cost or other advantage can be established) – leisure and tourism can be important elements in this strategy
- population control
- education and training projects
- infrastructure projects.

Plate 13 depicts continued tourism development in Koh Phi Phi, Thailand. Here, tourism development is characterized by SME development with modest capital requirements and strong local multiplier effects.

Development strategies may take place under a planning environment which can be either market- or government-led. However, the history of development projects includes a number of projects that have been inappropriate for the circumstances of the particular developing country. This particularly applies to technologies which require expert foreign management and costly imports and projects which are labour saving in countries with high unemployment. The following case studies show the contribution of the leisure and

Plate 13 Unloading building materials for beach accommodation, Koh Phi Phi, Thailand.
Source: The author.

tourism sector to economic development in China and Vietnam, illustrating different development strategies.

Leisure and tourism development in China

The characteristics of the Chinese economy are atypical of many developing countries, yet its population of over 1 billion and rapid rate of development will ensure its growing importance over the next few decades. It is atypical first because of its communist government and second because, despite its low per capita GNP and large agricultural sector, it has relatively high literacy, low mortality rates and its economic growth has recently been spectacular, averaging 7.8 per cent between 1985 and 1994 and generally exceeding 10 per cent since 1994. Its population growth has slowed rapidly with its one-child policy. Table 13.2 shows the increasing importance of Chinese tourism which by 2009 had become the fifth highest world earner of international tourism receipts which rose from about US$16 billion in 2000 to about US$40 billion in 2009.

It is expanding first because of China's open-door policy, which replaced a long period of mistrust of foreigners and barriers to tourism. Second, China is rich in cultural capital, and third, its low-wage economy makes tourism relatively cheap. However, investment in infrastructure and accommodation is crucial to tourism development and to counter the low level of investment associated with its low per capita GNP, China has encouraged private foreign investment in the form of joint ventures. This has been important in the accommodation sector for the development of hotels. In Beijing, for example, the Hotel Beijing-Toronto was financed with Canadian capital, is run by Japanese management and profits are shared with China. China's growth is fuelled primarily by its growth in exports. Here, China exploits its international advantage in wage costs. Exports cover a range of goods and include audio equipment, toys and sports goods from the leisure sector. The movement of labour from

Table 13.2 International tourism receipts (US$, billions)						
Country	2000	2005	2006	2007	2008	2009
USA	82.4	81.8	85.8	96.9	110.0	93.9
Spain	30.0	48.0	51.1	57.6	61.6	53.2
France	33.0	44.0	46.3	54.3	56.6	49.4
Italy	27.5	35.4	38.1	42.7	45.7	40.2
China	16.2	29.3	33.9	37.2	40.8	39.7

Source: UNWTO Barometer.

China's agricultural sector to the manufacturing and service sector has enabled labour productivity to increase.

Tourism in Vietnam

In 1975, the communist government of Vietnam emerged victorious from a long war with the USA. Vietnam entered a period of centrally planned economic development and international isolation, limiting its trade and tourism exchanges to those with the former USSR and its allies.

A change in direction was heralded in 1986 when strict central planning was relaxed in favour of free enterprise. Additionally, the period of international isolation finished as restrictions on foreign investment and ownership were lifted. Tourism was a key beneficiary of this change in policy direction. Vietnam is well endowed in many of the basic tourism factors of production – unspoiled beaches, interesting landscapes and cultural heritage. To this can be added a cheap and plentiful labour supply.

After 1986, capital, the missing ingredient for economic development was now supplied by foreign investors. Between 1988 and 1995, almost $2 billion was invested in over 100 hotel projects including those involving multinational hotel chains such as the Hyatt and Marriot (USA), Omni (Hong Kong) and Hotel Metropole (France). Tourism to Vietnam boomed with arrivals rising from 300,000 in 1991 to over 1.3 million by 1995 (Table 13.3). By 1995, tourism earnings were estimated to be over $400 million making a strong contribution to Vietnam's GNP. However, as a result of the Asian economic crisis, the number of foreign visitors declined in 1998. But by 2000, 130,000 jobs were provided directly by tourism as well as those in businesses related to the tourism industry. The industry's contribution to the country's GDP had reached 5.8 per cent. By 2002, the country could boast 1940 hotels, nearly 670 guest houses, bungalows and villas and 11 tourist villages.

There have been two major problems facing Vietnam in its progress towards economic growth. First is the problem of foreign debt. Vietnam went through a period as a severely indebted low-income country. This hampered the development process when Vietnam had to use a high proportio-n of its national income to repay interest and capital on its foreign debt. The second problem is one of

Table 13.3 Total visitors to Vietnam, 1990–2010 (million)

1990	1995	2000	2005	2010
0.2	1.3	2.1	2.5	5.0

Source: Adapted from www.vietnamtourism.com

multinational ownership. The lack of domestic capital has mean that much of Vietnamese investment in tourism has been supplied by multinational corporations. This enables tourism capacity to grow in the short run faster than otherwise might be the case. But multinational investment means that the multiplier effect of tourism to Vietnam is reduced with a high proportion of tourism expenditure being exported back to shareholders of the multinationals in the form of profits. Both of these factors limit the ability of low-income countries such as Vietnam to enjoy the full benefits of the expansion of tourism. Additionally, Vietnam has suffered from poor basic infrastructure (road networks, airports and communications) although these are being improved.

The year 2002 was a good year for tourism industry. It attracted a record of 2.6 million foreign tourists as well as 13 million domestic holidaymakers. This was an increase of over 11 per cent over the previous year and earned US$1.52 billion in revenues. But the SARS outbreak in early 2003 results in a big setback to the tourism industry and the number of incoming tourists was only one-third of the figure that was recorded over the same period in 2002 although the 22nd Southeast Asian Games which was held in Vietnam increased the volume of tourists towards the end of the year. Additionally in 2003, the Vietnam National Administration of Tourism (VNAT) announced that the Vietnamese Government would invest an additional VND450 billion (nearly US$30 million) in the tourism industry. The move demonstrated the government's strategy to harness the tourism industry to spearhead economic development and help to develop other industries. One important effect of the increased investment is that it acted as a catalyst in attracting more projects from domestic and foreign investors. Previous government investment into the local tourism (US$17.7 billion in 2001 and US$24 billion in 2002) focussed on localities such as Quang Ninh, Ninh Binh, Nha Trang, Khanh Hoa, Thua Thien-Hue, Hai Phong and Ho Chi Minh City and attracted other capital sources into tourism projects. For example, Quang Ninh attracted a combined domestic and foreign investment of nearly US$56.6 million in its tourist resorts, especially in the province's United Nations Educational Scientific and Cultural Organizations (UNESCO)-recognized World Cultural Heritage of Ha Long Bay.

Tourism in Vietnam has continued to prosper and by 2010 international arrivals exceeded 5 millions. The expansion in tourism is facilitated by a mixture of government and private sector projects and the following shows some of these highlights for 2010:

- A project for the planning of the Thang Long Imperial Citadel area.
- The Vietnam Institute of Culture and Arts was assigned to plan the Highland gong culture preservation project by the Ministry of Culture, Sports and Tourism.

- Italian government offers aid for the My Son World Heritage restoration project.
- The Intercontinental Hotels Group (IHG) signed a cooperation deal with the Lucky Star Joint Stock Company (JSC) and the Thinh Vuong Company to expand business in Vietnam.
- Work starts on five-star hotel joint project between the Saigontourist Holding Company (Saigontourist) and the Que Huong Liberty JSC in Ho Chi Minh City.
- Government plans two new airports.
- Starwood Hotels & Resorts Worldwide, Inc. signed an agreement with Robin-Hill Resort Limited Company, a member of Saigon Invest Group, to manage a Sheraton resort underway in the Central Highland's Dalat City.
- Petrocapital and Infrastructure Investment JSC started building a four-star hotel in the southern province of Tay Ninh, marking its first step into the hospitality sector.

REGENERATION

As well as being a source for national growth strategies, recreation, leisure and tourism are also used in regeneration schemes. Regeneration is the term used to describe the process of economic redevelopment generally in an area that has suffered decline because of structural changes in the economy. It can be applied both to urban and to rural contexts.

The economist J.M. Keynes noted that full employment is not a necessary equilibrium position in a market economy. In other words, there is no guarantee that a market economy will provide sufficient jobs for the population. The same idea may be applied to the level of economic activity in any particular localized area. Market economies are by their nature dynamic and markets are constantly signalling and causing change. But there is no reason that a decline in one aspect of a local economy should be automatically offset by a growth in another aspect. A local area will suffer economic decline where the rate of loss of existing jobs exceeds the rate of creation of new jobs. If this pattern is sustained, a point will be reached where an area becomes 'depressed' or 'deprived'. The economic indicators of localized economic depression include the level of unemployment and per capita incomes.

Just like at the national level, a recession can turn into a long depression without intervention, a similar process may occur at a localized level. Typically, the sequence of events illustrated in Figure 13.3 occurs and the circular effect shows how the multiplier process can exacerbate the situation.

Regeneration is therefore generally about replacing the gap left by declining industries by implanting new centres of economic activity. Leisure, recreation and tourism projects can provide a popular focus

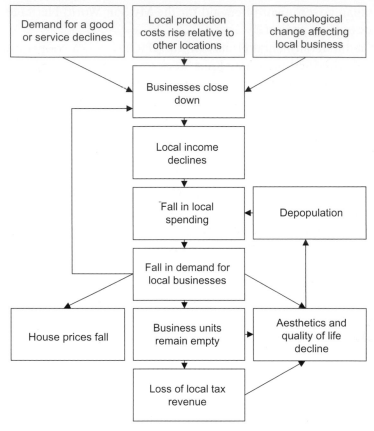

Figure 13.3 Local economic decline.

for this. There is generally a threefold impact of regeneration. First, local jobs are provided at the construction stage of new projects. Next, local jobs are generated when the new projects are commissioned. Third, leisure projects often attract spending from outside the local area. Where regeneration is successful, the whole multiplier process swings into reverse and increased spending attracts further investment.

Urban regeneration

Smith (2003) examined the role of the cultural industries in urban regeneration. Examples here include the Guggenheim Museum in Bilbao, northern Spain which has led to an increase in tourism to this area where traditional industries such as steel and shipbuilding were in decline. Similarly, Glasgow in the UK achieved the status of European City of Culture in 1990, enhancing its external image and attracting tourism and inward investment. Mega events are also used to kick-start local economies. Examples here include

Exhibit 13.3 The London Olympics 2012

London 2012 is much more than just a celebration of sport, culture and the Olympic ideals.

It is part of the most extensive transformation of the city for generations. And its legacy will transform one of the most underdeveloped areas of the country for generations to come. The key catalyst is the development of the 500-acre Olympic Park and the resulting transformation of the Lower Lea Valley. The Park, containing the main sporting facilities, is set in 1500 landscaped acres stretching from Hackney Marshes down to the Thames – one of the biggest new city centre parks in Europe for 200 years.

It has also revitalized a network of waterways serving new communities and businesses that have influenced regeneration stretching out from the Lea Valley through East London and beyond. Each of the Games venues has been conceived to meet long-term needs. And the Olympic Village would also have a designated post-Games use as housing. All development would form part of an enormous and tangible legacy, ranging from sport and venues through to infrastructure and environment.

The potential tourism benefits of the London Olympics have been estimated at £2.1 billion between 2007 and 2017. Additionally, thousands of jobs were created in construction, thousands more as the redevelopment created new businesses and communities. London 2012 changes the face of this part of the capital forever.

Source: www.london2012.org

the hosting of Expo and in 1998 the Lisbon Expo attracted over 8 million visitors and generated additional income to the city of $900 million. In London, the Millennium Dome was generally seen to be a failure in direct revenue terms. However, it brought a new underground rail line to a depressed area of southeast London and its surrounding area of the Greenwich peninsula is exhibiting signs of regeneration with new housing, leisure and tourism developments. Eventually, the empty Millennium Dome was transformed into the highly successful O_2 Arena hosting pop concerts.

The hosting of the Olympic Games is also seen as an opportunity to reinvigorate urban economies, and regeneration of the Lea Valley and Eastern Gateway is an important consideration in the bringing of the 2012 games to London (Exhibit 13.3). In respect of the Sydney Olympics in 2000, consultants Jones Lang LaSalle and LaSalle carried out an economic impact analysis. They reported that the games increased the international profile of Sydney, encouraged tourism and hotel development and acted as a catalyst for a range of residential, retail and business developments, as well as improving transport infrastructure. One of the sites – Homebush – now host to a leading sporting venue and popular residential community – was previously part swamp and part munitions dump.

However, it is also often reported that local communities may fail to benefit fully from regeneration activities – either through having no interest or access to new projects, or by being uprooted by new schemes, or by losing their traditional retailers or where the new jobs go to those from outside the local community.

Rural regeneration

Taking the UK as an example, the rural economy presents a mixed picture. The rural economy has not been immune from a range of restructuring processes which include European policy reforms, changes in economy and society, international trade patterns, development of new technologies, environmental pressures, the buying power and patterns of large supermarkets and the low perception of agriculture by potential workers. The effects of all these have been exacerbated by farming and food crises.

Farming is still an important industry though it accounts for only about 4 per cent of GDP in rural areas. It supplies much of the food of the UK and provides direct employment for around 600,000 people (although this includes seasonal and part-time workers). But farm incomes have witnessed a long-term decline and farming has gone through difficult periods over the last 50 years. These difficulties affect many related businesses as well as the prosperity of market towns.

Despite this, employment and self-employment are generally higher in rural areas than in urban areas and unemployment is lower. Against this, average earnings are lower and rural jobs are more likely to be casual or seasonal, than jobs in urban areas. The nature of employment is changing, with fewer jobs in primary industries such as farming, and other jobs moving to edge of town locations. Home-based working is on the increase especially driven by the opportunities offered by high-speed broadband access.

Sharpley (2003) noted that the UK Rural White Paper published in 2000 firmly established tourism as a vehicle for the social and economic regeneration of the British countryside. He further noted that the Foot and Mouth crisis in 2001 served to demonstrate both the interdependence of various elements of the rural economy and the fragility (or lack of sustainability) of the tourism and leisure industry in particular. He therefore points to the pressing need for the effective and integrated management of the countryside as a resource for tourism and leisure. In terms of the significance of leisure to the rural economy, it can be noted that rural tourism is worth over £11.5 billion and creates over 380,000 jobs in England alone.

It is because of the decline in the role of farming and the potential of recreation, leisure and tourism to provide an alternative source

Exhibit 13.4 The Eden project

The Eden Project is a visitor attraction in the south west of the UK in the county of Cornwall. The project is located in area of a disused tin mine. The project houses the world's largest greenhouse in the form of two gigantic artificial biodomes. One dome reproduces a tropical environment and the other a Mediterranean environment.

The Eden project cost £86 million and this was raised by a public/private sector partnership bringing together public sector regeneration and lottery funds (£43 million was provided by the Millennium Commission) with private sector loan finance and sponsorship. In terms of employment, the project's first 34 staff were all recruited locally and by its opening in 2001, it employed a full-time equivalent staff of 200 people – the majority from the local area. The project's construction partner, McAlpine Joint Venture also worked positively to follow this ideal – out of the 300 workers employed on the site, approximately 85 per cent were local. Due to its success, the project employed 600 local full-time staff and contributed an estimated £300 million incrementally to the Cornish economy by its third year of operation. Its anticipated contribution is £2 billion in its first decade. Additionally, the project has worked closely to co-ordinate the facilitation of local supplier networks. For example, bread, dairy products, meat and vegetables for the catering facilities are all sourced locally.

Source: Various.

of income and employment that this sector is seen as important in rural regeneration. Schemes that have been successful include the Eden project in Cornwall (see Exhibit 13.4) and the Tate Gallery in St Ives.

However, it would be naïve to presume that in the UK rural prosperity depends on either farming or tourism. There is an increasing movement of the population into rural areas, particularly in the south of England and increasing use of the Internet means that business opportunities are no longer confined to urban areas.

REVIEW OF KEY TERMS

- Economic growth: the increase in real output per capita.
- Per capita: per person.
- Net investment: gross investment – depreciation.
- Productivity: output per employee.
- Import substitution: producing goods that are currently imported.
- Infrastructure: social capital such as roads and railways.
- Joint venture: overseas and domestic investment partnership.

Data Questions

Task 13.1 The Bournemouth Artificial Surf Reef (UK)

Bournemouth is a seaside town on the south coast of England. Like many seaside towns in the UK, Bournemouth has witnessed mixed fortunes as UK residents have increasingly opted to take their beach holidays overseas. The Bournemouth Surf Reef is located off the beach at Boscombe and is an artificial reef designed to improve the quality and quantity of surfing waves. There are three other artificial reefs in the world in Narrowneck, Queensland; Cables, Western Australia and Mt Maunganui, New Zealand.

The reef in Bournemouth is about the size of a football pitch and is 225 metres from the shore. The main reason for building the reef is for regeneration and leisure. It is designed to replicate the effects of a natural reef acting as a ramp, pushing waves upwards and increasing their size. It is built from large geo-textile bags pumped hard with sand. Before the reef could be built, there was extensive consultation and research to ensure the reef would not have a negative impact on coastal erosion or marine ecology.

The £3.03 million reef was funded by Bournemouth Borough Council which raised the Boscombe Regeneration Project funds through the sale of a seafront car park. A Council Economic Impact Assessment suggested that:

> the reef will create an image value of £10million per annum resulting from a variety of publications and media interest on a national scale. It will generate a huge stimulus for equipment retailing, surf-training schools, accommodation, drink and food and would create an estimated 60 full-time and 30 part-time jobs. A recent survey in Cornwall revealed that surfers spend 8% more than other holidaymakers.

Support for the reef also came from the local Surfing Centre which commented:

> The reef spells a boom time for the area: Surfing first hit our beaches in the 1960's and today Bournemouth has the third largest population of surfers in the country. For the 10,000 locals and a catchment that includes London, the reef promises to be a huge attraction, the nearest thing to an Atlantic roller this side of Cornwall. The reef will not only boost the area's already thriving tourist industry but will encourage other watersports such as diving, windsurfing and provide a habitat for greater biodiversity.

However, after 1 year in operation the reef was not performing as expected.

Source: Adapted from www.bournemouthsurfreef.com

Recap Questions

1 What is regeneration and why is it needed?
2 Do you think the Bournemouth Artificial Surf Reef is an effective regeneration project?
3 What is the opportunity cost of the Bournemouth Artificial Surf Reef?
4 What possible economic multiplier effects might arise from the Bournemouth Artificial Surf Reef?

5 Why should local government spend public money on a project to improve surfing?

Task 13.2 Journal article: Ilieva, L. 1998. Development of sustainable rural tourism in Bulgaria. In: Hall, D., O'Hanlon, L. (Eds.), Rural Tourism Management: Sustainable Options Conference Proceedings. SAC, Ayr.

The following are extracts from Ilieva's (1998) strengths, weaknesses, opportunities, threats (SWOT) analysis of the potential for rural tourism in Bulgaria:

Strengths:

- Natural and anthropological potential.

Weaknesses:

- Superstructure: in many cases facilities do not meet the requirements of the modern tourist.
- Infrastructure: outdated traffic and telecommunications systems.

Opportunities:

- National advertising budget: financial resources for national tourist advertising.
- Educational programmes: there are five higher education institutions and many colleges where tourism students are being taught.

Threats:

- Macroeconomic frame: the slow pace of reforms, the unstable economic, political and legal situation … hamper the development of tourism.

Recap Questions

1 What other factors affecting Bulgaria should be included in a SWOT analysis?
2 Evaluate the potential for tourism to contribute to Bulgaria's rural economic development in view of this SWOT analysis.
3 What are the main arguments for, and potential benefits arising from, the development of rural tourism in Bulgaria?
4 In what ways have other countries successfully developed rural tourism and with what economic benefits and costs?

Task 13.3 Leisure and tourism development in France

Leisure and tourism is central to French economic prosperity. France is one of the world's most popular international tourist destinations and tourism makes an important contribution to its balance of payments with international tourism receipts of around US$50 billion in 2009 as illustrated by Table 13.2. France has a diverse and well-balanced tourism industry. Its winter sports tourism attracts millions of arrivals each year excluding day trips. Disneyland Paris is a leading short-break destination in Europe, and the Eiffel Tower is an iconic marker in Paris.

As well as being the premier international destination, France is the premier destination for its own residents. Tourism in France accounted for over 6 per cent of GDP in 2009 and a considerable proportion of this expenditure was by French domestic tourism. One reason for this is that, in contrast to US and Japanese workers, French workers receive a minimum of 5 weeks paid leave and this represents considerable potential

Data Questions

Task 13.3 **continued**

domestic demand. As well as tourism services, France exports leisure goods, particularly skiing and camping equipment, and has domestic air and ferry capacity in the form of Air France and Brittany Ferries. The latter was set up specifically to promote tourism to Brittany so as to promote that region's economic development. The demand for tourist facilities stimulates considerable private investment in hotels and other provision, but there is also a history of state encouragement. In terms of infrastructure, for example, France has a well-developed system of roads and railways. Recent investment in the high-speed train (TGV) has resulted in links between Paris and Lyons, Lille, Nantes and Bordeaux.

The Maison de France, mainly financed from public funds, was set up in 1987 to promote French tourism products. It is estimated that every euro spent by the Maison de France generates €15 in tourism receipts and its main activities include information, advertising, sales promotion and public relations. Maison de France maintains offices abroad, but as with many National Tourism Organizations it is often subject to pressures from government funding. There have been a number of major government-assisted regional development schemes based on tourism. For example, the Languedoc-Roussillon project was supported by more than €1 billion of state funding and commenced in 1963. It stimulated private investment and increased tourist visits to the area from 500,000 in 1964 to over 3.5 million by the late 1980s, and it has been estimated that 30,000 new jobs were created in the region between 1965 and 1980. Another government initiative was the Aquitaine scheme which planned a big increase in tourism capacity on the Atlantic coast south of La Rochelle.

French tourism was negatively affected by the recession of 2008–2009 when international tourism arrivals fell sharply, with impacted on airlines, hotels, attractions, bars and restaurants. Despite this, France remained the world's number one tourist destination. The recession brought about some changes in consumer behaviour such as:

- the search for value for money
- staycations
- trading down
- a decrease in business travel
- the closure of smaller tourist agencies.

Recap Questions

1 What special features does France have that put it top of the international arrivals table?
2 What factors may account for the fact that France has more international tourist arrivals than the USA but lower receipts? How could this issue be addressed?
3 What are the key economic impacts of recreation, leisure and tourism on the economy of France?
4 What are the arguments for and against state intervention as against the free market as an effective means of encouraging economic growth through leisure and tourism in France?
5 In what ways does a recession impact on tourism and what steps could be taken by:
   (a) the industry?
   (b) the government to assist tourism in recessionary times?

MULTIPLE CHOICE

1 Which of the following is false for real per capita growth in GNP?
   (a) It takes into account the total population.
   (b) It takes into account inflation.
   (c) It falls if the rate of growth of the population exceeds the rate of growth of the economy.
   (d) It is always greater than zero.
2 Which of the following is false?
   (a) A large subsistence sector will mean that the value of GNP is underestimated.
   (b) Reducing taxation is a 'supply side' policy for stimulating economic growth.
   (c) HIPCs are high-investment poor countries.
   (d) Iraq is a MENA country.
3 Which of the following is not a policy designed to improve economic growth in developing countries?
   (a) Import substitution.
   (b) Export-led growth.
   (c) Investment in infrastructure projects.
   (d) Import-led growth.
4 Which of the following is not a typical feature of developing countries?
   (a) High level of savings.
   (b) Dependence on raw material exports.
   (c) Employment centred on the agricultural sector of economy.
   (d) International debt.
5 Which of the following is true of regeneration projects?
   (a) They always favour poor people.
   (b) They are designed to counter structural changes in a locality.
   (c) They are most successful when they have a low-multiplier value.
   (d) They often cause local investment to fall.

REVIEW QUESTIONS

1 What is real GNP per capita?
2 What are the key determinants of economic growth?
3 What is balanced growth?
4 What factors led to the importance of leisure and tourism in the economy of Spain?

5 What are the advantages and problems of joint ventures for the Chinese economy?

6 Why is China successful in exporting electronic goods?

7 Compare private foreign investment with government investment in a hotel as alternative development strategies.

Websites of interest

New Zealand Statistics: www.stats.govt.nz

Australian Bureau of Statistics: www.abs.gov.au

Brazil Statistics: www.ibge.gov.br

Canada Statistics: www.statcan.gc.ca

World Bank: www.worldbank.org

International Monetary Fund: www.imf.org

World Tourism Organization: www.world-tourism.org

Bournemouth Surf Reef: www.bournemouthsurfreef.com

Virgin Galactic: www.virgingalactic.com

London Olympics: www.london2012.com

Eden Project: www.EdenProject.com

Maison de France: http://uk.franceguide.com/

Vietnam Tourism: www.vietnamtourism.com

PART 7

The Global Economy

CHAPTER

14

The balance of payments and exchange rates

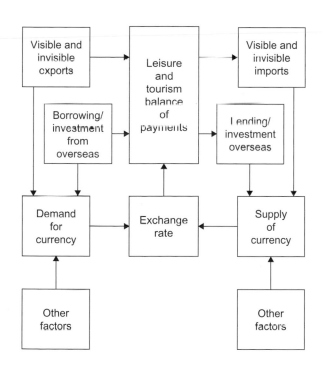

Objectives and learning outcomes

In addition to measuring the contribution of the recreation, leisure and tourism sector to the level of national income, we can consider its contribution at the international level to a country's balance of payments. The balance of payments records export earnings and import expenditure. Exchange rates are an important part of the picture. The exchange rate of a country's currency is inextricably linked with the balance of payments. Changes in a country's balance of payments may cause changes in the demand and supply for its currency and thus movements in its exchange rate. These currency movements may subsequently cause changes in the patterns of exports and imports which can cause feedback to the balance of payments. The balance of payments is also one of the key macroeconomic variables which government policy makers monitor closely. If the balance of payments should move into an unsustainable deficit, government policy would be changed to address the problem, causing repercussions throughout the rest of the economy.

By studying this chapter, students will be able to:

- understand the arguments for free trade, the role of the WTO and General Agreement on Trade in Services (GATS);
- understand the balance of payments accounts;
- analyse the contribution of the sector to net export earnings;
- describe and explain comparative data for balance of payments accounts;
- understand the significance of exchange rates to recreation, leisure and tourism organizations;
- distinguish between spot and forward rates of exchange;
- analyse exchange rate movements;
- understand government and EC policy in trade and international payments.

FREE TRADE, THE WTO AND GATS

The economist David Ricardo was instrumental in developing the idea through 'The theory of comparative advantage' that free trade could bring greater economic benefits to those involved than a position of no trade. The essentials of his argument were that different countries had different resource mixes and therefore differing costs for producing a range of goods and services. It therefore pays countries not to attempt to be self-sufficient in producing a complete range of goods and services but to specialize in those where its production costs are lowest and their production efficiency highest. They would then trade with other countries to meet their full range of demands. Ricardo argued that specialization and trade would lead to an increase in total output compared to a position of no specialization and trade, based upon greater efficiency of production.

Some countries are more efficient at producing across a whole range of goods and services than others (e.g. the USA), and in this sense they are said to possess an 'absolute advantage' in production. However, it will still benefit such countries to specialize in producing those goods and services which is the very best at producing (where it has a 'comparative advantage' over other countries) and trading where its comparative advantage is less strong. This is really an example of playing to your own strengths and specializing in those areas.

Once countries specialize their production in particular areas, additional benefits of economies of scale and acquired expertise are likely to arise. Consumers benefit from free trade in terms of wider choice and lower prices.

The WTO is the international agency that promotes free trade. It has three main treaty agreements that summarize its rules of free trade. These are:

- The General Agreement on Tariffs and Trade (GATT) which covers trade in goods.
- The GATS which covers trade in services.
- The WTO's intellectual property agreement which covers trade and investment in ideas and creativity.

Free trade liberalization under the WTO is based on three specific pillars:

1 *Market access*: Foreign-owned companies have free access to domestic markets.
2 *Most favoured nation status*: Concessions granted to any one country must also be made available on a non-discriminatory basis to all other signatories of the agreement.
3 *National treatment*: Foreign investors must be treated on an equal basis with domestic investors, domestic investors must not receive any favourable treatment that could be conceived as protectionist.

Diamantis and Fayed (2002) consider two main issues relating to GATS, namely its impact on the labour market and on its relevance to developing countries.

However, in the real world practical issues arise that can militate against the benefits of free trade. First, there are extra costs involved in currency conversion and risk. Second, transport costs can add to production costs. Third, extra costs are involved in adapting goods and services for local markets. Fourth, many countries seek to protect their home markets by protectionist policies. Fifth, most countries wish to maintain some balance of production in key strategic goods and services so as not to expose themselves to over-dependence on foreign countries. Sixth, although overall there are significant gains to be made from trade, which particular countries benefit most will depend on the terms of trade. Many developing nations feel that the terms of trade are unfairly weighted against them resulting in cheaper prices for raw materials and commodities (which they tend to export) and more expensive prices for manufactured goods and services (which the advanced economies tend to export).

TRADE AND TRADING BLOCS

A trading bloc is a group of countries who join together to liberalize trade between member states. There are four major trading blocs in the world.

The European Union

The EU has become the most powerful trading bloc in the world with a GDP now exceeding that of the USA. The EU continues to liberalize trade within member countries. The Single European Act, which came into effect in 1992, defines the single market as 'an area without internal frontiers in which the free movement of goods, persons, services and capital is ensured in accordance with the provisions of this treaty'. Some of the specific outcomes of this act which impinge on the leisure and tourism sector include the dismantling of EU internal border checks (some exceptions remain), and more competition in air and shipping services. On 1 January 1999, 11 EU countries fixed the exchange rate between their currencies in a landmark step towards full introduction of the Euro which occurred in January 2002. The EU members are:

Austria	Greece	Poland
Belgium	Hungary	Portugal
Cyprus	Ireland	Slovak Republic
Czech Republic	Italy	Slovenia
Denmark	Latvia	Spain
Estonia	Lithuania	Sweden
Finland	Luxembourg	UK
France	Malta	Bulgaria
Germany	The Netherlands	Romania

North American Free Trade Agreement

The USA has linked with Canada and Mexico to form a free trade zone, the North American Free Trade Agreement (NAFTA). It hopes to extend NAFTA to the rest of Latin America to create a Free Trade Area of the Americas. The USA is already negotiating with Chile to join NAFTA, but that has caused controversy with some other South American countries. The NAFTA agreement covers environmental and labour issues as well as trade and investment. Its members are:

- Canada
- Mexico
- USA.

The Asia-Pacific Economic Cooperation Forum

The Asia-Pacific Economic Cooperation (APEC) forum is a loose grouping of the countries bordering the Pacific Ocean who have pledged to facilitate free trade. Its 21 members account for 45 per cent of world trade. Progress on free trade initiatives was seriously dented by the Asian crisis, which affected the economies of the fast-growing newly industrialized countries like South Korea and Indonesia. Its members are:

Australia	Japan	Philippines
Brunei	South Korea	Russia
Canada	Malaysia	Singapore
Chile	Mexico	Taiwan
China	New Zealand	Thailand
Hong Kong	Papua New Guinea	USA
Indonesia	Peru	Vietnam

The Cairns group

The Cairns group of agricultural exporting nations was formed in 1986 to lobby at world trade talks in order to free up trade in agricultural products. Highly efficient agricultural producers, including those in both developed and developing countries, want to ensure that their products are not excluded from markets in Europe and Asia. Its members are:

Argentina	Columbia	Paraguay
Australia	Fiji	Philippines
Brazil	Indonesia	South Africa
Canada	Malaysia	Thailand
Chile	New Zealand	Uruguay

THE TERMS OF TRADE

The terms of trade measures the relative prices of what a country exports in relation to the prices of its imports. It is expressed by the formula:

$$\frac{\text{The average price of exports}}{\text{The average price of imports}}$$

If the terms of trade rise (i.e. export prices rise faster than import prices), the terms of trade are said to improve. This is because more imports can now be bought with a given amount of exports. Changes in the terms of trade are brought about by changes in the demand and supply of exports and imports and movements in exchange rates.

A persistent argument put forward by developing countries is that they face unfavourable terms of trade in comparison with developed countries. This is because the raw materials and commodities which are characteristic of the exports of developing countries generally command much lower prices than the manufactured and services exports characteristic of developed countries' exports.

THE BALANCE OF PAYMENTS

The balance of payments is an account which shows a country's financial transactions with the rest of the world. It records inflows (+) and outflows (−) of currency. For example, if a UK resident flies on Emirates airlines a service has been 'imported' and a payment is made overseas to purchase this. Although the accounting conventions of presenting these accounts differ from country to country, there are some basic similarities in that the balance of payments generally has four main components:

1 the current account
2 the capital account
3 the financial account
4 net errors and omissions.

The main difference between these parts is that the current account mainly measures the value of goods and services traded, whilst the capital account measures flows of capital, for example, investments and the financial account measures financial transactions involving the claims on, and liabilities to, non-residents. In addition, there is a net errors and omissions item which arises because, due to inaccurate data collection, the figures do not always add up as they should. This is to compensate for mistakes that have been made (errors) and items that have not been counted (omissions). Table 14.1 shows recent balance of payments data for the UK.

Date	Current account	Capital account	Financial account	Net errors and omissions
Table 14.1 UK balance of payments (£ million)				
2006	−44,934	975	41,974	1,985
2007	−36,482	2,566	24,790	9,126
2008	−23,776	3,241	25,811	−5,276
2009	−15,506	3,219	5,597	6,690

Source: Adapted from ONS The Pink Book (2010 edition).

The balance of payments account always balances in an accounting sense. Every expenditure of foreign currency must be offset by a receipt, otherwise the expenditure could not take place. For poorer countries (as with poorer people), this means that expenditure (on imports) cannot exceed earnings (from exports) because they simply run out of (foreign) currency. However, for countries with a developed financial sector, current import expenditure may exceed current export income. This can be financed perhaps by borrowings, or perhaps by selling assets. In such a case, although the account would balance in an accounting sense, it would show structural imbalance. This is because such a position could not be sustainable over a long period. Sources of borrowing would dry up and there is only a finite stock of assets to be sold. The implications of such a structural deficit are discussed below in the section on government policy. In the UK balance of payments account for 2009 shown in Table 14.1, it can be seen that the four parts of the balance of payments sum to zero:

$$-15506 + 3219 + 5597 + 6690 = 0.$$

The current account

The current account records payments for trade in goods and services and income and transfers. It is thus divided into four parts:

1 visibles
2 invisibles
3 total income
4 current transfers.

Visibles

Visibles represents exports and imports in goods or tangibles and is typically divided into the following sections:

- food, beverages and tobacco
- basic materials

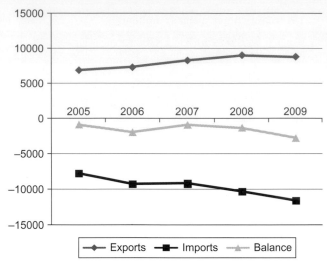

Figure 14.1 Value of foreign trade in ships and aircraft (£ million). *Source: Adapted from CSO; The Pink Book 2010.*

- fuels
- semi-manufactures
- manufactures
- others.

The leisure sector is represented in this part of the account, for example, by trade in alcoholic beverages, electrical goods, sports equipment and sportswear. Figure 14.1 shows the balance of trade in ships and aircraft. The information for ships and aircraft demonstrates similar characteristics to that for UK visible trade as a whole exhibiting a deficit, with imports exceeding imports. This has been caused by uncompetitive UK exchange rates and cheaper overseas production costs – particularly labour costs.

Table 14.2 shows the UK total visible trade balance over recent years. The information shows the deficit steadily rising, peaking in 2008 and falling back in 2009. This demonstrates the relationship between growth in the economy as a whole and the balance of payments. During the period 1999–2007, the UK experienced a period of sustained growth and increased spending power which sucked in ever more imported goods. The sharp recession of 2008–2009 meant a decline in spending power and this fed through to a drop in the demand for imported goods. In the UK, as in most countries, there is a strong link between economic growth and import demand.

Invisibles

Invisibles record the trade in services or intangibles and is typically organized under the following headings:

- transportation
- travel

Table 14.2 UK trade in goods (£ million)	
1999	−29,051
2000	−32,976
2001	−41,212
2002	−47,705
2003	−48,607
2004	−60,900
2005	−68,589
2006	−76,312
2007	−89,754
2008	−93,116
2009	−81,875

Source: Adapted from ONS The Pink Book (2010).

- communications
- construction
- insurance
- financial
- computer and information
- royalties and license fees
- other business
- personal, cultural and recreational
- government.

The key items of relevance to the leisure and tourism sector are transportation, travel and cultural and recreational items.

Table 14.3 shows how tourism makes an important contribution to Australia's export earnings. For example, in 2009–2010, international visitors consumed AUS$27,636 million worth of goods and services produced by the Australian economy. However, in the period 2002–2010, Australia's tourism expenditure overseas has grown faster than its earnings from overseas tourists. Whilst the balance of tourism payments for Australia showed a surplus in 2002–2003, by 2009–2010 there was a deficit of some AUS$6338 millions. Note that the value of tourism earnings depends not just upon the number of visitors but also their average expenditure and Exhibit 14.1 illustrates this point.

The data in Table 14.4 shows the more general data for Australia's trade in goods and services. It can be seen that between 2007 and 2010 Australia has run a deficit in its trade in services (and an imbalance in its tourism trade contributed to this). Its trade in goods has

Table 14.3 Inbound and outbound tourism expenditure in Australia

	2002–2003	2003–2004	2004–2005	2005–2006	2006–2007	2007–2008	2008–2009	2009–2010
Total consumption by Australian residents on outbound trips ($ million)	17,309	19,738	22,742	24,565	26,648	31,837	32,880	33,974
Total consumption by non-residents on inbound trips ($ million)	22,603	23,430	23,995	24,976	26,296	27,942	29,232	27,636

Source: Australian Bureau of Statistics, Tourism Satellite Account 2009–2010.

Exhibit 14.1 They came, they saw … but did not spend much

The following extract from the *International Tourism Reports* comments on East European tourists to Paris:

'Paris has long represented a dream destination for many East Europeans. When they were suddenly free to travel after so many years of isolation from the western world it was natural that the French capital would be their first goal. It should nevertheless be pointed out that most East Europeans travelling to France in the early 1990s slept in their coaches travelling to and from and at their destinations and took much of their food with them. As a result their contribution to the country's inter-national tourism receipts was minimal.'

Source: International Tourism Reports, 1998, Vol. 3, Travel and Tourism Intelligence, London.

Table 14.4 Selected items from Australia current balance of payments

Year	Balance on goods and services	Goods	Services
2007–2008	−24,852	−21,902	−2,950
2008–2009	7,622	10,915	−3,293
2009–2010	−3,775	−3,027	−748

Source: Australian Bureau of Statistics, Australian Economic Indicators (January 2011).

shown a more mixed and quite volatile picture ranging from a substantial deficit in 2007–2008 to a surplus in 2008–2009 and back to deficit in 2009–2010.

Exhibit 14.2 shows the relationship between visitor numbers, visitor spend and total tourism consumption in Australia, illustrating that an increase in visitor numbers does not always lead to an increase in total tourism consumption.

Tourism is a net earner to the balance of payments of some countries and for example Blazevic and Jelusic (2002) discuss the

Exhibit 14.2 Changes in tourism in Australia: visitor numbers, spend and total consumption

- Tourism consumption by same-day domestic visitors in 2009–2010 increased by 6.7 per cent. This resulted from an increase in the number of visitors (up 6.7 per cent) and a relatively unchanged per visitor spend.
- For overnight domestic visitors, there was a small decrease in the number of visitors of 1.0 per cent but an increase in the per visitor spend of 3.4 per cent leading to an overall increase in tourism consumption of 2.3 per cent.
- International tourism consumption in 2009–2010 fell by 2.1 per cent since although there was an increase in the number of visitors of 2.7 per cent, per visitor spend fell by 4.7 per cent.

Source: Adapted from Australian Bureau of Statistics, Tourism Satellite Account 2009–2010.

Table 14.5 Aspects of international tourism to the USA

	1999	2000	2001	2002	2003	2004	2005	2006	2007	2008	2009
Change in arrivals	+5	+6	−8	−7	−5	+12	+7	+4	+10	+3	−5
Change in export value	+3	+9	−13	7	−4	+16	+10	+5	+14	+15	−15

Source: US Travel and Tourism Industries: A Year in Review, http://tinet.ita.doc.gov/pdf/2009-year-in-review.pdf

importance of tourism to the Croatian balance of payments. France and Spain boast large tourism surpluses, and tourism surpluses are rising rapidly for Turkey and China. On the other hand, Germany and Japan both have significant deficits in their tourism payments accounts, and the UK has a steadily deteriorating deficit. Table 14.5 shows the changes in the fortunes of international tourism to the balance of payments of the USA. The global economic recession made 2009 the most difficult environment for the tourism industry since the aftermath of 11 September 2001 with 3 million fewer international arrivals, a US$21 billion decline in tourism exports and the loss of 392,000 jobs in the industry.

Total income

Income is made up from income earned by domestic residents from non-residents and vice versa. It includes:

- workers earnings
- investment income.

Workers earnings include wages earned by individuals from economies other than those in which they are residents. Investment income comprises income earned or paid from the provision of financial capital. Of significant here are interest, profit and dividends, which records payments relating to overseas business investments. For example, profits returned to the French-owned Brittany Ferries from its activities in the UK would represent an income debit under this section.

Current transfers

These represent sums to approximate to the value of resources given or received overseas where no money has changed hands (e.g. short-term aid).

The capital and financial account

Whilst the current account of the balance of payments records the export and import of goods and services, this part of the account deals mainly with movements of capital. Such capital movements are generally considered under the headings of:

* the capital account
* the financial account.

Capital account

The capital account consists of capital transfers as well as the purchase and sales of non-produced, non-financial assets such as copyrights.

Financial account

This account records money flows under five main sections:

1 direct investment
2 portfolio investment
3 financial derivatives
4 other investments
5 reserve assets.

Direct investment is the direct purchase of firms of land or buildings abroad. Portfolio investment is the purchase of securities or shares abroad. These activities lead to an initial outflow of funds but a potential future inflow of funds under the 'total income' section of the current account. Financial derivatives include options (e.g. currency options), traded financial futures and currency and interest swaps. Other investment covers trade credits, loans and deposits. Here, for example, a loan to an overseas company will lead to an outflow of capital but future inflows of interest payments in the 'total income' part of the current account. Reserve assets are those foreign financial assets that are controlled by the monetary authorities such as the central bank. For example, government use of

Table 14.6 The balance of Disneyland Paris payments for France

	Exports/credits	Imports/debits
Current account		
Visible trade	Exports of Disneyland Paris merchandise Souvenirs bought by overseas residents	Purchase of overseas equipment Merchandise imported from the USA and Far East for sale Imported foods for catering
Invisible trade	Admission charges paid by overseas residents Meals bought by overseas residents	Royalties and management fees paid to US parent company Overseas marketing
Total income		Interest paid on loans to overseas banks Dividends paid to overseas shareholders Private transfers by overseas workers employed
Capital and financial account		
Investment in France by overseas residents	Direct investment from the US parent company of 49 per cent of Disneyland Paris Purchase of Disneyland Paris shares by overseas residents	Sales of Disneyland Paris shares by overseas residents to French residents
Investment overseas by French residents banking transactions	Borrowings from overseas banks	Capital repayments to overseas banks

official reserves of foreign currencies is recorded here. An increase in reserves would lead to a corresponding outflow of capital from the balance of payments account.

The balance of leisure and tourism payments

The complex effects of leisure and tourism activities on a country's balance of payments are illustrated in Table 14.6 by an example of international currency flows associated with Disneyland Paris.

Overall, we can predict that the economic impact of Disneyland, Paris, would make a positive contribution to the balance of payments of France. However, potential earnings can be diminished in several ways. First, consider the element of overseas ownership. The greater the share of overseas ownership (through direct and portfolio investment), the more profit is exported in the form of dividends to overseas shareholders. Second, the role of overseas banks

Plate 14 Tourism leakages: an Italian Coffee machine unloaded on a Thailand beach.
Source: The author.

is significant. A high initial loan from foreign banks results in significant capital and interest repayments flowing overseas. Third, the degree of import content of goods sold must be considered. Tourists buying Disney *Toy Story* video tapes are making more of a contribution to the US balance of payments than the French one in the form of royalty payments. Fourth, some projects employ a high proportion of foreign nationals who repatriate some of their earnings. Finally, the construction of a project may entail the use of overseas contractors and importation of equipment. A further example of potential leakages is demonstrated in Plate 14. Tourism represents a key export earner for Thailand, but some expenditure leaks out of the economy to purchase imports to satisfy the demands of international tourists. In this case an Italian coffee making machine is being imported represents an outflow of currency to Thailand's current account in goods (visibles).

Comparisons

Table 14.7 shows comparative current account data for a range of surplus and deficit countries for the second quarter of 1999. This illustrates some of the key global imbalances in the international trade of goods and services with Australia, Canada, the UK and the USA all posting substantial deficits, whilst Germany, Norway, Japan and especially China all earned substantial surpluses.

Table 14.7 Current account of balance of payments (Q2 2009) ($ million)	
Australia	−10,252
Canada	−10,672
Denmark	2,161
Germany	36,496
Greece	−9,226
Japan	40,582
Korea	13,257
Norway	13,373
Spain	−17,279
Switzerland	13,441
Turkey	−3,555
UK	−17,712
USA	−84,447
Brazil	−3,142
China	134,460
Source: OECD www.stats.oecd.org	

Government policy

In the short term a balance of payments deficit on current account is not necessarily a problem. It can be offset by borrowing from overseas, or overseas inward investment, or selling of assets overseas. There are, however, limits to borrowing and the selling of assets abroad, and so an acute long-term current account deficit will require government intervention. This may take the form of:

- devaluation or currency depreciation
- deflation
- protectionism.

Each of these will affect leisure and tourism organizations.

Devaluation or currency depreciation

This is a policy of allowing a country's currency to fall in value or depreciate under a system of floating exchange rates, or moving to a lower rate under a fixed exchange rate system. The aim is to stimulate exports by making their foreign currency price cheaper and to curb imports by increasing their price in the domestic currency. An example of the effects of devaluation is shown in Table 14.8. Here

Table 14.8 The effects of currency movements on prices

		Local currency price	Purchase price: £1 = $1.50	Purchase price: £1 = $2.00
Visible import	Apple Music iPod	$300	£200	£150
Invisible import	Hotel for week in Miami	$600	£400	£300
Visible export	Litre of Scotch whiskey (before tax)	£5	$7.50	$10.00
Invisible export	Night at Heathrow hotel	£100	$150	$200

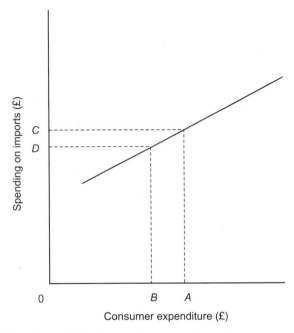

Figure 14.2 The effects of deflationary policy on export spending.

the dollar falls against sterling from £1 = $1.50 to £1 = $2.00. This should stimulate demand for US exports in the UK (in this case the £ price of i-Pods and US hotel accommodation goes down) and reduce US demand for UK exports (the dollar price of Scotch whiskey and UK hotel accommodation goes up).

Success of the policy will depend upon demand elasticities. For example, devaluation will only increase total foreign currency earnings from exports if demand is elastic, so that the fall in the foreign currency price per unit is compensated for by a larger proportionate rise in demand.

Deflation

A deflationary policy involves the government reducing spending power in the economy. The rationale is that, since imports form a significant proportion of consumer expenditure, a reduction in spending power will in turn reduce imports. Figure 14.2 shows the relationship between imports and the overall level of consumer spending in an economy.

Deflation is achieved through increasing interest rates or increasing taxes. If deflationary policy reduced consumer expenditure from 0A to 0B, then import spending would fall from 0C to 0D.

Protectionism

This entails direct controls on imported goods, including taxes on imports (tariffs) and limits on import volumes and values (quotas). The threat of retaliation and the rules of international treaties such as the EU and GATT (which exists to reduce protectionism) make protectionism a difficult option.

EXCHANGE RATES

Significance of exchange rates

The exchange rate is the price of one currency expressed in terms of another currency. Exchange rates are important to leisure and tourism organizations for a number of reasons. Firms selling or manufacturing goods may import either the finished good or the raw materials to make the finished good. For example, ski equipment is mainly imported into the UK and a fall in the value of sterling against the currency of the exporting country will mean a rise in the sterling cost of equipment.

The purchase of tourism facilities abroad is classed as an invisible import and so a fall in the value of the domestic currency will increase the local price of such services. A fall in the value of domestic currency will however reduce the foreign currency price of visible exports and invisible exports, stimulating inbound tourism.

Organizations selling imported goods and services may favour a higher exchange rate, whereas those exporting goods and services may favour a lower one. Exhibit 14.3 links a fall in the value of the Fiji dollar to tourism growth and a rise in the value of the Costa Rican colon to a fall in tourism revenues. Above all, stability of the exchange rate is crucial for organizations whose operations involve significant foreign currency transactions. This was a key argument for the creation of a single EU currency – the Euro. However, exchange rates are only part of the equation determining export competitiveness and Dwyer et al. (2002) outline a method that allows the various determinants of tourism price competitiveness, such as exchange rate and price changes, to be highlighted and their influence on the indices to be identified.

Exhibit 14.3 Currency ups and downs: tourism downs and ups

Costa Rica: Costa Rica's tourism businesses have been negatively affected by the 15 per cent increase in the value of its currency, the colon in 2010. The tourism industry receives most of its revenue in dollars and pays most expenses in colones. This means that in 2009 a $1500 hotel booking for a hotel reservation generated revenue of 862,500 colones to cover their costs. But the same $1500 booking in 2010 only generated 757,500 colones, a decline in income of about $200.

Fiji: Chief executive of Tourism Fiji Josefa Tuamoto said that in 2009 the devaluation of the Fiji dollar was a major boost for the tourism industry. He said 'In a nutshell, the devaluation means there has never been a better time to holiday in Fiji ... the devaluation will bring the Fiji dollar in line with the currencies in our major source markets – especially Australia and New Zealand – where we will be driving the value for money message as part of our overall marketing of the destination.'

Source: Press cuttings.

Determination of floating exchange rates

A floating exchange rate is one which is determined in the market without government intervention. Here the exchange rate is determined, like most prices, by the forces of demand and supply. For example, on the foreign exchange markets, the £ sterling is demanded by holders of foreign currency wishing to buy sterling and sterling is supplied by holders of sterling wishing to buy foreign currency. Using the Australian dollar to stand for all foreign currencies, we can identify the main determinants of the demand for and supply of sterling as follows:

Demand for sterling (supply of Australian dollar)

- Demand for UK visible exports.
- Demand for UK invisible exports.
- Demand for funds for direct and portfolio investment in the UK.
- Demand for funds for overseas deposits in sterling bank accounts.
- Speculation.
- Government intervention.

Supply of sterling (demand for Australian dollar)

- Demand for Australian visible exports.
- Demand for Australian invisible exports.
- Demand for funds for direct and portfolio investment in Australia.
- Demand for funds for deposits in Australian bank accounts.
- Speculation.
- Government intervention.

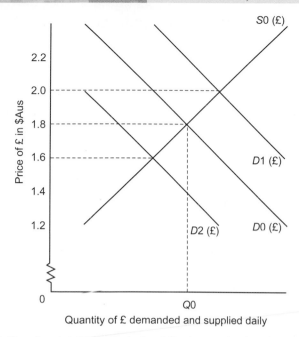

Figure 14.3 The price of sterling in Australian dollar (see text for details).

Figure 14.3 shows typical demand and supply curves for sterling against the Australian dollar. The demand for pounds is represented by the demand curve D0, and S0 shows the supply of pounds. The equilibrium exchange rate is at £1 = AUS$1.8, where the number of pounds being offered on the foreign exchange market is equal to the number of pounds demanded (0Q0).

Should any of the determinants of the demand or supply of sterling change, the demand and/or supply curves will shift position and a new equilibrium price will be achieved. The price of sterling will rise if the demand curve for sterling shifts to the right. In Figure 14.3 a shift of the demand curve from D0 to D1 causes the exchange rate to rise to AUS$2.0. This could be caused, for example, by a significant increase in the value of UK exports, or a rise in UK interest rates causing foreign currency holders to switch their deposits into sterling accounts to earn higher interest rates.

A leftward shift of the supply curve for sterling would have a similar effect on the exchange rate. The price of sterling will fall if the demand curve for sterling shifts to the left. In Figure 14.3 a shift of the demand curve from D0 to D2 causes the exchange rate to fall to AUS$1.6. This could be caused, for example, by a significant fall in the value of UK exports, or a fall in UK interest rates causing foreign currency holders to switch their deposits out of sterling accounts to earn higher interest rates abroad. A rightward shift of the supply curve for sterling would have a similar effect on the exchange rate.

Determination of fixed exchange rates

A fixed exchange rate system is where the price of one currency is fixed in terms of another currency. For example, for a period before full monetary union and the introduction of the Euro, most EU member states fixed their currencies at an agreed rate. Similarly, some countries peg their exchange rate to the US dollar. The idea behind fixed exchange rates is to avoid the sudden changes to trading conditions that can accompany large and sudden fluctuations in exchange rates. However, a key problem is maintaining a fixed rate. This generally involves substantial intervention by the government directly to buy or sell its own currency or indirectly by changing interest rates to make its currency more or less attractive as a medium for international savings.

The Euro

On 1 January 1999, 11 EU countries (Austria, Belgium, Finland, France, Germany, Ireland, Italy, Luxembourg, Netherlands, Portugal and Spain) fixed their exchange rates in the final preparations for the introduction of the Euro – the single European currency. The Euro was introduced fully in 2002, although the UK, Norway and Denmark retained their national currencies. The Maastricht Treaty, signed in 1992, laid the foundations for the Euro and set the economic conditions necessary for member states to join. These were known as the convergence criteria. In 1994, the European Monetary Institute was set up. This is the institution that has the responsibility for the introduction and the managing of the Euro. In effect it is a European central bank. The introduction of the Euro was held up because too few countries had met economic convergence criteria, but by 1998, the 11 founder members had all met the criteria.

The main advantages of joining the Euro for member countries are a reduction in the transaction costs of trading: a reduction in foreign currency risk and greater competition that comes from easier price comparisons across the Eurozone. The main drawback is the acceptance of a single interest rate across member states. This may be inappropriate if member states are experiencing differing economic conditions. For example, high unemployment would generally dictate a fall in interest rates whilst high inflation would call for a rise in interest rates. Many EU consumers also felt that the introduction of the Euro was seen by producers as an opportunity to raise prices.

Spot and forward foreign exchange markets

The spot market is the immediate market in foreign currency and represents the current market rate. Payment is made today and the transaction takes place today at today's rate. There is a margin making dealers' selling prices slightly more than buying prices. However, some organizations seek protection from exchange rate fluctuations, particularly if they need to quote for contract prices involving a large foreign currency consideration. The forward market exists to satisfy demand for a guaranteed future exchange rate. A rate of exchange is set today at a guaranteed rate for a future date. This rate may be above or below current market rates depending on predictions about the future.

Exchange rate trends and government policy

In theory a floating exchange rate should provide an automatic adjustment mechanism to changes in a country's trading position. A deficit would cause the exchange rate to fall, thus stimulating the demand for exports and reducing import demand as relative prices changed. In practice there are many factors that mean that this self-adjusting role of the exchange rate rarely happens. For example, where demand or supply is particularly inelastic, exchange rate-induced price changes may have a limited effect on sales. At the same time, speculation and interest rate effects can each cause currencies to rise or fall to levels that do not reflect a country's balance of payments position.

In the past, governments have often intervened in the market (a process called dirty floating) in an attempt to influence the exchange rate. Policy instruments to affect the exchange rate consist of interest rates and direct buying and selling of currency by the Central Bank. Raising interest rates will generally increase the demand for a currency as savings are moved from overseas banks to domestic banks to benefit from higher interest rates.

The government faces a dilemma in its exchange rate policy as in many other policy areas. A lower exchange rate makes export prices competitive and discourages imports, whilst a high exchange rate, by cutting import prices, helps to combat inflation.

REVIEW OF KEY TERMS

- Terms of trade: relative prices of imports and exports.
- Balance of payments: record of one country's financial transactions with the rest of the world.
- Exchange rate: price of one currency in terms of another.
- Current account: value of trade in goods and services.
- Visible trade: trade in goods.
- Invisible trade: trade in services.
- Devaluation or currency depreciation: movement to a lower exchange rate.

- Deflationary policy: government policy to reduce economic activity.
- Protectionism: policy to control imports.
- GATT: General Agreement on Tariffs and Trade.
- GATS: General Agreement on Trade in Services.
- Floating exchange rate: one which is determined in the market without government intervention.
- Fixed exchange rate: constant rate of exchange maintained by market intervention.
- Spot market: the immediate market in foreign currency.
- Forward market: futures market for currency.

 Data Questions

Task 14.1

Table 14.9 shows the exchange rate between the Australian dollar and the UK pound in the period 2004–2011.

Table 14.9 Exchange rate of Australian dollar to UK pound								
Year	2004	2005	2006	2007	2008	2009	2010	2011
£1 = AUS$?	2.37	2.46	2.35	2.50	2.20	2.18	1.77	1.58

Source: Adapted from XE Exchange Rates http://www.xe.com/

Recap Questions

1 Comment on the changes shown in the data.
2 Draw a demand and supply graph to illustrate the likely causes of the change in the exchange rate between 2007 and 2011.
3 What are the likely impacts of these changes on inbound and outbound tourist statistics for Australia?
4 How important are exchange rates in determining overall visitor flows to a country?

Task 14.2 The Euro: from christening to crisis

2002: The 11 European Member States of Austria, Belgium, Finland, France, Germany, Ireland, Italy, Luxembourg, the Netherlands, Portugal and Spain were all in the first wave of the Eurozone. On 1 January 1999, exchange rates between their currencies were fixed and the Euro became legal currency. From 1 January 2002, Euro notes and coins replaced those of domestic currencies and all transactions have been in Euros. The agreement of European Monetary Union (EMU) was ratified by the Treaty of Maastricht and the ERM provided a practical rehearsal. The European Central Bank in Frankfurt was established in 1998 to regulate the new currency. Jacque Santer, the former President of the European Commission, cited the following benefits of the Euro in a speech in Chicago in May 1998:

1 The future Eurozone is roughly comparable in size and economic weight to the United States. It will have nearly 300 million

inhabitants, and account for almost 20 per cent of the world GDP and of world trade, comparable to the United States.

2 The Eurozone will have a high degree of stability. The European Central Bank, whose independence has constitutional rank, will guarantee price stability, defined in operation terms as inflation between 0 and 2 per cent.

3 It will continue to spur economic growth, and will therefore indirectly stimulate job creation.

4 The Euro will also have a profound microeconomic effect on the functioning of Europe's internal market. By removing transaction costs and completely eliminating currency fluctuations and currency risk, trade, investment and travel in the Eurozone will be greatly facilitated, and prices driven downwards through greater competition.

5 In the financial sector, the potentially positive impact of the Euro is especially large.

6 The big unknown is the Euro's international impact. Will it become a truly international currency, performing the role of the unit of account, means of payment and reserve currency?

Willem Buiter, Professor of International Macroeconomics at the University of Cambridge, gave a more measured support for the Euro at a speech in London in December 1998:

'EMU will succeed in generating greater Euroland-wide prosperity than would have been likely under any alternative monetary arrangement. As regards macroeconomic stability it will make a modest positive contribution, provided the national countries redesign their automatic fiscal stabilizers to generate more strongly anti-cyclical deficits. Lower transaction costs and greater price transparency will help complete the single market, limit price discrimination and other restrictive practices. These are worthy and worthwhile gains, but it is unlikely to add up to a hill of beans.'

Those opposed to EMU draw attention to the following questions:

• Would joining EMU create better conditions for firms making long-term decisions to invest in an EMU country?

• How would being part of the single currency affect trade?

• Are business cycles compatible so that those economies in the EMU zone can prosper under a single Euro interest rate?

• If economic problems or currency problems do emerge, is there sufficient flexibility to deal with them?

• Will joining the EMU help to promote higher growth, stability and a lasting increase in jobs?

2011: The Eurozone is facing a major crisis. The governments of Portugal, Ireland, Greece and Spain have all had to seek emergency funding arrangements from the European Financial Stability Facility to help meet their mounting problems of financing their national debt. The European Financial Stability Facility was especially created to support Eurozone members facing a financial crisis. There is even discussion about the disintegration of the Euro. Many Germans would dearly like to see a return to the mighty Deutschmark and commentators are pointing to the deep divisions opening up in the Eurozone between the strong economies of Germany, France and the Netherlands versus the weak ones of Portugal, Italy, Ireland, Greece and Spain. Perhaps even the Eurozone might collapse into two halves.

Task 14.2 **continued**

Source: The European Commission (http://europa.eu.int/euro/html/), The Bank of England (http://www.bankofengland.co.uk), Newspapers: The Guardian and The Daily Telegraph, The BBC.

Recap Questions

1 Explain the meaning and importance of the following terms to a named leisure or tourism organization: *macroeconomic stability, single Euro interest rate, anti-cyclical deficits, restrictive practices.*
2 Evaluate the impact of the Euro on consumers of leisure and tourism goods and services.
3 Evaluate the impact of the Euro on producers of leisure and tourism goods and services.
4 Evaluate the decision of the UK and Denmark to opt out of the initial Eurozone.
5 Why was the Eurozone in crisis in 2011?
6 Examine the impacts of a collapse of the Eurozone.

Task 14.3 **Journal article: Lee, S.K., Jang, S., 2011. Foreign exchange exposure of US tourism-related firms. Tourism Management (in press).**

Lee and Jang's (2011) study included the following main points:

- [It] examined the exchange rate exposure of US tourism-related firms.
- [The] study revealed that travel services and recreation industries constitute a unique case for exchange rate exposure.
- The study also found that a relatively high percentage of firms significantly exposed to exchange rate risks.
- As expected, a significant percentage (78 per cent) of the tourism-related firms was exposed, in terms of their operation, to changes in exchange rates.
- A considerable percentage of domestic firms (58 per cent) without foreign income were also exposed to exchange rate risk in terms of their financing and investing activities, suggesting that as a firm's activities are interconnected, the impact of exchange rate on a firm's operations can influence all activities of the firm.
- The existence and characteristics of foreign exchange exposure is dependent on the respective firm's operating, investing, and financing profiles.
- Firms in tourism-related industries need to make an effort to identify and address the risks associated with exchange rate changes.
- If a firm's products are purchased by consumers whose buying power is subject to a foreign exchange rate, or can be substituted with any good priced by foreign currency, the lurking effect of exchange rates may significantly influence corporate cash flows.
- For tourism-related firms business diversification seems to be of considerable importance in order to operationally hedge against exchange rate risks.
- Constructing a hedge against currency value deviation among tourist markets … may be an attainable counter measure as well.
- Foreign inputs should also be considered where commercially feasible.

Recap Questions

1 What is foreign exchange exposure?
2 What examples are there of US firms that are likely to have high foreign exchange exposure?
3 What problems does high foreign exchange exposure cause?
4 How can firms minimize their exposure to foreign exchange risk?
5 Why is foreign exchange exposure less of a problem in Europe?

MULTIPLE CHOICE

1 The terms of trade will improve if.

(a) The price of exports rises faster than the price of imports.

(b) The price of imports rises faster than the price of exports.

(c) Export earnings are greater than import expenditure.

(d) Import expenditure is greater than export earnings.

2 Which of the following is not a benefit of specialization and trade?

(a) Self-sufficiency.

(b) Economies of scale.

(c) A rise in total output.

(d) Acquired expertise.

3 The exchange rate for US dollar falls. Which of these will be a direct consequence to 'Leisurewear', a US organization which imports raw materials and exports finished products?

(a) Import costs will fall.

(b) Import costs will rise.

(c) Import costs will remain unchanged.

(d) US labour costs will fall

4 In 2009–2010 the estimated tourism balance of payments for the Australia was as follows:

Overseas tourism spending in Australia: AUS$27,636 millions.

Australia tourism spending overseas: AUS$33,974 millions.

Which of the following statements are true?

(i) There was a deficit of tourism payments of AUS$6338 million.

(ii) There was a surplus of tourism payments of AUS$6338 million.

(iii) Australia's GNP rose by AUS$61,610 million.

(iv) Government debt was reduced by AUS$27,636 million.

(a) (i) only.

(b) (ii) only.

(c) (i) and (iii) only.

(d) (iii) and (iv) only.

5 Which of the following is true?

(a) A rise in interest rates will tend to make the exchange rate fall.

(b) Tourism is classified as an invisible trade item.

(c) A fall in the exchange rate will tend to reduce inbound tourism.

(d) The purchase of an overseas leisure company represents an outflow under the current account.

REVIEW QUESTIONS

1 Illustrate which parts of the balance of payments account are affected by the activities of a named organization in the leisure and tourism sector.

2 Under what circumstances would a fall in the value of the Euro (a) increase and (b) decrease earnings of US dollars for Greece?

3 How might persistent current account deficits affect organizations in the leisure and tourism sector?

4 Explain how a fall in the value of the domestic currency would affect three different organizations in the leisure and tourism sector?

5 Explain what factors have caused fluctuations in exchange rates over the past few years?

Websites of interest

Australian Bureau of Statistics: www.abs.gov.au

UK Office of National Statistics: www.ons.gov.uk/

US Travel and Tourism Industries: www.tinet.ita.doc.gov/

OECD: www.stats.oecd.org

XE Exchange Rates: www.xe.com/

The Euro (EU site): http://europa.eu.int/euro/

CHAPTER

15

Globalization

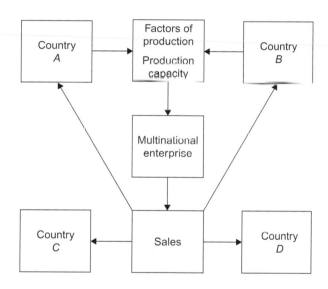

Objectives and learning outcomes

A significant trend in the last 25 years has been the globalization of the economic environment. This means that goods and services are increasingly being produced and sold across national economic boundaries. This chapter investigates the rise of globalization and the multinational enterprise (MNE) and analyses the motives for multinational operations as well as the effects of MNEs on consumers, parent countries and host countries. It also considers the relationship between MNEs and governments in parent and host economies. The significance of MNEs cannot be underestimated since it has been estimated that the 200 largest MNEs have a combined sales equal to about one-third of the world's GDP.

By studying this chapter, students should be able to:

- explain the meaning of globalization;
- explain the meaning of an MNE;
- understand the motives for extending operations overseas;
- analyse the effects of MNEs;
- evaluate government policy relating to MNEs.

GLOBALIZATION

Robertson (1992: 8) describes globalization as:

> the compression of the world and the intensification of consciousness of the world as a whole...concrete global interdependence and consciousness of the global whole in the twentieth century.

Under globalization, people around the world are more connected to each other than ever before in a variety of ways. Information and money flow more quickly than ever and between more people and at greater distances. Goods and services produced in one part of the world are increasingly available to the rest of the world. International travel is more frequent. International communication is commonplace. In fact, globalization has a variety of dimensions including cultural, political and environmental ones. This chapter will concentrate on the economic dimensions of the term. In this sense, Friedman (1999: 7–8) offers the following definition:

> [T]he inexorable integration of markets, nation-states, and technologies to a degree never witnessed before – in a way that is enabling individuals, corporations and nation-states to reach around the world farther, faster, deeper and cheaper than ever before...the spread of free-market capitalism to virtually every country in the world.

Economic globalization represents a development of markets and expansion of global linkages. It would be possible to identify four main stages of this development from subsistence (little market interaction) to the development of local and regional markets through to the importance of national and finally to the ready access to international markets. It refers to the increasing integration of economies around the world. This integration is evident mainly through trade and capital flows but it also includes the movement of people (labour) and knowledge (technology) across international borders:

- *Trade*: International trade has risen dramatically over the past 25 years. This has lead to a big increase in the range of leisure goods and services available as global markets offer greater opportunity for consumers to tap into more and larger markets around the world. Trade has increased as transport has become cheaper and faster so that resource differentials in different countries can be exploited. Markets promote efficiency through competition and the division of labour encouraging greater specialization that allows people and economies to focus on what they do best, but at the same time entailing more trade. The strongest rise has been in the export of manufactured goods whilst the share of primary commodities in world exports, such as food and raw material, has declined. The increase in world trade has also hastened the structural changes in economies. Advanced industrial economies have witnessed rapid de-industrialization as manufacturing has become relocated in newly industrialized developing countries, particularly in Asia.

- *Capital movements*: This aspect relates to funds to finance investment and there were rapid increases in private capital flows, particularly to developing countries during much of the 1990s and direct foreign investment is the most important category.

- *Movement of people*: This has been one of the less spectacular aspects of globalization. Given the vast differentials in wages and living conditions it might be expected that more workers would move from one country to another to exploit better employment opportunities. However, whilst trade and capital movements have been liberalized, labour migration has not. Most countries still operate restrictive immigration policies.

- *The spread of knowledge (and technology)*: Knowledge, information and technology transfer is a significant aspect of globalization. It can occur at two levels. For example, countries may benefit from technical innovation from direct foreign investment. However, knowledge about management techniques, export markets production methods and economic policies is also much more readily available and at comparatively low cost to companies and individuals who wish to benefit from it.

The rise of globalization has been facilitated by technological advances. In particular, there has been a revolution in communications based on information technology, the Internet and mobile devices and a steady increase in the efficiency of transportation. These have made it easier, cheaper and quicker to complete international transactions – both trade and financial flows.

Globalization is seen by some as a power for good whilst others see it as laden with threats. Those who advocate its benefits refer to improved communications, a more open world, the advent of new, better and cheaper products, the reduction in barriers to trade and its contribution to faster economic growth. For this group globalization offers significant opportunities for world development and they see the major problem that it is not progressing evenly. They note that some countries have been integrated into the global economy more quickly than others and that these are seeing faster growth and reduced poverty. For example, free-trade policies have brought dynamism and greater prosperity to much of East Asia, transforming it from one of the poorest areas of the world 40 years ago.

However, to others, globalization is a pejorative term sometimes used as shorthand for the ills of capitalism. Here concerns are expressed about the deterioration in the well-being of particular groups (these range from whole countries, to workers in developed countries who have seen their jobs exported, to workers in developing countries who work under conditions of exploitation), the sovereignty and identity of countries, the disparities of wealth and opportunities among countries and people, the health of the environment and the greater exposure it brings countries to sudden and profound economic shocks.

Tourism is a particularly significant aspect of globalization (Mules, 2001). Its supply and demand are global and its operation creates and recreates new identities at the consumer, organizational and national levels. Above all, it is a very significant economic activity in global terms as Table 15.1 and Plate 15 illustrate. Sugiyarto et al. (2003) examined the economic impact of globalization and tourism in Indonesia and found that tourism growth amplifies the positive effects of globalization and lessens its adverse effects. Production increases and welfare improves, while adverse effects on government deficits and the trade balance are reduced.

Globalization is sometimes thought of as a synonym for global business. However, at the same time as businesses have organized themselves at a global level so have other agencies – some representing governments and some representing non-governmental interests. The United Nations and its variety of subsidiary offices are a good example of the former. Greenpeace, Friends of the Earth, the WorldWide Fund for Nature, are examples of the latter.

Table 15.1 Global significance of tourism (2010)	
Tourism contribution to worldwide economic activity .	5%
Tourism contribution to worldwide employment	6–7%
Tourism contribution to worldwide exports of services	30%
Tourism contribution to worldwide total exports	6%

Source: Adapted from UN World Trade Organization Tourism Highlights
http://www.unwto.org/facts/menu.html

Plate 15 Same (but different greeting): MacDonald's, Thailand. *Source: The author.*

MEANING AND EXTENT OF MNE

An MNE is one which has production or service capacity located in more than one country. The MNE has a headquarters in a parent country and extends its operations into one or more host countries. The headquarter countries for many of the key MNEs in travel and tourism are the USA, the UK, Ireland, France, Germany, Japan and Hong Kong. The main ways in which multinational operations are extended are by investment in new or 'greenfield' capacity, by taking an equity stake in a foreign company (i.e. buying up shares) or by operating a franchise or alliance with a foreign company. Coca-Cola is

Exhibit 15.1　Coca-Cola worldwide

- The Coca-Cola Company is the world's leading owner and marketing organization of non-alcoholic beverage brands.
- The Coca-Cola Company's products account for approximately 1.6 billion of the 54 billion beverage servings of all types consumed worldwide every day.
- The Coca-Cola Company's operating structure is as follows:
  - Eurasia and Africa
  - Europe
  - Latin America
  - North America
  - Pacific
  - Bottling Investments
  - Corporate.
- During 2009 the Coca-Cola Company introduced a variety of new brands worldwide including:
  - Cascal, a fermented fruit beverage, in the USA
  - Glaćeau smartwater in Canada
  - Hugo (fruit juice and milk protein) in Chile
  - Valle Fruit, a fruit pulp juice in Brazil, Colombia, Ecuador, Costa Rica, Mexico, Nicaragua and Panama.
  - Schuss Gaseosa in Spain
  - Lift Pear (sparkling, with real fruit juice) in Poland and Bulgaria
  - Schweppes Dark Malt Beverage in Ghana
  - Mazoe dilutable juice drinks in South Africa
  - Cappy Lemonade in Turkey
  - Dobry Lemonade (with traditional Russian flavors) in Russia
  - I LOHAS (a new water brand) in Japan
  - Minute Maid Pulpy Super Milky (fruit juice, milk powder, whey protein and coconut bits in China
  - Vitaminwater in South Africa, France, South Korea, Japan, Belgium, Portugal, Hong Kong, China, Sweden and Macau.
- Comparative worldwide operating revenues by region 2010 were:

  - Eurasia and Africa　　07.22%
  - Europe　　　　　　　15.85%
  - Latin America　　　　14.91%
  - North America　　　　25.10%
  - Pacific　　　　　　　15.23%
  - Others　　　　　　　21.68%

Source: The Coca-Cola Company Annual Report.

a good example of a global corporation as illustrated in Exhibit 15.1. The exhibit demonstrates its significant share of the global market, the contribution of global regions to its operating revenues and its product innovation aimed at satisfying local tastes.

MOTIVES FOR GOING MULTINATIONAL

The general motive for companies going multinational is profit maximization. In this respect, investment overseas can be viewed in a similar way to any investment. The criterion for profit maximization for an investment is that the rate of return should be better than other possible uses for the capital that is to be employed. The rate of return will be related to the cost of, and the revenue derived from, the investment. Thus, motives for overseas investment will include cost reductions or increased sales resulting from production or service provision overseas.

Companies involved in manufacturing leisure as well as other goods now have much weaker ties with any particular region or national economy. The increase in international trade has made the market place more competitive and companies much more aware of the need for achieving price leadership or adding value to their products in order to achieve market share and profitability. Thus, firms are more ready to transfer production to another location should circumstances favour this. Service sector companies that wish to extend their services to overseas markets generally have little option other than to invest in capacity overseas.

Specific motives for multinational expansion can include the following:

- lower labour costs
- lower other costs
- exploiting 'national diamonds'
- marketing advantages
- scale economies, integration and competition
- extension of product life cycles
- tariff avoidance
- incentives in host economies.

Labour costs

In order to achieve price leadership, firms are constantly attempting to lower their costs below those of their rivals. One of the key factor costs that can be reduced by globalization is labour costs. Countries such as China, Malaysia, Vietnam and Thailand are popular destinations for production plants for MNEs because of their cheap labour rates. As well as cheap rates, labour and health and safety legislation are much less onerous on organizations in these countries. Union power is also very limited. So, for example, the Japanese Sony Company has products assembled in Malaysia. It is not uncommon for UK publishers to have books printed in Singapore and Hong Kong. A similar trend towards investment in tourism destinations can be observed with countries such as Egypt offering lower wage rates than those found in Spain and France.

Other costs

MNEs have access to international capital markets; so local interest rates are rarely a consideration. Land costs and planning regulations, though, can be an important factor, particularly in 'greenfield' developments. The rate of exchange between the parent and the host economy will also be significant.

'National diamonds'

Porter (1990) investigated the source of different countries' competitive advantage in the production of goods and services. He suggested an important factor which he calls the 'national diamond' effect. Why should the Japanese, for example, be so competitive in the production of cars when they have few local raw materials and relatively high wages? Porter's answer is that intense competition and demanding consumers in the home market are key factors which cause firms to improve technology, quality and marketing. In other words, the product is polished and reworked into a national diamond. This then enables such companies to compete successfully in overseas markets where local products are comparatively uncompetitive since they have not been similarly honed.

Marketing advantages

Some companies have an internationally renowned corporate image which can be exploited by extending operations overseas. Examples here include Holiday Inn (hotels), McDonald's (fast food) and Disney (entertainment). The name is important for two reasons. First, it guarantees a standard. This may encourage use, for example, by tourists in foreign destinations who may want their hotel room to represent 'a slice of home,' or who are sceptical about using unknown hotels. Second, foreign branded names, particularly US ones, are popular status symbols in some less-developed countries. The queues around McDonald's in Beijing and Moscow are testimony to this.

Scale economies, integration and competition

Multinational expansion may be a way of extending profits through vertical integration. For example, tour operators and airlines invest in accommodation overseas to extend their profits. Similarly, a strong incentive for horizontal integration may be the reduction in competition that occurs from buying foreign competitors. There are also considerable economies of scale to be achieved through transnational ownership. Economies of scale are discussed more fully in

Chapter 5, and include bulk purchasing, advertising economies and utilization of specialist inputs from different geographical areas.

Extension of product life cycles

Product life cycle refers to the different stages in the marketing of a product. Products which have reached the mature end of their product life cycle in their initial market and are thus suffering a decline in sales may be revived by launching them in overseas markets – particularly in less-developed economies.

Tariff avoidance

Where the exports of a country are affected by tariffs, companies affected may elect to set up production within the tariff area. This is perhaps one of the reasons why the UK has attracted so much investment from Japanese MNEs in the past decade. Such companies can thereby market freely into the EC without tariff barriers.

Incentives in host economies

Investment and running cost can often be reduced by operating overseas and taking advantage of government incentive packages.

MNEs IN LEISURE AND TOURISM

Examples of significant MNEs in leisure and tourism include:

Airlines	Electronics	Entertainment	Consumer products
Emirates	Apple	Walt Disney	Coca-Cola
UAL (United)	Toshiba	Anheuser-Busch	McDonald's
BA	Sony	Virgin	Nike
Delta		Merlin	
Qantas			

Air travel

There is a growing tendency for global strategies in major airline companies. The two main directions to this strategy are horizontal globalization and diversification. Horizontal globalization involves extending service networks worldwide. The motives for this include the general benefits of horizontal integration as discussed in Chapter 5, but increased market share is clearly a key motive. For example, whilst BA's turnover is highest in Europe there is significant potential growth in passengers in the Americas, Southern and Pacific regions.

Exhibit 15.2 Oneworld

1998: BA announced its new global partnership – Oneworld – which started as an alliance between BA, American Airlines, Canadian Airlines International, Cathy Pacific and Qantas. The heart of this alliance is a 'code-sharing' agreement where one airline sells a ticket on another carrier's flight, but issues a ticket carrying its own two-letter code. Oneworld is taking its activities further by joint marketing activities and the pooling of the frequent-flyer programmes of it members. Such agreements help airlines to extend their marketing and fill empty seats.

The popularity of alliances is the fact that there are financial and political difficulties which face airlines attempting traditional takeovers and mergers. Alliances allow airlines many of the benefits of merger without the related problems.

The main advantage is to establish a global network where passengers can be sold tickets in any part of the world to travel between any airports in the world. This helps to reduce passenger wastage when customers are forced to change carriers to reach destinations outside the network of their initial carrier.

2011: Current members of the Oneworld alliance are shown in Figure 15.1 Oneworld statistics:

- Members serve 900 destinations in nearly 150 countries.
- Alliance carries around 350 million passengers each year.
- Has a combined fleets of 2500 aircraft.
- Schedules around 9500 flights each day
- Earns more than US$90 billion in annual revenues.

Source: The author. Press Releases and www.oneworld.com

Hence BA's global strategy has involved investment in foreign airlines to provide global representation and extend BA's passenger base. Its merger with Iberia gives it improved access to routes to South America. Airlines may opt for alliance membership to extend their global reach where an added advantage is that allied airlines can use code sharing. Under code sharing, connecting flights of an airline group can share a common flight number. So a passenger flying from the UK to Perth, Australia will see the flight as one BA flight number rather than a BA flight and a Qantas transfer. Exhibit 15.2 records the announcement of BA's 'Oneworld' alliance. Most of the world's major airlines have entered similar global alliances and Figure 15.1 shows some of the major airline partnerships. Fayed and Westlake (2002) examined the impacts of globalization and GATS on air transport industries and noted the trends towards the privatization of airline companies in the context of the development of so-called global 'alliances' or 'partnerships' and liberalization at regional level and within trade groups such as the EU.

There is also an incentive for airlines to diversify into complementary activities. The logic behind this is that the airlines have

Oneworld	American Airlines	LAN
	BA	Malév
	Cathay Pacific	Mexicana
	Finnair	Qantas
	Iberia	Royal Jordanian
	JAL Japan Airlines	S7 Airlines
Sky Team	Aeroflot	Delta Air Lines
	Aeromexico	Kenya Airways
	Air Europa	KLM
	Air France	Korean Air
	Alitalia	TAROM
	China Southern Airlines	Vietnam Airlines
	Czech Airlines	
Star Alliance	Adria Airways	LOT Polish Airlines
	Aegean Airlines	Lufthansa
	Air Canada	Scandinavian Airlines
	Air China	Singapore Airlines
	Air New Zealand	South African Airways
	ANA	Spanair
	Asiana Airlines	Swiss International Air Lines
	Austrian Airlines	TAM Airlines
	Blue1	TAP Portugal
	BMI	Thai Airways International
	Brussels Airlines	Turkish Airlines
	Continental Airlines	United Airlines
	Croatia Airlines	US Airways
	EgyptAir	

Figure 15.1 World airline alliances.

customers who are likely to require related travel services – primarily car hire and accommodation. Thus it is not uncommon for airlines to have alliances with or equity stake in or ownership of car-hire companies and hotel operators.

Shipping

Ferry and cruise operations tend to be multinational in their operations. Many UK, US and Scandinavian cruise companies operate in the Caribbean. Typically, such ships are registered not in the country of their parent firm but in countries which offer flags of convenience, such as Panama and the Bahamas. In doing this, shipping companies can benefit from less stringent shipping regulations and lower taxes. The crewing of such ships is often provided from low-wage countries to cut costs, whilst the officers tend to be recruited from parent countries. Purchases of ship's stores and refittings can be done in ports which offer lowest costs. Papathanassis (2009) indicates some of the key issues facing cruise tourism which include:

- capacity increases
- larger vessels
- product differentiation
- labour recruitment

- working conditions
- industry governance
- environmental impacts.

Hotels and hospitality

Major MNEs in the hotel sector include corporations such as Accor, IHG Starwood and Marriott.

The recent history of the IHG illustrates some of the key issues of globalization. IHG started in 1946 as part of Pan American Airlines. It was sold in 1981 to Grand Metropolitan. The Saison Group acquired ownership in 1988. In 1998, Bass paid nearly £1.8 billion for the Intercontinental Hotel chain. Bass, a UK brewing group, had expanded significantly into a global hotel presence during the late 1980s. It bought the Holiday Inn chain outside North America in 1988 and the remainder in 1990 and 1993. The acquisition of Intercontinental Hotels (ICH) added 117 hotels with 44,000 rooms and a handful of mid-range Forum hotels to its global hotel portfolio. Globalization is able to bring important cost savings to hotel chains. For example, Bass was able to develop a single reservation system covering both Holiday Inns and InterContinental. MNE hotels are also able to exploit their international brand names and can often take advantage of cheap land prices at an early stage of the development of a tourist destination. The move towards globalization is driven by economies of scale, marketing benefits and the good growth prospects for international tourism.

With its acquisition of Intercontinental Hotels, Bass achieved good coverage across price ranges and is able to offer four-star hotels in addition to its mid-market Holiday Inns. It also added to its geographic coverage in Europe and Asia. In 2001, Bass plc changed its name to Six Continents plc and in 2002 Six Continents announced the separation of the group into Mitchels and Butlers plc and the ICH Group plc. By 2004, the ICH Group PLC owned a portfolio of well-recognized brands, including InterContinental, Crowne Plaza, Staybridge Suites, Candlewood Suites, Holiday Inn and Express by Holiday Inn. By 2010, IHG was able to offer more hotel rooms than any other hotel group in the world with around 4400 hotel rooms in almost 100 countries.

Whitla et al. (2007, p.207) found that in the hotel sector:

global strategy is most influenced by market factors, other drivers having much less influence. Cost drivers are constrained by limited economies of scale and standardization opportunities. Globalization is most marked in the thrust for a broad geographic presence in key overseas markets, the pursuit of global branding, positioning and uniform service standards.

EFFECTS OF MULTINATIONALS ON HOST ECONOMIES

The effects of MNEs on host economies are mixed. The main benefits can include:

- extra investment and related effects (growth, exports and employment);
- technology and skills transfer.

However, some of the problems that can arise from MNE activities include:

- leakages from the economy
- prices and bargaining power
- exporting of externalities
- threat to local competition
- power to pull out
- enclaves and dual development
- resource grabbing
- labour exploitation.

Benefits of multinationals to host country

Extra investment

The key benefit to host economies is the introduction of new investment. Such investment will represent investment which is extra to that which a host economy is able to generate itself and is important because capital tends to be scarce in developing countries and such capital shortages can retard economic development. In terms of the benefits of globalization to developing countries, it is those countries which have encouraged direct foreign investment that have seen dramatic increases in living standards over recent years. This is particularly true for China and countries in Southeast Asia. The effects of such investment will be the primary effects (resulting from construction of facilities, etc.) and the secondary effects (resulting from running of the facilities). As discussed in Chapter 12, the investment will give rise to extra income and growth in the economy and the associated benefits in terms of employment and foreign currency earnings.

Technology and skills transfer

It may be that the use of skilled labour and advanced technology introduced to an area by MNEs transfers to the local economy by way of demonstration effects. This depends partly upon the training and level of skilled employment offered by the MNE.

Problems of multinationals for host country

Leakages from the economy

MNE investment in an economy will generally generate more leakages than investment funded locally. This is because MNEs will remit profits to the parent company, often employ more foreign staff and sometimes use more imported inputs.

Prices and bargaining power

MNEs which represent monopoly or near-monopoly purchasers of a local input (e.g. hotel rooms) will be able to negotiate low prices with suppliers and thus reduce the impact of foreign expenditure in a local host area.

Exporting of externalities

It is sometimes alleged that the reaction of MNEs to environmental pressures and legislation in parent countries is to set up overseas in order to avoid extra compliance costs. In this view, externalities of production are simply exported, often to less-developed countries which are sometimes keen to accept such externalities in order to retain international competitiveness.

Threat to local competition

The low-cost, high-technology and high-quality goods and services associated with MNEs may make it difficult for new local firms to enter the industry. This is illustrated in Figure 15.2. LRAC represents a typical long-run average cost curve is associated with the production of a particular product. It is downward sloping, reflecting the considerable economies of scale that are derived from large-scale production. Because of its size and international buying power, an MNE is likely to enjoy low average costs of $0C$ at a large global level of output $0B$. New domestic firms trying to enter the market will face higher average costs of $0D$ associated with their small size $0A$, and thus find it difficult to compete.

Power to pull out

MNEs, like other private-sector organizations, seek to maximize profits. They are therefore constantly monitoring the environment to exploit changes in international costs or demand patterns. They thus have no particular loyalty to an area and can pull out, taking with them foreign expenditure (in the case of tour operators) or employment (in the case of manufacturers).

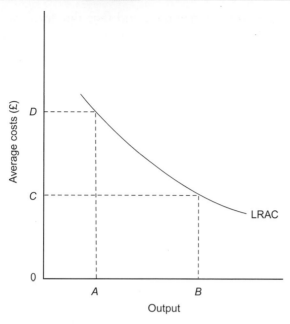

Figure 15.2 Costs for MNEs and local firms. LRAC.

Enclaves and dual development

One possible result of MNE investment is that a development will be exclusively for foreigners and exclude local people. For example, the Coral Resort owned by a Japanese company on the island of Cebu in the Philippines is guarded by armed security personnel and the beach area is only accessible to Coral Resort guests. Exclusive developments such as these are termed enclaves.

Dual development describes the situation where the economies of developing countries witness the growth of a sophisticated part of the economy often based around MNEs, with high wages, good working conditions and developed infrastructure. However, this may not be well integrated into the rest of the economy, so there may exist alongside this sector an impoverished economy which does not benefit from MNE investment.

Resource grabbing

Local resource prices in developing countries (particularly land) are often low in international terms, and developing countries are generally short of capital and foreign exchange. MNEs tend to have ready access to capital and thus are granted planning permission. One result of this is that MNEs may purchase large areas of land relatively cheaply. This resource is then lost to local exploitation which might be appropriate at a future stage of a country's development. At a Japanese golf course development in the Philippines, it was calculated that 150 hectares of land were bought for 150 million yen, a fraction of land prices in Japan, and that the development would yield 600 million yen of income by recruiting just 300 members out of an eventual target of 1600 members.

Labour exploitation

One attraction of investment in developing countries for MNEs is that labour legislation is generally more relaxed and trades unions, less evident or powerful. This means that labour costs can be reduced significantly through low wages, longer working hours, avoidance of sick, pension or holiday pay. Additionally, it is generally easier to hire and fire labour as production fluctuates.

GOVERNMENT POLICY AND MULTINATIONALS

Governments view the activities of MNEs with mixed feelings, on the one hand attempting to encourage them and the increased income, employment and foreign exchange earnings they can bring, but on the other hand conscious of less-attractive characteristics.

Government assistance for multinationals

Because of the potential benefits to a host economy, governments often offer incentive packages to MNEs to attract their projects. For example, estimates for Disneyland Paris suggested that the project would create 18,000 jobs in the construction phase and 12,000 jobs in the operating phase as well as earning US$700 million in foreign currency each year. Because of this there was considerable competition between the governments of France, the UK and Spain to provide the most attractive incentive package to attract Disneyland and enable their national economies to benefit from its effects. In the event, the French government provided a comprehensive infrastructure package including new roads and rail connections. It assisted Disneyland Paris with land purchase, provided a loan at preferential interest rates and gave planning permission for future-linked developments.

Forsyth and Dwyer (2003) examined the benefits and costs of foreign investment in Australian tourism are identified including effects of increased tourist numbers, balance of payments effects, regional socioeconomic impacts, technology transfer, changes in industry structure, loss of equity and control and transfer pricing. They concluded that Australia can maximize the economic gains it achieves from tourism industry by maintaining a liberal attitude towards foreign investment.

Exhibit 15.3 Virgin protests

Virgin Atlantic protested strongly to the competition authorities about BA's Oneworld alliance, despite having its own agreement with Continental Airlines, British Midlands, Malaysian and Ansett. It argues that these mega-alliances are formed to squeeze out smaller independent airlines and will lead to less competition. This view is supported by travel agents who note that there is no evidence that the new alliances have brought down prices or raised service standards.

Source: The author.

Government resistance to multinationals

Competitive threat

In some cases, governments may think that MNE expansion in their country may pose a danger to domestic companies and thus may attempt to limit MNE expansion. Exhibit 15.3 illustrates an airline lobbying government and protesting about the threat to its own business from the creation of global networks through airline alliances.

Power and accountability

Another government concern regarding MNEs is that of their power and accountability. Some MNEs have turnovers that exceed the GNPs of smaller economies, and this can make some governments feel impotent in terms of policy. Similarly, MNEs, through their substantial resources, can exert considerable powers lobbying governments to protect and promote their interests. In some cases, the nature of a MNE's product or service can be threatening to governments. This is particularly so in media services. News Corporation has worldwide ownership of newspaper titles as well as world satellite television interests. News Corporation is thus able to exert a considerable influence on public opinion.

Transfer pricing and tax losses

Because MNEs conduct business across national frontiers, they can often rearrange their accounts to minimize their tax position. This is known as transfer pricing. Transfer pricing takes advantage of different rates of corporation tax in different countries.

For example, assume there are two countries. Country A has business profit tax of 40 per cent and country B has a tax of 20 per cent. It will clearly pay an MNE that operates across countries A and B to ensure that most of its profits are earned in country B and thus pay a smaller amount of tax. It does this by adjusting the internal prices of goods traded within the company. For example, if it imports raw materials for its manufacturing plant in country A from its plant in country B, it can charge itself an artificially high price for these materials. In doing so it will make high profits in country B but pay the lower rate of 20 per cent corporation tax on them. The results of this will mean that profits on finished goods sold in country A will have been lowered due to the high import charges, thus payments of high corporation tax (40 per cent) in country A are minimized. This means that more profits are retained across the MNE's international operations and that country A loses tax revenue.

REVIEW OF KEY TERMS

- Globalization: organization of a firm's production and sales on a worldwide basis.
- MNE: one which has production or service capacity located in more than one country.
- Parent country: base country of MNE.
- Host country: country in which MNE is operating.
- Greenfield development: new investment on a new site.
- National diamond: product or service for which a country has built a world reputation.
- Product life cycle: stages in marketing of product from growth to maturity and decline.
- Tariff barriers: taxes on goods imported into a geographic area (e.g. the EU).
- Code sharing: packaging of interconnecting flights of linked airlines into one flight code.
- Demonstration effect: method by which skills and technology are transferred to a host economy by participation of local labour.
- Enclave: local MNE development which is isolated from the main host economy.
- Resource grabbing: MNE utilizing of host country's resources which prevents later domestic utilization.
- Transfer pricing: adjusting the prices of goods traded internally within MNEs to minimize tax.

Data Questions

Task 15.1 Coca-Cola-nization

The following are some of the risk factors that the Coca-Cola Company reported in its 2009 annual report that might impact on its operations, earnings, share of sales and volume growth:

- 'Obesity and other health concerns may reduce demand for some of our products.

- Water scarcity and poor quality could negatively impact the Coca-Cola system's production costs and capacity.
- Changes in the nonalcoholic beverages business environment could impact our financial results.
- The recent global credit crisis and its effects on credit and equity market conditions may adversely affect our financial performance.
- Increased competition could hurt our business.
- If we are unable to expand our operations in developing and emerging markets, our growth rate could be negatively affected.
- Fluctuations in foreign currency exchange rates could affect our financial results.
- If interest rates increase, our net income could be negatively affected.
- We rely on our bottling partners for a significant portion of our business. If we are unable to maintain good relationships with our bottling partners, our business could suffer.
- If our bottling partners' financial condition deteriorates, our business and financial results could be affected.
- Increases in income tax rates or changes in income tax laws could have a material adverse impact on our financial results.
- Increased or new indirect taxes in the United States or in one or more of our other major markets could negatively affect our business.
- If we are unable to renew collective bargaining agreements on satisfactory terms, or we or our bottling partners experience strikes, work stoppages or labor unrest, our business could suffer.
- Increase in the cost, disruption of supply or shortage of energy could affect our profitability.
- Increase in the cost, disruption of supply or shortage of ingredients or packaging materials could harm our business.
- Changes in laws and regulations relating to beverage containers and packaging could increase our costs and reduce demand for our products.
- Significant additional labeling or warning requirements may inhibit sales of affected products.
- Unfavorable general economic conditions in the United States or in other major markets could negatively impact our financial performance.
- Unfavorable economic and political conditions in international markets could hurt our business.
- Changes in commercial and market practices within the European Economic Area may affect the sales of our products.
- Litigation or legal proceedings could expose us to significant liabilities and damage our reputation.
- Adverse weather conditions could reduce the demand for our products.
- If we are unable to maintain our brand image and corporate reputation, our business may suffer.
- Changes in the legal and regulatory environment in the countries in which we operate could increase our costs or reduce our net operating revenues.
- Changes in accounting standards could affect our reported financial results.

Task 15.1 **continued**

- If we are not able to achieve our overall long-term goals, the value of an investment in our Company could be negatively affected.
- If we are unable to protect our information systems against data corruption, cyber-based attacks or network security breaches, our operations could be disrupted.
- We may be required to recognize additional impairment charges which could materially affect our financial results.
- If we do not successfully integrate and manage our Company-owned or controlled bottling operations, our results could suffer.
- Climate change may negatively affect our business.
- Global or regional catastrophic events could impact our operations and financial results'.

Source: Adapted from Coca-Cola Company, 2009 Annual Report. http://www. thecoca-colacompany.com/investors/pdfs/form_10K_2009.pdf

Recap Questions

1 Describe and analyse the global opportunities and threats to the Coca-Cola Company under as many of the above headings as possible.
2 What are the advantages and disadvantages of Coca-Cola's global operations to:
  (a) Shareholders?
  (b) Host countries?
  (c) Workers?
3 What are the six major risk factors affecting the Coca-Cola Company today? Explain and justify your answer.
4 What are the six major risk factors affecting:
  (a) A major cruise company?
  (b) A major airline?
  (c) A major manufacturer of leisure products?

Task 15.2 **Millennium developments in Zanzibar**

Zanzibar is an idyllic island off the east coast of Africa. In Nungwi, villagers use rough red planks to make dhow boats and live on a harvest of mangoes, almonds, coconuts, cloves and citrus fruit, and by netting fish from the Indian Ocean. Its future looks set to for radical change with a significant tourism development planned.

The UK-owned East Africa Development Company (EADC) in 1999 announced a massive $4 billion investment proposal in northern Zanzibar on the Nungwi peninsula. The EADC was granted a 49-year lease renewable for another 49 years for $1 a year to develop the peninsula. As part of the deal, the government has taken a 26-per cent stake in the venture. Forte Meridien, the UK-based hotel group, is one of several UK companies which are partners in the proposals which will become East Africa's biggest holiday resort. The scale of the proposals include a harbour for cruise ships, 14 luxury hotels, holiday villas, three golf courses and a world trade convention centre.

The Nungwi scheme will be one of the world's biggest building projects. The benefits to the multinational companies involved are clear. Zanzibar is a destination with a good year-round climate, land prices are cheap and so is labour. There is also the prospect of a greenfield site on a large scale. There are also potential benefits to local people in terms of higher paid jobs and better living conditions, if clean water and electricity are introduced. Nungwi village recently suffered an outbreak of cholera when raw sewage contaminated its well.

But Sue Wheat, writing in the *Guardian*, was keen to point out the strong counter-arguments against this development. She noted that although 20,000 people currently live on the site, the plans make no mention of them and suggest that the area is uninhabited. Sue Wheat poses some other key questions raised by the development of the site:

1 Water rationing is currently the norm in this area. How will the development affect water supplies?
2 How will local needs and environment issues be tackled?
3 Where will the 20,000 residents go?
4 Will any jobs created be suitable for the largely fishing and farming communities?
5 Will the resort use local produce and benefit local farmers or will it import foodstuffs to cater for visitor tastes?

Patricia Barnett, Director of the pressure group Tourism Concern, was also sceptical whether benefits promised to local people will materialize and is campaigning to protect Nungwi.

Source: The author from press reports.

Recap Question

1 Evaluate the costs and benefits of the Nungwi development to:
  (a) The host country.
  (b) The local host community.
  (c) The EADC.
  (d) Forte Meridian.
2 How is Zanzibar currently affected by MNE investments in leisure and tourism?

Task 15.3 Journal article: Hjalager, A.M., 2007. Stages in the economic globalization of tourism. Annals of Tourism Research 34, 437–457.

Aims of Paper: 'There is more to the globalization of tourism than cross-border flows of customers and purchasing power. This paper distinguishes four stages and different manifestations of the globalization of the tourism industry, and shows that it, like many other business systems, is undergoing an irrevocable globalizing process (p. 437)'.

Defining Globalization: 'Globalization, as one of today's most controversial issues, can be defined as the increasing integration of economies, societies, and civilizations. It includes, and goes beyond, the more simple internationalization defined as relations among and within nations. Globalization is a restructuring process that works across units and affects all aspects of human life: from capital flows, through political collaboration, to the flow of ideas. It also includes environmental pollution, criminal behavior, disease, and, ultimately, terror. Travel and tourism are among the many causes and results of globalization processes (pp. 437–438)'.

A Four-Stage Model: 'Stage one embraces the attempts of the national tourism system to reach out to new markets. Stage two describes the

Task 15.3 **continued**

integration and incorporation of its business across borders. Stage three addresses the fragmentation and flexible relocation in space of production processes. Finally, in stage four, the industry identity will be challenged, and new market types and business concepts will appear that go beyond previous definitions of tourism. Although the model suggests a logical progression toward the last more complex phase, in practice they overlap (pp. 440–441)'.

Some Implications of the Model: 'Potentially, the model can guide tourism policymaking by helping actors discard outdated modes of operation in time, and review and renew their policies according to the real global potential. If applied to the level of national and destination policies, there is in most countries in northern Europe a scope for far more advanced globalization formats than simple market representation and promotion. A better understanding of globalization potentials and a hedging of the threats require increased innovation and the structural development of commercial tourism industries, and also that government bodies enter into new types of alliances. Models of boundary crossing systems in other industries, such as pharmaceuticals or music and entertainment, may also apply to tourism... There is a particular need to address the political implications of globalization in much greater detail (pp. 452–453)'.

Recap Questions

1 Discuss Hjalager's definition of globalization with reference to an example from leisure or tourism.
2 Apply and explain Hjalager's four-stage model to an example from leisure or tourism.
3 Explain what Hjalager means by the statement 'there is in most countries…a scope for far more advanced globalization formats than simple market representation and promotion'.
4 Explain what Hjalager means by the statement 'There is a particular need to address the political implications of globalization in much greater detail'.

MULTIPLE CHOICE

1 Which of these is the least pronounced effect of globalization?
   (a) Trade in goods and services.
   (b) Capital movements.
   (c) Movement of people.
   (d) The spread of knowledge.

2 IHG opens a new Holiday Inn hotel in India. Which of the following will not benefit the host country?
   (a) The demonstration effect.
   (b) The increased capital expenditure effect.
   (c) The leakage effect.
   (d) The technology transfer effect.

3 Which of the following is not a possible disadvantage to the host economy of MNEs?

(a) Leakages from the economy.

(b) Threat to local competition.

(c) Improved know-how.

(d) Enclaves and dual development.

4 Which of the following statements is false?

(a) An enclave may discriminate against local people.

(b) Transfer pricing may be used by MNEs to avoid taxes.

(c) MNEs may set up in foreign countries to avoid tariff barriers.

(d) Multinational investment mean less leakages from the economy than domestic investment.

5 Which of the following is not an argument against globalization?

(a) Workers in developed countries may see their jobs exported.

(b) A reduction in tariff barriers.

(c) Loss of sovereignty in economic policy.

(d) More exposure to economic shocks.

REVIEW QUESTIONS

1 What MNEs exist in the leisure goods, leisure services and tourism sectors of the economy? What makes these companies MNEs?

2 Why and how are airlines 'going global'?

3 Using a named overseas project of an MNE, evaluate:

(a) The benefits of the project to the host country.

(b) The problems of the project to the host country.

(c) The benefits of the project to the MNE.

4 What is meant by transfer pricing?

5 Why do MNEs invest from and to the UK?

Websites of interest

Emirates: www.emirates.com

Marriott International: www.marriott.com

McDonald's Corp.: www.mcdonalds.com

Apple: www.apple.com

Oneworld Alliance: www.oneworld.com

Sony Corporation: www.sony.com

Intercontinental Hotel Group: www.InterContinental.com

The Coca-Cola Company: www.thecoca-colacompany.com

Virgin Atlantic: www.virgin-atlantic.com

UN World Trade Organization: www.unwto.org

PART 8

Environmental Economics

Environmental impacts

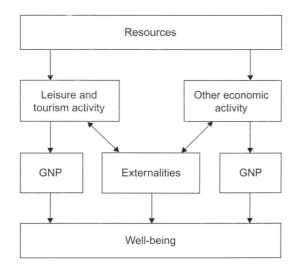

Objectives and learning outcomes

Chapters 12–14 examined the contribution of recreation, leisure and tourism to countries' national economies. Traditionally, economic analysis has measured impacts in terms of readily measurable variables such as employment, balance of payments and GNP.

In contrast, the objective of this chapter is to examine the issues raised by environmental economics. Environmental economics involves a wider view of the impact of economic development and growth, taking into account well-being rather than just measuring how much richer people become in monetary terms. Here, issues such as global warming, acid rain and resource depletion have been highlighted as threats to economic growth and even to the future of our species, and critiques and techniques developed by environmental economists can be readily used in the recreation, leisure and tourism sector.

This chapter lays the theoretical ground for understanding environmental economics as applied to leisure and tourism. First, it revisits the concept of externalities – especially the undesirable side effects of leisure and tourism on the environment. Next, questions are raised about the validity of measures of success that focus solely on the uncritical use of GNP data. Here, alternative methods of measurement of economic success are discussed which include consideration of the environment and human happiness. Third, the basic circular flow model, at the centre of much traditional macroeconomic analysis, is critiqued and extended to add an environmental dimension. Fourth, the particular economic problem of open-access resources is considered in relation to the environment. The second part of the chapter examines the specific environmental impacts of leisure and tourism both at the local level and at the global level with a particular emphasis on the pressing issues of global warming and the contribution of air travel to this. Finally, the chapter notes that when subjected to environmental scrutiny, the recreation, leisure and tourism sector can display examples of previously unaccounted overall benefits as well as costs. Additionally, as well as being the perpetrator of negative environmental effects, the sector is sometimes the victim of environmental pollution caused elsewhere.

By studying this chapter, students will be able to:

- understand environmental externalities;
- distinguish between growth in GNP and growth in well-being;
- understand a model of the economy that incorporates the significance of resources (sources) and waste disposal capacity (sinks);
- analyse environmental impacts;
- distinguish between renewable and non-renewable resources (sources) and analyse the use of such resources;
- analyse the effects of the existence of open-access resources on resource use;
- identify the existence of externalities and their contribution to well-being.

EXTERNALITIES AND THE ENVIRONMENT

The notion of externalities has already been briefly discussed in Chapter 7. Externalities are those costs or benefits arising from production or consumption of goods and services which are not reflected in market prices. Because of this, there is little incentive for firms to curb external costs since they do not have to pay for them. Externalities can be positive or negative (good or bad). The concept of negative externalities in particular is crucial to the understanding of environmental economics. Airlines provide a good example of environmental impacts and externalities for the leisure and tourism sector. As well as producing intended effects (satisfied consumers), air travel also produces undesirable side effects. Prominent here are noise pollution and CO_2 emissions. These represent significant costs to individuals and society, but neither airlines nor their passengers pay for these costs. Environmental economics seeks to identify and quantify such costs and find ways of diminishing the undesirable side effects of economic activity on the environment. Externalities can be divided into the following categories:

- *Production on production*: This is where one firm's external costs interfere with the operation of another firm, for example, noise from discos and clubs which creates a noise nuisance to hotel residents.
- *Production on consumption*: This is where industrial externalities affect individuals' consumption of a good or service, for example, aircraft noise affects people trying to listen to music; increase in crime levels in resorts; visual pollution of hotels, caravans and car parks affects enjoyment of landscape.
- *Consumption on production*: This occurs when external costs of consuming a good or service interfere with a firm's production process, for example, traffic jams caused by a leisure park cause transport delays to local firms.
- *Consumption on consumption*: This is where the external effects of an individual's consumption of a good or service affect the well-being of another consumer, for example, holidaymakers destroying coral reef, congestion around a football stadium causing inconvenience to other people.

Figure 16.1 shows how firms tend to overproduce goods and services which are subject to externalities. Demand curve D shows the marginal private benefit of consuming the good and, assuming there are no external benefits, it also represents the marginal social benefit. It shows how much consumers are willing to pay for extra units of output. Supply curve S shows the marginal private costs of production, that is, costs per extra unit of output. Producers will wish to expand their output to $0Q0$ since the price they receive from extra units of production will exceed the costs of extra units

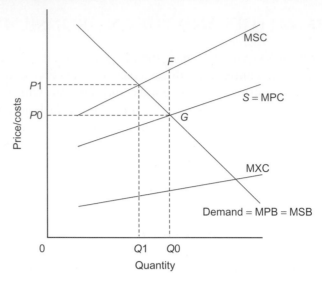

Figure 16.1 External costs, private costs and optimum output.

of production up to that point. Beyond that point, the extra costs of producing each good will exceed the price received for it. Thus, $0Q0$ represents the optimal market level of production.

Curve MXC represents marginal external costs, perhaps because of noise or other pollution effects. Adding MXC to MPC generates the marginal social cost curve MSC. Notice that now we include external costs, that is, previously unpriced environmental resources, the level of output $0Q0$ is no longer optimal. This is because marginal social costs exceed marginal social benefits by the amount FG. A reduction in output to $0Q1$ where MSC = MSB would need to take place to provide the optimal social level of production.

The case of sewage discharges into the sea illustrates this point. Whilst there is little marginal private cost to the water companies for pumping sewage into the sea, it represents a loss of well-being to people who want to use the sea. There is a considerable marginal external cost which takes the form of cleaning costs to surf equipment, medical costs to treat infections and loss of earnings caused by sickness. These are readily quantifiable costs to which must be added the general unpleasantness of contact with sewage. These points are illustrated in Exhibit 16.1.

ECONOMIC GROWTH, THE ENVIRONMENT AND WELL-BEING

Environmental economics provides a strong critique of conventional measures of economic growth and points out that well-being is insufficiently considered. Chapter 13 considered the contribution of the leisure and tourism sector to economic growth and development.

Exhibit 16.1 Surfing in the sewers

'I've just come back from a surf. The water quality wasn't too bad today because the wind was blowing offshore and the tide was going out. When the wind blows on to the shore and when the tide is high you still get the occasional pad or condom floating by'.

The surfers are far from happy. And it is not hard to see why. A quick walk on to the headland and you notice the air begins to smell rich, sweet and vile. A brown slick drifts out to sea off the point. Tucked away beneath the cliffs is its source – the same old sewage outflow pipe, pumping out output all day long.

Source: Adapted from The Guardian.

Economic growth was measured by examining changes in real GNP per capita. Environmental economists point out that such figure may give a misleading impression about improvements in economic well-being for the following reasons:

- The environmental costs of producing goods and services which appear in GNP are not always accounted for. These are the environmental externalities discussed in the "Externalities and the Environment" section.
- The distribution of the benefits of economic growth is not always even.
- GNP figures may include 'defensive' expenditure. Defensive expenditure is that which would not be otherwise undertaken but is necessary to offset environmental externalities.
- The loss of resources to future generations is not accounted for.
- The destruction of the natural environment that can occur from economic development is not given a monetary value.

Exhibit 16.2 demonstrates some of these concepts in relation to the development of an airport. The discussion in Exhibit 16.2 shows the need for caution in equating growth in GNP with growth in well-being. Indeed, some economists have argued that when a wider view of economic growth is taken, the costs may exceed the benefits. Such analysis has caused the questioning of policies which lead to fastest economic growth without regard to the wider consequences and some environmental economists have called for a halt or limit to economic growth.

The New Economics Foundation (NEF) has been at the forefront of efforts to produce alternative measures of 'growth' which take account of externalities. It produced an Index of Sustainable Economic Welfare (ISEW) as an alternative measure of economic progress to that of GDP. The ISEW adjusts GDP accounts to take account of a wider understanding of welfare. Its five main adjustments are:

1 Defensive expenditure (spending to offset social environmental costs) is deducted.

Exhibit 16.2 Development and well-being

The building and the running of an airport will add to GNP in terms of expenditure on building materials, fixtures and fittings, and access, staffing and consumables. However, local residents will suffer from increased noise and atmospheric pollution as well as traffic congestion – none of these costs will appear in GNP data.

Whilst some local residents may benefit in terms of job opportunities, gainers and losers are often different people. The main gainers from the development are the shareholders of the airport company, airlines and tour operators, employees and travellers themselves. Local residents are likely to form only a small fraction of these categories and so the benefits of such growth will be unevenly shared. GNP per capita figures only show average effects of growth.

Because of the extra noise, some residents will buy double glazing, more petrol will be used because of traffic congestion, and roofing contractors will gain more work because of vortex effects of aircraft (the tendency of aircraft engine thrust to cause intense patches of air currents which remove roof tiles). This is defensive expenditure. It is expenditure made to try to combat some of the ill effects of the development. It does not leave anyone better off than before the development, but it contributes to GNP data, exaggerating the apparent benefits of the development.

Finally, the development will involve loss of the natural environment. This represents the loss of an amenity to some people in terms of views or tranquillity or open space, but again this loss fails to register in GNP data.

2 An allowance is made for long-term environmental damage.

3 Net investment is included.

4 Changes in the distribution of income are valorized to reflect the higher marginal utility derived by extra income earned by poorer people.

5 A value for household labour is included.

More recently NEF has developed a 'Happy Planet Index (HPI)'. The HPI measures the degree to which long and happy lives are achieved per unit of environmental impact. The HPI is compiled using the formula:

HPI = Happy life years / Ecological footprint

- Happy life years = life satisfaction $\times$ life expectancy.
- Life satisfaction is found from surveys (such as the Gallup World Poll) which include the question 'All things considered, how satisfied are you with your life as a whole these days?' Responses are made on a numeric scales from 0 to 10, where 0 is dissatisfied and 10 is satisfied.
- Average life expectancy at birth is taken from the Human Development Index report.

Table 16.1 Happy planet?					
HPI rank	Country	Life expectancy	Life satisfaction	Ecological footprint	HPI
1	Costa Rica	78.5	8.5	2.3	76.1
9	Brazil	71.7	7.6	2.4	61.0
20	China	72.5	6.7	2.1	57.1
60	Croatia	75.3	6.4	3.2	47.2
74	UK	79.0	7.4	5.3	43.3
76	Spain	80.5	7.6	5.7	43.2
84	Hong Kong	81.9	7.2	5.7	41.6
102	Australia	80.9	7.9	7.8	36.6
105	Denmark	77.9	8.1	8.0	35.5
114	USA	77.9	7.9	9.4	30.7
143	Zimbabwe	40.9	2.8	1.1	16.6

Source: (Un)Happy Plant Index 2.0 www.happyplanetindex.org/public-data/files/happy-planet-index-2-0.pdf

- Ecological footprint data is taken from the WWF's Living Planet Report. Its meaning and measurement is outlined by NEF (Abdallah et al., 2009, p. 12) in its '(Un)Happy Planet Index 2.0'.

> The ecological footprint of an individual is a measure of the amount of land required to provide for all their resource requirements plus the amount of vegetated land required to sequester (absorb) all their CO_2 emissions and the CO_2 emissions embodied in the products they consume. This figure is expressed in units of 'global hectares' ... Dividing this by the world's total population, we can calculate a global per capita figure on the basis that everyone is entitled to the same amount of the planet's natural resources. Using the latest footprint methodology ... the figure is 2.1 global hectares. This implies that a person using up to 2.1 global hectares is, in these terms at least, using their fair share of the world's resources – one-planet living.

Table 16.1 records the HPI for selected countries. Notable results include that Costa Rica tops the table having good scores across the three criteria. The USA is quite far down because of its high ecological footprint and Zimbabwe is bottom of the table largely due to its very low scores on life expectancy and life happiness.

In relation to this section, it is interesting to compare the National Tourism Strategies of various countries. For many, there is still an obsession with very narrow measures of success based on growth in visitor numbers and foreign exchange earnings with little regard to wider measures of welfare. One notable exception to this is New Zealand where the strategy focusses on improving quality and value as well as growing visitor numbers.

DEVELOPING A MACROECONOMIC MODEL THAT INCORPORATES ENVIRONMENTAL DIMENSIONS

Figure 16.2 recalls the simple circular flow of income model used earlier to underpin introductory macroeconomic analysis. Factors of production are purchased by firms from households and combined to produce goods and services which are then sold to households. Household expenditure is financed from the income derived from selling factors of production to firms. Additionally, there are leakages from the system in the form of taxes, savings and imports, as well as injections into the system of government spending, investment and exports.

However, in its simple form, the model fails to illustrate some key points about the relationship of the economy to the environment. In particular, it fails to show the production of waste materials (use of sinks) and the using up of resources (use of sources). In fact, the production of waste materials is partially covered by the model and partially not. Exhibit 16.1 illustrates this point.

The article is about Newquay in Cornwall, UK, whose population of 100,000 is swollen by up to a million summer visitors. A key product of the tourism industry is sewage. This waste is collected and

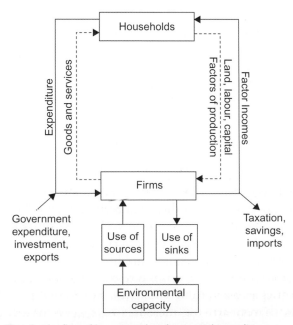

Figure 16.2 The circular flow of income and environmental capacity.

partially treated by South West Water, and this activity is picked up by traditional economics in the simple circular flow diagram as the use of factors of production to perform a service. However, the raw sewage that is discharged directly into the sea represents the use of a waste sink and the simple circular flow model does not reflect this.

The circular flow model can show an increase in economic growth caused by tourism – increased expenditure, generating increased incomes which in turn allow increased expenditure – without high-lighting a significant threat to such growth in terms of pollution effects. The use of the waste sink is free to South West Water and thus there is little incentive for it to amend its behaviour. There is, although, clearly a limit to the capacity of the sea to assimilate this waste. Where this assimilative capacity is exceeded, degradation of the sea occurs.

Environmental economics seeks to make the link between:

- economic consumption and production – in this case in leisure and tourism;
- the relationship between consumption, production and resources;
- the ability of the ecosystem to absorb waste.

It therefore amends the basic macroeconomic model to incorporate this relationship so that such economic development can take place without causing feedback which would threaten economic develop-ment or cause an unacceptable level of pollution. Thus, Figure 16.2 adds an environmental dimension to the simple circular flow model to highlight the fact that consumption and production uses sources and sinks and that the environment has a limited capacity (sources) to meet these demands.

THE PROBLEM OF OPEN-ACCESS RESOURCES

There is a particular problem posed by open-access to resources. It is what Hardin (1968) referred to as the tragedy of the commons. The sea is an example of an open-access resource. It does not have a clear owner, and therefore it is difficult to exert property rights over it – for example, preventing waste dumping. Because of this, there is little incentive to reduce outflows into the sea. The problem becomes more difficult with seas such as the Mediterranean. The Mediterranean coastline is shared by a number of countries. If one country should decide to reduce outflows of sewage into the sea, it will still suffer the ill effects of the outflows from other countries who might even think that there is now more capacity for their sewage. Of course, this is exactly the same problem that confronts efforts to achieve interna-tional agreements on CO_2 emissions and global warming. The atmo-sphere is a free access resource – shared by all of the countries that make up the planet earth. So there is no incentive for any country to take the lead and to curb its CO_2 emissions irrespective of the policy

Exhibit 16.3 Reefs under threat

It took thousands of years to create the majestic coral reefs that lie under the earth's oceans. These vast limestone structures have been laid over the centuries by reef-building corals. They are home to a huge diversity of plants and over 200 species of fish.

The Great Barrier Reef, off the coast of Australia extends for some 2000 kilometre and is a magnet for scuba divers. The Belize Barrier Reef stretches for some 250 kilometre off the coast of Belize in Central America.

But the reefs are under threat from industry, from agriculture and from tourism. Industrial fishing techniques using dynamite can blow up the fragile polyps that create the reefs. Rainforest clearance smothers the Belize Reef as thickly polluted run-off flows out of the rivers into the oceans.

Meanwhile, the tourism trade is set to kill one of its golden gooses. Whilst some boat operators practise good conservation methods and coach and cajole their clients to respect the coral, the growing size of the tourist tide threatens reef preservation. Boatloads of inexperienced snorkellers and divers regularly inflict unintentional damage, by touching sensitive polyps or smashing coral branches with a kick of a flipper.

But not all the damage is accidental. Some boat operators let their anchors drop on the reefs – the damage is evident by the clouds of debris thrown up. And some tourists seem unable to resist taking home just one small momento (that will not make any difference). For those who do not make the dive themselves, there are plenty of willing hands – and souvenir shops in reef resorts are often full of rare shells and coral curios.

Source: The author, from press cuttings.

of other countries. It would still suffer the effects of global warming caused by the actions of others. So the skies are another open-access resource and because of this there is less incentive to reduce pollution, for example, by aircraft.

Exhibit 16.3 goes beneath the sea to record the destruction of an open-access resource. On the same subject, Rodgers and Cox (2003) examined the effects of trampling on the survival of Hawaiian corals against different levels of human use. They found that survival dropped from 70 per cent at the low impact site to 55 per cent at the medium impact site. Total loss (0 per cent survival) was reported from the high impact site after only 8 months. High impact was equivalent to less than 200,000 total visitors or 63 people in the water per hour.

RECREATION, LEISURE, TOURISM AND THE ENVIRONMENT

The environment plays a unique role to much recreation, leisure and tourism for it provides the stage upon which much recreation is enacted. The sector very much depends on the environment for its

Exhibit 16.4 Intergovernmental Panel on Climate Change

In 1999, the IPCC published a study of the impact of aircraft pollution on the atmosphere and its main findings included:

- Aircraft release more than 600 million tonnes of the world's major GHG CO_2 into the atmosphere each year.
- Aircraft cause about 3.5 per cent of global warming from all human activities.
- Aircraft greenhouse emissions will continue to rise and could contribute up to 15 per cent of global warming from all human activities within 50 years.
- Nitrogen oxides (NO_2) and water vapour have a more significant effect on the climate when emitted at altitude than at ground level. Hence, any strategy to reduce aircraft emissions will need to consider other gases and not just CO_2.
- An increase in supersonic aircraft flying could further damage the ozone layer as aircraft emissions of NO_2 deplete ozone concentrations at high altitudes, where these aircraft would typically fly.
- Aircraft vapour trails or contrails, often visible from the ground, can lead to the formation of cirrus clouds. Both contrails and cirrus clouds warm the Earth's surface magnifying the global warming effect of aviation.

Source: Adapted from www.ipcc.ch/index.htm

success. But this provides the dangerous irony for the sector. For the richer the environment, the more recreational activities are drawn to it. The more economic activity, the more the potential negative impacts on the environment, and therefore the sector has the potential to destroy the very environment upon which it depends – pristine beaches, coral, attractive countryside, flora and fauna (loss of biodiversity).

Additionally, recreation, leisure and tourism are very dynamic growth sectors in the global economy. By virtue of this, they are set to generate more and more environmental impacts as they grow. In particular, transport is a key aspect of this sector. The growth in car use and air travel both have potentially serious impacts on the environment in terms of air pollution, casualties, concretization, noise pollution, congestion, CO_2 emissions, global warming (Exhibit 16.4), ozone depletion, acid rain and health. Another key aspect of the sector is the physical structures and infrastructures that support it and their associated impacts. Add to this the huge amount of waste generated by the sector and the energy consumption of the sector and it is not difficult to see why the sustainability of the sector has become such an important issue. For example, Gielen et al. (2002) have noted that whilst a move towards environmentally benign service industries is widely considered a key strategy for sustainable development, the environmental impact of these industries is not negligible. They analysed the environmental impact of Japanese leisure and tourism and their results suggested that leisure and tourism was responsible for 17 per cent of the national greenhouse gas emissions, 13 per cent of the national primary energy use and that a considerable part of the national land-use is affected by leisure and tourism. They further noted that leisure and tourism impact on biodiversity is hard to quantify because of inadequate monitoring systems.

Recreation, leisure and tourism can contribute to environmental impacts at the local and global level.

Local environmental impacts

At the local level these can be classified as:

- impacts on natural resources
- pollution
- physical impacts
- displacement.

Impacts on natural resources

Environmental economics distinguishes between two types of resources.

1 *Non-renewable resources* are those which have a fixed supply. Once they have been used up, there will be none left for future generations.
2 *Renewable resources* are those which are capable of being replenished.

Landscapes, views, open spaces and tranquillity represent local *non-renewable resources* in the leisure and tourism sector. They are used up by general economic development as well as by leisure and tourism development itself. An important consideration concerning the use of non-renewable resources is the rate of depletion and hence the level of resources bequeathed to future generations. It is also possible to identify less obvious, distant, external, environmental costs of tourism and leisure developments. For large-scale resort developments, for example, consideration should be given to the sources of raw materials for building and the subsequent effect of quarrying for stone or forest depletion for timber.

The urgency of this problem can be illustrated as follows: economic development uses up such resources. It also generates increases in incomes and leisure time and thus the demand for such resources. Thus, we have the prospect of dwindling natural resources having to provide for increasing demands and thus degeneration occurring at a quickening pace.

An important local *renewable resource* for large-scale tourism development in some parts of the world is water. Large-scale development requires considerable resources of fresh water. It is here that the technique of impact assessment is important. Forecasts need to be made of water use against water renewal although in some circumstances the latter may be supplemented by water diversion schemes. If water is obtained from underground aquifers, these will eventually run dry or be subjected to salt or other pollution if the rate of extraction exceeds the rate of replenishment. This problem is compounded by the free access problem, where it is not in anyone's interests to preserve water if everyone is drawing it from the same source. Golf courses require large amounts of water for their every day maintenance, and according to Tourism Concern a golf course in a tropical country such as Thailand uses as much water as 60,000 rural villagers. Over extraction of water from wells can cause saline intrusion into groundwater.

Resources such as footpaths, public parks and golf courses also have a renewable resource element to them. If the rate of wear of footpaths, for example, exceeds the rate of regeneration of protective vegetation, degradation will occur. This is illustrated in Exhibit 16.5 and Plate 16 which point to the potential damaging effects of biking to the environment. In a similar context, Havitz and Adkins (2002) discuss the circumstances in which it might be necessary to de-market municipal golf courses where the natural surfaces of the golf course are negatively impacted by overuse.

One of the reasons for such overuse and degradation is that the use of footpaths and public parks is free to the user. In markets where prices prevail, price is an important factor in rationing the demand for scarce resources. Consumers economize on use so as to conserve their limited money income. Where price is zero, there is no incentive to economize. The use of unmetered water illustrates

---

Exhibit 16.5 Calls for brake on mountain biking – Nicholas Schoon

Governments in many countries have been considering whether restrictions on mountain bikes may be necessary because their growing popularity is damaging some of the sites used by mountain bikers.

For example, a report published by the Council for the Protection of Rural England highlighted mountain biking as one of the ways in which unrestricted countryside leisure and tourism is increasingly harming the environment. The cyclists often use footpaths although the law says that they should be restricted to bridleways and byways. The broad, high grip tyres they use are stripping out vegetation and leaving deep, muddy furrows.

Walkers and ramblers complain that they are irritated and frightened by mountain bikes that pass them at speed. Some regard the bicycles as an inappropriate, unnatural leisure pursuit in cherished landscapes such as the 11 national parks of England and Wales.

Source: Adapted from The Independent.

Plate 16 Erosion from trampling and cycling. *Source: The author.*

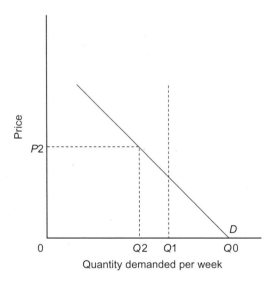

Figure 16.3 Effects of zero price on demand.

this point. For example, many people leave the tap on when they are cleaning their teeth, using a couple of pints of water where only half a cupful is needed since there is no incentive to economize on use. Figure 16.3 shows the economics behind this. Curve D represents the demand curve for the use of a footpath. As price falls, demand rises. At price $P2$ demand would be $Q2$. If zero price is charged, demand rises to $0Q0$. For some paths, this may result in usage which exceeds the limits where the resource can regenerate itself. If $0Q1$ represents the point of use beyond which regeneration cannot take place, then $Q1Q0$ represents use which causes degeneration of the resource at zero price.

Recreational and tourism demands can also put pressure on local resources like energy, food and other raw materials particularly where they are already be in short supply. Overfishing is a possible impact here. Many forests have suffered negative impacts of tourism. These include forest fires, clearance for development and tree cutting for fuel. For example, a single trekking tourist in Nepal can use up to 5 kilogram of wood a day.

The idea of carrying capacity is related to the regenerative capacity of resources. It has been defined as 'the maximum number of people who can use a site without an unacceptable alteration in the physical environment and without an unacceptable decline in the quality of experience gained by visitors' (Mathieson and Wall, 1982). It should be noted that this definition includes not just the possible degeneration of the physical environment but also the fact that too many visitors may spoil the visitor experience.

Leisure and tourism can also consume high amounts of energy at a local level. Hotels in particular can have high energy demands for heating, lighting and air conditioning. Some attractions are also very high energy users (e.g. indoor ski facilities in Dubai). In the main, energy is consumed in the form of electricity which is generated predominantly from *non-renewable* sources – particularly oil and gas. However, some energy is produced from *renewable* sources such as solar, wind and hydro power.

Pollution

Recreation and tourism, although often seen as clean in comparison with chemical and smokestack manufacturing and power generation industries, can cause similar pollution as other industries. These effects include:

- air pollutants
- noise pollution
- solid waste
- littering
- sewage
- noxious discharges
- visual pollution.

Recreation and tourism place particular demands on air, road and rail transport. Tourism accounts for more than 60 per cent of air travel and is therefore an important source of air emissions. As incomes increase, so long-haul travel becomes more popular. Air pollution from transportation for recreation and tourism has impacts at the local and global level. At the global level carbon dioxide (CO_2) emissions are significant, whilst at the local level pollution around London's Heathrow Airport, for example, often exceeds European Community maximum permitted levels due to a combination of traffic congestion and aircraft movements. This pollution includes carbon monoxide, sulphur dioxide as well as carbon particulates from diesel fuel and can cause asthma and other health problems.

Noise and air pollution also emanates from recreational vehicles such as snowmobiles and jet skis. A survey of snowmobile impacts at Yellowstone National Park, WY, USA found that snowmobile noise could be heard 70 per cent of the time at 11 of 13 sample points.

On average, passengers on cruise ships in the Caribbean each generate 3.5 kilogram of waste daily which is more than 4 times the average 0.8 kilogram generated by the local inhabitants. In mountain areas, trekking tourists generate waste so that the Machu Pichu trail in Peru and Nepal trails have been nicknamed the 'Coca-Cola trail' and 'Toilet paper trail'. Exhibit 16.6 considers some of the environmental effects caused by tourism development in Greece – focussing particularly on litter and plastic bottles. It demonstrates the fine balance that has to be achieved in tourism development, with overdevelopment causing degradation of the place itself, which can threaten future demand and prosperity.

Construction and use of hotels, recreation and other facilities often leads to increased sewage pollution and this has polluted seas and lakes particularly in countries where sewage treatment is undeveloped.

Recreational development can also cause severe visual pollution using cheap and standardized buildings which may be totally out of character with local vernacular architecture, or grossly out of proportion or which fail to harmonize with natural features in and around a destination. Cheap land and lack of planning and building

---

Exhibit 16.6 Tourism curse visited on this blessed Aegean isle

The Greek Island of Amorgos is rugged, barren and beautiful.

But over the past 20 years the economy has changed fast and locals can now make more money through tourism in 2 months than they could otherwise make in a year.

The tourism boom has taken its environmental toll. There are growing problems with water, sewage and rubbish although officials have been reluctant to acknowledge them.

'If we're careful we'll be all right. Our only real problem is plastic water bottles', commented a local mayor. 'You know the quality of our lives has really improved with tourism'.

And indeed it has. It has meant a huge rise in living standards and the acquisition of luxury goods for local inhabitants, but these are luxuries that may ultimately be at the expense of Amorgos.

Source: Adapted from The Guardian.

regulations can cause a sprawl of tourism and recreation facilities as well as the supporting infrastructure.

Physical impacts

The development and use of recreation and tourism facilities and infrastructure may require blasting, sand and stone mining, concretization and cause erosion, loss of wildlife habitats and loss of natural drainage. Some ecosystems such as alpine regions, rainforests, wetlands, mangroves, coral reefs and sea grass beds are particularly fragile and sensitive to development and change of use. Similarly, the development of marinas and beach breakwaters can cause changes in currents and coastlines.

Specific impacts from recreational activities include damage by trampling or mountain bikes on vegetation, the impact of water-based recreation on marine ecosystems such as coral reefs and animal distress and displacement from safaris.

Displacement

Another consequence that may stem from leisure, tourism and recreation development is that price inflation and property prices may rise, making it increasingly difficult for those not participating in the development and thus benefiting from rising wages and profits to remain in the area. This effect is termed economic displacement and occurs where a traditional and a growing sector of the economy exist side by side creating in effect a dual economy. The growing sector may increasingly threaten the traditional sector, and participants in the traditional sector may only be able to access limited parts of the growing sector.

Global impacts

At the global level, environmental impacts of recreation and tourism include:

- loss of biological diversity
- depletion of the ozone layer
- climate change
- resource depletion and peak oil.

Loss of biological diversity

Biological diversity means the variety of plant and animal species. Recreation and tourism can lead to loss of biodiversity where species are hunted, removed or trampled or where the use of natural resources (e.g. vegetation, wildlife, mountain and water) exceeds the carrying capacity. Tourists and suppliers may also import species that can disrupt and destroy local ecosystems.

Depletion of the ozone layer

The ozone layer is situated in the upper atmosphere and protects life on earth by absorbing the harmful wavelengths of the sun's ultraviolet (UV) radiation. In particular, high exposure to UV radiation can cause skin cancer. The tourism industry seems to contribute to ozone depletion mainly through emissions from jet aircraft with predictions that by 2015 half of the annual destruction of the ozone layer will be caused by air travel.

Climate change

Climate change, or global warming, seems to be worsening because of an increase in the production, and effects, of greenhouse gases (GHGs) in the atmosphere. These GHGs act as an insulation layer in the atmosphere and trap heat from the sun. CO_2 is one of the most significant GHGs. CO_2 is generated when fossil fuels such as coal, oil and natural gas are burned (e.g. in industry, electricity generation and automobiles). Additionally, since vegetation is an important source of CO_2 absorption, the loss of large areas of forest to clearance adds to the accumulation of CO_2. The main conclusions of the Summary for Policy makers of Working Group I of the Intergovernmental Panel on Climate Change (IPCC) Second Assessment Report (1995) include the following:

- Increases in greenhouse gas concentrations since pre-industrial times (i.e. since about 1750) have led to climate change, tending to warm the surface of the Earth as well as other changes.
- The atmospheric concentrations of the GHGs have grown significantly:
  carbon dioxide (+30 per cent)
  methane (+145 per cent)
  nitrous oxide (+15 per cent).
- These trends can be attributed largely to human activities, mostly:
  fossil-fuel use
  land-use change
  agriculture.
- Many GHGs remain in the atmosphere for a long period.
- Our ability to quantify the human influence on global climate is currently limited because of natural variability and uncertainties in key factors.
- The balance of evidence suggests that there is a discernible human influence on global climate.
- Estimates of the rise in global average surface air temperature by 2100 relative to 1990 range from 1°C to 3.5°C.

Table 16.2 Emissions from global tourism (2005, including same-day visitors)

Activity	CO_2 (Mt)
Air transport	517
Other transport	468
Accommodation	274
Activities	45
Total	1307
Total world	126,400
Share of Global Tourism	4.95

Source: UNWTO Climate Change and Tourism (2007).

- Estimates of the sea-level rise due to climate change induced polar ice cap melting by 2100 relative to 1990 range from 15 to 95 centimetre.
- Warmer temperatures mean prospects for more variation in severe droughts and/or floods.

Recreation and tourism are significant contributors to CO_2 production. It is estimated that recreation and tourism accounts for more than 50 per cent of road traffic and currently air traffic contributes about 2.5 per cent of the total world production of CO_2. Table 16.2 shows UN World Tourism Organization (UNWTO) estimates for the relative contribution of travel and tourism at about 5 per cent of total global CO_2 emissions. However, passenger jets are also the fastest growing source of greenhouse gas emissions with the number of international travellers expected to increase from 0.6 million in 1996 to 1.6 billion by 2020. For the UK, the total contribution of air traffic to carbon emissions in 2007 was about 10–19 per cent, but this is expected to rise to 27–54 per cent by 2050.

In the preface to Becken and Hay's (2007, p. xvii) book on *Tourism and Climate Change*, the directors of the UNWTO and the World Meteorological Association (WMO) stated:

> Climate change will not only impact on tourism directly by changes in temperature, extreme weather events and other climatic factors, but also indirectly as it will transform the natural environment which attracts tourist in the first place – for example, by accelerating coastal erosion, damaging coral reefs and other sensitive ecosystems and by reducing snowfall and snow cover in mountainous regions. It will also affect the basic services that are so critical for tourism such as water supplies, especially during periods of peak demand.

It should be noted that not only are the physics and the chemistry of global warming fraught with uncertainty, but so are the economics.

It is difficult to predict the rate of economic growth and the subsequent demand for fossil-fuel burning for energy provision. Also, there is a time lag between the emission of GHGs and the effect on global warming.

Resource depletion and peak oil

At the global level, one of the most important areas of resource depletion is fossil fuels which are *non-renewable resources* – particularly oil. Recreation and tourism can be intensive users of fossil fuels through their consumption of energy and especially the use of kerosene for air travel. A significant recent development here is the concept of 'peak oil'. The issue here is that we may have reached (or will soon reach) the point of the maximum rate of global extraction of oil. After this the rate of production will decline and combined with an ever-increasing demand this would cause shortages and significant price spikes.

Becken (2011) makes the following observations about peak oil and tourism:

- Tourism is very oil intensive. The aviation industry alone consumes 243 million tonnes of fuel per year; 6.3 per cent of world refinery production.
- The analysis of knowledge on tourism and oil shows that reduced oil availability and increasing prices will have far-reaching impacts on tourism as they will on society as a whole.
- Society and tourism are intimately interrelated, and impacts go beyond economic ones, including pervasive changes such as people's lifestyles and the role of tourism within these.
- Just like societies in countries of origin will change, tourist destinations and communities will transform in response to higher oil prices.
- Some destinations may find it easier to adapt, whereas others – possibly more remote places – are more vulnerable.
- Tourism businesses are essential parts of destinations and their ability to adapt will be critical for the development and sustainability of their associated communities.
- Changes in tourism products and associated experiences are, in turn, likely to act as a driver of social change for tourists in their home countries.

ENVIRONMENTAL EFFECTS OF OTHER SECTORS ON THE LEISURE AND TOURISM SECTOR

The general environmental concerns of global warming, unpredictable climate, ozone depletion, acid rain and atmospheric pollution each have impacts on the leisure and tourism sector. The early 1990s for example witnessed successive years of poor snow conditions in European ski resorts. Global warming would clearly have an impact on the height of snow cover, thus putting low-level resorts out of business and shortening the length of the ski season. For example, as noted earlier the IPCC estimates a rise in global average surface air temperature by 2100 relative to 1990 range from 1°C to 3.5°C. This is based on estimated outputs and effects of GHGs. The results are bad news for the low-lying ski resorts since more of the precipitation that falls on these will be in the form of rain rather than snow. Exhibit 16.7 demonstrates alarming possible effects of global warming as low-lying islands are under threat of flooding. Here, global warming is associated with a rise in sea levels. Freak weather conditions have seen hurricane Katrina devastate the once popular tourism destination of New Orleans, forest fires in Victoria, Australia and severe flooding in Brazil and Queensland, Australia. Of course, hurricanes, floods and forest fires are not new but scientists of global warming predict that these events will become more common and more accentuated.

Ozone depletion may also affect the leisure and tourism sector. The ozone layer is a layer of gas around the earth which protects it from UV radiation from the sun. Recent thinning of the ozone layer has been attributed to use of CFCs – chlorofluorocarbons – which

Exhibit 16.7 'Paradise' Islands unite against sea-level threat: alarm over global warming – Geoffrey Lean

Fakaofu Atoll, the main island of the watery territory of Tokelau, has just one of the world's 400 million automobiles and it is making a lonely contribution to the island's impending extinction.

Tokelau, a group of islands administered by New Zealand – just 12 km² of land in more than 250,000 km² of Pacific Ocean – is expected, literally, to be wiped off the map by pollution. So are six other scattered strings of atolls, including similar dependencies and independent nations, among them the 1196-island state of the Maldives in the Indian Ocean.

As CO_2 emitted by fuel burned in the world's cars, homes and industries heats up the climate, many scientists believe that the seas will rise and eventually drown such low-lying islands.

Although small may be beautiful, however, it is also vulnerable. These islands' water supplies are usually limited and are increasingly being depleted by the tourism on which at least half of their economies depend. Tourism increases pollution – only one-tenth of the sewage produced by the 20 million people who visit the Caribbean each year receives any kind of treatment. Increasingly dirty seas and oil spills imperil economies.

But the greatest threat of all comes from global warming. The highest point on the main island of Kiribas, in the Pacific Ocean, is 2 foot above sea level; and scientists' best estimate is that the seas will rise higher than this over the next century.

Source: Adapted from The Independent on Sunday.

have been used in the manufacture of spray cans and refrigerators although these have now been banned. The main harmful effects of ozone depletion are to increase the danger of skin cancer after exposure to the sun. Clearly, this may affect the demand for holidays based around sunbathing especially in areas of high ozone depletion such as Australia and New Zealand.

Acid rain is the term given to acidic deposits caused mainly by the emission of sulphur dioxide into the atmosphere by industry. Its main effects in the leisure and tourism sector include:

- corrosion of buildings (particularly the stonework found on cathedrals)
- damage to trees (making forest areas less attractive to tourism)
- pollution of rivers and lakes.

The external effects of specific industrial developments can also have an impact on the leisure and tourism sector. Exhibit 16.8 illustrates the effects of the film industry on the tourism sector although it is interesting to note that Maya Bay subsequently become a major tourist attraction because of its starring role in *The Beach*. Additionally, oil spills, like the oil tanker disaster that occurred off the Galapagos Islands (Ecuador) in January 2001, can cause severe short-term damage to tourist attractions. There, a ship loaded with 160,000 gallons of diesel fuel and 80,000 gallons of other petroleum products ran aground spilled nearly its entire load. The tourism potential of the area was seriously affected. Berrittella et al. (2006) investigated the economic impacts of climate change on tourism. They noted that in the medium to long term, the tourism effects of climate change may have a negative

---

Exhibit 16.8 Lights, camera, destruction

Twentieth-century Fox, searching for a location to film Alex Garland's best-selling novel, *The Beach*, chose Maya Bay on Phi Phi Ley Island, situated off southern Thailand. The film stars Leonardo DiCaprio and Tilda Swington. However, Maya Bay's natural state of scrub bushes did not quite fit the imagination of the producer of the film, Andrew Macdonald. He wanted coconut trees and long clear views over sand and sea and gained permission from the Thai forestry department to give the beach a makeover. The government added its blessing to the project saying that the film would benefit the economy by promoting Thailand.

However, John Vidal reported in *The Observer* that 'More than half of the level section of the beach [was] dug up and the sand dunes broken up. Hundreds of holes [were] dug, destroying the roots of plants that hold the dunes together'. The actions of the film unit attracted the attentions of local environmental groups. They staged a demonstration on the beach wearing DiCaprio masks and protested that the damage caused by digging up plants was damaging the ecosystem and would lead to beach erosion.

effect on global GDP but that effect will be uneven with some countries (e.g. in the cooler northern regions) attracting more tourists while those with hotter climates (e.g. the Mediterranean countries) will become less attractive to tourists.

Finally and somewhat ironically, one of the solutions to CO_2 emissions is to generate more electricity from renewable resources. Wind and solar power are rapidly developing sectors here. But the installation of large wind farms and solar panel farms can have a very high visual impact on the landscape and therefore have a negative external effect on leisure and tourism. This is particularly true where landscapes are valued for their pristine nature such as in remote and mountainous areas and seascapes.

POSITIVE ENVIRONMENTAL EFFECTS OF LEISURE AND TOURISM

Although much of the environmental debate focusses on the detrimental effects of economic development, there are also benefits which can be noted. The inflow of foreign tourists to London for example sustains a breadth of theatres that could not be supported by the indigenous population. The existence of tourism in remote rural areas can make the difference between local shops remaining profitable, and therefore open, or not. Similarly, the income and interest derived from tourists help to preserve heritage sites, contributing to restoration and upkeep. National parks and forest provide not only facilities for tourism but also preserve habitats for flora and fauna.

Exhibit 16.9 illustrates the potential for tourism to counter global deforestation.

REVIEW OF KEY TERMS

- Environmental economics: analysis of human well-being as well as the flow of money in the economy.
- Externalities: those costs or benefits arising from production or consumption of goods and services which are not reflected in market prices.
- Defensive GNP expenditure: expenditure that takes place to defend or protect one party from the external effects of the activities of another (e.g. double glazing as a defence from noise pollution).
- ISEW: Index of Sustainable Economic Welfare.
- HPI: Happy Planet Index.

Exhibit 16.9 Deforestation: the tourism alternative

The Amazonian rainforest is rapidly declining in size. The forest is being subjected to a series of developments which involve its wholesale destruction. These include industrial-scale agriculture schemes, cattle ranching and tropical timber cutting. To support these schemes, there have been forest highway projects, energy distribution schemes and resettlement programmes.

The environmental consequences of this destruction are threefold. First, the Amazon rainforest is home to Amerindian settlements. Second, it contains almost 50 per cent of the world's terrestrial species and is a crucial site for maintaining biodiversity. The Amazon rainforest also plays an important role in the global carbon and water cycles. Trees are essential in reducing CO_2 levels in the atmosphere and about one-fifth of the earth's fresh water flows down the river Amazon. Meanwhile, carbon emissions from slash-and-burn clearance programmes add to global warming.

The World Resources Institute and environmental champions in the Brazilian government have suggested alternative uses of the forest to prevent its destruction, emphasizing the role leisure and tourism can play. A joint declaration stated: 'Brazil is receiving hundreds of millions of dollars in international assistance administered by the World Bank to reduce deforestation. More careful use of these G-7 funds could go a long way towards combating the crisis … Investments could be made in alternative development, such as community forestry, non-timber products, education and tourism, instead of subsidizing rainforest destruction'.

Source: The author.

- Non-renewable resources: those which have a fixed supply.
- Renewable resources: those which are capable of being replenished.
- Waste sink: part of the environment where waste products are deposited.
- Assimilative capacity: ability of sink to absorb waste.

 Data Questions

Task 16.1 Journal article: Stern, N., 2008. The economics of climate change. *American Economic Review* 98, 1–37.

The main findings of the Stern Report on the economics of climate change include the following:

- The level of GHGs in the atmosphere has risen from 280 ppm CO_2 equivalent (CO_2e) to their current level of 430 ppm CO_2e.

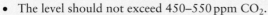

- The level should not exceed 450–550 ppm CO_2.
- Excessive GHGs in the atmosphere mean that there is a high possibility of major change to the climate.
- Climate change presents a special challenge for economics.
- It is the greatest and most widest-ranging market failure ever seen.
- Average temperatures could rise by 5°C compared to pre-industrial levels if climate change is not averted.
- All countries are likely to be affected by climate change, but especially the poorest countries.
- The effects of climate change may include:
  - rising sea levels, heavier floods and drought
  - species extinction
  - threats to global food production.
- The economic analysis of climate change needs to be global, include long-term time horizons and risk and uncertainty.
- Deforestation is responsible for more CO_2 emissions than the transport sector.
- A failure to prevent significant climate change could cost the world at least 5 per cent of GDP and possibly more than 20 per cent of GDP in a worst case scenario.
- Each tonne of CO_2 emitted causes damages worth at least $85.
- Emissions can be cut at a cost of less than $25 a tonne.
- Adopting a low-carbon path for the world economy could eventually benefit it by $2.5 trillion a year.
- Actions taken now will have only a limited effect on the climate over the next 40 or 50 years but may have a profound effect on the climate in the second half of this century.

Recap Questions

1 What is meant by the statement climate change is 'the widest-ranging market failure ever seen'?
2 What are the predicted impacts of climate change?
3 What are the major contributions from leisure and tourism to climate change?
4 What are the special challenges that climate change poses for economics?
5 The article suggests that each tonne of CO_2 emitted causes damages worth at least $85. What might these damages be?

Task 16.2 Leisure and tourism: blessing or blight?

Table 16.3 illustrates some of the possible economic benefits and costs of recreation, leisure and tourism. Critically review the comprehensiveness of the table, add to it where necessary and use it as a basis to analyse the effects of a leisure or tourism development or provision.

Task 16.2 continued

Table 16.3 Leisure and tourism costs and benefits

Benefits	Costs
Satisfaction of wants	Distortion of local prices
Employment	Satisfaction of some wants at the expense of others
Foreign exchange earnings	Imports
Technology transfer	Congestion
Improved health	Aesthetic degradation
Better understanding of things	Pollution
Regeneration in depressed areas	Resource depletion
Engine for economic growth	Erosion
Source of profit	Loss of natural environment Loss of local control of resources CO_2 emissions

Task 16.3 Fasten your seat belts and prepare for unsustainable take-off

The Heathrow Association for the Control of Aircraft Noise (HACAN) published data from a number of sources about the effects that airports have on their local environment. These include:

- Sedative use increases by 8 per cent in areas affected by aircraft noise.
- Fourteen per cent more anti-asthma drugs are consumed by people living within 10 kilometre of an airport.
- Transport 2000 calculates that every return air ticket generates an average of four car journeys.
- It has been estimated that every passenger on a return flight to Florida is responsible for a discharge of 1.8 tonnes of CO_2.
- The IPCC shows that aircraft emissions are responsible for about 10 per cent of the world's CO_2 production.
- Mortality rates near Los Angeles Airport are 5 per cent higher than in quieter places.
- The reading ability of 12- to 14-year olds who attend schools under flight paths is reduced by 23 per cent.
- Children exposed to aircraft noise are more likely to develop anxiety disorders.
- Airport expansion means more noise and less countryside.
- CO_2 emissions are forecast to increase by 500 per cent by 2100.
- High-altitude carbon emissions from aircraft are less likely to be reabsorbed by forests or oceans than other emissions and are therefore more serious threats to the greenhouse effect.
- Sulphur dioxide emissions from aircraft on the polar routes contribute to ozone depletion.

Source: HACAN.

Recap Questions

1 What externalities are associated with air travel?
2 Assess the impact of air travel on renewable and non-renewable resources.
3 Are the skies an example of open-access overuse?
4 What evidence is there to suggest that the market equilibrium of air traffic exceeds the optimum social equilibrium?
5 How should GDP figures be adjusted to take account of the externalities of air travel?

MULTIPLE CHOICE

1 Environmental economists would argue that the value of suncream should not appear as part of a country's GNP. The main reason for this is because:
   (a) The price of suncream includes sales tax.
   (b) Suncream consumption is unevenly distributed throughout the population.
   (c) The purchase of suncream represents 'defensive' expenditure.
   (d) Suncream is not a necessity.

2 Which of the following externalities represents the disruption to local traders' profits of an international fixture at a large sports stadium?
   (a) Production on consumption.
   (b) Consumption on consumption.
   (c) Consumption on production.
   (d) All of the above.

3 Which of the following statements is not true?
   (a) Externalities are those costs arising from production of goods which are not reflected in market prices.
   (b) Water is a non-renewable resource.
   (c) Non-renewable resources have a fixed supply.
   (d) Renewable resources are capable of being replenished.

4 The use of renewable resources is necessarily unsustainable:
   (a) In the long term.
   (b) In the short term.
   (c) Where their use is greater than their regenerative capacity.
   (d) Where their use is less than their regenerative capacity.

5 Which of the following statements is true?
   (a) There are no positive environmental effects of leisure and tourism.
   (b) Making resources free will protect them from overuse.
   (c) Air travel gives rise to defensive expenditure.
   (d) GNP underestimates overall well-being.

REVIEW QUESTIONS

1 What additions and what subtractions would environmental economists like to see with regard to GNP figures?
2 Distinguish between the four types of externalities.
3 What unpriced externalities arise from the:
    (a) Location of a football stadium?
    (b) Building of the channel tunnel?
    (c) Development of a lakeside campsite?
4 Under what circumstances are renewable resources exhaustible?
5 What environmental problems arise from open-access resources?

Websites of interest

New Economics Foundation: www.neweconomics.org

Tourism Concern: www.tourismconcern.org.uk

Happy Planet Index: www.happyplanetindex.org

Intergovernmental Panel on Climate Change: www.ipcc.ch

Friends of the Earth: www.foe.co.uk

Surfers against Sewage: www.sas.org.uk

Heathrow Association for the Control of Aircraft Noise (HACAN): www.hacan.org.uk

United National Environmental Programme: www.unep.org

Action for sustainability

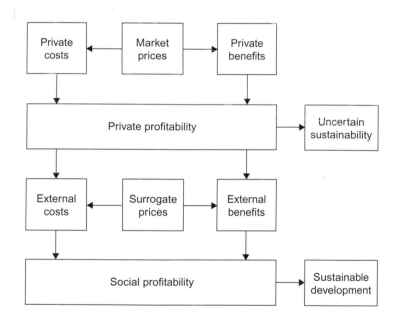

Objectives and learning outcomes

Chapter 16 examined the environmental impacts of the leisure and tourism sector. It considered ways in which the market failed to signal long-term problems of resource depletion, waste production and disposal and other unpriced externalities. It highlighted the distinction between what was most profitable for firms and for society as a whole. It chronicled a wealth of evidence of undesirable results if the market was left to dictate future developments without any regard for wider environmental considerations.

This chapter examines strategies for utilizing environmental economics to enable development of the leisure and tourism sector to take place with due regard to possible side effects. The aim of such analysis is to prevent the side effects of development causing socially unacceptable damage to the environment or indeed to stifle the very developments themselves. By studying this chapter, students will be able to:

- explain the meaning of sustainable development;
- understand the meaning of sustainable tourism as a subset of sustainable development;
- understand the limitations of the price mechanism in allocating resources in respect of environmental considerations;
- utilize different instruments for mitigating environmental impacts;
- evaluate a variety of methods to impute value to unpriced externalities;
- understand the meaning of adaptation to environmental impacts.

MEANING OF SUSTAINABLE DEVELOPMENT

There is considerable debate about the precise definition of sustainable development. It should also be noted that several levels of sustainability may be considered. Sustainable development itself is a generic term whilst sustainable tourism and leisure refers to a specific sector of this development. At the widest level, sustainable development embraces those planet-threatening issues of global warming, resource depletion and ozone loss. Sustainability can also be considered at a national economy level, at a local level and at an individual leisure or tourism project level.

Key milestones in the development of environmental understanding and policy include:

- The United Nations Conference on the Human Environment held in Stockholm, 1972: A key outcome here was the creation of the United Nations Environmental Programme (UNEP).

- The 1987 *Brundtland Report* for the World Commission on Environment and Development which defined sustainability as 'development that meets the needs of the present without compromising the ability of future generations to meet their own needs' (World Commission on Environment and Development, 1987: 43). It therefore laid considerable emphasis on what is termed 'intergenerational equity'.

- The 1992 Earth Summit held in Rio, 1992: Here, 182 governments agreed to adopt Agenda 21 – a comprehensive action plan for the environment.

- 1995: Agenda 21 guidelines produced for the Travel and Tourism Industry by the UN WTO, with the World Travel and Tourism Council (WTTC) and the Earth Council (WTO, 1997a).

- Lanzarote Charter for Sustainable Tourism, 1995 (UNWTO, UNEP, UNESCO, EU).

- The Kyoto Conference in 1997: This led to the Kyoto Protocol which set out a 5-year commitment period (2008–2012) for signatories to meet emission targets for GHGs.

- World Summit on Sustainable Development (WSSD) in Johannesburg, South Africa in 2002: Of relevance to recreation and tourism here was guidance for changing unsustainable patterns of consumption and production; promotion of sustainable tourism development as an issue of protecting and managing the natural resource base for economic and social development; sustainable tourism that contributes to social, economic and infrastructure development and sustainable development in the developing parts of the world.

- Québec Declaration on Ecotourism, 2002.

- The World Tourism Organization (UNWTO) convened the First International Conference on Climate Change and Tourism in Djerba, Tunisia, 2003.

- Climate Change 2007: This was the Fourth IPCC Assessment Report and was a comprehensive assessment of the evidence on climate change.

- The UNWTO Davos Declaration 2007: 'The tourism sector must rapidly respond to climate change, within the evolving UN framework and progressively reduce its GHG contribution if it is to grow in a sustainable manner; This will require action to:

  mitigate its GHG emissions, derived especially from transport and accommodation activities;

  adapt tourism businesses and destinations to changing climate conditions;

  apply existing and new technology to improve energy efficiency;

  secure financial resources to help poor regions and countries'.

- The UNWTO Report on 'Climate Change and Tourism –
  Responding to Global Challenges' released in 2008.
- The 2009 United Nations Climate Change Conference in
  Copenhagen (COP-15): A disappointing meeting where delegates
  approved a motion to 'take note of the Copenhagen Accord'
  recognizing the case for keeping temperature rises below 2°C.
  However, the Accord did not contain agreements for the reduced
  emissions necessary to achieve that aim.

Common elements in the *Brundtland* approach to sustainable
development are, first, the rate of use of renewable and non-renewable
resources and maintenance of natural capital. Implicit here is that
renewable resources should not be used beyond their regenerative
capacities. Additionally, where non-renewable resources are used up,
future generations should be compensated by the provision of substitute capital in some form so that, at the minimum, a constant stock
of capital is maintained across generations. The second key element
in the *Brundtland Report* is consideration of the effects of development on local and global waste sinks.

Sustainability has also been defined as growth which is not threatened by feedback, for example, pollution, resource depletion or
social unrest. This can be related to tourism destination development.
In this case, sustainability would be that level of development which
did not exceed the carrying capacity of the destination and thus cause
serious or irreversible changes to the destination. It is development
that can sustain itself in the long run. It is also possible to consider
environmental costs and benefits when considering specific projects.
This approach considers the total social and private costs against the
total private and social benefits of a project with a view to summarizing its total social value, taking into consideration environmental
impacts as well as market profitability.

The key principles of sustainability can be summarized as:

- consideration of externalities (i.e. undesirable, harmful side
  effects);
- consideration of depletion of non-renewable resources
  (i.e. conservation of scarce resources);
- tailoring of economic activity to the carrying capacity of the
  environment (i.e. avoiding over-exploitation of resources);
- the precautionary principle (i.e. even where there is some doubt
  as to the science we should err on the side of caution);
- the 'polluter pays' principle (i.e. the cost of sustainable measures
  should be borne by those who create negative environmental
  impacts).

Since the operation of the free market in its present form does not
guarantee the inclusion of the above principles in resource allocation,

it follows that the implementation of sustainable development will involve modifications of free market activity.

SUSTAINABLE TOURISM POLICY

It is difficult for a country or a sector to introduce effective plans for sustainable tourism development without having a guiding strategy. Intergovernmental organizations such as the UNWTO (http://www. world-tourism.org/frameset/frame_sustainable.html) provide policy guidelines and it defines sustainable tourism as follows:

'Sustainability principles refer to the environmental, economic and socio-cultural aspects of tourism development, and a suitable balance must be established between these three dimensions to guarantee its long-term sustainability. Thus, sustainable tourism should:

1 Make optimal use of environmental resources that constitute a key element in tourism development, maintaining essential ecological processes and helping to conserve natural heritage and biodiversity.

2 Respect the socio-cultural authenticity of host communities, conserve their built and living cultural heritage and traditional values and contribute to inter-cultural understanding and tolerance.

3 Ensure viable, long-term economic operations, providing socio-economic benefits to all stakeholders that are fairly distributed, including stable employment and income-earning opportunities and social services to host communities, and contributing to poverty alleviation'.

THE PRICE MECHANISM AND THE ENVIRONMENT

The market economy does in fact have an in-built tendency to conserve resources. In the model where competing firms seek to maximize their profits, since profit is defined as total revenue minus total costs, there is a constant pressure to economize minimize costs and hence on resources. Where environmental costs also appear as a firm's costs (e.g. energy use) business objectives and environmental objectives will coincide. This is particularly true in an era of rising energy prices when firms will be constantly seeking to economize and find alternative technologies.

However, the current market price of resources is not always an accurate measure of their true cost. This is because of unpriced externalities such as emissions and noise. This is also the case for unpriced

17

open access resources such as the sea. Chapter 16 explored the fact that, whilst the costs of sewage pumping into the sea were minimal for water companies, considerable pollution costs are incurred by other users of the sea. Similarly, the loss of landscape and views caused by tourism destination development is not apparent in the profit and loss accounts of the organizations involved. Equally, the price mechanism does not give due regard to the future. Overexploitation of non-renewable resources such as coastline, countryside, rivers and mountains may leave future generations materially worse off than the current population. These considerations mean that the market often leads to overproduction and overdevelopment of projects where there are considerable unpriced externalities.

APPROACHES TO SUSTAINABILITY: MITIGATION

Mitigation involves action to regulate the causes of negative environmental impacts of tourism and recreation. There are a variety of different mitigation approaches to encourage sustainability. These are identified in Table 17.1 under the three categories of:

1 regulations
2 market approaches
3 soft tools.

These approaches function at different operational levels. Regulation generally functions at the national and international level. The next level is the market level. Here, it is possible to use taxes and subsidies to influence the demand and supply of goods and services towards improved environmental ends. Soft tools such as eco-labelling may also be used to influence consumption at the consumer level.

Table 17.1 Approaches to environmental control and improvement

Regulations	Market approaches	Soft tools
Permissions and permits	Ownership	Tourism eco-labelling
Environmental impact assessment	Taxes subsidies, grants and special projects	Certification/award schemes
Controls and laws	Tradable rights and permits	Guidelines and treaties
Special designation	Deposit–refund schemes	Citizenship, education and advertising
CSR	Product and service charges	Voluntary schemes Altruism Ecotourism

Regulation

Direct regulation methods, sometimes known as command and control (CAC), involve the government setting environmental standards. These might take the form of water quality standards or planning regulations. Regulations include:

- permissions and permits
- environmental impact assessment
- controls and laws
- special designation
- corporate social responsibility (CSR).

Permissions and permits

These form a type of preventative control and by and large these are more effective. They are aimed at preventing damage by requiring permissions to engage in possibly harmful activities. For example, planning permission is a preventive control seeking to stop developments that do not meet planning guidelines. Planning guidelines are devised to ensure that developments consider wider environmental issues and impacts. Enforcement is relatively straightforward since building may not commence without the necessary permit. Similarly, permits may be used to enforce maximum visitor numbers at sites or maximum cars admitted to a national park. This type of control would include suggestions for 'personal carbon allowances' whereby individuals would be allocated a limited personal allocation of carbon each year.

Environmental impact assessment

Projects over a certain size are often required to undertake an environmental impact assessment. This generally takes the form of a cost–benefit analysis that it includes the wider costs and benefits to society in addition to those accruing privately to firms and individuals. For a project or development to be socially acceptable, the sum of the benefits to society (including external and private benefits) must exceed the sum of the cost to society (including external and private costs). This may be written as:

$$\Sigma B > \Sigma C$$

where Σ means 'the sum of', B the benefits to society and C the costs to society.

A problem arises from using this equation in its raw form. When we measure costs and benefits, some happen immediately and some happen at some future date. People would prefer to have money today than in the future. This is because £100 today is worth more than a promise of £100 in 10 years since it can earn interest in the intervening period. Therefore, future values must be adjusted to give present values. This is known as discounting and the rate used to discount is generally related to the long-term interest rate. The formula for finding a present value is:

$$\frac{B_t}{(1 + r)_t}$$

where B_t is the benefit in year t and r is the discount rate.

Thus, incorporating discounting techniques to the formula for social acceptability for projects gives:

$$\frac{B_t}{(1 + r)_t} > \frac{C_t}{(1 + r)_t}$$

where C_t is the benefit in year t.

There is considerable debate amongst environmental economists about the use of discount rates since, if environmental damage resulting from a project results in the distant future, then its effects are minimized in cost–benefit analysis by discounting. It is felt by some that this attributes too little significance to, for example, the potential damage caused by storing nuclear waste.

These types of control are sometimes criticized for their bureaucratic nature and the extra costs that are generated.

Controls and laws

Controls and laws are ways of setting and policing environmental control targets. Sometimes, these are introduced retrospectively after the externality-producing activity has commenced. These include limits to aircraft and other noise and water quality levels. Litter laws and penalties also fall under this category. Critics argue that such control methods themselves use considerable resources in monitoring and policing the limits and that non-compliance rates can be high. Figure 17.1 in the following section compares their effectiveness with green taxes.

Special designation

Some sites have been granted special status designation as a way of promoting conservation and controlling development. These designations have varying degrees of statutory backing. For example, in the UK, there are designated sites of special scientific interest (SSSIs) and areas of outstanding natural beauty (AONBs). SSSIs are sites which are considered to be of special interest because of flora, fauna, geological or physiographical features. AONBs are designated by the Countryside Commission to conserve areas of natural beauty.

The IUCN (the World Conservation Union) has also identified categories of protected areas, with a view to international collaboration and standardization for conservation. The categories include:

- *Strict nature reserve/wilderness area*: protected area managed mainly for science or wilderness protection.
- *National park*: protected area mainly managed for ecosystem protection and recreation.
- *Natural monument*: protected area managed mainly for conservation of specific natural features.
- *Habitat/species management area*: protected area managed mainly for conservation through management intervention.
- *Protected landscape/seascape*: protected area managed mainly for landscape/seascape conservation and recreation.
- *Managed resource protected area*: protected area managed mainly for the sustainable use of natural ecosystems.

Corporate social responsibility

Many governments now oblige large organizations to devote a section of their Annual Report to CSR as part of their governance requirements. CSR is a wide term that includes issues such as not only employment, human rights, ethical trading, the community but also the environment. Increasingly, individual firms are appointing environmental managers, compiling environmental policies and conducting environmental audits and action plans. Leadership in this area has come from the WTTC, the WTO both of which have published guidelines. Organizations such as BA produce a regular environmental report setting and monitoring targets for:

- noise
- emissions
- waste
- congestion
- tourism and conservation.

Market approaches

Market approaches focus on manipulation of prices rather than use of regulations as a method of achieving environmental goals. The key to economic approaches is the adjustment of market prices in an attempt to reflect more fully the environmental costs and benefits of activities. The aim is to make producers and consumers adapt their behaviour in the light of these adjusted prices. In this way, pursuit of self-interest can bring environmental improvements. Approaches under this category include:

- ownership
- taxes

- subsidies, grants and special projects
- tradable rights and permits including ETS
- deposit-refund schemes
- product and service charges.

Ownership

Since free-access resources are often overused (e.g. the sea as a waste sink), privatization of such resources is sometimes advocated. For example, ownership of a lake is an incentive to enforce property rights. In such a case, the use of the lake as a waste sink (e.g. for sewage disposal) would have to be bought and thus a price would be charged for a hitherto free service. The price would fluctuate, like all market prices, to reflect the demand and supply of the service.

Rental also gives a less strong incentive for environmental care than ownership. In New Zealand, this has been addressed by offering concessions to operate in some national parks and some conservation areas on a tradable basis. This means that if concessionaires move on, they may sell their permit. This gives a strong incentive to tenants to invest in environmental improvements that can be recouped in an improved selling price of a concession.

Some argue that there may be little incentive for an organization in the private sector to consider cost–benefit analysis when appraising a project. It will, instead, attempt to satisfy its shareholders by seeking to maximize profits. Public ownership is thus advocated to improve environmental performance. In principle, a public-sector organization has an incentive to consider social costs and benefits, since external costs will fall upon the electorate. The actual way in which public-sector organizations approach externalities will depend upon the demands of the government. Voluntary sector organizations may have aims and objectives which encompass consideration of the full social costs and benefits. Exhibit 17.1, describing the National Trust's approach to conservation work, illustrates this.

Taxes

Typical of economic approaches are taxes which can be used to raise prices to discourage consumption of goods and services with harmful environmental impacts, and subsidies which can be used to reduce prices and encourage consumption of goods and services with beneficial environmental impacts. Taxation is also a way of promoting the polluter pays principle adopted by OECD in 1972. In this case, producers of goods and services who cause environmental impacts are required to pay taxes which are sufficient to cover the costs of mitigating environmental impacts.

Curtis (2002) investigated CO_2 emissions per tourist bed which he found to average 748.8 kilogram CO_2 per year in the Cairns region

Exhibit 17.1 Conserving national heritage

As a major conservation charity, the National Trust does its utmost to practise what it preaches. It has a policy to guide its conservation:

'Conservation is defined as the careful management of change'. It is about revealing and sharing the significance of places and ensuring that their special qualities are protected, enhanced, understood and enjoyed by present and future generations.

We base our conservation work around six main conservation principles. These are:

- *Integration*: Integrating the conservation of natural and cultural heritage.
- *Change*: Working with change, adapting and mitigating.
- *Access and engagement*: Benefiting society and gaining support.
- *Skills and partnership*: Developing skills and experience with others.
- *Accountability*: Recording decisions and sharing knowledge.
- *Significance*: Understanding values and spirit of place'.

Source: The National Trust – 'Our Conservation Principles' http://www.nationaltrust. org.uk/main/w-chl/w-places_collections/w support-what_is_conservation/w-support-conservation_principles.htm

of Queensland, Australia. He noted that moderate emissions reductions can be made by way of increased energy efficiency but that excess emissions by luxury hotels/resorts need further action. An investment in carbon sinks was recommended (i.e. in forests or other means of CO_2 absorption) or alternately a carbon tax amounting to $5.23 per bed per year, or based on emissions, $15.38 per tonne of CO_2 per year.

Transport is a key issue here. The importance of transport to countryside tourism and recreation has been emphasized by National Parks authorities which found that over 90 per cent of the visits made annually to UK National Parks are made by car. Because the environmental effects and impacts of air and car travel are considerable, there are repeated calls for taxation to make transport prices more fully reflect environmental costs. In particular, there is pressure to increase taxes on car and air travel. Friends of the Earth (UK) also have a campaign directed at air travel. Called The Right Price for Air Travel, it is pressing for air ticket prices to reflect the true environmental costs of flying. It notes that currently plane tickets and kerosene are free of VAT. In addition, there are no excise duties on kerosene. It is ironic that there is no tax on kerosene given that air travel is responsible for significant noise pollution, CO_2 and nitrogen oxide emissions. It is forecasted that half of the annual destruction of the ozone layer will be caused by air traffic in 2015 (De Clerck and Klingers, 1997: 4–5).

A carbon tax, based on emissions of GHGs, is one way of reducing such emissions. The effects of such a tax would be to:

- encourage users of carbon-based fuel and processes to substitute to other cleaner processes and fuels;
- encourage innovation and the development and production of cleaner fuels;
- reduce demand for goods and services affected by the tax.

Because taxes hit the poor more than the rich, it has been suggested that increasing taxes on flying does so at the expense of the poor (i.e. the reduction in passengers would be mainly from lower income earners). In response to this, it has been suggested that 'Green Air Miles Allowance' could be introduced by which frequent flyers are taxed at a higher rate. Under a 'Green Air Miles Allowance' scheme, everyone would be entitled to a tax-free allowance of flying each year – for example one short-haul return flight per year either tax-free or at a standard rate of tax. Once this allowance was used up, additional flights would be charged at a higher rate of tax.

Tol (2007, p. 129) investigated the impact of a carbon tax on international tourism, and a simulation model of international tourist flows was used to estimate the impact of a carbon tax on aviation fuel. The author summarizes the research as follows:

> The effect of the tax on travel behaviour is small: A global tax of \$1000/tonne of CO_2 would change travel behaviour and reduce carbon dioxide emissions from international aviation by 0.8%. A carbon tax on aviation fuel would particularly affect long-haul flights, because of high emissions, and short-haul flights, because of the emission during take-off and landing. Medium distance flights would be affected least. This implies that tourist destinations that rely heavily on short-haul flights or on intercontinental flights will see a decline in international tourism numbers, while other destinations may see international arrivals rise.

Control of production of waste may also be achieved using taxation. For example, taxes on non-returnable beverage containers (e.g. Finland) can encourage the use of returnable containers and therefore reduce the amount of containers left as litter. Landfill taxes which impose charges on waste companies using landfill sites to bury solid waste aim to discourage the production of waste and encourage the recovery of more value from waste and to seek more environmentally friendly methods of waste disposal.

Figure 17.1 compares the operation of an environmental tax with a direct environmental control. *D* represents the demand curve and marginal private benefit for a product. *S* represents the supply curve and marginal private costs (MPCs) of production. Profit-maximizing firms will continue to produce where the price paid for extra sales

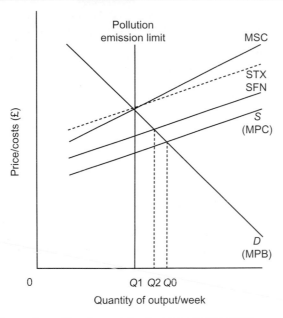

Figure 17.1 Comparison of taxation and direct environmental control).

(indicated by the demand curve) is greater than the extra costs of production (MPC). They will thus produce a level of output of $0Q0$.

However, in this example, production causes pollution and external costs. Adding these to MPC generates the marginal social cost (MSC) curve. The socially optimum level of output is now found at $0Q1$ since production should be increased at all points where marginal private benefit (MPB; indicated by how much consumers are willing to pay for extra units of the good) exceeds marginal social cost.

The imposition of a pollution tax is designed to make the firm internalize the previously external costs of pollution and integrate environmental considerations. A pollution tax which raised the S or MPC curve to STX would cause the firm's private profit-maximizing level of output to coincide with the social profit-maximizing level of output at $0Q1$. A similar result could be achieved by imposing a pollution emission limit at $0Q1$. A system of fines would be needed to enforce such pollution limits. The system of monitoring of standards and imposition of fines is not totally effective, though. If, considering the likelihood and level of fine, the firm's MPC were only increased to SFN, then the firm would produce a level of output of $0Q2$ – thus, the system of direct control would be less effective than the system of taxation. It would also incur administrative costs.

One of the economic justifications for taxes on alcohol is to reduce consumption and thus minimize externalities in use (being drunk and disorderly). It is interesting to speculate whether scenes such as those described in Exhibit 17.2 are less common in countries such as Norway and Sweden where there are much higher alcohol taxes than in the UK.

Exhibit 17.2   Emergency: Britons having fun – Sandra Barwick

It was New Year's Eve, but the mood was not exactly festive in the accident and emergency department of St Thomas' Hospital. 'We do not normally have vomit bowls laid out at reception', sighed the assistant director...'but those are what we are going to need'. The first casualty arrived, at 11.25, prone on his trolley, visible only in patches: large hairy legs, a pair of immobile trainers, some vomit-speckled hair. 'He's had a combination of beer, champagne and something else', said the ambulanceman, deadpan. 'We think he's Spanish'. A faint cry of 'Waaaa-aaaa' came from the trolley as it was wheeled away.

At midnight, the chimes of Big Ben came over the television. In they came, one after the other, bound to their trolleys. Almost all were men in their late teens or early 20s, in dirty jeans over which they had vomited. Outside the minor surgeries department a line of men sat or lay: punchmarks embedded on their cheeks, bottled broken on their heads, noses broken, lips cut. One had been bitten, one had had a cigarette stubbed out on his eye.

'Happy New Year', the ambulanceman said with ironic detachment to their prone charges.

Source: Adapted from The Independent.

In reality, although administrative costs are lower than for direct controls, there are several problems in setting an environmental tax. These include imputing monetary value to pollution costs, long-term pollution costs and the relating of pollution levels to output levels. A further criticism of environmental taxes and environmental charging is their regressive nature, in that their effects will hit the poor proportionately more than the rich. In theory, this problem might be addressed by compensating the poor by income tax adjustments.

Subsidies, grants and special projects

In contrast to taxes, subsidies (e.g. to public transport) are often used to encourage the supply of goods and services which have positive environmental impacts. So for example the UK government offers a £5000 grant to customers who wish to purchase an electric car to offset their higher price and encourage the switch to greener fuels. In some countries, the government subsidises gym membership. The logic here is that gym membership provides a positive social externality in the form of healthier people. This leads to less need for government spending on health and medical services. The subsidy should therefore increase the uptake of gym membership and be offset by savings in government health spending. Carbon sequestration projects are being developed to remove carbon from the atmosphere. These include the deliberate planting of forests to capture carbon naturally as well as the artificial capture of carbon and its storage in underground reservoirs.

Cycling is a prime example of a sustainable form of transport and so it is not surprising that governments seek to promote cycling by a variety of schemes. These include:

- subsidised purchase
- giving grants to organizations that promote cycling
- city-centre cycle-hire systems (e.g. Vienna, Seville, Barcelona, London)
- infrastructure schemes (e.g. Amsterdam's world-leading urban cycleways).

Tradable rights and permits including ETS

Tradable rights and permits are often associated with quotas that are set by governments for pollution levels. Tradability means that the overall quota can be achieved flexibly with companies buying and selling quotas to each other. Permits are issued allowing a given level of pollution. For example, the total number of noise units for aircraft could be stipulated for a particular airport. These permits are then tradable. Supporters of this system stress its flexibility. Some aircraft operators can reduce noise pollution more cheaply than others. They can do so and sell permits to those who find it expensive to reduce noise pollution. Thus the total amount of pollution is limited, but how it is achieved is likely to involve flexibility and lowest costs.

The Waitomo glow worms cave (Plimmer, 1994: 2–3) demonstrates the use of permits applied to environmental impacts. CO_2 emissions from visitor numbers were threatening the glow worms. A permit was introduced which did not stipulate visitor numbers but rather fixed a maximum quota for CO_2 levels. This left the way of achieving environmental improvement flexible, so that revenues could be protected by appropriate visitor management.

Since global warming and the limitation of carbon emissions were key aspects of the Kyoto agreement, carbon trading has become more closely studied. Exhibit 17.3 outlines the operation of the EU ETS which is extended to include airlines in 2012. This works by:

- Setting a maximum limit of emissions.
- Allocating quotas to polluting companies within this limit.
- Fining companies who exceed their quotas.
- Companies may purchase, sell or save quotas.
- The ETS allows companies flexibility in deciding how to manage their emissions whilst maintaining overall limits which themselves can be progressively lowered.

Similar schemes can involve not just firms (such as airlines) trading carbon emission quotas amongst themselves but could involve trading emission rights against the carbon-sink functions of forests. The sink function of forests comes from their ability to absorb carbon

---

Exhibit 17.3 The EU ETS

The EU Emissions Trading System (EU ETS) is a cornerstone of the European Union's policy to combat climate change and its key tool for reducing industrial greenhouse gas emissions cost-effectively. Being the first and biggest international scheme for the trading of greenhouse gas emission allowances, the EU ETS covers some 11,000 power stations and industrial plants in 30 countries.

The EU ETS, a system based on the "cap and trade" principle

The EU ETS works on the "cap and trade" principle. This means there is a "cap", or limit, on the total amount of certain greenhouse gases that can be emitted by the factories, power plants and other installations in the system. Within this cap, companies receive emission allowances which they can sell to or buy from one another as needed. The limit on the total number of allowances available ensures that they have a value.

At the end of each year each company must surrender enough allowances to cover all its emissions, otherwise heavy fines are imposed. If a company reduces its emissions, it can keep the spare allowances to cover its future needs or else sell them to another company that is short of allowances. The flexibility that trading brings ensures that emissions are cut where it costs least to do so.

The number of allowances is reduced over time so that total emissions fall. In 2020 emissions will be 21% lower than in 2005.

Growing bigger and stronger

The ETS now operates in 30 countries (the 27 EU Member States plus Iceland, Liechtenstein and Norway). It covers CO_2 emissions from installations such as power stations, combustion plants, oil refineries and iron and steel works, as well as factories making cement, glass, lime, bricks, ceramics, pulp, paper and board.

Nitrous oxide emissions from certain processes are also covered. Between them, the installations currently in the scheme account for almost half of the EU's CO_2 emissions and 40% of its total greenhouse gas emissions.

Airlines will join the scheme in 2012. The EU ETS will be further expanded to the petrochemicals, ammonia and aluminium industries and to additional gases in 2013.

Making a difference

The EU ETS has put a price on carbon emissions and shown that it is possible to trade in greenhouse gas emissions. Emissions from installations in the scheme are falling as intended. The changes to be introduced in 2013, notably a progressive move towards auctioning of allowances, will further enhance its effectiveness.

The success of the EU ETS has inspired other countries and regions to launch cap and trade schemes of their own. The EU hopes to link up the ETS with compatible systems around the world to form the backbone of a global carbon market.

Source: European Commission Climate Action: http://ec.europa.eu/clima/policies/ets/index_en.htm

---

from the atmosphere, and Thoroe (2003) argues the need for a more intensive inclusion of forest sinks in the international regulations, as well as the assignment of responsibility for the conservation of sinks.

Deposit-refund schemes

These schemes are aimed at reducing littering, rubbish and dumping and at encouraging recycling. They work by incentivising consumers to dispose of used items in an environmentally friendly way. A deposit is charged on for example a bottle and this deposit is refunded when the bottle is returned to the retailer. It is possible to introduce such schemes at a local outlet to encourage the return of cans and bottles and reduce littering at a site, but because visitors often bring in products bought from elsewhere, initiatives on a national scale are likely to be more successful.

Product and service charges

Charges for car parking can be used to encourage a switch towards the use of public transport. Additionally, road pricing for motorway use exists in some EU countries (e.g. France and Spain) but not in others (e.g. UK and Germany). London now operates a Congestion Charging scheme where motorists are charged £10 to enter the central zone. This has reduced traffic flows by approximately 25 per cent. Low-carbon-emitting vehicles are exempt from the scheme. The benefits of the scheme include:

- There has been a 6-per cent increase in bus passengers during charging hours.
- All net revenue raised by the charge (£148 million in financial year 2009/2010) has been invested in improving transport in London.
- Less traffic congestion (in fact congestion has risen back to pre-charging levels but would have risen more without the charge).
- Less traffic pollution.
- Less accidents.
- Encourages substitution from high-carbon to low–carbon-emitting vehicles.

Soft tools

Soft tools represent another set of instruments to promote sustainability. They are voluntary by nature and attempt to change behaviour sometimes by improved information, sometimes by advice, sometimes by persuasion and sometimes by forming specific networks. They include the following:

- tourism eco-labelling
- certification/award schemes
- guidelines and treaties

- citizenship, education and advertising
- voluntary schemes
- altruism
- ecotourism.

Tourism eco-labelling

The focus of this approach to sustainability is the consumer in the marketplace. Leisure and tourism consumers themselves have power to change the environmental effects of goods and services by purchasing those which are environmentally friendly. The idea here is to supply consumers with additional environmental information to enable them to make a more informed choice in the purchase of goods and services. The food industry (prompted by governments) now routinely provides information on energy and other values as well as information on suggested daily maximums. This offers consumers sufficient information to make better decisions on their diet consistent with healthy living and avoiding weight gain. For example, the recommended daily calorie intake is about:

- 2000 kilocalories per day for women
- 2500 kilocalories per day for women for men.

On the other hand, typical calorific content of foods and drinks include:

- A bowl of cornflakes with skimmed milk: 172 kilocalories.
- A Big Mac: 490 kilocalories.
- A portion of fries: 250 kilocalories.
- A can of Coca-Cola: 139 kilocalories.
- A full-size pizza: 1000 kilocalories.
- A bag of crisps: 184 kilocalories.
- A Snickers bar: 313 kilocalories.

So a woman eating just the above items would consume 2548 kilocalories and most likely start to increase weight.

Just as foods are labelled to indicate their contents, an eco-label can provide information concerning key environmental data related to a good or service supplied. The rationale behind eco-labelling is first to give consumers additional environmental information upon which to base their comparison of goods and services before purchase. Second, an eco-label can stimulate producers to achieve environmental improvements in the products in order to gain competitive advantage. Third, consumers would be able to make a rough calculation about their 'fair' usage of say carbon. The complex nature of tourism services makes eco-labelling in this area difficult, but a number of examples exist such as the Green Globe scheme. However, there has been little progress in for example carbon-rating of goods and services. So, whilst we can generally monitor our diet to maintain healthy living, we do not have the equivalent information about our carbon consumption. For consumers to be self-monitoring in terms of their carbon footprint, they need information on:

- recommended individual limit for carbon consumption
- carbon consumption data for items consumed.

Very few people are aware of either of these. It is particularly noticeable that airline tickets do not include carbon consumption data or any indication of what a 'fair' share of individual carbon consumption might be.

Certification/award schemes

Certification schemes exist in order to authenticate and give credibility to environmental claims made by organizations and to provide marks that can be recognized by consumers and producers. The Blue Flag scheme for beaches is a good example here. The Blue Flag is awarded to beaches which have achieved acceptable standards for water quality as well as facilities, safety, environmental education and management, and around 3500 beaches have achieved Blue Flag status in 41 countries. Flying the Blue Flag can act as an effective and powerful environmental marketing device. Equally, the absence of a Blue Flag can act as a disincentive for tourists who may have worries about water quality at such beaches. The scheme has provided a strong incentive over a number of years for beach managers and local governments to improve the environmental quality of coastal areas under their control.

Many schemes such as the Blue Flag incorporate Environmental Management Systems (EMS) as part of the certification process. EMS requirements are based on the management philosophy known as the Deming Cycle. This consists of four points of simple and sound management practice summarized as Plan-Do-Check-Act.

- *Plan*: The EMS is based around the environmental policy of an organization. This identifies and states the environmental commitments the organization intends taking. The policy provides the direction for the remaining Plan-Do-Check-Act elements of an EMS which creates a closed-loop system of management. The 'Plan' is an assessment of the environmental impact of the organization leading to a plan of environmental performance improvements.
- *Do*: Doing ensures the actions identified in the plan (i.e. the environmental performance improvements) are carried out.
- *Check*: This defines the checking and corrective action part of the system which is simply an audit of the previous sections

of the Deming Cycle. An EMS requires verification or assessment of some kind. This should be carried out internally through the audit and review process. The audit will assess how successfully the commitments and direction set out in the organization's environmental policy are being followed and developed.

- *Act*: This is where the conclusions of the check are reviewed and acted upon. The review establishes what should be changed to improve the EMS and how the process should move forward. This final stage is the implementation of corrective action and subsequent monitoring which forms the closed loop system of management.

Buckley (2002) discusses the other examples of effective eco-label schemes such as Green Globe 21 and the National Eco-tourism Accreditation Programme for Australia. Award schemes are often used as ways of rewarding and publicizing good practice. The Tourism for Tomorrow (UK) is an annual award given for contribution to sustainable tourism.

Guidelines and treaties

A variety of organizations produce guidelines and codes of conduct for good environmental practice in countryside areas. For example, the World Conservation Union (IUCN, 1995) has published a guide for conservation planning in countryside areas. These are a series of guidance notes supported by illustrative case studies. Similarly, the Federation of Nature and National Parks of Europe (FNNPE, 1993) produced a report *Loving Them to Death* which includes guidelines for managers for developing sustainable tourism in protected areas, along with case studies and recommendations to governments. Other guidelines include:

- Sustainability Guidelines by the Federation of Tour Operators www.fto.co.uk/responsible-tourism/sustainability-guidelines/
- Sustainable Cultural Tourism Guidelines in Historic Towns and Cities http://www.historic-towns.org/documents/downloads/SustainableTourismGuidelines.pdf
- The South Australian Tourism Commission's Design Guidelines for Sustainable Tourism http://www.tourism.sa.gov.au/tourism/plan/design_guidelines.pdf

Citizenship, education and advertising

The focus of this approach to sustainability is on the individual acting in the role of consumer or worker or opinion former. In order for consumers to fulfil their full power in purchasing 'green' goods and services, they first need raised consciousness about the environmental effects of their purchases. Here, improved environmental education is an important method so that citizens are more aware of the environmental effects of actions and consequently act to change their own actions and influence others to do the same. Examples include:

- building environmental education into the curriculum
- providing specialist courses
- information and interpretation for visitors to tourism sites
- interest groups to raise consciousness
- advertising campaigns to change behaviour.

The Institute for Public Policy Research (UK) issued a report urging the government to introduce vivid health warnings similar to those found on smoking materials to be included on all advertising for holidays that include flights, and at airports. They argue that it is important to raise consciousness of the global warming threat to air passengers and that highly visible information about the impacts of flying may help encourage people to reduce their flying. They recommend a simple, large, visible warning that 'Flying Causes Climate Change'. Plate 17 illustrates a campaign in Bondi Beach, NSW, Australia to discourage the dropping of litter on the beach. The name of the campaign was 'Don't be a Tosser'.

Voluntary schemes

Voluntary schemes exist to allow consumers to mitigate the impacts of any environmental damage they may cause. Prominent amongst these are carbon offset schemes offered by many airlines. Here, as part of the booking process, passengers are asked if they wish to

Plate 17 Do not be a tosser. *Source: The author.*

offset the carbon costs of their air travel. A calculation based on distance reveals to the passenger:

- the amount of CO_2 that will be emitted into the atmosphere as a result of their journey;
- an amount of money that will offset or compensate for this.

The scheme works by purchasing an offset by a firm specializing in projects that save carbon emissions. So for example to offset the carbon emissions of a flight the offset firm might distribute low-energy replacement light bulbs or plant trees to sequestrate carbon.

Altruism

Some firms extend their interest and actions in the environment beyond that required by the law or that prompted by commercial considerations. This action would constitute a form of altruism where the good of other parties is placed above the good of the organization.

Ecotourism

Ecotourism is a special type of tourism that has an emphasis on sound ecological principles. The International Ecotourism Society (TIES) defines ecotourism as: 'Responsible travel to natural areas that conserves the environment and improves the well-being of local people'. TIES further notes the key principles of ecotourism should aim to:

- Minimize impact.
- Build environmental and cultural awareness and respect.
- Provide positive experiences for both visitors and hosts.
- Provide direct financial benefits for conservation.
- Provide financial benefits and empowerment for local people.
- Raise sensitivity to host countries' political, environmental and social climate.

The promotion of ecotourism is therefore seen as a way of minimizing negative and maximizing the positive external impacts of tourism. However, critics note that ecotourism will always remain a minority form of tourism and therefore it does not hold the key to achieving sustainable tourism more generally.

PRICING THE ENVIRONMENT

In the realm of purely private costs and benefits, it is relatively straightforward for firms to determine a profit-maximizing level of output. The costs of inputs are readily available and selling prices can be gauged from scanning the competition, from historical data and, ultimately, are determined in the market. There are thus some firm figures which inform production levels.

However, when we move into the arena of external costs and benefits, we encounter the problem of missing markets and thus find pricing difficult. We can easily calculate the costs of aircraft use in terms of fuel, staffing and depreciation, but how do we measure the cost of aircraft noise? We clearly need to address this problem, if we are to attempt to modify economic behaviour. For without some indication of the costs of environmental impacts, it is impossible to set effective levels of taxation or decide upon other interventions in a rational way. Several methods have been developed by environmental economists to impute value for unpriced goods or services:

- willingness to pay (WTP) method
- hedonic pricing method (HPM)
- travel cost method (TCM)
- dose–response method
- replacement cost technique
- mitigation behaviour method.

WTP method

Here, survey techniques are used to find households' WTP for the preservation of an environmental asset – for example, a piece of woodland threatened by a road development. The survey can include people who are currently visiting the asset and those who do not visit it but care about it. The total valuation of the asset can then be found by multiplying the average WTP by the number of people who enjoy the asset. The main difficulty of using the WTP method is whether respondents reply to the hypothetical WTP question in the same way as they would if faced with actual payment. In other words, people often over-report their WTP.

Hedonic pricing method

Hedonic pricing values environmental resources by considering their effect on the prices of goods or services that have readily observable market prices. House prices are a convenient yardstick for this exercise. House prices are affected by a number of factors – condition, number of rooms, central heating, garden size and nearness to transport and shops. They are also affected by environmental factors, for example, prices will be depressed by the presence of aircraft noise and increased by the presence of a park.

HPM involves the collection of data recording price and the presence or absence of all the salient determinants of price. Once a price can be established to reflect the non-environmental factors (number of rooms, etc.), then the effects of the environmental factor under analysis (e.g. aircraft noise) can be attributed to variations in the price of houses with otherwise similar characteristics. An imputed cost can then be attributed for aircraft noise nuisance. For example, the author lives in a house in West London, UK, next to the River Thames. However, this idyllic setting is somewhat spoiled by the fact that it is also under the flight path to runway 28L at London Heathrow airport. This means that planes overfly the house at 55-second intervals starting as early as five o'clock in the morning. Similar properties without this environmental disbenefit sell for prices that are 30–40 per cent higher than the author's house and this price differential gives an important clue as to how the negative environmental impacts of flights can be valued. Difficulties involved with HPM mainly centre on the large number of differences that occur between houses and the changes in other factors such as interest rates during data collection.

Goffele (2000) used the HPM to assign monetary values to some of the external effects of agricultural and silvicultural activities in France. The renting price of rural self-catering cottages or gîtes was examined and it was found that intensive livestock farming caused the renting price of gîtes to decrease, whereas permanent grassland had the opposite effect.

Travel cost method

The assumption behind this method of environmental asset valuation is that there is a relationship between the travel costs that a visitor has incurred to visit a tourism or recreational site and their valuation of that site. The attraction of this method is that travel costs for visitors by car are readily measurable as they consist mainly of petrol costs. A survey records the distance visitors travelled to the site and technical details about their car. From this, travel costs are calculated. This is then compared to the number of visits the individual makes per year to the site.

Figure 17.2 illustrates a typical scatter diagram which might result from plotting travel costs against number of visits, after adjusting for other factors such as income differences. A typically shaped demand curve $D0$ relates the price of visiting the site (measured by travel costs) to the demand (the number of visits per year). A total value of the site for recreational use can be obtained from this information.

There are however problems which arise in using TCM. First, travelling involves use of time which represents an additional cost for many people. Second, some people may arrive on bicycle or on foot and thus register no travel cost, even though their actual valuation of the site may be positive. Third, people may combine visiting the site with other activities on the same journey and it is difficult to unscramble the contribution of travel costs to each.

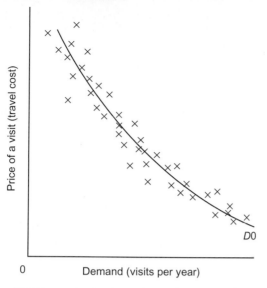

Figure 17.2 Use of TCM to construct a demand curve for a tourism/recreational site.

Dose–response method

This valuation method depends upon the availability of data linking the effects of pollution to a response in, for example, human health or crop production. The effects of sewage pollution in the sea could be measured in terms of medical resources needed to remedy pollution-induced sickness and loss of earnings.

Replacement cost technique

This might offer a way of measuring some of the environmental effects of acid rain. For example, the cost of restoration of buildings damaged by such pollution could be measured and thus the cost of acid-rain pollution measured.

Mitigation behaviour method

Some pollution effects result in households undertaking defensive expenditure which can be measured in the market. The existence of aircraft noise pollution, for example, may lead households to fit double glazing to mitigate its effects. This defensive expenditure can be summed to find costs incurred from the pollution.

Exhibit 17.4 provides estimates of the economic environmental costs of climate change, local noise and local air quality (LAQ) of UK passenger air traffic, and the study was commissioned by government in order to inform its environmental management policy for air travel.

Exhibit 17.4 Aviation and the environment: using economic instruments

1 The 'cost of carbon'

This represents the cost to society resulting from climate change effects caused by releasing carbon into the atmosphere as CO_2. The cost of global environmental damage caused by climate change is estimated and then related to the amount of carbon released as CO_2, giving a damage cost per tonne of carbon.

It was concluded that 'a value of approximately £70/tC (2000 prices, with equity weighting) seems like a defensible illustrative value for carbon emissions in 2000. This figure should then be raised by £1/tC in real terms for each subsequent year'.

The £70 per tonne of carbon value takes no account of uncertainties including the probability of:

- the so-called 'climate catastrophe' (e.g. melting of the West Antarctic ice sheet, Gulf Stream suppression and so on);
- the 'socially contingent impacts' of climate change (e.g. famine, mass migration and so on);
- the costs of impacts post 2100.

The estimated CO_2 emissions from UK passenger flights are:

- 2000: 30 millions of tonnes.
- 2030: 70 millions of tonnes.

2 Total climate change costs

As well as CO_2 effects, air travel also causes climate change due to the emissions of other gases and vapour trails. The total of these are called radiative effects. Taking all radiative effects into account, the estimated total climate change costs of UK passenger flights are:

- 2000: £1.4 billion.
- 2030: £4.8 billion.

3 Noise costs

Estimates of the cost of noise were made by estimating the effect of a sustained increase in noise on house prices, using 'hedonic pricing' techniques. Based on the these studies, monetary values for the effect of aircraft noise at Heathrow Airport ranged between 36 and 40 pence per passenger. The total cost of noise impacts for all airports has been estimated at around £25 million for 2000.

4 LAQ

The study by CE Delft in 2002 on the *External Costs of Aviation* estimates that the external LAQ costs of aviation vary between Euros1 and 2 per passenger (equivalent to £119–236 million for all UK passengers).

Source: Adapted from http://www.hm-treasury.gov.uk/media//8E752/Aviation_Environment.pdf

APPROACHES TO SUSTAINABILITY: ADAPTATION

Adaptation approaches mean finding solutions to impacts caused by unsustainable practices and especially to global warming, rather than trying to control the causes of the impacts. The following are examples of adaptive strategies to deal with specific environmental threats:

- *Rising sea levels*: Evacuate and relocate populations, build higher sea defences and flood protection.
- *Droughts*: Increase reservoir capacity; build desalination plants.
- *Depletion of ozone layer*: Public health campaigns to warn of dangers of skin cancer.
- *Loss of snow cover in ski resorts*: Increase capacity of artificial snow making.

NEED FOR A PARADIGM CHANGE

What the discussion in Chapters 16 and 17 suggest is that as individuals, as nations and as a species, we have over-concentrated on materialism, the short term, and we have established and continue to develop lifestyles based on high carbon consumption. If we are to divert our path from unsustainable growth at any costs to a sustainable future, we need a radical change in our paradigm of living and working. Individual action is important, but of paramount importance are international agreements on how to deal with sustainability issues that affect the whole planet. We have to confront the tragedy of the commons as it relates to our earth's atmosphere.

We have to move from	To
GNP	Gross National Welfare
Short termism	Long termism
Someone else's problem	My problem
Material growth	Sustainable growth
Private benefit	Social benefit
Local awareness	Planetary awareness
Passive	Action for change

REVIEW OF KEY TERMS

- Sustainable development: development which can endure over the long run.
- Intergenerational equity: ensuring future generations do not inherit less capital than the current one.
- Natural capital: raw materials and the natural environment.
- Regenerative capacity: limit to harvesting of renewable resource whilst maintaining stock level.
- Social cost–benefit analysis: comparison of full social costs and benefits of a project.

- Discounting: adjusting future monetary values to present monetary values.
- WTP method: discovery of what people would be prepared to pay for a currently unpriced resource.
- HPM: imputing a price for an environmental externality by determining its effect on other prices.
- TCM: imputing the value of a site by measuring the cost of travel to it.
- Dose–response method: measuring effects of pollution in monetary terms.
- Replacement cost technique: measuring costs of pollution by calculating restoration costs.
- Mitigation behaviour method: measuring costs of pollution by counting defensive expenditure.
- CAC: direct regulations (e.g. water quality regulations).
- Market-based incentives: adjusting prices to reflect external costs.
- Polluter pays principle: polluter pays the full cost of pollution effects.

Data Questions

Task 17.1 **Journal article: Miller, G., Rathouse, K., Scarles, C., Holmes, K., Tribe, J., 2010. Public understanding of sustainable tourism. *Annals of Tourism Research* 37, 627–645.**

This article argues that 'if tourism is to become part of a more sustainable lifestyle, changes are needed to the patterns of behaviour adopted by the public. This paper presents the results of research conducted amongst members of the public in England on their understanding of sustainable tourism, their response to four desired tourism behaviour goals, and expectations about the role of government and the tourism industry in encouraging sustainable tourism. The research shows a lack of awareness of tourism's impact relative to day-to-day behaviour, feelings of disempowerment and an unwillingness to make significant changes to current tourism behaviour'.

Its conclusions include the following comments:

- 'This research has shown a low level of awareness about the impacts of the tourism industry and appropriate response options.
- Where there was greater awareness, this tended to be on the tangible impacts such as littering rather than the intangible impacts of global warming.
- Respondents were resistant to change their behaviour unless other people and developing countries changed.
- [They] often express[ed] a sense of entitlement to enjoy their holidays as they chose.
- The research identified drivers and inhibitors for each of the four behaviour goals, revealing potential to encourage more domestic holidays and more sustainable travel methods, while encouraging people to travel less, combine travel and to undertake different activities seems certain to face greater resistance.

- Respondents seem to place greater responsibility on government to address the problem than any other group, including themselves.
- The challenge then will become to develop a sense of personal responsibility for the impacts developed by taking a holiday.
- A number of possible practical actions can be drawn from the research such as: the need for labelling of the sustainability of tourism products; the promotion of personal carbon allowances and a "carbon calculator" to understand tourism's relationship with these allowances; the creation of priority lanes for boarding planes (or similar) for those who have offset their emissions; and the introduction of "metering" in hotels to allow guests to be charged for the resources they consume.
- Further, pro-environmental behaviour could be encouraged through physical and virtual networks to develop and cement the connections between people, and the connections between people and their actions. The "weight-watchers" programme may provide an example of how difficult changes to behaviour are made possible with group support.
- Hence, initiatives like community based social marketing and utilising social networking tools such as "facebook" may have currency for the tourism industry to overcome public disempowerment and lack of understanding to support pro-environmental behaviour change.
- Any behaviour changes will of course be contingent on there being a supply of pro-environmental holiday options available to absorb new-found motivations to act.
- Further research will be needed on the segmentation model to see if there are groups of consumers who are more or less receptive to messages of change, for what reasons and how receptive they may be to ideas of responsibility'.

Recap Questions

1 What is meant by the 'public understanding of sustainable tourism' and why is it important?
2 How would you account for the 'low level of awareness about the impacts of the tourism industry'?
3 How can tourists be helped 'to develop a sense of personal responsibility for the impacts developed by taking a holiday'?
4 Evaluate the practical actions suggested in this article to encourage more sustainable practices.
5 In what ways could taxes on tourism be used to minimize environmental damage?
6 Is it possible to devise a fair tax on aviation?
7 What are the policy implications of this research?

Task 17.2 **Under deafening skies**

1993: Residents of the tiny village of Longford barely flinch any more. Living within a few hundred yards of one of London Heathrow Airport's two runways, they have become accustomed to the deafening roar of transatlantic jumbos as they heave themselves into the skies. Lunchtime conversation under umbrellas outside the White Horse stops involuntarily every few minutes to allow the ear-splitting din to die down. The plane passes, chatter resumes … for a moment. 'You get used to it', the locals shrug philosophically.

Task 17.2 continued

Many work or have worked at the airport. They have learned to rely for their sanity on the hours of relative peace when Heathrow switches its operations to the south runway. Until then, those at home tend to spend most of the time locked behind double glazing. It might seem bad now, but with a dramatic increase in the number of passengers forecast by the aviation industry and consequent expansion plans, environmentalists are fearful of what lies ahead.

1995: At Heathrow, already the world's busiest international airport, work is nearing completion on a fifth terminal (T5) which will double the airport's annual capacity to nearly 80 million passengers. Clusters of opposition groups have mushroomed around the country's main airports to fight the expansion plans. The argument they have to counter is the creation of much-needed jobs and the economic shot-in-the-arm which the aviation industry claims they would bring. Rita Pearce, who has lived in Longford for 23 years and worked for Pan-American at Heathrow for 16, now believes enough is enough.

The pollution has already taken its toll on her family's health, she says – she has had pleurisy 5 times in 2 years and her two daughters have developed asthma – and she believes increased air traffic and the introduction of night flights from October will make life there unbearable. 'It is going to be absolute hell', she said. If planning permission for the fifth terminal is granted, in addition to the main terminal building with up to three satellites, there are plans for three giant car parks, with access provided by a new spur road from the M25 spanning the Colne Valley Park, described by Friends of the Earth as a unique river valley in the capital, important for wildlife and recreation. The plans also assume the M25 will be widened to 14 lanes in the Staines area to the south-west. The sewage works, meanwhile, occupying the site of T5 has been shifted on to green belt land to the north-west of the airport.

2004: Families in the area do not believe reassurances that T5 will not require a third runway. A report has suggested that BA had drawn up plans for a new Heathrow runway to the south of the existing two.

2006: Sipson is a village between London Heathrow airport and the nearby M4 motorway. This year the people of Sipson have been told that their village will be 'wiped off the map'. The government, the airlines and the airport owners have decided that Heathrow should have a third runway. Sipson will be buried under airport concrete by 2020 if the government approves a third runway for Heathrow – R3

2008: The first passengers arrived at T5 on flight BA026 from Hong Kong. T5 is Heathrow's new £4.3-m Terminal 5 which is as big as the whole of London's second airport – London Gatwick.

2010: The new government in the UK ruled out the building of a third runway (R3) at Heathrow and introduced a 'green tax' on flights.

Source: Adapted from The Guardian *(23 July 1993, 1995, 2004, 2006, 2008, 2010).*

Recap Questions

1 Draw up a list of private and social costs and benefits of the development of T5.
2 In what ways could you attempt to measure the monetary value of the costs and benefits?
3 Why should the village of Sipson be saved?

4 The airline industry argues that without R3, Heathrow will just lose air traffic to the other major European hubs of Frankfurt (Germany), Charles de Gaulle (Paris) and Schipol (Amsterdam) airports and that carbon emissions will be unaffected. Discuss.

Task 17.3 Recommended actions from The Stern Report on Climate Change

The recommended actions from The Stern Report on Climate Change included the following:

- There is a need for three elements of policy for effective action against climate change, that is:
  - carbon pricing
  - technology policy
  - energy efficiency.
- *Carbon pricing* could be achieved through regulation, taxation or an ETS to reveal the full social costs of a carbon intensive economy.
- A global carbon price across countries and sectors is an important aim.
- ETS should be expanded and globally linked.
- *Technology policy* should encourage the development and use of low-carbon and high-*energy efficiency* products and services.
- Support for energy research and development and the deployment of low-carbon technologies should be a priority.
- There should be a move towards international standards.
- Ways to curb deforestation should be implemented.
- Climate change awareness and policy should be integrated into development policy.
- Rich countries should support less-developed countries through overseas aid.
- Improved information on regional climate change impacts needed.
- International funding needed for research into new crop varieties that will be climate change tolerant.

Source: The Stern Report on Climate Change http://webarchive.nationalarchives. gov.uk/+/http:/www.hm-treasury.gov.uk/sternreview_index.htm

Recap Questions

1 What is carbon pricing, why is it needed and how can it be introduced?
2 Which is the best option for carbon pricing – regulation, taxation or an ETS?
3 Why is climate change important for the tourism and recreation industries?
4 Have you changed any of your travel habits because of the threat of climate change? Explain your answer.
5 What technological options are worth developing to counter climate change?
6 Distinguish between mitigation and adaptation strategies in the above extract.

MULTIPLE CHOICE

1 The setting of air noise limits around airports is an example of:
(i) An attempt to control external costs.
(ii) A Command and Control method of environmental damage control.
(iii) Privatization of a free-access resource.
(iv) A perfect market.

Which of the above is true?
(a) All of the above.
(b) (i) only.
(c) (i) and (ii) only.
(d) (ii) and (iii) only.

2 Measurement of the social costs of sewerage dumping at sea, by counting the costs to surfers of sewerage related illness, uses which of the following methods?
(a) Hedonic pricing.
(b) Dose–response method.
(c) Willingness to Pay method.
(d) Polluter pays principle.

3 Which of the following is true of 'intergenerational equity'?
(a) It was the main policy outcome of the Kyoto conference.
(b) It means not causing resource impoverishment for the future.
(c) It means trying to reduce extremes of poverty.
(d) It involves equating marginal private and marginal social costs.

4 Which of the following is not true?
(a) Greenhouse gases are a main cause of global warming.
(b) Ozone depletion causes an increase in penetration of UV rays.
(c) CO_2 is a key Greenhouse gas.
(d) CO_2 is a key cause of ozone depletion.

5 Which of the following is not a principle of sustainable development?
(a) The endogenous growth principle.
(b) Tailoring of economic activity to the carrying capacity of the environment.
(c) The precautionary principle.
(d) The 'polluter pays' principle.

REVIEW QUESTIONS

1 List the various stakeholders that would wish to influence a named leisure or tourism development and identify their viewpoints.

2 Explain the various ways in which the cost of aircraft noise could be imputed.

3 What is the approximate present value of £100 due in a year's time, if the discount rate is 10 per cent?

4 What are the essential elements of sustainable development?

5 What are the five key stages in social cost–benefit analysis?

Websites of interest

The Brundtland Report: www.un-documents.net/wced-ocf.htm

The Davos Declaration: www.unwto.org/media/news/en/press_det. php?id=1411&idioma=E

UNWTO Sustainable Tourism Policy: http://www.world-tourism.org/ frameset/frame_sustainable.html

The International Ecotourism Society: www.ecotourism.org/

The Stern Report on Climate Change: http://webarchive.nationalarchives. gov.uk/+/http:/www.hm-treasury.gov.uk/sternreview_index.htm

Green Globe: a worldwide environmental management and awareness programme for the travel and tourism industry: www.greenglobe.org/

UNEP – tourism: www.unepie.org/tourism/home.htm

The National Trust: www.nationaltrust.org.uk

European Commission Climate Action: http://ec.europa.eu/clima/ policies/ets/index_en.htm

Critique, alternative perspectives and change

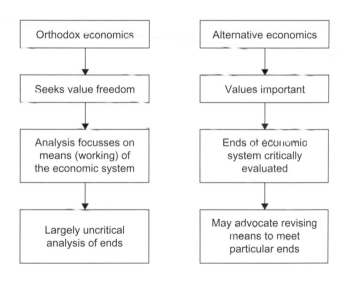

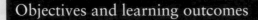

Objectives and learning outcomes

The purpose of this chapter is to question the way orthodox or conventional economics explains how things work according to what appear to be natural or neutral principles. This chapter invites a critical look at the economic aspects of the world of recreation, leisure and tourism as it has developed and asks normative questions. Has this world developed in a way that is good? Are there better ways of constructing this world and how could we go about achieving this?

By studying this chapter, students will be able to:

- critique the assumptions of conventional economics;
- understand the Marxian critique of capitalism;
- critically evaluate the economic state of recreation, leisure and tourism;
- articulate desirable economic ends;
- explain alternative approaches to reaching desired economic ends.

CRITIQUE

The point of departure for this chapter is Richard Lipsey's (1973) once ubiquitous economics textbook that went under the title *Positive Economics*. This text represents the influential core of orthodox economics. It is likely that this or similar economic texts were the undergraduate bibles of those representatives of the IMF, who travel the world lecturing the poorest countries on the importance of a balanced State budget, the merits of privatization and tight monetary control.

The problem with this text was that it sold its approach – *positive* economics – as the only meaningful approach to economics. It elevated this approach to an orthodoxy that was eloquently critiqued by Omerod (1994) in *The Death of Economics*. In doing so, it reduced economics to a set of theories laden with restrictive assumptions. The theory of perfect competition is a good example. The theories had to simplify the world because the actual real world of economics is too complex and messy to model otherwise. So the theories were constructed with many limiting assumptions that allowed them to function with mathematical precision. But of course the more assumptions that preceded theory building, the less useful the theories became in explaining or predicting real-world behaviour.

At the same time, *Positive Economics* promoted the free market as a natural and irrefutable entity. It elevated it to the status of say gravity. That is, something that was natural and that humans were subservient to. The counterpart to this was that it also demoted human agency to the periphery of the stage of free-market economics.

Humans were assigned the role of *homo economicus* that is to say they made rational economic decisions based around maximizing their satisfaction from a limited income. Firms were assigned the role of profit maximizers, and the world was therefore assigned a set of economic rules by which to develop itself.

The world which *Positive Economics* so confidently pitched itself against was the world of normative thought. Positive economics dealt with facts. Disputes over facts could be resolved by resort to evidence or logic. In contrast, normative thought was based on opinion or values or aspirations. Since, the argument went that there was no way of resolving a dispute over opinion, normative thought should be banished from economics which could make its case more securely based on facts. A positive approach put economics on the same kind of secure foundations as physics, chemistry and biology.

So *Positive Economics* explained why there were differences in wages, the benefits of Free Trade, how markets acting freely would deliver economic and allocative efficiency and how consumers maximized their satisfaction. In other words individual markets, national economies and indeed the global trading economy could all theoretically work like a well-oiled machine. Indeed this approach to economics seems to devote its entire effort to understanding the means by which the economy works rather than putting the ends of economic endeavour up for scrutiny.

To quote Omerod (1994: 3):

> The world economy is in crisis ... [and] the orthodoxy of economics, trapped in an idealized, mechanistic view of the world, is powerless to assist.

It is interesting to note that Omerod wrote this in 1994 and the world economy is once again in crisis. This chapter will open up the economics of leisure, recreation and tourism to scrutiny and in particular focus on some key questions which are unresolved. It starts its journey with an introduction to Marxian economics.

MARX VERSUS ORTHODOX ECONOMICS

Joan Robinson (1942) in her *Essay on Marxian Economics* wrote of the fundamental differences between Marxian and traditional orthodox economists. She notes first, that 'orthodox economists accept the capitalist system as part of the eternal order of nature while Marx regards it as a passing phase in the transition from the feudal economy of the past to the socialist economy of the future'. Second, she notes that orthodox economists assume that all of the members of economic society share a common interest while 'Marx conceives of economic life in terms of a conflict of interest between owners of property [the bourgeoisie] who do no work and workers [the proletariat] who own no property'. Robinson is thereby advertising to the fact that orthodox economists take the market or capitalist economic system for granted and work within it to explain its mechanisms. They take it as a given. Marx on the other hand holds the whole system up for inspection and examines its consequences paying particular attention to the conflict of class interests and the possibility of another system – that of socialism.

Marx's *Manifesto of the Communist Party* represents a powerful critique of capitalist economics and Exhibit 18.1 reproduces some key extracts from it.

Exhibit 18.1 Karl Marx and Frederick Engels: Manifesto of the communist party 1848 (extracts)

The history of all hitherto existing society is the history of class struggles…

The modern bourgeois society that has sprouted from the ruins of feudal society has not done away with class antagonisms. It has but established new classes, new conditions of oppression, new forms of struggle in place of the old ones.

Our epoch, the epoch of the bourgeoisie, possesses, however, this distinct feature: it has simplified class antagonisms. Society as a whole is more and more splitting up into two great hostile camps, into two great classes directly facing each other – bourgeoisie and proletariat…

Each step in the development of the bourgeoisie was accompanied by a corresponding political advance in that class…. The bourgeoisie has at last, since the establishment of Modern Industry and of the world market, conquered for itself, in the modern representative state, exclusive political sway. The executive of the modern state is but a committee for managing the common affairs of the whole bourgeoisie.

The bourgeoisie … has resolved personal worth into exchange value, and in place of the numberless indefeasible chartered freedoms, has set up that single, unconscionable freedom – Free Trade. In one word, for exploitation, veiled by religious and political illusions, it has substituted naked, shameless, direct, brutal exploitation. The bourgeoisie has stripped of its halo every occupation hitherto honoured and looked up to with reverent awe. It has converted the physician, the lawyer, the priest, the poet, the man of science, into its paid wage labourers. The bourgeoisie has torn away from the family its sentimental veil, and has reduced the family relation into a mere money relation.

The bourgeoisie cannot exist without constantly revolutionizing the instruments of production, and thereby the relations of production, and with them the whole relations of society…. The need of a constantly expanding market for its products chases the bourgeoisie over the entire surface of the globe. It must nestle everywhere, settle everywhere, establish connections everywhere…

All old-established national industries have been destroyed or are daily being destroyed. They are dislodged by new industries, whose introduction becomes a life and death question for all civilized nations, by industries that no longer work up indigenous raw material, but raw material drawn from the remotest zones; industries whose products are consumed,

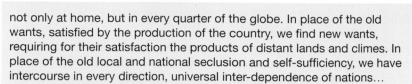

not only at home, but in every quarter of the globe. In place of the old wants, satisfied by the production of the country, we find new wants, requiring for their satisfaction the products of distant lands and climes. In place of the old local and national seclusion and self-sufficiency, we have intercourse in every direction, universal inter-dependence of nations…

The bourgeoisie, by the rapid improvement of all instruments of production, by the immensely facilitated means of communication, draws all, even the most barbarian, nations into civilization. The cheap prices of commodities are the heavy artillery with which it forces the barbarians' intensely obstinate hatred of foreigners to capitulate. It compels all nations, on pain of extinction, to adopt the bourgeois mode of production; it compels them to introduce what it calls civilization into their midst, i.e., to become bourgeois themselves. In one word, it creates a world after its own image.

The bourgeoisie has subjected the country to the rule of the towns. It has created enormous cities, has greatly increased the urban population as compared with the rural, and has thus rescued a considerable part of the population from the idiocy of rural life. Just as it has made the country dependent on the towns, so it has made barbarian and semi-barbarian countries dependent on the civilized ones, nations of peasants on nations of bourgeois, the East on the West.

The bourgeoisie … has agglomerated population, centralized the means of production, and has concentrated property in a few hands. The necessary consequence of this was political centralization. Independent, or but loosely connected provinces, with separate interests, laws, governments, and systems of taxation, became lumped together into one nation, with one government, one code of laws, one national class interest, one frontier, and one customs tariff…

In proportion as the bourgeoisie, i.e. capital, is developed, in the same proportion is the proletariat, the modern working class, developed – a class of labourers, who live only so long as they find work, and who find work only so long as their labour increases capital. These labourers, who must sell themselves piecemeal, are a commodity, like every other article of commerce, and are consequently exposed to all the vicissitudes of competition, to all the fluctuations of the market.

Owing to the extensive use of machinery, and to the division of labour, the work of the proletarians has lost all individual character, and, consequently, all charm for the workman. He becomes an appendage of the machine, and it is only the most simple, most monotonous, and most easily acquired knack, that is required of him. Hence, the cost of production of a workman is restricted, almost entirely, to the means of subsistence that he requires for maintenance, and for the propagation of his race. But the price of a commodity, and therefore also of labour, is equal to its cost of production. In proportion, therefore, as the repulsiveness of the work increases, the wage decreases. What is more, in proportion as the use of machinery and division of labour increases, in the same proportion the burden of toil also increases, whether by prolongation of the working hours, by the increase of the work exacted in a given time, or by increased speed of machinery, etc.

Modern Industry has converted the little workshop of the patriarchal master into the great factory of the industrial capitalist. Masses of labourers, crowded into the factory, are organized like soldiers. As

Exhibit 18.1 continued

privates of the industrial army, they are placed under the command of a perfect hierarchy of officers and sergeants. Not only are they slaves of the bourgeois class, and of the bourgeois state; they are daily and hourly enslaved by the machine, by the overlooker, and, above all, in the individual bourgeois manufacturer himself. The more openly this despotism proclaims gain to be its end and aim, the more petty, the more hateful and the more embittering it is…

The proletariat goes through various stages of development. With its birth begins its struggle with the bourgeoisie. At first, the contest is carried on by individual labourers, then by the work of people of a factory, then by the operative of one trade, in one locality, against the individual bourgeois who directly exploits them. They direct their attacks not against the bourgeois condition of production, but against the instruments of production themselves; they destroy imported wares that compete with their labour, they smash to pieces machinery, they set factories ablaze, they seek to restore by force the vanished status of the workman of the Middle Ages.

At this stage, the labourers still form an incoherent mass scattered over the whole country, and broken up by their mutual competition…. But with the development of industry, the proletariat not only increases in number; it becomes concentrated in greater masses, its strength grows, and it feels that strength more. The various interests and conditions of life within the ranks of the proletariat are more and more equalized, in proportion as machinery obliterates all distinctions of labour, and nearly everywhere reduces wages to the same low-level. The growing competition among the bourgeois, and the resulting commercial crises, make the wages of the workers ever more fluctuating. The increasing improvement of machinery, ever more rapidly developing, makes their livelihood more and more precarious; the collisions between individual workmen and individual bourgeois take more and more the character of collisions between two classes. Thereupon, the workers begin to form combinations (Trade Unions) against the bourgeois; they club together in order to keep up the rate of wages; they found permanent associations in order to make provision beforehand for these occasional revolts. Here and there, the contest breaks out into riots.

Now and then the workers are victorious, but only for a time. The real fruit of their battles lie not in the immediate result, but in the ever-expanding union of the workers. This union is helped on by the improved means of communication that are created by Modern Industry, and that place the workers of different localities in contact with one another. It was just this contact that was needed to centralize the numerous local struggles, all of the same character, into one national struggle between classes. But every class struggle is a political struggle…

Finally, in times when the class struggle nears the decisive hour, the progress of dissolution going on within the ruling class, in fact within the whole range of old society, assumes such a violent, glaring character, that a small section of the ruling class cuts itself adrift, and joins the revolutionary class, the class that holds the future in its hands…

Of all the classes that stand face to face with the bourgeoisie today, the proletariat alone is a genuinely revolutionary class. The other classes decay and finally disappear in the face of Modern Industry; the proletariat is its special and essential product…

In the condition of the proletariat, those of old society at large are already virtually swamped. The proletarian is without property; his relation to his wife and children has no longer anything in common with the bourgeois family relations; modern industry labour, modern subjection to capital, the same in England as in France, in America as in Germany, has stripped him of every trace of national character. Law, morality, religion, are to him so many bourgeois prejudices, behind which lurk in ambush just as many bourgeois interests…

All previous historical movements were movements of minorities, or in the interest of minorities. The proletarian movement is the self-conscious, independent movement of the immense majority, in the interest of the immense majority. The proletariat, the lowest stratum of our present society, cannot stir, cannot raise itself up, without the whole superincumbent strata of official society being sprung into the air…. The modern labourer … instead of rising with the process of industry, sinks deeper and deeper below the conditions of existence of his own class. He becomes a pauper, and pauperism develops more rapidly than population and wealth. And here it becomes evident that the bourgeoisie is unfit any longer to be the ruling class in society, and to impose its conditions of existence upon society as an overriding law…. Society can no longer live under this bourgeoisie, in other words, its existence is no longer compatible with society.

The essential conditions for the existence and for the sway of the bourgeois class is the formation and augmentation of capital; the condition for capital is wage labour. Wage labour rests exclusively on competition between the labourers. The advance of industry, whose involuntary promoter is the bourgeoisie, replaces the isolation of the labourers, due to competition, by the revolutionary combination, due to association. The development of Modern Industry, therefore, cuts from under its feet the very foundation on which the bourgeoisie produces and appropriates products. What the bourgeoisie therefore produces, above all, are its own grave-diggers. Its fall and the victory of the proletariat are equally inevitable.

Marx develops a number of key ideas which include:

- history can be seen as a series of class struggles;
- the basic conflict between the bourgeoisie and the proletariat;
- the representation of bourgeois interests by government;
- the deterioration of the conditions of the proletariat;
- the globalization of capitalism;
- the constant change of capitalism;
- the commercial crises of capitalism;
- the inevitable victory of the proletariat over the bourgeoisie.

So what is the relevance of Marx to the economic provision of recreation, leisure and tourism? Perhaps we should start with its problems. Although communism represented an important force in the twentieth century, by the twenty-first century it is largely on the wane. Some interesting exceptions remain. China in name is still communist but hardly in action, Cuba is both in name and action and Nepal is subject to regular attack from Marxist revolutionary groups. But in general there appears to be no threat of imminent revolution. Indeed in many parts of the world worker power (particularly as measured by Trade Union membership) is in decline. Capitalism has its recurrent minor and major crises but government economic intervention has been successful in preventing prolonged or profound crises. The conditions of workers have generally improved by most measures – more holidays, better conditions and better pay so that they are able to become part of consumer society.

But Marxian analysis still offers some important insights. First, it encourages a deep inspection of the whole project of capitalism rather than blind acceptance of it. It reminds us that the prevailing economic system is not a natural or given phenomenon and critique encourages us to ask whether the system is providing the kind of economic ends that we desire. Second, it encourages us to ask whose interests are being served by capitalism. Third, it encourages us to ask whose interests are served by governments. Fourth, whilst it is clear that the absolute poverty of the proletariat has declined, the relative gap between owners of capital and workers seems to be widening. Perhaps more significantly there seems to be an underclass of those who are unable to access the mainstream economic system and thus we can witness the extraordinary contrasts of poverty and plenty a few blocks away in major cities of the world. Fifth, we may see the globalization of capitalism as replacing other competing value systems in societies throughout the world through its overwhelming power. But perhaps most significantly whilst national class antagonisms seem to have subsided, internationally the gap between rich and poor is extreme. Indeed, it appears that in many parts of the world the conditions of the poor remain stubbornly wretched (Plate 18).

Plate 18 Delivering coal by handcart. *Source: The author.*

RECREATION, LEISURE AND TOURISM: THE STATE WE ARE IN

So, as we journey through the twenty-first century we may remark upon how wrong Marx was in his analysis of capitalism. Revolutions have been taking the world population not into communism but out of it. Capitalism is as brash, dynamic and delivering goods and services by the bucket load. In terms of leisure and tourism those on average incomes in the North America, the EU and Australasia have access to a dazzling array of recreation, leisure and tourism opportunities in the form of gyms, satellite television, sports, recreational activities and domestic and foreign holidays. Moreover there has, in general, been a release from the harsh conditions of work described by Marx. Fewer people work in factories or endure hard physical work. In short we have never had it so good.

Economic development in some parts of the world based on tourism means that generations of workers have been able to completely miss out the squalid conditions associated with the Industrial Revolution of the UK, for example, and achieve economic growth using the relatively clean industry of tourism.

Karl Marx famously said that religion was the opium of the masses. By this he meant that strong religious beliefs meant that people were not alive to their plight in the world. Religion provided both a discipline encouraging unquestioning respect for authority and a kind of a drug providing meaning and the promise of a good after-life in return for a well-spent life on earth and good deeds. It could be said that in the present age leisure and tourism are the opium of the people. They provide a feel good factor and a diversion from more profound politico-economic issue.

It therefore seems appropriate to end this book with a wake-up call concerning the less desirable ends that are delivered as part and parcel of our economic prosperity based upon free market economics. This will take the form of a number of paradoxes for consideration. They are paradoxes because leisure is often thought of as what we do when our work is done. But as the following list shows there is still much work left undone. The overall question to be asked is whether conventional economics can help to solve any of these issues.

TWENTY-ONE PARADOXES IN LEISURE AND TOURISM

1. Poverty amongst plenty

Poverty estimates published by the World Bank (2008) show that 1.4 billion people in the developing world (one in four) were living on less than US$1.25 a day in 2005. This figure is down from 1.9 billion (one in two) in 1981 but the recent figures show that poverty has been more widespread across the developing world over the past 25 years than previously estimated. The problem is particularly acute in Sub-Saharan Africa where the $1.25 a day poverty rate remains at 50 per cent of the population. However, population growth means that the absolute number of poor people in the region has nearly doubled, from 200 million in 1981 to 390 million in 2005.

Table 18.1 shows examples of world poverty where in Bangladesh 81 per cent and Ethiopia 78 per cent of the population are living on less than $2 a day. This notion of poverty, disease and starvation in a world of unparalleled affluence is surely the most profound disgrace to the modern world. It is particularly stark when viewed in contrast to the luxurious world of leisure and tourism. Table 18.2 shows the distribution of world GDP amongst the world population. Note the paradox in distribution between India which has a population of 1.182 millions but only 5 per cent of world GDP and the USA which has a population of 310 millions and an 20 per cent share of world GDP. Despite their disproportionate populations the

Table 18.1 World poverty

Year of survey	Country	Percentage of population below $1.25 a day	Percentage of population below $2 a day
2005	Bangladesh	50	81
2005	Ethiopia	40	78
2005	India	42	76
2006	Mali	51	77
2005	Uganda	52	76
2006	Vietnam	22	48

Source: Adapted from IMF, www.worldbank.org/data

Table 18.2 Distribution of world output (2011)

Area/example	Percentage of world GDP	Population (m)
Advanced economies	55	–
e.g. *United States*	*20*	*310*
Emerging and developing economies	45	–
e.g. *India*	*5*	*1,182*

Source: Adapted from IMF, World Economic Outlook.

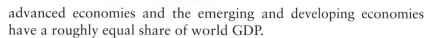

advanced economies and the emerging and developing economies have a roughly equal share of world GDP.

- Are we happy with the intense poverty that we have to step over and around in many parts of the world as we travel from airport to hotel, from museum to restaurant?
- Why has the economic system failed the poor of the world?
- Will continuing asymmetries of wealth and poverty threaten global economic stability?

And even limited travel in our own countries also raises questions about poverty:

- Why is there such a big gap between rich and poor?
- Why does the economy generate squalor and affluence within close proximity?

2. Working for peanuts

Factory life and harsh working conditions are disappearing from the developed world. However, the production of many leisure goods – computers, mobile devices, sports shoes, equipment and clothing – often takes place in factories and sweatshops in less-developed countries with poor wages and tough working conditions. Exhibit 18.2 reports on conditions of work on some cruise ships. Cruise ships provide an

---

Exhibit 18.2 Sweatships

The following include the main findings of a report titled 'Sweatships – What It's Really Like to Work on Board Cruise Ships', joint-produced by the anti-poverty charity War on Want and the International Transport Workers' Federation (ITF).

- Workers are sourced especially from Eastern Europe, Asia and Latin America.
- Typical jobs are in staff engine rooms, laundries, kitchens and restaurants on cruise ships.
- As ships get bigger the passenger to crew ration will grow from 2:1 to 3:1 to help cut costs.
- Wages can be as low as US$45 per month for waiters and waitresses.
- Contracts are often short and insecure.
- An ITF survey found that 95 per cent are working 7 days a week.
- Just under a third worked up to 14 hours a day.
- Workers reported widespread authoritarian and aggressive behaviour by managers and supervisors.
- Discipline includes on-the-spot fines or being moved to heavy work where tips are poor.
- Cases are reported of instant dismissal and repatriation home.

Exhibit 18.2 continued

- There have been many accusations of sexual harassment against those in authority on board.
- In one extreme case 'there were only two showers and one working toilet for a hundred men and women crewmembers and staff had to sleep six to each tiny cabin containing only three bunks'.

Source: War on Want www.waronwant.org/past-campaigns/sweat-ships

alarming example of the very good life on the upper decks and the very bad life below decks:

- Are we happy that others work long hours with low pay and in bad working conditions to provide us with cheap goods?
- Why do those who work hardest often get the lowest wages?

3. The travelling elite

Travel has given us the opportunity to move freely around the globe, dropping in and out of distant lands and cultures. But just as an EU or a US passport is a passport to freedom many other nationalities face severe restrictions on where they may travel to. This raises two questions:

1 Why is travel and tourism the confined to an elite group of mobile travellers?
2 Is it just that many people are excluded and denied access to developed countries in search of better conditions?

4. Getting hotter

Global warming is potentially the most significant crisis to confront human development.

- Why are we still operating a high carbon dependent economy?
- Why is climate change the most important market failure ever?

5. Loving the planet

We all share a common planet. Economic growth brings higher wages and material prosperity but all our resources are extracted from the planet's limited sources and all of the rubbish we produced stays with all of us.

- Are we happy with the balance between economic growth and environmental damage including:
    atmospheric pollution

traffic congestion

noise pollution

the concretization of the natural environment.

- How do we move our thinking and actions 'from cowboy economy to spaceship earth?'

6. Cultural clashes

We have seen major wars in Iraq and Afghanistan. We have seen major terrorist incidents including the plane-bombing of the Twin Towers and the London Tube bombs. The cultural clashes behind these events have the potential to curb the mobility and security that tourism depends upon:

- Why are we still plagued by war and terrorism – are there any economic reasons for this?

7. The generation gap

An economic generation gap seems to be opening up in developed countries. Many older people enjoyed free university education, they own properties, have high incomes, paid holidays, have good pension schemes and are able to enjoy the very best that leisure and tourism has to offer. On the other hand, the younger generation faces difficulties in finding jobs, accommodation, financing education and accessing worthwhile pension schemes.

- Is an unsustainable economic generation gap opening up and what are the consequences for leisure and tourism?

8. Visible and invisible walls

In some countries, there is still explicit discrimination against groups of people on the grounds of gender, caste, sexual orientation, race and age. But even in countries which have equal opportunities legislation invisible walls and ceilings exits which prevent some groups from obtaining equal access. For example, when we examine the profiles of Chief Executive Officers and board members of major companies including those in leisure and tourism we find a strong imbalance:

- Can we defend the disproportionate representation of white males in positions of economic power?
- How can we promote equality of opportunity throughout the world?

It appears that in a free market we all have access to recreation, leisure and tourism:

- Why do some groups seem to suffer from social exclusion from these and other areas of life?

9. Beauty and the beast

We cannot fail to be moved by the natural beauty of planet and the universe that it is part of. As we develop the planet there are examples of the grace and beauty of human architecture and buildings. But there are many examples of deeply unattractive built environments, lacking soul, the human dimension or aesthetic qualities. Exhibit 18.3 illustrates one of many lists of ugly buildings.

- Why do we sometimes replace beauty with ugliness?
- Why do we give so little attention to aesthetics in planning?

10. Crime and violence

As economic growth increases crime seems to grow too. This is also observable as destinations attract more tourists. The fear and effects of crime can be profound:

- Have we properly understood the relationship between crime and the economy?
- Is tourism worth the increase in crime that accompanies it?

Exhibit 18.3 Awful architecture

The website travelindia-guide.com has produced a list of 10 famous buildings that are rated as ugly eyesores. They are:

1. Boston City Hall, Boston (US): dreary façade, bad fit with the surrounding architecture
2. Montparnasse Tower, Paris (France): size, functional design, visibility from rest of Paris
3. Luckyshoe Monument, Tuuri (Finland): kitsch
4. Metropolitan Cathedral, Liverpool (England): looks like a space capsule
5. Port Authority Bus Terminal, New York City (US): iron monstrosity, looks unfinished
6. Torres De colon, Madrid (Spain): overbearing effect on the city
7. Liechtenstein Museum of Fine Arts, Vaduz (Liechtenstein): angular, monolithic design
8. Scottish Parliament Building, Edinburgh, (Scotland): strange mix of stone, oak and bamboo textures
9. Birmingham Central Library, Birmingham (England): 'Brutalist' style
10. Peter The Great Statue, Moscow (Russia): overbearing height

Source: Adapted from www.travelindia-guide.com

11. Weapons or welfare?

The government collects taxes and spends them on our behalf:

- Are we happy with the amount of taxes raised?
- Are we happy with the way in which our money is spent on for example, education, health, defence, leisure and so on?

12. Unintended leisure

Leisure and tourism require holidays, weekends and spare time. Indeed many of those in work find themselves in the position of being money rich and time poor and so their ability to engage in leisure and tourism may be restricted. On the other hand, unemployment is rife in capitalist economies. The unemployed find themselves in the opposite position of being time rich and money poor so their ability to engage in leisure and tourism is also severely restricted.

- Why does capitalism generate unemployment?
- Why do we tolerate unemployment?
- What can be done to reduce unemployment?
- Why do we not find a more flexible and fair way of sharing out employment giving more time to the employed and work to the unemployed?

13. The selfish tourist

By definition tourists are affluent members of society. Tourists also benefit from free access to many parts of the world – other people's spaces – where the contrast between their own wealth and those of the hosts can be stark.

- Why do many tourists still insist on hard bargaining when the amount under dispute is of little relative value to themselves but of significant value to the host population?
- Why do tourists so easily forget about the harsh economic conditions in the countries they travel to when they return home and give so little back?

14. Human rights and wrongs

On 10 December 10 1948, the General Assembly of the United Nations adopted and proclaimed the Universal Declaration of Human Rights. These rights include the right to life, liberty and dignity, equal treatment, freedom to travel, freedom of thought and speech, the right to education, adequate living standards, property rights, fair employment, the right to leisure and participation of cultural life and duties to the community.

- Do any aspects of the pursuit of leisure and tourism infringe the human rights of others?
- Are we happy to allow child prostitution and sex tourism?

15. Connected yet lonely

Many of us live in a highly connected society with access to mobile phones, texts, e-mail and social networks. Yet there is evidence that people are sometimes living more solitary lives as communities and families break down and lifestyles become more fluid and transient. Capitalism makes society members more competitive, more individualistic, more acquisitive and less community oriented.

- How does leisure and tourism contribute to the making or breaking of communities?

16. Surveillance society

In leisure and tourism as in many other areas of life we are under more and more surveillance by governments and private companies. This includes:

- The widespread use of CCTV (closed circuit television) to monitor shops, airports, railways, beaches, hotels, etc.
- The collection and sharing of data between governments (e.g. passport details between origin and destination country governments).
- The collection, use and selling of data about our spending patterns – generally collected form loyalty cards or frequent flyer programmes or Internet retailers such as Amazon.
- The fishing of data for illegal purposes especially for identity and bank fraud.
- The collection of data from participation websites such as social network sites.

This gives rise to a number of questions:

- Why have we become a 'surveillance society'?
- What are the dangers of data collection and storage?
- Should we be protected from data collection and storage?
- How does surveillance affect us?

17. Mac-Disneyfication of experience

The spread of globalization, the tendency towards mergers and bigger units of production, the attraction of economies of scale, the power of the American dream and its ability to circulate the world are all factors leading to the MacDonaldization and Disneyfication of production. The former means that goods and services become more globally similar and standardized. The latter means that culture becomes commodified – that is sold and packaged into easily digestible consumer packets.

- What are the consequences of more standardization of leisure and tourism?
- Is the commodification of culture desirable?

18. Crises of capitalism

The global economic crisis of 2007–2008 demonstrated huge faults in parts of the economy. These included:

- the tendency for capitalism to create periods of unsustainable boom and bust
- an overexposure to risk
- a lack of ethical behaviour
- cowboy banking
- a disjunction between those responsible for the crisis and those who suffered its effects.

Indeed the major economies came close to catastrophic collapse as part of the banking crisis and each has suffered painful economic adjustment – especially in tax increases and rising unemployment.

- Are we all just passive players in the economy or should there be more active management of the economy?
- Are we happy that profits are often put before ethics?
- How is leisure and tourism contribute to the crisis?
- How is leisure and tourism affected by the crisis?
- Why did economists fail to predict the crisis?
- Is neoliberalism a good code by which to run society?

19. Fit or flabby?

A richer society, and one with many opportunities for leisure and tourism does not appear to be a healthier one:

- Why are so many people anxious/depressed and taking medicines to get by each day?

- Why are many children in advanced economies diagnosed with attention deficit disorder (ADT)?
- Are we happy to encourage cigarette smoking to cause terrifying death by lung cancer?
- Why are alcohol and drugs consumed to excess?
- Why is obesity such a problem in wealthy societies?

20. Blindness and apathy

Many of us live in a highly educated society. We have spent many years learning about ourselves and the world. We have passed exams which affirm our educated state. We have access to news stories, news pictures and the internet all of which can tell us about injustices in the world.

- If we can see injustice, if we are aware of it why do we often appear blind to it?
- Why do we do so little about it?
- Why do we carry on with our everyday lives ignoring injustice?

21. Human (un)happiness

Leisure and tourism are very much cantered on pleasure. But although we seem to grow richer each year it is not clear that we grow happier:

- Are governments over-obsessed by measures of GNP?
- Are we satisfied with our work/life balance?
- Why have we lost touch with the rhythms of time, seasons, weather and nature?
- Do we work too many hours?
- Has consumerism meant the loss of our spiritual dimension?
- What makes us happy?

PRACTICAL APPROACHES

This section examines some practical approaches to some of the issues outlined in the previous sector. In fact in some cases the issues have been covered in previous chapters. For example, the issues surrounding environmental economics have been discussed in Chapters 16 and 17. Similarly policies to discourage demerit goods (cigarettes) and encourage merit goods (fitness) were tackled in Chapter 7. Work/leisure issues were covered in Chapter 4.

Trade Unions

Trade Unions can act as powerful groups to protect the interest of workers. This is because they are able to provide collective bargaining which means that the power of the group is much greater than the power of individual members. So the main business of Trade Unions is to improve the working conditions, pay and pensions of its members. It may be argued that the growth of Trade Unions had an important effect in raising the living standards and working conditions of the proletariat so that the kind of revolutionary class conflict predicted by Marx failed to occur.

Exhibit 18.4 illustrates the aims and activities of the International Transport Workers' Federation (ITF). This is an international trade union federation of transport workers' unions meaning that its members are Transport Workers Unions worldwide. The ITF represents workers on cruise ships and ferries in the tourism sector.

Exhibit 18.4 The International Transport Workers' Federation

'The International Transport Workers' Federation (ITF) is an international trade union federation of transport workers' unions. Any independent trade union with members in the transport industry is eligible for membership of the ITF.

781 unions representing over 4,600,000 transport workers in 155 countries are members of the ITF. It is one of several Global Federation Unions allied with the International Trade Union Confederation (ITUC).

The ITF's headquarters is located in London and it has offices in Nairobi, Ouagadougou, Tokyo, New Delhi, Rio de Janeiro, Amman, Moscow and Brussels.

Objectives

The aims of the ITF are:

- to promote respect for trade union and human rights worldwide
- to work for peace based on social justice and economic progress
- to help its affiliated unions defend the interests of their members
- to provide research and information services to its affiliates
- to provide general assistance to transport workers in difficulty.

Although the range of ITF activities is very wide, they can be best summed up under three key headings:

- representation
- information
- practical solidarity.

The ITF represents the interests of transport workers' unions in bodies which take decisions affecting jobs, employment conditions or safety in the transport industry, such as the International Labour Organisation (ILO), the International Maritime Organisation (IMO) and the International Civil Aviation Organisation (ICAO).

Exhibit 18.4 **continued**

A major function of the ITF is informing and advising unions about developments in the transport industry in other countries or regions of the world. The ITF also maintains a specialist education department, dedicated to the development of strong and democratic transport unions.

The ITF organises international solidarity when transport unions in one country are in conflict with employers or government and need direct help from unions in other countries.

The kind of solidarity needed can range from

- protest messages
- demonstrations
- political pressure
- direct industrial action in the form of strikes
- boycotts etc.

The ITF's worldwide campaign in the maritime industry against the use by ship owners of Flags of Convenience (FOCs) to escape from national laws and national unions is a good example of solidarity.'

Source: The International Transport Workers' Federation http://www.itfglobal.org/about-us/index.cfm

Pressure groups

There are a number of pressure groups that exist to achieve particular aims in leisure, recreation and tourism and engage in broader campaigns which have relevance to these subjects. The point to remember about most of these pressure groups is that they are non-industry based. So they represent an independent voice.

Tourism Concern

The vision of Tourism Concern is 'A world free from exploitation in which all parties involved in tourism benefit equally and in which relationships between industry, tourists and host communities are based on trust and respect' and its mission is 'to ensure that tourism always benefits local people'. Tourism Concern has five key principles that govern its work:

1 '*Independence:* Tourism Concern is a non-industry based organization and strongly believes that its independence is vital to its role.

2 *Listening:* We ensure that we listen to the opinions and perspectives of our partners in destination communities. Our campaigns are often initiated when communities and organizations come to us with requests for help.

3 *Shared values and vision:* We strongly believe in working with organizations that share our values and vision and we strive to work towards common goals throughout the collaborative process.

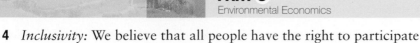

4 *Inclusivity:* We believe that all people have the right to participate in all decision-making that affects them both internally and in the work we do.

5 *Ethical practices:* We strive to adopt low impact "green" policies and practices and to purchase and promote fair trade products.'

Past and present campaigns organized by Tourism Concern have included:

- *Water equity:* to promote and protect the right to water of local communities in the face of increasing competition from the tourism industry.
- *Putting tourism to rights:* a campaign to end to human rights abuses in tourism.
- *Tsunami of tourism:* raising awareness around tourism issues and helping to build the capacity of tsunami-hit communities threatened with displacement and unsustainable developments.
- *Burma:* From 1998 to 2010 a tourism boycott to Burma was organized. It was argued that money earned from tourism helped to finance one of the most brutal military regimes in the world associated with severe human rights abuses linked to tourism developments.
- *Sun sea and sweatshops:* uncovered and publicized evidence of exploitative labour conditions and campaigned to force tour operators to make made improvements to labour conditions in the tourism industry.
- *Trekking wrongs:* to publicize and improve the conditions of works faced by porters supporting tourist groups on trekking trips.

Greenpeace

Greenpeace is a pressure group that is 'passionate about protecting the Earth – the only life support system we have'. It was started in 1971 by a small group of activists and now has a strong global presence. Its message is an urgent one:

> Now we are poised at a pivotal point in human history where even more must be done, and urgently, if life on Earth is to survive. What's needed now is a new map to steer by – nothing less than a radically new way of understanding and living in this world we call home.

The vision of Greenpeace is:

> to transform the world by fundamentally changing the way people think about it. We want governments, industry and each and every person to stop viewing the Earth as an inexhaustible resource and start treating it as something precious that needs our protection and careful management. We all need a planet that is ecologically healthy and able to nurture life in all its diversity.

Greenpeace tries to achieve desirable change through action which includes:

- investigating and exposing environmental abuse
- lobbying governments and decision-makers
- championing environmentally responsible and socially just solutions
- Taking nonviolent direct action.

Greenpeace does not accept donations from governments or corporations but relies on contributions from individual supporters and foundation grants. It does this to maintain its independence.

Greenpeace focusses on worldwide threats to biodiversity and the environment and its main campaigns seek to:

- Stop climate change
- Protect ancient forests
- Save the oceans
- Stop whaling
- Say no to genetic engineering
- Stop the nuclear threat
- Eliminate toxic chemicals
- Encourage sustainable trade.

Oxfam

One of the main aims of this charity and pressure group is the relief of poverty. To achieve this, it offers direct help to those in poverty, lobbies governments for change and organizes campaigns:

- It seeks to help people organize so that they might gain better access to the opportunities they need to improve their livelihoods and govern their own lives. It also works with people affected by humanitarian disasters, with preventive measures, preparedness, as well as emergency relief.
- It conducts high-level research and lobbying aiming to change international policies and practices in ways which would ensure that poor people have the rights, opportunities and resources they need to improve and control their lives.
- It instigates popular campaigning, alliance building and media work designed to raise awareness among the public of the real solutions to global poverty, to enable and motivate people to play an active part in the movement for change and to foster a sense of global citizenship.

The main areas that Oxfam is active in are:

- climate change
- conflict and natural disasters
- health
- education

- debt and aid
- gender equality
- the right to be heard
- trade
- private sector
- poverty
- global economic crisis.

An example of its campaigning was its NikeWatch Campaign:

> Ever wondered, as you slipped on your sneakers or pulled on a pair of jogging shorts, what life might be like for the person who made them? Nike promotes sport and healthy living, but the lives of workers who make Nike's shoes and clothes in Asia and Latin America are anything but healthy. They live in severe poverty and suffer stress and exhaustion from overwork. Oxfam Community Aid Abroad is part of an international campaign to persuade Nike and other transnational corporations to respect workers' basic rights (www.caa.org.au/campaigns/nike/).

However, we should be careful not to paint an overly negative picture of employment conditions in leisure and tourism. For example, Cukier (2002) conducted research that challenged the negative image of tourism employment that he argues has largely been derived from a developed country context and has not been based on empirical research within the tourism sector. His research is based on interviews conducted with 240 tourism workers in the coastal resort villages of Sanur and Kuta in Bali, Indonesia. The study examined the appropriateness of existing conceptions of tourism employment and determined empirically the degree to which these conceptions are appropriate to developing countries. He concluded that tourism employment is a generally positive phenomenon from the perspective of tourism employees. Tourism employment is accorded a relatively high status, provides many opportunities for women and migrant workers and is generally well remunerated, especially when compared to traditional employment options.

Intergovernmental organizations

Several intergovernmental organizations operate that have an impact on human development in leisure and tourism. These include:

- the UN Organization
- the UN World Tourism Organization
- the Intergovernmental Panel on Climate Change
- the International Labour Organization
- the United Nations Development Programme
- United Nations Children's Fund
- the World Bank.

An important initiative from the United Nations Organization was the Millennium Development Goals (MDGs). These were agreed in 2000, following a decade of preparatory discussions, when world leaders assembled at the United Nations Headquarters in New York. Here they agreed to adopt the United Nations Millennium Declaration which committed countries to a global programme to reduce extreme poverty and set out a series of milestones with a deadline of 2015. The MDGs are:

- end poverty and hunger
- universal education
- gender equality
- child health
- maternal health
- combat HIV/AIDS
- environmental sustainability
- global partnership.

The New Economics Foundation

The New Economic Foundation (NEF) is an independent think and do tank which exists to 'inspire and demonstrate real economic well-being'. Its strap line is 'economics as if people and the planet mattered'. It aims to improve quality of life by promoting innovative solutions that challenge mainstream thinking on economic, environment and social issues. Economic, social and environmental justice are central to its philosophy and it aims to put people and the planet first. NEF seeks to combine rigorous analysis and policy debate with practical solutions on the ground, often run and designed with the help of local people. The main ways in which NEF works are through:

- practical local projects and tools for change
- in-depth research
- campaigning
- policy discussion
- raising awareness through the media and publications
- incubation of new organizations and campaigns that can create long-term change in society.

The NEF is working on a number of projects where it feels that traditional economics has lost its way. These include:

- *'The Great Transition:* Finding ways to survive and thrive through financial crises, climate change and the peak and decline of global oil production.
- *Banking for the Great Transition:* Our new campaign to build a banking system that is fit for purpose.

- *Reimagine Your High Street:* Fight clone towns with Reimagine Your High Street – a new project helping communities protect, enhance and benefit from the places that matter to them.
- *National Accounts of Well-being:* The first comprehensive international analysis of well-being provides an alternative measure of national progress to GDP (see next section).
- *A new economic model:* The pursuit of growth has failed on its own terms, and for people and the planet. We are working on a new way to structure the economy.'

The HPI and gross national happiness

The NEF also supports the development of the HPI. The rationale behind the HPI project is that our central measures of progress continue to be the narrow economic indicators of GDP. But this measure misses the rich possibilities of human development as well as many of the environmental and social costs of growth. The HPI seeks to put human happiness and ecological sustainability at the heart of its measurement of success and development. It does this by measuring three key indicators:

1 ecological footprint
2 life-satisfaction
3 life expectancy.

Bhutan also demonstrates a radical and human-centred approach to measuring progress. Its king, Jigme Singye Wangchuck, has declared a commitment to advance Bhutan's culture based on Buddhist spiritual values. As a result of this it has developed GNH an alternative measure to GDP. GNH measures Gross National Happiness and defines the quality of life in more holistic and psychological terms than GDP.

The four pillars of GNH are:

1 the promotion of equitable and sustainable socioeconomic development
2 preservation and promotion of cultural values
3 conservation of the natural environment
4 establishment of good governance.

Free trade/fair trade

Chapter 14 discussed the theoretical arguments for free trade and the GATS agreement. However, as well as bringing lower consumer prices, more choice and greater economic efficiency, free trade also has key drawbacks. In particular, there appears to be an imbalance of power and trading terms between rich and poor countries. Exhibit 18.5 offers a critique from Tourism Concern of aspects of GATS.

Exhibit 18.5 The downside of GATS

There is evidence that GATS may promote the interests of companies over people and the environment. GATS and the corporate globalization it promotes, does not necessarily support sustainable development. Many countries have made commitments to liberalize tourism under GATS, but few are able to retain powers to restrict developments that threaten eco-systems and local communities.

There are various obligations under the GATS. One called 'most favoured nation' means that companies can always set up tourism businesses in countries signed up to GATS. Another obligation – termed 'national treatment' – means that foreign businesses must be treated in the same way as domestic businesses.

Consequently, host governments, cannot compel tourism transnationals to employ local labour or use local materials and products instead of importing them. This prevents destinations from optimizing local economic benefits. Nor will governments be able to implement special measures to secure a competitive base for domestic businesses against foreign investment.

On paper the purpose of these commitments is to ensure a transparent and anti-discriminatory 'level playing field'. They should also help companies benefit from liberalized trade in other countries. Having such 'reciprocal rights' is particularly important for Southern countries wanting to gain market access in Northern countries. However, in a very unequal world, this may benefit some rather than all.

GATS could definitely pose problems for destinations with a large proportion of small or underdeveloped businesses, with a lot of informal sector tourism businesses, or with poor technological and capital resources. If countries also have weak, political and democratic governance which prevents poor communities from gaining access to national and international markets, the implications for ordinary people involved in tourism are also negative.

Far from reducing poverty, liberalization under GATS has meant Southern countries are bracing themselves for an onslaught of foreign investment in the form of takeovers and acquisitions within their newly budding tourism industries. Northern countries are, however, not reciprocating equally by opening up their markets to the service exports of Southern countries. This is particularly the case in relation to labour under the mode of 'supply of natural persons'. Barriers to a two-way flow of labour include restrictive immigration rules in developed nations. Other barriers include licensing, technical standards setting and grant subsidies for the domestic sectors in tourism for Southern countries.

GATS entails no specific obligation on companies to trade in host countries according to internationally agreed conventions on environmental sustainability and human rights, including labour rights. Consequently, governments could face real difficulties in trying to limit negative environmental, social and cultural impacts in their country. These include trying to restrict the mushrooming of foreign-owned developments including all-inclusive hotels, which are often highly controversial amongst local people because they contribute so little to the local economy. Governments also face difficulties in making the employment of local workers or the use of local products and materials a condition of foreign investment. It could also render a government powerless to stop tourism development on indigenous land and sacred sites, in response to community protests. If host governments attempted to control foreign investment in any way, once they had committed to GATS they could be legally challenged by investing companies under the dispute settlement procedure within the WTO.

Source: Fair Trade in Tourism, the bulletin of Tourism Concern's Fair Trade in Tourism Network, Issue 3.

It is because of concerns of Free Trade on the interests of poorer countries that the Fair Trade lobby has arisen.

The key principles of Fair Trade (Fair Trade Federation, 2003) include:

- *Creating opportunities for economically disadvantaged producers*: At the heart of Fair Trade is the aim of poverty alleviation and sustainable development. It lays a particular emphasis on creating opportunities for workers and suppliers who have been economically disadvantaged or marginalized by the conventional trading system.
- *Gender equity*: Another key principle is to ensure that women's work is properly valued and rewarded. The aim of Free Trade is to ensure that women are always paid for their contribution to the production process and are empowered in their organizations.
- *Transparency and accountability*: Fair Trade advocates transparent management and commercial relations so that trading partners and customers are fully aware of the way in which the business works.
- *Capacity building*: Fair Trade aims to develop producer independence and growth in similar organizations. This can be achieved by assistance in developing management skills, improved access to markets and financial and technical expertise.
- *Payment of a fair price*: This is at the heart of Fair Trade. A fair price is one that has been agreed through dialogue and participation and is set in the regional or local context. It should cover production costs but additionally enable production that is socially just and environmentally sound. It includes the principle of equal pay for equal work by women and men and prompt payment by trading partners.
- *Working conditions*: Fair Trade entails ensuring a safe and healthy working environment. Where children are part of the labour force the principles of the UN Convention on the Rights of the Child are adhered to.
- *Environmental sustainability*: Fair Trade encourages producers to engage in production practices that manage and use local resources sustainably.

Pro-poor tourism

Ashley et al. (2000) note that:

> In the tourism sector, national governments and donors have generally aimed to promote private sector investment, macro-economic growth and foreign exchange earnings, without specifically taking the needs and opportunities of the poor into account in tourism development.

They make the additional point that:

> Donor-supported tourism master plans focus on creating infrastructure, stimulating private investment and attracting international tourists. Investors are often international companies and local élites, whose profits are generally repatriated abroad or to metropolitan centres. Links with the local economy are often weak, with the possible exception of employment.

This view is supported by various case studies including that of Mvula (2001) who reports on the impacts of wildlife tourism to South Luangwa National Park, Zambia on the rural local communities that reside there. She assesses local people's attitude towards tourism in the area and solicits their views on how the benefits to the community could be increased. Her findings show that the community want more involvement with tourism and tourists. She indicates, however, that the benefits of tourism currently reach few local people and that in some instances inequality and discrimination are evident in the employment practice of the local tourism industry. Mvula points to community tourism based on cultural heritage as a potential way of maximizing the benefits of tourism to communities, while minimizing the impacts.

 These observations have given rise to the concept of pro-poor tourism (PPT). PPT is tourism that results in increased net benefits for poor people. PPT is not a specific product or niche sector but rather it is an approach to developing and managing tourism and its aim is to enhance the linkages between tourism businesses and poor people. In this way tourism's contribution to poverty reduction can be increased and poor people can be empowered to participate more effectively in the development and provision of tourism products. There are a variety of links with different types of 'the poor' that need to be considered. These include staff, neighbouring communities, landholders, producers of food, fuel and other suppliers, operators of micro-tourism businesses, craft-makers, other users of tourism infrastructure (roads) and resources (water), etc. PPT strategies are various and can range from increasing local employment to building mechanisms for consultation. The critical success factor in PPT is not the type of company or the type of tourism, but that an increase in the net benefits that go to poor people can be demonstrated. By net benefits is meant the surplus of gains over the costs of tourism to the target 'poor' population.

The SNV-Nepal project is a good example of PPT in action and provides a good example of the import substitution process – whereby the goods and services required by the tourism industry are encouraged to be produced and supplied locally rather than from Kathmandu. In this project, the Dutch Development Agency SNV, works through its District Partners Programme (DPP) with district and village development committees, NGOs and the private sector to 'benefit women and disadvantaged groups at village level' in the remote Humla district of north-west Nepal.

The focus of the project is at the local level – on specific enterprises and communities along a trekking trail. The emphasis of the PPT strategy is on local mobilization through the development of community-based organizations and business planning and training designed to enable the poor to develop micro-enterprises and to take up employment opportunities. The outcomes of the project include:

- the development of micro-enterprise plans, of which 32 have been approved;
- plans to develop hot springs and village tours;
- plans for a multiple use Visitors Centre to provide a focal point for the local provision of tourism services such as portering, mules, horses, etc. and produce, such as vegetables, to trekking agents and tourists;
- construction of toilets along the trekking trail;
- a US$2 per tourist trail maintenance tax;
- an understanding of the challenges of breaking into the existing well-established and connected tourism elite.

ENDNOTE: MARKETS, ETHICS, POWER AND PARTICIPATION

It should be clear that the study of economics does not include any real analysis of power or ethics in society. The study of positive economics implies a quite passive analysis of how the economy works. Power is seen as something neutral and a study of positive economics only describes power in economics in terms of what causes market changes. So where does power lie in the economic world? Clearly, it lies mainly with those who have highest incomes, accumulated capital and healthy profit. For it is this spending power which dictates the answers to those questions posed at the beginning of this book:

- What to produce?
- How to produce it?
- Where to produce it?
- Who is it produced for?

It is therefore equally clear that those with low incomes and no accumulated capital have very little influence in determining how these basic economic questions will be answered.

At the same time it can be seen that economics does not necessarily deliver solutions that are ethically sound. Ethics is concerned with our values – and our distinctions between good and bad. What this chapter has attempted to show is that the ends that result from economic activity (i.e. the outcomes of the playing out of economic forces) may not be the ones that we would choose from an ethical perspective. For when we examine the outcomes of:

- What has been produced?
- How it has been produced?
- Where it has been produced?
- Who has benefited from production?

We may well feel that from an ethical point of view these outcomes are not always appropriate. Hence our list of 21 substantive paradoxes.

And so it seems appropriate to end this book on a power/political/ personal note. On the one hand, we may not mind about the outcomes of economic activity and just accept them as inevitable. Or we might agree that economic outcomes are the best that we can have. But if we have a vision of alternative, of better ends of economic activity, then we must intervene to initiate change. And we can do that at many levels:

- We all have some power at the individual level and here we may change our own consumption patterns. We can effectively withhold our money votes from economic outputs we disapprove of and vote for those we favour.
- At the individual level we can also make our ethical views known by joining Internet groups and discussion boards. We can influence our friends by discussion and argument.
- We can also lever up our individual power by grouping with other people. This can mean contributing to or joining a pressure group that campaigns on an issue we support.
- Or it may mean supporting or joining a broader political party.
- At the very least it must mean exercising our right to vote where we have one.

REVIEW OF KEY TERMS

- Positive economics: deals with facts.
- Normative economics: includes values and opinions.
- Marxian analysis: conflict of interest between owners of property [the bourgeoisie] who do no work and workers [the proletariat] who own no property.

- *The Real World Economic Outlook's* critique: globalization brings problems of debt and deflation.
- Ricardo: expounded theory of the benefits of Free Trade.
- Fair Trade: payment of a fair price for traded goods and services.
- PPT: tourism that results in increased net benefits for poor people.

 Data Questions

Task 18.1 **The German Ideology**

The ideas of the *ruling class* are in every epoch *the ruling ideas*, that is the class which is the *ruling material force* of society, is at the same time its *ruling intellectual force*. The class which has the means of material production at its disposal has control at the same time over the means of material production, so that thereby, generally speaking, the ideas of those who lack the means of material production are subject to it.

Source: From Marx and Engels The German Ideology.

Recap Questions

1 What is meant by the terms in italics?
2 What did Marx and Engels mean by this statement?
3 To what extent is this statement true today?

Task 18.2 **Journal article: Tribe, J. 2007. Tourism: a critical business.** *Journal of Travel Research*, **245–255.**

The following are key extracts from this article:

Critical research can play an important part in extending, supplementing and challenging the dominant discourses that pervade the management and governance of tourism. It can question taken-for-granted recipes and responses and lead to a deeper engagement with aims and ends. It can illuminate tourism's blind spots.

Higgins-Desbiolles (2005) offers two examples of critical research:

- First she 'offers a critical polemic focusing on terrorism and tourism ... [referring to] "Hostile Meeting Grounds." She states "No one seems to ask why there is terrorism, and if a war against terrorism will solve any problems at all." Justice and justice alone will bring peace ... as long as the world is asymmetrical, there will be no peace (p. 5).'
- She also 'provides an alternative system of analytical binaries, which include wretched/rich, and world as playground/world as home and workplace. These binaries serve to demonstrate basic asymmetries in the tourism system leading Higgins-Desbiolles to conclude that Tourism must serve the "wretched" as well as the "rich" if it is to continue to enjoy the open access it has been given to the world's resources and the faith that has been instilled in it for improving the lives of people (p. 29).'

Task 18.2 **continued**

'If we look to the key issues that are likely to affect the tourism industry into the future, they fall into two categories. On the one hand, there are issues such as the changing nature of tourists (often referred to as new tourists or post-tourists); the rapid pace of change in information and communication technologies; destination competitiveness; the rise of China as a tourism generating and receiving country; new business models; and tourism satellite accounts. On the other hand, there are issues such as sustainability (in environmental terms, including global warming and tourism's contribution to it via the carbon emissions of air travel, and in terms of the very survival of tourism); terrorism and peace; globalization and community tourism; ethical tourism and social exclusion; equity; and poverty elimination. The successful management of the first group of issues will generally call on research of a technical nature, which must typically be undertaken using positivist methods. The second group of issues also generates some technical research issues (e.g., measurement of air emissions and tourism multipliers).'

'But an important distinction between each group of issues is their relationship to power. Current configurations of power structures and the operation of the free market will generally assist in the delivery of better management for the first set of issues. However, progress for the second set of issues can often be inhibited by current configurations of power and the operation of dominant ideological practices. For example, Rowe (2005) argues that an ideological deployment of culture and tourism can hide the need for more profound structural remedies to social and economic problems. Here, critical research is uniquely placed to contribute to better management and governance of tourism. For ideology and power relations and particularly those that are well disguised and taken for granted, are a key focus for critical tourism research. If we are to make genuine and deep progress in sustainable tourism in both its environmental and survival senses, there is an urgent need to understand the operation of ideology and power as a prelude to better management and governance.'

If we ignore the deep asymmetries and paradoxes that are evident in tourism this will be 'sure to lead to tourism's alienation and catastrophic demise long before any serious effects of global warming come into play'.

References

Higgins-Desbiolles, F. 2005. Encounters Between the Wretched of the Earth and the Tourist. Ecumenical Coalition on Tourism, China.
Rowe, D. 2005. Some critical reflections on research and consultancy in cultural tourism planning. Tourism Culture and Communication 5 (3), 127–37.

Recap Questions

1 Why should tourism be a critical business?
2 In what ways does conventional economics lack a critical dimension?
3 Explain some of the major asymmetries of leisure and tourism and why these are significant.
4 Why does Tribe distinguish between two categories of issues that affect leisure and tourism?
5 Explain the relevance of power and ideology to solving some key issues in leisure and tourism.

6 What does Tribe mean when he states that we might reach 'tourism's alienation and catastrophic demise long before any serious effects of global warming come into play?'

Task 18.3 Journal article: Tribe, J. 2002. Education for responsible tourism action. *Journal of Sustainable Tourism* 10 (4), 309–24.

We need more than just rules for ethical tourism. Rules are often ignored or flouted according to expediency. They do not necessarily result in improved outcomes. Therefore this article is concerned with two main themes. First, it is about ethical tourism action. The term action is deliberately used to locate the discussion in contrast to the discourse that is mainly about reflection. The reflective discourse around ethical tourism has attracted criticism as 'promise without practice'. Indeed it was well over a decade ago when Krippendorf cautioned that:

> ...the 'thinkers' who sit in their studies are political lightweights. Their recommendations will remain politically anaemic theories as long as there is no pressure on the politicians from the general public – both tourists and their hosts... What we need then are rebellious tourists and rebellious locals. (1987: 107)

The second theme of the article is education and students. What is sought is not necessarily rebellious students but students who act in the tourism world – whether as tourists, or tourism professionals or political activists – with a strong and developed sense of critical knowing. This is a knowing not just of the narrow professional competence that may be characterized as vocationalism but which extends to an ethical competence. Action thus informed is designed to promote change for the promotion of a better tourism society and world.

Recap Questions

1 What is ethical tourism and what might be its typical features?
2 How might ethical tourism differ from current tourism products?
3 Why is there a difference between ethical tourism and actual tourism?
4 To what extent does the study of economics help us to understand ethical tourism?
5 In what ways can we promote ethical tourism?

MULTIPLE CHOICE

1 Which of the following is a criticism of Paul Omerod of orthodox economics?

(a) It is trapped in an idealized, mechanistic view of the world.

(b) It explains differences in wages.

(c) It explains the benefits of Free Trade.

(d) It deals in values.

2 Which of the following is not part of Marxian analysis?
  (a) History can be seen as a series of class struggles.
  (b) There is basic conflict between the bourgeoisie and the proletariat.
  (c) The victory of the proletariat over the bourgeoisie is inevitable.
  (d) International trade brings gains to all its participants.

3 Which of these is not a feature of the GATS agreement on Free Trade?
  (a) Signatories of the agreement are free to impose import duties.
  (b) Foreign-owned companies must have free access to domestic markets.
  (c) Concessions granted to any one country must also be made available to all other signatories of the agreement.
  (d) Foreign investors must be treated on an equal basis with domestic investors.

4 Which of the following is not a feature of Fair Trade?
  (a) Gender equity.
  (b) Payment of a fair price.
  (c) A safe and healthy working environment.
  (d) Guaranteed quality of goods traded.

5 In a free market economy what is produced is determined by:
  (a) Ethical considerations.
  (b) Fairness.
  (c) Purchasing power.
  (d) Human needs.

REVIEW QUESTIONS

1 What is orthodox economics?

2 How does the economics of the New Economics Foundation differ from that of orthodox economics?

3 What are the key points in Marx's analysis of capitalism?

4 Why did Marx's prediction of a proletariat revolution not materialize?

5 How does Fair Trade differ from Free Trade – what are its advantages and disadvantages?

6 How could consumers and producers ensure that their tourism is pro-poor?

7 What are your personal points of satisfaction and dissatisfaction with the recreation, leisure and tourism opportunities offered by the market economy?

Websites of interest

Greenpeace: www.greenpeace.org

Pro-poor Tourism: www.propoortourism.org.uk

Tourism Concern: www.tourismconcern.org.uk

Oxfam: www.oxfam.org.uk

Fair Trade Federation: www.fairtradefederation.com

New Economics Foundation: www.neweconomics.org

Happy Planet Index: www.happyplanetindex.org

The United Nations Organization: www.un.org

Bibliography

Abdallah, S., Thompson, S., Michaelson, J., Marks, N., & Steuer, N. (2009). *The (UN)Happy Planet Index 2.0*. London: New Economics Foundation.

ABS. (2009). *Tourism Satellite Account 2007–2008*. Canberra: Australian Bureau of Statistics.

Aguiar, M., & Hurst, E. (2007). Measuring trends in leisure: The allocation of time over five decades. *Quarterly Journal of Economics, 122*, 969–1006.

Aguiló, E., Alegre, J., & Sard, M. (2003). Examining the market structure of the German and UK tour operating industries through an analysis of package holiday prices. *Tourism Economics, 9*(3), 255–278.

Aksu, A., & Tarcan, E. (2002). The Internet and five-star hotels: A case study from the Antalya region in Turkey. *International Journal of Contemporary Hospitality Management, 14*(2), 94–97.

Andersson, T. D., & Getz, D. (2009). Tourism as a mixed industry: Differences between private, public and not-for-profit festivals. *Tourism Management, 30*, 847–856.

Araña, J. E., & Leon, C. J. (2008). The impact of terrorism on tourism demand. *Annals of Tourism Research, 35*, 299–315.

Archer, B. (1996). Economic impact analysis. *Annals of Tourism Research, 23*(3), 704–707.

Archer, B., & Fletcher, J. (1996). The economic impact of tourism in the Seychelles. *Annals of Tourism Research, 23*(1), 32–47.

Archer, B. H. (1982,). The value of multipliers and their policy implications. *Tourism Management, 3*(4), 236–241.

Archer, B. H. (1984). Economic impact: Misleading multipliers. *Annals of Tourism Research, 11*, 517–518.

Archer, B. H. (1995). Importance of tourism for the economy of Bermuda. *Annals of Tourism Research, 22*, 918–930.

Archer, B. H., & Owen, C. A. (1971). Toward a tourist regional multiplier. *Regional Studies, 5*(4), 289–294.

Ashley, C. (2000). *The impacts of tourism on rural livelihoods: Experience in Namibia*. ODI Working Paper No. 128.

Ashley, C., & Roe, D. (1998). *Enhancing community involvement in wildlife tourism: Issues and challenge*. Wildlife and Development Series No. 11. London: IIED.

Ashley, C., Boyd, C., & Goodwin, H. (2000). *Pro-poor tourism: Putting poverty at the heart of the tourism agenda*. Natural Resource Perspectives. London: ODI.

Ashworth, G. J., & Dietvorst, A. G. J. (Eds.). (1995). *Tourism and spatial transformations: Implications for policy and planning*. Wallingford: CAB International.

Ashworth, G. J., & Voogd, H. (1990). *Selling the city*. Chichester: Wiley.

Balaguer, J., & Cantavella-Jordá, M. (2002). Tourism as a long-run economic growth factor: The Spanish case. *Applied Economics, 34*(7), 877–884.

Barke, M., Towner, J., & Newton, M. (Eds.). (1995). *Tourism in Spain*. Wallingford: CAB International.

Becken, S. (2011). A critical review of tourism and oil. *Annals of Tourism Research*, (in press).

Becken, S., & Hay, J. E. (2007). *Tourism and climate change: Risks and opportunities*. Bristol: Multilingual Matters Ltd.

Begg, D., Fischer, S., & Dornbusch, R. (2002). *Economics* (7th ed.). Europe: McGraw-Hill Education.

Benckendorff, P., Moscardo, G., & Pendergast, D. (2010). *Tourism and generation Y*. Wallingford: CAB International.

Bergstrom, J. A., Cordell, H. A., Ashley, G. A., & Watson, A. A. (1990). Economic impacts of recreational spending on rural areas: A case study. *Economic Development Quarterly*, 4(1), 29–39.

Berrittella, M., Bigano, A., Roson, R., & Tol, R. S. J. (2006). A general equilibrium analysis of climate change impacts on tourism. *Tourism Management*, 27, 913–924.

Blake, A., & Sinclair, M. T. (2003). Tourism crisis management: US response to September 11. *Annals of Tourism Research*, 30, 813–832.

Blazević, B., & Jelusić, A. (2002). Croatian balance of payment and tourism. *Tourism and Hospitality Management*, 8(1/2), 127–142.

Boakye, K. A. (2010). Studying tourists' suitability as crime targets. *Annals of Tourism Research*, 37, 727–743.

Bouchet, P. (2002). A new consumer trend amongst the elderly: High-end tourism. *Loisir et Societe*, 25(2), 377–396.

Bourdieu, P. (1984). *Distinction: A social critique of the judgement of taste*. London: Routledge and Kegan Paul.

Boviard, A., Tricker, M., & Stoakes, R. (1984). *Recreation management and pricing*. London: Gower.

Bramham, P., Henry, I., Mommaas, H., & Van der Poel, H. (1993). *Leisure policies in Europe*. Wallingford: CAB International.

Braun, B., & Soskin, M. (1999). Theme park competitive strategies. *Annals of Tourism Research*, 26(2), 438–442.

Briguglio, L., Archer, B., Jafari, J., & Wall, G. (Eds.). (1996). *Sustainable tourism in islands and small states: Issues and policies*. London: Pinter.

Briguglio, L., Butler, R., Harrison, D., & Filho, W. (Eds.). (1996). *Sustainable tourism in islands and small states: Case studies*. London: Pinter.

Brooker, M. (2002). How to raise finance for the small hotel enterprise – a way forward. *Hospitality Review*, 4(1), 13–20.

Brown, F. (1998). *Tourism: Blight or blessing?* Oxford: Butterworth-Heinemann.

Bryman, A. (1995). *Disney and his worlds*. London: Routledge.

Buckley, R. (2002). Tourism ecolabels. *Annals of Tourism Research*, 29(1), 183–208.

Buhalis, D. (2003). *eTourism: Information technology for strategic tourism management*. Harlow: Prentice-Hall.

Buhalis, D., & Law, R. (2008). Progress in information technology and tourism management: 20 years on and 10 years after the internet – The state of eTourism research. *Tourism Management*, 29, 609–623.

Buhalis, D., & Zoge, M. (2007). The strategic impact of the Internet on the tourism industry: *Information and communication technologies in tourism 2007*. In M. Sigala, Mich., L., & Murphy, J. (Eds.), *proceedings of the international conference in Ljubljana, Slovenia*, 2007. Berlin: Springer Verlag. pp. 481–492.

Bull, A. (1995). *The economics of travel and tourism*. Harlow: Longman.

Burns, P. (1998). From Communist to common-weal: Reflections on tourism training in Romania. *Tourism Recreation Research*, 23(2), 45–52.

Burns, P., & Holden, A. (1995). *Tourism: A new perspective*. Hemel Hempstead: Prentice-Hall.

Butler, R., Hall, R., & Jenkins, M. (Eds.). (1998). *Tourism and recreation in rural areas*. Chichester: Wiley.

Canina, L. (2001). Acquisitions in the lodging industry: Good news for buyers and sellers. *Cornell Hotel and Restaurant Administration Quarterly, 42*(6), 47–54.

Canina, L., Walsh, K., & Enz, C. (2003). The effects of gasoline-price changes on room demand: A study of branded hotels from 1988 through 2000. *Cornell Hotel and Restaurant Administration Quarterly, 44*(4), 29–37.

Carney, D. (Ed.). (1998). *Sustainable rural livelihoods: What contribution can we make?* London: DFID.

Casellas, A., & Pallares-Barbera, M. (2009). Public-sector intervention in embodying the new economy in inner urban areas: The Barcelona experience. *Urban Studies, 46*, 1137.

Cater, E., & Lowman, G. (1994). *Ecotourism: A sustainable option*. Chichester: Wiley.

Coalter, F. (1998). Leisure studies, leisure policy and social citizenship: The failure of welfare or the limits of welfare? *Leisure Studies, 17*(1), 21–36.

Coccossis, H., & Nijkamp, P. (Eds.). (1995). *Sustainable tourism development*. London: Ashgate.

Commonwealth of Australia. (2003). *Tourism white paper*. Canberra: Department of Communications.

Conlin, M., & Baum, T. (Eds.). (1995). *Island tourism: Management principles and practice*. London: Wiley.

Cooke, A. (1994). *The economics of leisure and sport*. London: ITBP.

Cooper, C., & Wanhill, S. (Eds.). (1997). *Tourism development: Environmental and community issues*. Chichester: Wiley.

Croall, J. (1995). *Preserve or destroy? Tourism and the environment*. London: Calouste Gulbenkian Foundation.

Cukier, J. (2002). Tourism employment issues in developing countries: Examples from Indonesia. In R. Sharpley & D. Telfer (Eds.), *Tourism and development: Concepts and issues*. Clevedon: Channel View Publications.

Cullen, P. (1997). *Economics for hospitality management*. London: ITBP.

Curtis, I. (2002). Environmentally sustainable tourism: A case for carbon trading at Northern Queensland hotels and resorts. *Australian Journal of Environmental Management, 9*(1), 27–36.

Cushman, G., Veal, A. A., & Zuzanek, J. (Eds.). (1996). *World leisure participation: Free time in the global village*. Wallingford: CAB International.

Dardis, R., Soberon Ferrere, H., & Patro, D. (1994). Analysis of leisure expenditures in the United States. *Journal of Leisure Research, 25*(4), 309–321.

Davidson, R. (1994). *Business travel*. Harlow: Longman.

Davidson, R. (1998). *Tourism in Europe* (2nd ed.). Harlow: Longman.

Davidson, R., & Maitland, R. (1997). *Tourism destinations*. London: Hodder and Stoughton.

Dawson, S., Blahna, D., & Keith, J. (1993). Expected and actual regional economic impacts of Great Basin National Park. *Journal of Park and Recreation Administration, 11*(1), 45–57.

De Clerck, P., & Klingers, J. (1997). The right price for air travel? *Tourism in Focus, 25*.

Deegan, J., & Dineen, D. A. (1997). *Tourism policy and performance: The Irish experience*. London: ITBP.

Deloitte and Oxford Economics. (2010). *The economic contribution of the visitor economy: UK and the nations*. London: Visit Britain.

Deloitte and Touche, IIED and ODI. (1999). *Sustainable tourism and poverty elimination study*. A Report to DFID, UK.

Department of the Environment. (1990). *Tourism and the inner city*. London: DOE.

Diamantis, D., & Fayed, H. (2002). The general agreement on trade in services (GATS) and its impact on tourism. *Travel and Tourism Analyst*, *3*, 87–99.

Dickinson, B., & Vladimir, A. (1996). *Selling the sea: An inside look at the cruise industry*. Chichester: Wiley.

Doganis, R. (1991). *Flying off course: The economics of International Airlines*. London: Routledge.

Doganis, R. (1992). *The airport business*. London: Routledge.

Dumazedier, J. (1967). *Toward a society of leisure*. London: Macmillan.

Dwyer, L., Forsyth, P., & Prasada, R. (2002). Destination price competitiveness: Exchange rate changes versus domestic inflation. *Journal of Travel Research*, *40*(3), 328–336.

Eadington, W. R., & Redman, M. (1991). Economics and tourism. *Annals of Tourism Research*, *18*, 41–56.

Eaton, B. (1996). *European leisure business: Strategies for the future*. Cambridge: Elm Publications.

Eckard, E. (2001). The origin of the reserve clause: Owner collusion versus 'public interest'. *Journal of Sports Economics*, *2*(2), 113–130.

Edgecombe, S. (2003). Leisure provision as a public good and the need for another bottom line. *Australian Parks and Leisure*, *6*(1), 22–23.

Elliot, J. (1997). *Tourism: Politics and public sector management*. London: Routledge.

English, D. B. K., & Bergstrom, J. C. (1994). The conceptual links between recreation site development and regional economic impacts. *Journal of Regional Science*, *34*(4), 599–611.

Fair Trade Federation. (2003). *Report on fair trade trends in US, Canada and the Pacific Rim*. Washington, DC: Fair Trade Federation.

Fayed, H., & Westlake, J. (2002). Globalization of air transport: The challenges of the GATS. *Tourism Economics*, *8*(4), 431–455.

Fleming, W. R., & Toepper, L. (1990). Economic impact studies: Relating the positive and negative impacts to tourism development. *Journal of Travel Research*, *29*(1), 35–42.

Fletcher, J. E. (1989). Input–output analysis and tourism impact studies. *Annals of Tourism Research*, *16*, 514–529.

FNNPE (The Federation of Nature and National Parks of Europe). (1993). *Loving them to death?* Grafenau, Germany: FNNPE.

Forsyth, P., & Dwyer, L. (2003). Foreign investment in Australian tourism: A framework for analysis. *Journal of Tourism Studies*, *14*(1), 67–77.

France, L. (Ed.). (1997). *Earthscan reader in sustainable tourism*. London: Earthscan.

Frechtling, D. (2001). *Forecasting tourism demand*. Oxford: Butterworth-Heinemann.

Frechtling, D. C. (2010). The tourism satellite account: A primer. *Annals of Tourism Research*, *37*, 136–153.

Fredman, P., & Heberlein, T. (2003). Changes in skiing and snowmobiling in Swedish mountains. *Annals of Tourism Research*, *30*(2), 485–488.

Friedman, T. (1999). *The lexus and the olive tree*. New York: Anchor Books/ Doubleday.

Gee, C. Y. (Ed.). (1997). *International tourism: A global perspective*. Madrid: World Tourism Organisation.

Gee, C. Y., Makens, J. C., & Choy, D. J. L. (1997). *The travel industry*. New York: Van Nostrand Reinhold.

Gielen, D., Kurihara, R., & Moriguchi, Y. (2002). The environmental impacts of Japanese tourism and leisure. *Journal of Environmental Assessment Policy and Management*, *4*(4), 397–424.

Glover, P., & Prideaux, B. (2009). Implications of population ageing for the development of tourism products and destinations. *Journal of Vacation Marketing*, *15*, 25.

Glyptis, S. (Ed.). (1993). *Leisure and the environment: Essays in honour of professor J. A. Patmore*. London: Belhaven Press.

Go, F. M., & Pine, R. (1995). *Globalization strategy in the hotel industry*. London: Routledge.

Goffele, P. (2000). Hedonic pricing of agriculture and forestry externalities. *Environmental and Resource Economics*, *15*(4), 397–401.

Goodwin, H. J., Kent, I., Parker, K., & Walpole, M. (1997). *Tourism, conservation and sustainable development*. Final report to the Department for International Development.

Grant, B. (2002). Over 65 and ready to play. *Australian Leisure Management*, *35*, 36–38.

Gratton, C., & Kokolakakis, T. (2003). A bright future. *Leisure Management*, *14*(9), 38–40.

Gratton, C., & Taylor, P. (2000). *Economics of sport and recreation*. London: E & FN Spon.

Hall, C. M. (1994). *Tourism and politics: Policy, power and place*. Chichester: Wiley.

Hall, C. M. (1997). *Tourism in the Pacific Rim: Development impacts and markets* (2nd ed.). Harlow: Longman.

Hall, C. M., & Jenkins, J. M. (1995). *Tourism and public policy*. London: ITBP.

Hall, C. M., & Lew, A. (Eds.). (1998). *Sustainable tourism: A geographical perspective*. London: Addison Wesley.

Hall, C. M., & Page, S. J. (1996). *Tourism in the Pacific: Issues and cases*. London: ITBP.

Hall, M. (Ed.). (1998). *Sustainable tourism: A geographical perspective*. Harlow: Longman.

Hamzaee, R., & Vasigh, B. (1997). An applied model of airline revenue management. *Journal of Travel Research*, *35*(4), 64–68.

Hanlon, P. (1996). *Global airlines: Competition in a transnational industry*. Oxford: Butterworth-Heinemann.

Hardin, G. (1968). The tragedy of the commons. *Science*, *162*, 1243.

Harris, R., & Leiper, N. (Eds.). (1995). *Sustainable tourism: An Australian perspective*. Oxford: Butterworth-Heinemann.

Harris, R., Heath, N., Toepper, L., & Williams, P. (1998). *Sustainable tourism: A global perspective*. Oxford: Butterworth-Heinemann.

Harrison, D. (Ed.). (1992). *Tourism and the less developed countries*. Chichester: Wiley.

Harrison, L. C., & Husbands, W. (Eds.). (1996). *Practising responsible tourism*. Chichester: Wiley.

Havitz, M., & Adkins, K. (2002). Demarketing leisure services: The case of municipal golf courses. *Journal of Park and Recreation Administration*, *20*(2), 90–110.

Haywood, L., & Butcher, T. (1994). *Community leisure and recreation: Theory and practice*. London: Focal Press.

Higgins-Desbiolles, F. (2005). *Encounters between the wretched of the Earth and the tourist*. Hong Kong: Ecumenical Coalition on Tourism.

Higgins-Desbiolles, F. (2007). Hostile meeting grounds: Encounters between the wretched of the Earth and the tourist through tourism and terrorism in the 21st century. In P. M. Burns & M. Novelli (Eds.), *Tourism and politics: Global frameworks and local realities* (pp. 309–323). Oxford: Elsevier.

Hjalager, A. M. (2007). Stages in the economic globalization of tourism. *Annals of Tourism Research, 34*, 437–457.

Holloway, C. J. (1998). *The business of tourism*. Harlow: Longman.

Hyland, A., Puli, V., Cummings, M., & Sciandra, R. (2003). New York's smoke-free regulations: Effects on employment and sales in the hospitality industry. *Cornell Hotel and Restaurant Administration Quarterly, 44*(3), 9–16.

Indra, D. (2001). The effect of the events of September 11, 2001 on world tourism. *Turizmus Bulletin, 5*(4), 47–50.

Inkpen, G. (1998). *Information technology for travel and tourism* (2nd ed.). Harlow: Longman.

Inskeep, E. (1997). *Tourism planning*. New York: Van Nostrand Reinhold.

Ioannides, D., & Debbage, K. G. (Eds.). (1998). *The economic geography of the tourist industry: A supply-side analysis*. London: Routledge.

IUCN (The World Conservation Union). (1995). *Best practice for conservation and planning in rural areas*. Gland, Switzerland: IUCN.

Jamieson, W. (2001). *Promotion of investment in tourism infrastructure*. New York: UN ESCAP.

Jensen, T. (1998). Income and price inelasticities by nationality for tourists in Denmark. *Tourism Economics, 4*, 2.

Johnson, J. (2003). Grey power: The future is now. *Parks and Recreation Canada, 60*(5), 26–27.

Johnson, P., & Thomas, B. (Eds.). (1992). *Perspectives on tourism policy*. London: Mansell.

Johnson, P., & Thomas, B. (Eds.). (1992). *Choice and demand in tourism*. London: Mansell.

Johnson, R. L., & Moore, E. (1993). Tourism impact estimation. *Annals of Tourism Research, 20*, 279–288.

Jones, P., & Pizam, A. (Eds.). (1993). *The international hospitality industry: Organisational and operational issues*. Harlow: Longman.

Knowles, T. (1996). *Corporate strategy for hospitality*. Harlow: Longman.

Knowles, T., & Egan, D. (2000). Recession and its implications for the international hotel industry. *Travel and Tourism Analyst, 6*, 59–76.

Koch, F., de Beer, G., & Elliffe, S. (1998, Summer). SDIs, tourism-led growth and the empowerment of local communities in South Africa. *Development Southern Africa, 15*(5), 809–826.

Kotas, R., Teare, R., Logie, J., Jayawardena, C., & Bowen, J. (Eds.). (1996). *The international hospitality business*. London: Cassell.

Kottke, M. (1988). Estimating economic impacts of tourism. *Annals of Tourism Research, 15*, 122–133.

Krippendorf, J. (1987). *The holiday makers*. Oxford: Butterworth-Heinemann.

Lashley, C., & Rowson, B. (2010). Lifestyle businesses: Insights into Blackpool's hotel sector. *International Journal of Hospitality Management, 29*, 511–519.

Lawson, F. (1998). *Tourism and recreation development*. London: Focal Press.

Lea, J. (1998). *Tourism and development in the third world*. London: Routledge.

Lee, S. K., & Jang, S. (2011). Foreign exchange exposure of US tourism-related firms. *Tourism Management* (in press).

Leiper, N. (1999). A conceptual analysis of tourism-supported employment which reduces the incidence of exaggerated, misleading statistics about jobs. *Tourism Management*, *20*(5), 605–613.

Li, G., Wong, K. K. F., Song, H., & Witt, S. F. (2006). Tourism demand forecasting: A time varying parameter error correction model. *Journal of Travel Research*, *45*, 175.

Linder, S. (1970). *The harried leisure class*. New York: Columbia University Press.

Lipsey, R. (1973). *An introduction to positive economics*. London: Weidenfeld and Nicolson.

Lockhart, D. G., & Drakakis-Smith, D. (Eds.). (1996). *Island tourism: Trends and prospects*. London: Pinter.

Lundberg, D., Stavenga, M., & Krishnamoorthy, M. (1995). *Tourism economics*. Chichester: Wiley.

Mathieson, A., & Wall, G. (1982). *Tourism: Economic, physical and social impacts*. Harlow: Longman.

McCormack, F. (1994). *Water based recreation: Managing water resources for leisure*. Cambridge: Elm Publications.

McNeill, L. (1997). *Travel in the digital age*. Chichester: Bowerdean Publishing.

Medlik, S. (1994). *The business of hotels*. Oxford: Butterworth-Heinemann.

Middleton, V. T. C., & Hawkins, R. (1998). *Sustainable tourism: A marketing perspective*. Oxford: Butterworth-Heinemann.

Miller, G., Rathouse, K., Scarles, C., Holmes, K., & Iribe, J. (2010). Public understanding of sustainable tourism. *Annals of Tourism Research*, *37*, 627–645.

Milne, S. S. (1987). Differential multipliers. *Annals of Tourism Research*, *14*, 499–515.

Mowforth, M., & Munt, I. (1998). *Tourism and sustainability: New tourism in the third world*. London: Routledge.

Mules, T. (2001). Globalization and the economic impacts of tourism. In B. Faulkner, G. Moscardo & E. Laws (Eds.), *Tourism in the twenty-first century: Reflections on experience*. London: Continuum.

Munoz, T. G. (2007). German demand for tourism in Spain. *Tourism Management*, *28*, 12–22.

Mvula, C. (2001). Fair trade in tourism to protected areas – A micro case study of wildlife tourism to South Luangwa National Park, Zambia. *International Journal of Tourism Research*, *3*(5), 393–405.

National Park Service. (1990). *Economic impacts of protecting rivers, trails, and greenway corridors – a resource book*. Washington: US Department of the Interior National Park Service.

Newman, T., Curtis, K., & Stephens, J. (2003). Do community-based arts projects result in social gains? A review of the literature. *Community Development Journal*, *38*(4), 310–322.

O'Hagan, J., & Jennings, M. (2003). Public broadcasting in Europe: Rationale, licence fee and other issues. *Journal of Cultural Economics*, *27*(1), 31–56.

Omerod, P. (1994). *The death of economics*. London: Faber and Faber.

Oppermann, M. (Ed.). (1997). *Pacific Rim tourism*. Wallingford: CAB International.

Oppermann, M., & Chon, K. -S. (1997). *Tourism in developing countries*. London: ITBP.

Page, S. (1994). *Transport for tourism*. London: ITBP.

Page, S. A., & Getz, D. (Eds.). (1997). *The business of rural tourism: International perspectives*. London: ITBP.

Papathanassis, A. (2009). *Cruise sector growth*. Wiesbaden: Gabler.

Pattullo, P. (1996). *Last resorts: The cost of tourism in the Caribbean*. London: Cassell.

Peacock, M. (1995). *Information technology in the hospitality industry*. London: Cassell.

Pettifor, A. (2003). *Real world economic outlook*. Hampshire: Palgrave Macmillan.

Pitegoff, B., & Smith, G. (2003). Measuring the return on investment of destination welcome centres: The case of Florida. *Tourism Economics*, *9*(3), 307–323.

Plaza, B. (2004). Valuing museums as economic engines: Willingness to pay or discounting of cash-flows? *Journal of Cultural Heritage*, *11*, 155–162.

Plaza, B., & Haarich, S. N. (2009). Museums for urban regeneration? Exploring conditions for their effectiveness. *Journal of Urban Regeneration and Renewal*, *2*, 259–271.

Plimmer, N. (1994). Everyone benefits? The case of New Zealand: *Environment and development report*. London: WTTC.

Poon, A. (1993). *Tourism, technology and competitive strategies*. Wallingford: CAB International.

Porter, M. (1980). *Competitive strategy: Techniques for analysing industries and competitors*. New York: Free Press.

Porter, M. (1990). *The competitive advantage of nations*. Basingstoke: Macmillan.

Porter, M. E. (1985). *Competitive advantage* (15th ed.). New York: Free Press.

Price, M. F. (Ed.). (1996). *People and tourism in fragile environments*. London: Wiley.

PricewaterhouseCoopers (2002). Analysis of UK hotel employment trends and hotel sector performance. *Hospitality Directions – Europe Edition*, *6*, 8–12.

PricewaterhouseCoopers (2003). UK hotel sector must wait until 2004 for a strong rebound. *Hospitality Directions – Europe Edition*, *8*, 21–27.

Priestley, G. K., Edwards, J. A., & Coccossis, H. (Eds.). (1996). *Sustainable tourism? European experiences*. Wallingford: CAB International.

Putnam, R. (2000). *Bowling alone: The collapse and revival of American community*. New York: Simon and Schuster.

Ravenscroft, N. (1992). *Recreation planning and development*. Basingstoke: Macmillan.

Riley, M., Ladkin, A., & Szivas, E. (2002). *Tourism employment: Analysis and planning*. Clevedon: Channel View Publications.

Ritchie, J. R., Amaya Molinar, C. M., & Frechtling, D. C. (2010). Impacts of the world recession and economic crisis on tourism: North America. *Journal of Travel Research*, *49*, 5.

Ritzer, G. (1993). *The McDonaldization of society*. Thousand Oaks, CA: Pine Forge Press.

Robertson, R. (1992). *Globalization: Social theory and global culture*. London: Sage.

Robinson, J. (1942). *An essay on Marxian economics*. Basingstoke: Macmillan.

Robinson, L., & Taylor, P. (2003). The performance of local authority sports halls and swimming pools in England. *Managing Leisure, 8*(1), 1–16.

Rodgers, K., & Cox, E. (2003). The effects of trampling on Hawaiian corals along a gradient of human use. *Biological Conservation, 112*(3), 383–389.

Russell, B. (1994). *In praise of idleness and other essays*. London: Routledge. (Original work published 1932.)

Ryan, C. (2003). *Recreational tourism: Demand and impacts*. Clevedon: Channel View Publications.

Sable, K., & Kling, R. (2001). The double public good: A conceptual framework for 'shared experience' values associated with heritage conservation. *Journal of Cultural Economics, 25*(2), 77–89.

Salma, U. (2002). Indirect economic contribution of tourism to Australia. Bureau of Tourism Research. *Tourism Research Report, 4*(2), 43–47.

Schiff, A. & Becken, S. Demand elasticity estimates for New Zealand tourism. *Tourism Management*. (in press).

Schor, J. (1992). *The overworked American: The unexpected decline of leisure*. New York: Basic Books.

Schroder, A., & Widmann, T. (2007). Demographic change and its impact on the travel industry: Oldiesùnothing but goldies? *Trends and Issues in Global Tourism 2007*, 3–17.

Shackley, M. (1996). *Wildlife tourism*. London: ITBP.

Shah, K. (2000). *Tourism, the poor and other stakeholders: Asian experience*. ODI Fair-Trade in Tourism Paper. London: ODI.

Sharpley, R. (2003). *Tourism and leisure in the countryside*. Cambridge: Elm Publications.

Shaw, G., & Williams, A. (Eds.). (1997). *The rise and fall of British coastal resorts: Cultural and economic perspectives*. London: Pinter.

Sheldon, P. J. (1990). A review of tourism expenditure research. In C. P. Cooper (Ed.), *Progress in tourism, recreation and hospitality management*. London: Belhaven Press.

Sheldon, P. J. (1997). *Tourism information technology*. Wallingford: CAB International.

Shone, A. (1998). *The business of conferences in the hospitality and leisure industries*. Oxford: Butterworth-Heinemann.

Sinclair, M. T., & Stabler, M. J. (Eds.). (1991). *The tourism industry: An international analysis*. Wallingford: CAB International.

Sinclair, M. T., & Stabler, M. J. (1997). *The economics of tourism*. London: Routledge.

Smeral, E. (2003). A structural view of tourism growth. *Tourism Economics, 9*(1), 77–93.

Smith, M. K. (2003). *Issues in cultural tourism studies*. London: Routledge.

Song, H., Romilly, P., & Liu, X. (2000). An empirical study of outbound tourism demand in the UK. *Applied Economics, 32*(5), 611–624.

Spotts, D. M., & Mahoney, E. (1991, Spring). Segmenting visitors to a destination region based on the volume of their expenditures. *Journal of Travel Research*, 24–31.

Stabler, M. J. (Ed.). (1997). *Tourism and sustainability: Principles to practice*. Wallingford: CAB International.

Stern, N. (2008). The economics of climate change. *American Economic Review, 98*, 1–37.

Sugiyarto, G., Blake, A., & Sinclair, M. T. (2003). Tourism and globalization: Economic impact in Indonesia. *Annals of Tourism Research, 30*(3), 683–701.

Swarbrooke, J., & Horner, S. (1998). *Consumer behaviour in tourism: An international perspective*. Oxford: Butterworth-Heinemann.

Szymanski, S. (2000). Hearts, minds and the restrictive practices court practice. In S. Hamil, J. Michie, C. Oughton & S. Warby (Eds.), *Football in the digital age: Whose game is it anyway?* (pp. 191–204). Edinburgh: Mainstream Publishing Co. (Edinburgh) Ltd.

Tate, P. (2002). The impact of 9/11: Caribbean, London and NYC case studies. *Travel and Tourism Analyst, 5*, 1.1–1.25.

Taylor, D., Fletcher, R., & Clabaugh, T. (1993). A comparison of characteristics, regional expenditures, and economic impact of visitors to historical sites with other recreational visitors. *Journal of Travel Research, 32*(1), 30–35.

Taylor, F. (1993). *To hell with paradise: A history of the Jamaican tourism industry*. Pittsburgh, PA: University of Pittsburgh Press.

Teare, R., & Olsen, M. (Eds.). (1992). *International hospitality management: Corporate strategy in practice*. London: Longman.

Teare, R., Canziani, B. F., & Brown, G. (Eds.). (1997). *Global directions: New strategies for hospitality and tourism*. London: Cassell.

Theobald, W. (Ed.). (1998). *Global tourism: The next decade* (2nd ed.). Oxford: Butterworth-Heinemann.

Thomas, B., & Townsend, A. (2001). New trends in the growth of tourism employment in the UK in the 1990s. *Tourism Economics, 7*(3), 295–310.

Thomas, R. (Ed.). (1996). *The hospitality industry, tourism and Europe*. London: Cassell.

Thoroe, C. (2003). Sink effects of forestry inadequately rewarded? *Forst und Holz, 58*(3), 55–58.

Tol, R. S. J. (2007). The impact of a carbon tax on international tourism. *Transportation Research Part D: Transport and Environment, 12*, 129–142.

Torkildsen, G. (1992). *Leisure and recreation management*. London: Spon.

Tourism Forecasting Council. (1998). A major new investment tool. *Forecast – Tourism Forecasting Council, 4*(2), 28–31.

Tribe, J. (1997). *Corporate strategy for tourism*. London: ITBP.

Tribe, J. (2007). Tourism: A critical business. *Journal of Travel Research, 46*, 245–255.

Tribe, J. (2010). *Strategy for tourism*. Oxford: Goodfellow Publishers.

Veal, A. (2002). *Leisure and tourism policy and planning*. Wallingford: CAB International.

Veblen, T. (1967). *The theory of the leisure class*. New York: Viking Press.

Waddoups, C. (2001). Unionism and poverty-level wages in the service sector: The case of Nevada's hotel-casino industry. *Applied Economics Letters, 8*(3), 163–167.

Wagner, J. E. (1997). Estimating the economic impacts of tourism. *Annals of Tourism Research, 24*(3), 592–608.

Wahab, S., & Pigram, J. J. (Eds.). (1997). *Tourism, development and growth: The challenge of sustainability*. London: Routledge.

Weaver, D. (1998). *Ecotourism in the less developed world*. CAB International.

Wells, A. T. (1993). *Air transportation*. London: ITBP.

West, G., & Gamage, A. (2001). Macro effects of tourism in Victoria, Australia: A nonlinear input–output approach. *Journal of Travel Research*, *40*(1), 101–109.

Wheatcroft, S. (1994). *Aviation and tourism policies: Balancing the benefits*. London: ITBP.

Whitla, P., Walters, P. G. P., & Davies, H. (2007). Global strategies in the international hotel industry. *International Journal of Hospitality Management*, *26*, 777–792.

Williams, A. M., & Shaw, G. (Eds.). (1991). *Tourism and economic development: Western European experiences*. Chichester: Wiley.

Williamson, P., & Hirsch, P. (1996). Tourism development and social differentiation in Koh Samui. In M. Parnwell (Ed.), *Uneven development in Thailand* (pp. 186–203). Aldershot: Avebury.

Witt, S. F., & Witt, C. A. (1992). *Modelling and forecasting demand in tourism*. London: Academic Press.

World Commission on Environment and Development. (1987). *Our common future*. Oxford: OUP.

WTO. (1991). *Tourism to the year 2000: Qualitative aspects affecting global growth*. Madrid: World Tourism Organisation.

WTO. (1993). *Investments and financing in the tourism industry*. Madrid: World Tourism Organisation.

WTO. (1994). *GATS implications for tourism*. Madrid: World Tourism Organisation.

WTO. (1996). *Tourism and environmental protection*. Madrid: World Tourism Organisation.

WTO. (1996). *Tourism and new information technologies*. Madrid: World Tourism Organisation.

WTO. (1997a). *Agenda 21 for the travel and tourism industry*. Madrid: World Tourism Organisation.

WTO. (1997b). *Asia tourism – Towards New Horizons*. Madrid: World Tourism Organisation.

WTO. (1997b). *Compendium of tourism statistics*. Madrid: World Tourism Organisation.

WTO. (1997d). *Multilateral and bilateral sources of financing for tourism development*. Madrid: World Tourism Organisation.

WTO. (1997e). *Senior tourism*. Madrid: World Tourism Organisation.

WTO. (1997f). *Yearbook of tourism statistics*. Madrid: World Tourism Organisation.

WTTC. (2009). *Economic impact research*. www.wttc.org [Online]

Yale, P. (1995). *The business of tour operations*. Harlow: Longman.

Yeoman, I., & Ingold, A. (Eds.). (1997). *Yield management: Strategies for the service industries*. London: Cassell.

Zhou, D., Yanagida, J. F., Chakravorty, U., & Leung, P. (1997). Estimating economic impacts from tourism. *Annals of Tourism Research*, *24*(1), 76–89.

Index